1992

LITERATURE IN THE MODERN WORLD

LITERATURE IN THE MODERN WORLD

Critical Essays and Documents

Edited by
DENNIS WALDER
at the Open University

OXFORD UNIVERSITY PRESS
in association with
THE OPEN UNIVERSITY
1990

Oxford University Press, Walton Street, Oxford OX2 6DP

Oxford   New York   Toronto
Delhi   Bombay   Calcutta   Madras   Karachi
Petaling Jaya   Singapore   Hong Kong   Tokyo
Nairobi   Dar es Salaam   Cape Town
Melbourne   Auckland
and associated companies in
Berlin   Ibadan

Oxford is a trade mark of Oxford University Press

Published in the United States
by Oxford University Press, New York

British Library Cataloguing in Publication Data
Literature in the modern world: critical essays and
documents.
1. Literature. Critical studies
I. Walder, Dennis
809
ISBN 0-19-871114-X
ISBN 0-19-871037-2 pbk

Library of Congress Cataloging in Publication Data
Literature in the modern world: critical essays and documents/
edited by Dennis Walder.
Includes index.
1. Criticism—History—20th century. 2. Literature, Modern—20th
century—History and criticism. 3. Developing countries—
—Literatures—Occidental influences. I. Walder, Dennis.
PN94.L494 1990   801'.95'0904--dc20   90-41917

ISBN 0-19-871114-X.
ISBN 0-19-871037-2 (pbk.)

Typeset at the Alden Press
Oxford, London and Northampton

Printed in Great Britain by
The Alden Press, Oxford

Contents

Introduction

The aim of this collection of critical essays and documents is to provide students, teachers, and other interested readers with the materials for a new approach to the study of literature—mainly, but not exclusively, English—in the twentieth century. The collection is addressed in the first place to the needs of Open University students following a course on 'Literature in the Modern World', so its structure and assumptions come directly from that course. On the other hand, since the course has been designed to engage relative newcomers to the field with some of the main texts, themes, and issues which can be expected to concern them as serious readers of literature today, this includes anyone who might regard themselves as fitting that bill.

The unifying principle of the book can be easily and briefly expressed: it is intended to represent both the construction of a notion of 'English Literature' in the reading and evaluation of literary texts from the twenties to the eighties; and the development of a variety of opposed or undermining critical perspectives over the same period. The presence of American, Irish, and Scottish writing, of 'New Writings' from the former colonial countries, and of European writing in translation, alongside the rise of a radical questioning of the traditional literary 'canon' in terms of class, gender, and race, mean that 'Literature in the Modern World' is today a more accurate formulation of the subject of 'Modern English Literature'.

This Reader, then, is an integrated part of a course which takes as its basis the assumption that there has been an unignorable change in what 'counts' as 'English Literature' in the twentieth century, a period of British imperial decline and national self-doubt. In 1920, Britain was the centre of a world-wide imperial power-structure; in 1980, it was one of a group of European states dominated by the hegemonic position of the United States of America. Literature students will not necessarily want to analyse what is, after all, a massively complex historical condition; but they will want to be able to identify, understand, and evaluate its 'cultural mediation' in various forms of writing, including the three traditional genres (novel, poetry, and drama).

The aim here is to foster an informed and critical awareness of this 'mediation'. No attempt is being made to 'cover' the major critical schools or tendencies of our times, whether 'new criticism', 'structuralism', 'post-structuralism', 'new historicism', or any other of the related or divergent 'isms' offered, with varying degrees of success, by the numerous survey-type anthologies on the market. Nor is there any attempt here at seeking out the 'latest' critical fashion; that is in any case an illusory aim, as some of the more recent, and recently dated, introductions to 'literary theory' reveal.

'Theory' itself is a dodgy word, which has shifted in application and meaning to an alarming extent. It used to have to do with clarifying assumptions, or method, so as to validate an approach—a sense highlighted half a century ago when the American critic and theorist René Wellek challenged the British critic F. R. Leavis to reveal his critical principles, only to be met with the response that this was not the critic's job. Leavis, and those who followed him (some still do), preferred to offer his own 'concrete' experience of particular literary texts as a way of stimulating others to share that experience. Fair enough. But only if you agreed with the prior choice of texts, and the grounds for evaluating them. That is, if you agreed about what has come to be called the literary 'canon'. The vulnerability of Leavis's position has been shown up, and Wellek's view vindicated, by a veritable flood of literary theorizing, challenging the traditional choices of literary texts, and critical approaches to them. Wellek's original attempt to establish an agreed, rational set of critical guidelines has long been overtaken by this new genre, a genre in which works frequently address each other across the boundaries of literary study, linguistics, anthropology, sociology, philosophy, and psychology, in a self-generating spiral of interpretations of interpretations.

In this context, to say that the aim here is to offer a 'new approach' may seem madly ambitious, even absurd. Haven't we got enough new approaches to literary studies already? And to want to draw on the developments which have led literary studies in the direction of theory may still seem an abdication of the critic's role. You don't have to be a 'Leavisite' to want to read for pleasure rather than instruction, and to believe that the study of literature has to do with the excitement of discovering new novels, plays, and poems (or new things in them), rather than abstract system-building.

But things are not so simple. In the first place, in so far as the more 'theoretical' discussion which has come to dominate debate among professional critics nowadays has been mainly concerned with questioning the basic principles and procedures of traditional literary study, it is too important to be ignored. However, this development has also meant that, for example, while many critics (including some represented in this volume, such as Terry Eagleton) have taken it upon themselves to show how the old 'Eng. Lit.' curriculum is in some sense a 'construction', without any certain validity in itself, they have at the same time continued to deal with the familiar monuments in practice (Shakespeare, Milton, Dickens, T. S. Eliot). But there are available alternative, new versions of the curriculum, incorporating less well-known or highly regarded literary texts, by writers such as Sorley Maclean, Chinua Achebe, and Athol Fugard. There are also available alternative, newly formulated traditions, such as those proposed by critics and scholars writing from previously marginalized points of view—most notably the feminist, black American, and 'post-colonial' perspectives. One of the most important aims of this collection is to offer adequate representation of these perspectives, still generally ghettoized within their own anthologies. Hence the presence of Cora Kaplan, Toni Morrison, Frantz Fanon, and Chinweizu.

Secondly, the intellectual challenge offered by recent developments in 'literary theory' is undeniable. The struggle to redefine the subject itself in terms of its linguistic, cultural, and even philosophic implications has led to important and lasting insights into how and why we read and understand as we do, and how our 'understanding' might also be changed. Of course this increase in critical self-awareness has also led to elitism, smugness, and jargon—although, as the inimitable French critic Roland Barthes observed in his own defence, 'Old criticism is one caste among others, and the "French clarity" it recommends is a jargon just like any other . . . language is clear only to the extent that it is generally accepted' (*Criticism and Truth*, 1966). New thinking involves new language. None the less, far too much of the writing to be found in the latest guides and handbooks for students of literature—not to mention the specialist journals themselves—appears to be addressed only to the initiated, to those already thoroughly imbued with the language and thought of those three great gendarmes (as Barthes once called them) of modern literary culture, Marx, Freud, and Saussure.

You will, of course, find here writing which has been deeply influenced by the social science of Marx, the psychoanalysis of Freud, and the linguistics of Saussure. Familiarity with their works is not, however, assumed. Nor, therefore, will you find here very many examples of the higher reaches of theoretical debate, the 'post-structuralist' work of Lacan and Derrida or the 'post-post-structuralist' work of those who have engaged with them, such as Catherine Belsey in this country, Fredric Jameson in the United States, or Luce Irigaray in France. But you should find those higher reaches more accessible once you have worked through what is here.

The writings of some of those included in any case do not fall easily into any such categorizing, and seem to have gone through it all and come out the other side: Umberto Eco, for example, here included for his typically witty account of the 'Semiotics of Theatrical Performance', which goes some way towards confronting the marked absence generally of theoretical discourse on drama. The work of other contributors, such as Jean-Paul Sartre and Theodor Adorno (both Marxists), and George Steiner (who is not), on language and the writer's role 'after Auschwitz', has been of an originating power which has been overlooked in the rush to catch up with recent theoretical utterances. And some sense of the more 'advanced' thinking (if that is really what it is) may be gathered from Edward Said on 'Yeats and Decolonization', for instance; or from Pierre Macherey and Etienne Balibar on 'Literature as an

Ideological Form'; or from Hélène Cixous' proclamation of the possibility of a feminine writing—*écriture féminine*—in 'The Laugh of the Medusa', itself an example of what she argues.

The overriding aim here has been to assemble the materials for understanding the issues and debates likely to dominate discussion of literary studies in the 1990s. Many of the extracts are originating or even classic expressions of these issues and debates, rather than 'theory', in any case: ranging from Virginia Woolf on the deletion of women from the notion of Englishness being promoted in the twenties and thirties, to Frantz Fanon on the three stages through which the writings of the colonized pass before becoming truly 'national' (and revolutionary). To think of European literature today means, of course, thinking also of Russian and Eastern European writing: here represented by Joseph Brodsky on Anna Akhmatova, and Czeslaw Milosz 'On Hope'. Every extract has been chosen for its contribution to shaping our sense of how we might proceed in thinking about literatures available in English today. Every extract has been chosen for being of sufficient *length, force,* and *clarity* to give somebody unfamiliar with the language and the debates an opportunity to engage with them. Inevitably, within the covers of a single book, that has meant leaving out a lot; but at least the agenda should be clear.

The Reader is divided into two parts, carefully organized so that the issues are raised by means of representative and alternative voices which suggest debate among themselves. Part One consists of three sections, each of which is intended to introduce different aspects of our general approach to the changing study of literatures in English. Part Two, like the course with which it is integrated, is very broadly chronological, and consists of eight sections, each of which focuses upon a single subject-theme or issue. All sections have brief introductions, and each extract is provided with a source note. Here, and in other bibliographical citations, the place of publication is London unless otherwise stated. Footnotes have been selectively added or deleted to clarify (where essential) allusions and foreign words or phrases.

In the opening section of Part One, the question of the 'canon' is established and then, in effect, debated by a series of different voices, each from a particular perspective. The order of the extracts generally reflects a progressive level of difficulty and complexity of argument. This sets the pattern for all the succeeding sections in the book, and provides a framework for Part Two. The question of interpretation is obviously central to any discussion of what and how a literary text 'means' anything; the value of that meaning in social and political terms is inescapable. Hence the other two sections in Part One, on 'Interpretation' and 'Commitment'. These questions weave their way throughout the wide range of more specific discussions which follow.

'Form and Genre', which opens Part Two, introduces certain formal methods of analysis (as in the Seymour Chatman and Umberto Eco extracts), then includes an attack (by Martin Esslin and John Barrell) upon the ahistorical assumptions embedded in such methods. The following sections develop the twin strands of the basic approach. Firstly, how literary texts register the larger cultural-historical movements of the twentieth century: in terms of 'Modernism', the construction of 'Englishness', and the consequent effects of 'End of Empire' and the rise of 'New Writings' from the former colonial countries. Secondly, the more theoretical discussion prompted by and used to understand these developments is represented under the headings of 'Literature and Ideology', 'Language and Gender', and 'Literature and History'.

It is now more than a quarter of a century since the American writer and critic Susan Sontag observed (in *Against Interpretation*, 1964) that the 'effusion of interpretations of art' was fast becoming, like 'the fumes of the automobile and of heavy industry which befoul the urban atmosphere', a poisonous threat to 'our sensibilities'. Interpretation and critical discussion, she continued, were 'the revenge of the intellect upon art'. They represented a 'philistine refusal to leave the work of art alone', reducing art's capacity to 'make us nervous' by making it 'manageable, comfortable'. This philistinism was 'more rife in literature than in any other art', as the 'naked power' of the works of Lawrence, Joyce, Beckett, and many others was increasingly stifled by endless exegesis. Anyone aware of the massive increase in the volume of discussion and critical commentary which has taken place in recent decades —much of it in a language so specialized that only experienced toilers in the field can hope to participate—will feel some sympathy for this position. And yet, Sontag herself could not leave it at that. She went on to admit that works of art can be described, even paraphrased. The question is, how? Her answer was that the kind of criticism we now need is the kind that 'would serve the work of art, not usurp its place'. We need a criticism which, at its best, 'dissolves considerations of content into form'. For example? The writings of Roland Barthes and Walter Benjamin—neither of whom, of course, fits easily into any of the numerous 'movements' in criticism.

The point is, it is no longer possible, much less desirable, to offer literary criticism to the unoffending public without some justification; and Sontag's position is better than most, both in terms of what she says, and how she says it. Worthwhile criticism sharpens and extends our 'sensibilities', our thoughts and feelings about works of art or literature. That may be obvious enough. Less obvious, and therefore more important today, it leads us to rethink, to question, our basic assumptions about how we respond to works of art or literature. This means scrutinizing not only, in the traditional phrase, 'the words on the page', but also our own approach to them—a procedure which involves us in uncovering things we did not notice before about a text, and in that sense serving, not usurping it; a procedure which also involves us in uncovering things we did not recognize or admit before in ourselves, and the world in which we live.

As I have been suggesting, what this means in practice is that we cannot talk or write as if the explosion in 'theory' of the last twenty or thirty years had not happened. David Lodge, who is both a notable apologist of critical theory and a brilliant parodist of its wilder extremes, has put it well: 'We have eaten the apple of knowledge and must live with the consequences'. More positively, it has now become possible to look back and identify some of the 'classic', originating texts, by writers as diverse as Virginia Woolf, Theodor Adorno, and Frantz Fanon, which set the agenda for much of the most forceful and challenging debate to be heard nowadays, although their own voices are too rarely admitted. Further, it has also become possible to search out and identify hitherto unanthologized pieces by writers and critics such as Laurence Lerner, Wole Soyinka, or Edward Said, which take the debate into areas which have been too quickly set aside or completely overlooked.

Finally, I would like to thank all my Open University course team colleagues for their support and advice; in particular, Dinah Birch, Angus Calder, Roger Day, Cicely Palser Havely, Graham Martin, and Michael Rossington, for their specific contributions.

Open University, 1990   D. W.

PART ONE
General Approaches

I *Questioning the 'Canon'*

The main purpose of this section is to establish the origin and nature of the growing debate about what, exactly, constitutes the subject of literary studies in English today. Marilyn Butler may be said to express the way in which the accepted 'canon' of literary texts to be studied has come to be questioned from within mainstream English studies itself; Edward Said, on the other hand, considers the work of a familiar, 'canonized' writer (Yeats) from a consciously alternative, 'Third World' perspective. While Butler's position involves attending to writings excluded by conventional literary history traditions as 'minor', such as the Romantic poet Southey, Said's involves bringing in for consideration more radical alternatives from abroad, represented by writers such as Theodor Adorno, Frantz Fanon, and Chinua Achebe.

Sandra Gilbert and Susan Gubar's 'classic' piece establishes the need to realign a patriarchal formation of the literary canon by considering how women writers, in particular poets, have been doubly marginalized by the inherited attitudes of a critical establishment. Terry Eagleton takes another tack, undermining the rise of the 'canon' by questioning what we understand by 'literature' as well as offering a historical account of the rise of English studies. Frank Kermode, on the other hand, opens up the possibility of a sceptical resistance to all this questioning, querying its underlying radicalism.

I *Repossessing the Past: The Case for an Open Literary History*[1]

MARILYN BUTLER

In October 1986 the Cambridge historian David Cannadine informed the readers of the *Times Literary Supplement* why, broadly, he was leaving Britain for the USA. He wrote of the pointlessness of specializing in British history, now that no one but the British were interested in it. In this respect scholars of past English literature look to be in a far more favourable situation than historians. The conditions affecting literature have been revolutionized from time to time. The invention of printing, the extension of literacy and leisure,

---

* Original version first given as a lecture at Cambridge, 10 Nov. 1987; reprinted from M. Levinson *et al.*, ed., *Rethinking Historicism: Critical Readings in Romantic History*, Basil Blackwell, Oxford, 1989, pp. 64–84.

the mechanization of book production, each in turn brought in new readers, and in the end the readers determine the books. We are now living through the greatest expansion yet of the reading public for serious books in English. Thanks to the world dominance of America, English is what Latin once was, a world language. By analogy, literature in English will become what the Roman Empire made Latin literature, and indeed Greek literature too. The literature in the language the world speaks is—or should be—a world literature.

But, as a matter of fact, 'literature in English' is not at all the same thing as 'English literature', in the sense that the English (or British, or those of Anglo-Saxon descent) have narrowly conceived it. Literatures in English have begun to proliferate since the late nineteenth century, in most cases accompanied by a strong will to independent nationhood, and a consciousness of linguistic particularity. The schoolchildren of Canada, Australia, Nigeria and the West Indies partly learn about national autonomy by studying cultural autonomy. They are increasingly likely to focus on their own national literatures before rather than after England's, and before rather than after America's too.

So where does that leave the 'canonical' literature of the past—Shakespeare, Milton and Wordsworth; Austen, the Brontës, George Eliot; Locke, Wortley Montagu and Ruskin; now the literature of a third-class power with a first-ranked language? The loss of British national prestige must entail a threat to the so-called authority of English literary classics—simply because the main motive for foreign children to learn about the British past, cultural as well as political, has in fact (as Cannadine perceived) been removed. Even if we suppose that America will and indeed has adopted England's literature *en bloc* as its own cultural heritage, America with its wealth and strength can afford the luxury of a cultural heritage. Will the largely third-world nations learning the language think it worth their while to follow rich Western nations on this point?

Most school students of English language are sitting, right now, at desks in China: they do not study English literature. Nations that have done so are showing signs of giving it up. Shakespeare has been for over a century on the syllabus in good Indian schools, but he is being declared too difficult, and anyhow irrelevant, and looks about to go. Schools, like universities, are in crisis where the humanities are concerned, because everywhere scarce resources are being diverted into the re-equipping, or creation, of industry. The sixties revolution that matters worldwide is not the Parisian one that gave Western academics post-structuralism, but the South Korean one that turned a war-devastated country into another Japan. The precondition of that technological miracle was a retrained workforce, and the moral is not lost on other governments. Where education is concerned, while not precisely saying so, Britain and the United States as well as India and Australia are increasingly interested in being Korean. The British Prime Minister acknowledges the utility of studying the English language, the medium in which buying, selling, and navigating ships and planes is conducted. She seems no more impressed than Rajiv Gandhi by English literature, which sells nothing, and may carry disagreeable ideological baggage along with it.

Somewhat against their own professional interest, intelligent young Indian academic teachers of English (who are numerous) question the relevance of so much time and money spent on the past writings of a country geographically far away, which imposed this literature upon them as part of its machinery of power. Read within Britain, much of the sub-Foucauldian[1] cultural history now pouring out of non-academic British presses—Methuen, Blackwell, Harvester, and the New Left imprint, Verso—may tend to give a crude and mechanistic account of the operation of power through literature and education. In the Third World, the iconoclasm of this type of work hearteningly confronts what otherwise looks like the white cultural monolith—for it's hard to deny the inequality of the cultural exchange between north and west on the one hand, south and east on the other. The bright young staff of Delhi University, readers of their own *Subaltern Studies* and of Gayatri Spivak's *In Other Worlds*, as well as of the brisk cheap left-wing semi-academic Western paperbacks, are provisionally willing enough to tolerate the canon, because they are so accomplished at turning it into cannon-fodder: apt material for a brutal, totalizing, highly political form of deconstruction, owing little to the manner of Yale and Cornell.

Aggressive manoeuvres of that kind, whether or not tactically appropriate in the Third World, are surely not good or even interesting choices for readers studying their own native tradition, or working in their own first language. We have all severally to work out our own models for how literary history is to be taught in our different countries. It must be for many of us a brutal simplification, and in the end a self-destructive one, to type all past literature as the voice of power, or of patriarchy, or of any other hateful institution. This form of pessimism or 'tragic essentialism', as it has been termed, is self-defeating because it glamorizes what it means to oppose. And a tactic devoted to exposing the bad faith of literature as a whole is hardly timely when, throughout much of the world, time and resources spent on research in the humanities have come under severe scrutiny from the central state. Yet this reductive position, under-researched, pseudo-intellectual, is able to pass professionally as a 'historical' approach to literature, for want of enough properly rigorous alternatives. At least the seriousness of the situation should belatedly force

---

[1] 'sub-Foucauldian': refers to the work of the influential historian of ideas, Michel Foucault (d. 1984). [Ed.]

Marilyn Butler

more ambitious literary critics to pay attention to the kind of issue that in the Romantic-modernist period they have characteristically evaded—the question of the relationship between culture and the state; more specifically, the role and rationale of past literature in education.

It can't be much more than 400 years since the centralized nation-states of Western Europe such as England began to cultivate their own pasts, including their vernacular literary pasts, as a means of raising national consciousness. For about half that time, the first 200 years or so, those who took a 'patriot' pride in native English (and in Scottish and Welsh) literatures were often not nationalists, in the modern sense of rallying behind the nation's leaders. From the seventeenth century on, amateurs among the gentry and middling sort collected vernacular books or the ephemera of popular culture. Pepys's huge collection of ballads, now in Magdalene College, Cambridge, has recently been published, and it illustrates the appeal of native alternatives to the aristocratic classical tradition. When the House of Commons debated the future of Latin in November 1987, the British public heard heartfelt references to 3,000 years of European culture. The same line of legitimacy was invoked in the eighteenth century to justify that period's truly conspicuous consumption in the arts—in architecture, or in classical statuary. But the classical heritage was articulately contested by other people's traditions. The new middle-class journals, with their largely provincial readership, encouraged the emergence of a more British, non-Latinate literary past, including ballads, Gothic tales, Elizabethan lyric and drama, and (for the learned like Cambridge's Thomas Gray) Anglo-Saxon, Celtic and Old Norse. The eighteenth-century writers who claimed that literature was originally simple and spontaneous were not themselves especially simple, and some of them invented their evidence, but they got what they wanted from history by remaking it. That generation, as well as the Victorian, is one of our possible models.

A single, official English literary history emerges only in the 1820s. The monoliths which European nation-states then made of their cultural traditions are deeply impressive, since they served all sorts of civic purposes, from mass literacy to nationalism, while remaining usefully economical. Critics around 1830 made the single great line of English poets, stretching (almost) unbroken from Chaucer to Tennyson. The so-called literary canon, a significantly theological term, was as characteristic of the age of its birth as the railway, and as much the symbol of British achievement. Together the single line of poets personified the national spirit, separately they were thoughtful, humane men—a little too like the ideal university professor perhaps, but wisdom and tolerance remain virtues. Wordsworth emerged *primus inter pares*[2] among the other five Romantics—then Coleridge, Scott, Byron, Shelley, Keats—because he taught a stoical, essentially optimistic acceptance of suffering, and because his vision of nature represented England as still a pastoral society, which was comforting in other ways.

The impact of the canon on all our perceptions is perhaps most striking when we reflect how quickly and how totally it changed posterity's understanding of the two literary generations before its acceptance. In the age of Adam Smith, large numbers of general readers were able to buy or borrow books for the first time. The novels and poems offered to these new readers were often quotidian in their concerns, and direct, non-specialized in their vocabulary and range of allusion. Many authors were women; some of the best poets, we might now agree—like Burns and Blake—came from the ranks. Nineteenth-century professionals, journalists and academics, made great writers into an officer class, and imposed restrictions on the entry of women and NCOs. The canon came to look harmonious rather than contentious; learned or polite rather than artless or common; national rather than provincial or sectarian on the one hand, or dispersed and international on the other. Literature is individualistic or pluralist; words such as 'canon' and 'heritage' impose a uniformity that had some practical advantages, especially at the outset, but was always artificial.

The Victorian canon must have been made for the 'general reader', more for consumption at home than in the classroom, since the process of canon-making clearly pre-dates the rise of English Literature as a school and university subject. By the second half of the nineteenth century, the era of mass secondary education, syllabus reform and the provision of academic school and university places for women, English literature was already so wholesome a field of study that its social utility was easy to argue for. Victorians, noted for their hardheadedness, saw the merits of a school subject that delivered the nation's traditions to pupils in an inspiring, unifying and easily digested form. On the most practical level, it provided models for using the language, most universal of all skills in advanced society; it opened the door to experience, personal and social, in the adult world. Given the large and steadily increasing numbers of women studying the subject, the supply of teachers was unlikely to run short. All these arguments still prevail, and are being rehearsed again in Britain, as a reforming government strives for an education system which will deliver, among other things, a mentally disciplined, trainable workforce. But what will the content of that school literature syllabus be? Must it still resemble the Victorian conception, simply because the Victorian conception is there?

The nature of the population has, after all, changed a great deal in a

---

[2] Latin: 'first among equals'. [Ed.]

century. It is now more urbanized and more ethnically diverse, and many of the non-formal aspects of its culture are new (radio, television, film, tabloid newspapers, sport). The adult work required of the populace in the twenty-first century will be very different from that required in the nineteenth. Without an empire to hold down, there seems less point in schooling young males in hearty nationalism (though many believers in educational reform still seem very keen on breeding patriots). There is, on the other hand, a valuable social lesson just as cogently drawn from studying past literature, that of learning to understand and tolerate the other person's position. Most literature does not speak for the official, London-based 'nation'. It expresses the view of a sect, a province, a gender, a class, bent more often than not on criticism or outright opposition. For literary purposes, the British Isles have always been what the Australian poet Les Murray recently termed them in the present day, 'the Anglo-Celtic archipelago'. As a social institution, literature models an intricate, diverse, stressful community, not a bland monolith.

There is now a logical and powerful case against mindlessly adopting any canon of great works as a basis of teaching literature in schools. It's hard not to smuggle in inappropriate ideas about what is most permissible, best sanctioned by an invisible, unexaminable 'authority'. And we have to acknowledge that reading a book sets up a transaction between author and reader, changing all the time as readers change. The consultation document which the Department of Education and Science in London sent out in July 1987 on the proposed new National Curriculum wisely acknowledged that its existing normal content must depend on who the pupils are now and where they have come from. We should ensure, it says, 'that all pupils, regardless of sex, ethnic origin and geographical location, have access to broadly the same good and relevant curriculum and programmes of study'. True, it goes on to speak of a body of pre-existent knowledge, the 'key content, skills and processes which they need to learn'. But it also respects 'relevance to the pupils' own experience' and 'continuing value to adult and working life'. Every pupil has a right to be given access to as much refined, musical poetry, as many great dramas and novels, as they can read with pleasure and profit to themselves. But that principle also implies a willingness to experiment with other materials, works of hitherto non-canonical status, which individual pupils, or minorities of pupils, would find more profitable. That is the syllabus problem as it affects schools, and it is in fact the greater and more pressing problem, with its own long-term repercussions on the teaching of literature in universities. But I want now to turn to look at the problem from the other end, not as a pedagogic issue in schools, but as an intellectual issue forced upon academics by radically changed modern circumstances. How in principle should we define the content of English Literature? How meet the objection that its existing normal content emerged at a particular time, for particular reasons, many of which no longer apply?

There is also a formidable case against continuing with the Victorian canon in its depleted version, as the basis either for teaching university students or for pursuing literary research. Over time the canon seems to have acquired a weird momentum of its own, and to have introduced various restrictive practices into criticism. Some originally pragmatic choices acquired fixity because, by the mid twentieth century, if you are a dead author and not in the canon you are probably not in print. The number of poets one *must* study gets fewer, and the number of poems by each writer gets much fewer, as time goes on. The questions that can be asked of major figures dwindle in number and importance with the fading of minor ones. The relations between texts are always of crucial significance, but it was left to twentieth-century scholars to claim that only major texts and major authors have meaningful relations. Keats now communes too often with Shakespeare, Wordsworth with St Augustine, everyone with the Bible. However much an artist is indebted to the mighty dead, he or she almost certainly borrows more from the living —that is, from writers no longer available for reading except in the better libraries. In the end, evaluation itself is threatened: how can you operate the techniques for telling who a major writer is, if you don't know what a minor one looks like?

Even in its adjusted modern form, the canon is being rapidly overtaken by events. Already within the last generation some academics at Columbia, Yale and Cornell have been redrafting literary history, while often denying that there is a literary history worth studying. M. H. Abrams, Geoffrey Hartman, Harold Bloom and their colleagues and pupils, encouraged by the Canadian Northrop Frye, have quietly installed their own line, which gives the modern East-coast intellectual his own appropriate intellectual genealogy, and is also, perhaps accidentally, conterminous with the independent history of the United States of America.

This line begins with Kant and runs through Blake, Wordsworth, Coleridge, Shelley to Hegel, Emerson, Carlyle, Whitman, Nietzsche, Freud and Wallace Stevens. German thinkers play a large part in the New England canon; many of the academics constructing it seem to have spoken German as their first language and to have trained in traditions that gave them no such personal motives for Anglophilia as old-style Ivy League professors often had. Since America has always been a multi-ethnic community, the British-built canon must often have tended to alienate, or at least fail to inspire, many of its students of literature. The strategic placing of Americans in the new one, and the skilful modernizing of the consciousnesses of the figures in it, does away, at first sight, with two of the more repellent features of old Eng. Lit. —its foreignness, and its historicity. On the other hand, it must be said that the new Modernist-Romantic canon hardly looks tailor-made for students: it is still Eurocentric and intimidatingly learned, through its range of allusion to the 2,000-year Hebraic religious tradition which the English Romantics allegedly revived. Wealth and prestige within the American university system continue to shift to California: it will be an interesting test of the responsiveness of the profession in America, to see if Emersonian New England gradually allows a pitch in the avant-garde parkland to California's Hispanics and Chinese.

It would be premature to offer rival international or British inner-city canons: those have to emerge with time, and with the raising of the consciousness of those currently marginalized. But an individual academic can at least begin to explore the unfortunate intellectual consequences of letting a small set of survivors, largely accidentally arrived at, dictate the model many of us seem to work with, of a timeless, desocialized, ahistorical literary community. What kind of critical difference would it make to study actual literary communities as they functioned within their larger communities in time and place? I propose that poets we have installed as canonical look more interesting individually, and far more understandable as groups, when we restore some of their lost peers. My example is a poet who was not accidentally overlooked but dropped by the curious consensus-making of the 1820s, for he was the Poet Laureate of the day, Robert Southey. . . .

Admitting Southey to the canon we have grown used to studying would not be a matter of enlarging it by one name. Several of the best-regarded poems of mainstream Romanticism interrelate so significantly with Southey's poems that they are no longer quite the same read without them. But if this is so, Southey's awkward status, neither canonical nor invisible to us, queries the formalist belief in the autonomous great poem, as well as the 'post-Romantic' faith in the independence of the great poet. Southey's position on the outside of the canon also raises the less palatable implications of that institution as a metaphor: it makes poets look like an exclusive club, an aristocracy, an old regime, a leadership of the righteously inclined.

Politics and the social needs of the day (progressive quite as much as oppressive) created in the nineteenth century these notions of literature, which history has delivered to us. It will be politics and new social needs that now induce us to revise them. The consequences of shirking a revision are great, for the opportunity facing teachers of literature in our lifetime may not recur in the next generation. Should millions of potential readers of great literature, in all parts of the world, be welcomed or repelled, given access to the past or in effect denied it? The barriers raised in their path at present include the intellectual and imaginative limitations, the conservativism or the possessiveness or the downright parochialism of entrenched literary professionals. A new historicism, newer and more open than most work attracting that description at present, seems a far healthier option.

2 Canon and Period*

FRANK KERMODE

I can best start this section on canon by reading an item from the US *Chronicle of Higher Education* dated 4 September 1985. This journal is widely circulated in American institutions of higher education. On this occasion, at the beginning of a new academic year, it ran a symposium in which twenty-two authorities in various fields told readers what developments to expect over the next few years. This is the forecast for literary studies:

The dominant concern of literary studies during the rest of the nineteen-eighties will be literary theory. Especially important will be the use of theory informed by the work of the French philosopher Jacques Derrida to gain insights into the cultures of blacks and women.

In fact the convergence of feminist and Afro-American theoretical formulations offers the most challenging nexus for scholarship in the coming years. Specifically the most exciting and insightful accounts of expressive culture in general and creative writing in particular will derive from efforts that employ feminist and Afro-American approaches to the study of texts by Afro-American writers such as Zora Neale Hurston, Sonia Sanchez, Gloria Naylor and Toni Morrison.

Among the promising areas for analysis is the examination of the concerns and metaphorical patterns that are common to past and present black women writers.

Such theoretical accounts of the cultural products of race and gender will help to undermine the half-truths that white males have established as constituting American culture as a whole. One aspect of that development will be the continued reshaping of the literary canon as forgotten, neglected or suppressed texts are re-discovered.

Literary theory is also full of disruptive and deeply political potential, which Afro-American and feminist critics will labor to release in coming years.

This manifesto, for such it appears to be, was written by the Professor 'of English and of Human Relations' at the University of Pennsylvania. It proposes what could well be called a radical deconstruction of the canon, putting in the place of the false elements foisted into it by white males a list of black females. These will be studied by methods specifically Afro-American. The writer points out the political implications of these developments, for he

* From Frank Kermode, 'Canon and Period', *History and Value*, Clarendon Press, Oxford, 1988, pp.113–170

knows that the changes he prophesies will not come to pass without alterations in more than the syllabus. He assumes that the literary canon is a
load-bearing element of the existing power structure, and believes that by
imposing radical change on the canon you can help to dismantle the power
structure.

What interests me most about this programme is not its cunning alliance
of three forces that might be thought to be in principle hostile to the idea of
the canon—Feminism, Afro-Americanism, and Deconstruction—so much as
its tacit admission that there is such a thing as literature and that there ought
to be such a thing as a canon; the opinions of the powerful about the contents
of these categories may be challenged, but the concepts of themselves remain
in place. Indeed the whole revolutionary enterprise simply assumes their
continuance. The canon is what the insurgents mean to occupy as the reward
of success in the struggle for power.

In short, what we have here is not a plan to abolish the canon but one to
capture it. The association of canon with authority is deeply ingrained in us,
and one can see simple reasons why it should be so. It is a highly selective
instrument, and one reason why we need to use it is that we haven't enough
memory to process everything. The only other option is not a universal
reception of the past and its literature but a Dadaist destruction of it. It must
therefore be protected by those who have it and coveted by those who don't.

Authority has invented many myths for the protection of the canon.
Religious canons can be effectively closed, even at the cost of retaining within
them books of which the importance is later difficult to discern, like some of
the briefer New Testament letters. They can be heavily protected, credited for
example with literal inspiration, so that it is forbidden to alter one jot or title
of them, diacritical signs, instructions to cantilators, even manifest errors.
And every word, every letter, is subject to minute commentary. Whatever is
included is sure to have its effect on the world. Suppose, for instance, that
Revelation had not got into the Christian canon, as it almost didn't; it would
have been just one more lost or apocryphal apocalypse, the province only of
specialist scholarship; instead it has had vast effects on social and political
behaviour over many ages, and continues to do so. The Fourth Gospel was at
one time under suspicion; had it not become so central a document for
Christian theology millions of people would have been required to believe
something quite different from the orthodox faith, and quite a lot of them
might have escaped burning if not burnt for some other reason.

So canons are complicit with power; and canons are useful in that they
enable us to handle otherwise unmanageable historical deposits. They do this
by affirming that some works are more valuable than others, more worthy of
minute attention. Whether their value is wholly dependent on their being
singled out in this way is a contested issue. There is in any case a quite

unmistakable difference of status between canonical and uncanonical books, however they got into the canon. But once they are in, certain changes come over them. First, they are completely locked into their times, their texts as near frozen as devout scholarship can make them, their very language more and more remote. Secondly, they are, paradoxically, by this fact, set free of time. Thirdly, the separate constituents become not only books in their own right but part of a larger whole—a whole because it is so treated. Fourthly, that whole, with all its interrelated parts, can be thought to have an inexhaustible potential of meaning, so that what happens in the course of time —as the original context and language of the collection grows more and more distant—is that new meanings accrue (they may be deemed, by a fiction characteristic of this way of thinking, to be original meanings) and these meanings constantly change though their source remains unchangeable. Since all the books can now be thought of as one large book, new echoes and repetitions are discovered in remote parts of the whole. The best commentary on any verse is another verse, possibly placed very far away from it. This was a rabbinical doctrine: 'I join passages from the Torah with passages from the Hagiographa, and the words of the Torah glow as the day they were given at Sinai.'[1]

The temporal gap between text and comment or application ensures that in practice something like the Gadamer-Jauss hermeneutics,[2] whether formalized or not, is always needed. The mutual influence of one canonical text on another, intemporal in itself, appearing in time only by means of commentary, is the essence of Eliot's idea of a canon, expressed in that famous passage in the essay 'Tradition and the Individual Talent'—'the whole of the literature of Europe . . . has a simultaneous existence and composes a simultaneous order', though he provides, as a secular canonist must, for additions to that order: 'The existing monuments form an ideal order among themselves, which is modified by the introduction of the new (the really new) work of art among them.[3] By this means 'order'—timeless order—'persists after the supervention of novelty', and it does so by adjusting itself to the new. Here the idea of canon is used in the service of an order which can be discerned in history but actually transcends it, and makes everything timeless and modern.

In this, as in the formulae of hermeneutics, in the rabbinical methodology and in the Marxist aspirations toward a theory of fruitful discrepancy, there is a clear purpose of making a usable past, a past which is not simply past but

---

[1] D. Patte, *Early Jewish Hermeneutic in Palestine* (1975), p. 44.
[2] Hans-Georg Gadamer, philosopher concerned with questions of meaning and interpretation, or 'hermeneutics'; Hans Robert Jauss, literary critic-scholar who argues that the historical 'horizon' of texts at various 'moments' alters how they are received and understood. [Ed.]
[3] *Selected Prose of T. S. Eliot*, ed. F. Kermode (1975), p. 38.

also always new. The object of all such thinking about the canonical monuments, then, is to make them *modern*. Indeed variants of this view are found in more than one writer of the period we now think of as 'Modernist'. At the same time there was a rival kind of Modernism that professed a desire to destroy the monuments, to destroy the past. But the ghost of canonicity haunts even these iconoclasts. And whether one thinks of canons as objectionable because formed at random or to serve some interests at the expense of others, or whether one supposes that the contents of canons are providentially chosen, there can be no doubt that we have not found ways of ordering our thoughts about the history of literature and art without recourse to them. That is why the minorities who want to be rid of what they regard as a reactionary canon can think of no way of doing so without putting a radical one in its place.

This is true even if one agrees with Benjamin that 'there is no document of civilization which is not at the same time a document of barbarism',[4] for every 'document of civilization' retains qualities that set it apart from possible substitutes 'in an age of mechanical reproduction'; and to Benjamin, with his unmatched sense of their qualities (which he subsumes under the name of 'aura'), the abolition of such documents was close to unthinkable. He believed that the historical materialist should in conscience dissociate himself from these works of art, indissolubly associated in their making and in their transmission with injustice and oppression, but he was no more able to do so than the materialists I've already talked about, including those who believed that the works of art in question should be preserved as the dearly bought heritage of the descendants of the victims. Benjamin approved of Proust, with his sense of aura, of 'the incalculable individual life'[5] (a rather bourgeois expression, surely), and he disapproved of Dada, which would destroy both aura and the past. There is no escaping it: if we want the monuments, the documents we value, we must preserve them in spite of their evil associations, and find ways of showing that their value somehow persists in our changed world. Moreover we cannot avoid seeing them as interrelated, as of the same family by reason of their distinctive features and qualities. So we have somehow to place them in relation to one another; and the way we do that will help to determine our attitude to the past. The canon, in predetermining value, shapes the past and makes it humanly available, accessibly modern.

---

[4] W. Benjamin, *Illuminations*, trans. H. Zohn (1968), p. 258.
[5] Ibid. p. 210.

3 Literature and the Rise of English*

TERRY EAGLETON

We have still not discovered the secret, then, of why Lamb, Macaulay and Mill are literature but not, generally speaking, Bentham, Marx and Darwin. Perhaps the simple answer is that the first three are examples of 'fine writing', whereas the last three are not. This answer has the disadvantage of being largely untrue, at least in my judgement, but it has the advantage of suggesting that by and large people term 'literature' writing which they think is *good*. An obvious objection to this is that if it were entirely true there would be no such thing as 'bad literature'. I may consider Lamb and Macaulay overrated, but that does not necessarily mean that I stop regarding them as literature. You may consider Raymond Chandler 'good of his kind', but not exactly literature. On the other hand, if Macaulay were a *really* bad writer—if he had no grasp at all of grammar and seemed interested in nothing but white mice —then people might well not call his work literature at all, even bad literature. Value-judgements would certainly seem to have a lot to do with what is judged literature and what isn't—not necessarily in the sense that writing has to be 'fine' to be literary, but that it has to be *of the kind* that is judged fine: it may be an inferior example of a generally valued mode. Nobody would bother to say that a bus ticket was an example of inferior literature, but someone might well say that the poetry of Ernest Dowson was. The term 'fine writing', or *belles lettres*, is in this sense ambiguous: it denotes a sort of writing which is generally highly regarded, while not necessarily committing you to the opinion that a particular specimen of it is 'good'.

With this reservation, the suggestion that 'literature' is a highly valued kind of writing is an illuminating one. But it has one fairly devastating consequence. It means that we can drop once and for all the illusion that the category 'literature' is 'objective', in the sense of being eternally given and immutable. Anything can be literature, and anything which is regarded as unalterably and unquestionably literature—Shakespeare, for example—can cease to be literature. Any belief that the study of literature is the study of a stable, well-definable entity, as entomology is the study of insects, can be abandoned as a chimera. Some kinds of fiction are literature and some are not; some literature is fictional and some is not; some literature is verbally self-regarding, while some highly wrought rhetoric is not literature. Literature, in the sense of a set of works of assured and unalterable value, distinguished by certain shared inherent properties, does not exist. When I use the words 'literary' and 'literature' from here on in this book, then, I place

* From Terry Eagleton, *Literary Theory: An Introduction*, Basil Blackwell, Oxford, 1983, pp. 10–15, 22–4.

them under an invisible crossing-out mark, to indicate that these terms will not really do but that we have no better ones at the moment.

The reason why it follows from the definition of literature as highly valued writing that it is not a stable entity is that value-judgements are notoriously variable. 'Times change, values don't,' announces an advertisement for a daily newspaper, as though we still believed in killing off infirm infants or putting the mentally ill on public show. Just as people may treat a work as philosophy in one century and as literature in the next, or vice versa, so they may change their minds about what writing they consider valuable. They may even change their minds about the grounds they use for judging what is valuable and what is not. This, as I have suggested, does not necessarily mean that they will refuse the title of literature to a work which they have come to deem inferior: they may still call it literature, meaning roughly that it belongs to the *type* of writing which they generally value. But it does mean that the so-called 'literary canon', the unquestioned 'great tradition' of the 'national literature', has to be recognized as a *construct*, fashioned by particular people for particular reasons at a certain time. There is no such thing as a literary work or tradition which is valuable *in itself*, regardless of what anyone might have said or come to say about it. 'Value' is a transitive term: it means whatever is valued by certain people in specific situations, according to particular criteria and in the light of given purposes. It is thus quite possible that, given a deep enough transformation of our history, we may in the future produce a society which is unable to get anything at all out of Shakespeare. His works might simply seem desperately alien, full of styles of thought and feeling which such a society found limited or irrelevant. In such a situation, Shakespeare would be no more valuable than much present-day graffiti. And though many people would consider such a social condition tragically impoverished, it seems to me dogmatic not to entertain the possibility that it might arise rather from a general human enrichment. Karl Marx was troubled by the question of why ancient Greek art retained an 'eternal charm', even though the social conditions which produced it had long passed; but how do we know that it will remain 'eternally' charming, since history has not yet ended? Let us imagine that by dint of some deft archaeological research we discovered a great deal more about what ancient Greek tragedy actually meant to its original audiences, recognized that these concerns were utterly remote from our own, and began to read the plays again in the light of this deepened knowledge. One result might be that we stopped enjoying them. We might come to see that we had enjoyed them previously because we were unwittingly reading them in the light of our own preoccupations; once this became less possible, the drama might cease to speak at all significantly to us.

The fact that we always interpret literary works to some extent in the light of our own concerns—indeed that in one sense of 'our own concerns' we are incapable of doing anything else—might be one reason why certain works of literature seem to retain their value across the centuries. It may be, of course, that we still share many preoccupations with the work itself; but it may also be that people have not actually been valuing the 'same' work at all, even though they may think they have. 'Our' Homer is not identical with the Homer of the Middle Ages, nor 'our' Shakespeare with that of his contemporaries; it is rather that different historical periods have constructed a 'different' Homer and Shakespeare for their own purposes, and found in these texts elements to value or devalue, though not necessarily the same ones. All literary works, in other words, are 'rewritten', if only unconsciously, by the societies which read them; indeed there is no reading of a work which is not also a 're-writing'. No work, and no current evaluation of it, can simply be extended to new groups of people without being changed, perhaps almost unrecognizably, in the process; and this is one reason why what counts as literature is a notably unstable affair.

I do not mean that it is unstable because value-judgements are 'subjective'. According to this view, the world is divided between solid facts 'out there' like Grand Central station, and arbitrary value-judgements 'in here' such as liking bananas or feeling that the tone of a Yeats poem veers from defensive hectoring to grimly resilient resignation. Facts are public and unimpeachable, values are private and gratuitous. There is an obvious difference between recounting a fact, such as 'This cathedral was built in 1612', and registering a value-judgement, such as 'This cathedral is a magnificent specimen of baroque architecture'. But suppose I made the first kind of statement while showing an overseas visitor around England, and found that it puzzled her considerably. Why, she might ask, do you keep telling me the dates of the foundation of all these buildings? Why this obsession with origins? In the society I live in, she might go on, we keep no record at all of such events: we classify our buildings instead according to whether they face north-west or south-east. What this might do would be to demonstrate part of the unconscious system of value-judgements which underlies my own descriptive statements. Such value-judgements are not necessarily of the same kind as 'This cathedral is a magnificent specimen of baroque architecture', but they are value-judgements nonetheless, and no factual pronouncement I make can escape them. Statements of fact are after all *statements*, which presumes a number of questionable judgements: that those statements are worth making, perhaps more worth making than certain others, that I am the sort of person entitled to make them and perhaps able to guarantee their truth, that you are the kind of person worth making them to, that something useful is accomplished by making them, and so on. A pub conversation may well transmit information, but what also bulks large in such dialogue is a strong element of what linguists would call the 'phatic', a concern with the act of communication itself. In chatting to you about the weather I am also signalling that I regard conversation with you as valuable, that I consider you a worthwhile person to talk to, that I am not myself anti-social or about to embark on a detailed critique of your personal appearance.

In this sense, there is no possibility of a wholly disinterested statement. Of course stating when a cathedral was built is reckoned to be more disinterested in our own culture than passing an opinion about its architecture, but one could also imagine situations in which the former statement would be more 'value-laden' than the latter. Perhaps 'baroque' and 'magnificent' have come to be more or less synonymous, whereas only a stubborn rump of us cling to the belief that the date when a building was founded is significant, and my statement is taken as a coded way of signalling this partisanship. All of our descriptive statements move within an often invisible network of value-categories, and indeed without such categories we would have nothing to say to each other at all. It is not just as though we have something called factual knowledge which may then be distorted by particular interests and judgements, although this is certainly possible; it is also that without particular interests we would have no knowledge at all, because we would not see the point of bothering to get to know anything. Interests are *constitutive* of our knowledge, not merely prejudices which imperil it. The claim that knowledge should be 'value-free' is itself a value-judgement.

It may well be that a liking for bananas is a merely private matter, though this is in fact questionable. A thorough analysis of my tastes in food would probably reveal how deeply relevant they are to certain formative experiences in early childhood, to my relations with my parents and siblings and to a good many other cultural factors which are quite as social and 'non-subjective' as railway stations. This is even more true of that fundamental structure of beliefs and interests which I am born into as a member of a particular society, such as the belief that I should try to keep in good health, that differences of sexual role are rooted in human biology or that human beings are more important than crocodiles. We may disagree on this or that, but we can only do so because we share certain 'deep' ways of seeing and valuing which are bound up with our social life, and which could not be changed without transforming that life. Nobody will penalize me heavily if I dislike a particular Donne poem, but if I argue that Donne is not literature at all then in certain circumstances I might risk losing my job. I am free to vote Labour or Conservative, but if I try to act on the belief that this choice itself merely masks a deeper prejudice—the prejudice that the meaning of democracy is confined to putting a cross on a ballot paper every few years—then in certain unusual circumstances I might end up in prison.

The largely concealed structure of values which informs and underlies our

factual statements is part of what is meant by 'ideology'. By 'ideology' I mean, roughly, the ways in which what we say and believe connects with the power structure and power-relations of the society we live in. It follows from such a rough definition of ideology that not all of our underlying judgements and categories can usefully be said to be ideological. It is deeply ingrained in us to imagine ourselves moving forwards into the future (at least one other society sees itself as moving backwards into it), but though this way of seeing *may* connect significantly with the power-structure of our society, it need not always and everywhere do so. I do not mean by 'ideology' simply the deeply entrenched, often unconscious beliefs which people hold; I mean more particularly those modes of feeling, valuing, perceiving and believing which have some kind of relation to the maintenance and reproduction of social power. The fact that such beliefs are by no means merely private quirks may be illustrated by a literary example.

In his famous study *Practical Criticism* (1929), the Cambridge critic I. A. Richards sought to demonstrate just how whimsical and subjective literary value-judgements could actually be by giving his undergraduates a set of poems, withholding from them the titles and authors' names, and asking them to evaluate them. The resulting judgements, notoriously, were highly variable: time-honoured poets were marked down and obscure authors celebrated. To my mind, however, much the most interesting aspect of this project, and one apparently quite invisible to Richards himself, is just how tight a consensus of unconscious valuations underlies these particular differences of opinion. Reading Richards' undergraduates' accounts of literary works, one is struck by the habits of perception and interpretation which they spontaneously share—what they expect literature to be, what assumptions they bring to a poem and what fulfilments they anticipate they will derive from it. None of this is really surprising: for all the participants in this experiment were, presumably, young, white, upper- or upper-middle-class, privately educated English people of the 1920s, and how they responded to a poem depended on a good deal more than purely 'literary' factors. Their critical responses were deeply entwined with their broader prejudices and beliefs. This is not a matter of *blame*: there is no critical response which is not so entwined, and thus no such thing as a 'pure' literary critical judgement of interpretation. If anybody is to be blamed it is I. A. Richards himself, who as a young, white, upper-middle-class male Cambridge don was unable to objectify a context of interests which he himself largely shared, and was thus unable to recognize fully that local, 'subjective' differences of evaluation work within a particular, socially structured way of perceiving the world.

If it will not do to see literature as an 'objective', descriptive category, neither will it do to say that literature is just what people whimsically choose to call literature. For there is nothing at all whimsical about such kinds of value-judgement: they have their roots in deeper structures of belief which are as apparently unshakeable as the Empire State building. . . .

THE RISE OF ENGLISH

Literature, in the meaning of the word we have inherited, *is* an ideology. It has the most intimate relations to questions of social power. But if the reader is still unconvinced, the narrative of what happened to literature in the later nineteenth century might prove a little more persuasive.

If one were asked to provide a single explanation for the growth of English studies in the later nineteenth century one could do worse than reply: 'the failure of religion'. By the mid-Victorian period, this traditionally reliable, immensely powerful ideological form was in deep trouble. It was no longer winning the hearts and minds of the masses, and under the twin impacts of scientific discovery and social change its previous unquestioned dominance was in danger of evaporating. This was particularly worrying for the Victorian ruling class, because religion is for all kinds of reasons an extremely effective form of ideological control. Like all successful ideologies, it works much less by explicit concepts or formulated doctrines than by image, symbol, habit, ritual and mythology. It is affective and experiential, entwining itself with the deepest unconscious roots of the human subject; and any social ideology which is unable to engage with such deep-seated a-rational fears and needs, as T. S. Eliot knew, is unlikely to survive very long. Religion, moreover, is capable of operating at every social level: if there is a doctrinal inflection of it for the intellectual elite, there is also a pietistic brand of it for the masses. It provides an excellent social 'cement', encompassing pious peasant, enlightened middle-class liberal and theological intellectual in a single organization. Its ideological power lies in its capacity to 'materialize' beliefs as practices: religion is the sharing of the chalice and the blessing of the harvest, not just abstract argument about consubstantiation or hyperdulia. Its ultimate truths, like those mediated by the literary symbol, are conveniently closed to rational demonstration, and thus absolute in their claims. Finally religion, at least in its Victorian forms, is a *pacifying* influence, fostering meekness, self-sacrifice and the contemplative inner life. It is no wonder that the Victorian ruling class looked on the threatened dissolution of this ideological discourse with something less than equanimity.

Fortunately, however, another, remarkably similar discourse lay to hand: English literature. George Gordon, early Professor of English Literature at Oxford, commented in his inaugural lecture that 'England is sick, and . . . English literature must save it. The Churches (as I understand) having failed, and social remedies being slow, English literature has now a triple function: still, I suppose, to delight and instruct us, but also, and above all, to save our souls and heal the State.'[1] Gordon's words were spoken in our own century, but they find a resonance everywhere in Victorian England. It is a striking thought that had it not been for this dramatic crisis in mid-nineteenth-century ideology, we might not today have such a plentiful supply of Jane Austen casebooks and bluffer's guides to Pound. As religion progressively ceases to provide the social 'cement', affective values and basic mythologies by which a socially turbulent class-society can be welded together, 'English' is constructed as a subject to carry this ideological burden from the Victorian period onwards.

4 *Women Poets**

SANDRA M. GILBERT AND SUSAN GUBAR

Despite a proliferation of literary ancestresses . . . Elizabeth Barrett Browning commented mournfully in 1845 that 'England has had many learned women . . . and yet where are the poetesses? . . . I look everywhere for grandmothers, and see none'.[1] In 1862, moreover, Emily Dickinson, articulating in another way the same distinction between women's prose and women's verse, expressed similar bewilderment. Complaining that

> They shut me up in Prose—
> As when a little Girl
> They put me in the Closet—
> Because they liked me 'still'[2]

she implied a recognition that poetry by women was in some sense inappropriate, unladylike, immodest. And in 1928, as if commenting on both Barrett Browning's comment and Dickinson's complaint, Woolf invented a tragic history for her 'Judith Shakespeare' because she so deeply believed that it is 'the poetry that is still denied outlet'.

Why did these three literary women consider poetry by women somehow forbidden or problematical? Woolf herself, after all, traced the careers of Anne

---

[1] Quoted by Chris Baldick, 'The Social Mission of English Studies' (unpubl. D. Phil., Oxford, 1981), p. 156. I am considerably indebted to this excellent study, to be published as *The Social Mission of English Criticism* (Oxford, 1983).

* From Sandra M. Gilbert and Susan Gubar, 'Introduction', *Shakespeare's Sisters: Feminist Essays on Women Poets*, Indiana University Press, Bloomington and London, 1979, pp. xvi–xxii.

[1] *The Letters of Elizabeth Barrett Browning*, ed. Frederick G. Kenyon (2 vols. in 1, New York: Macmillan, 1899), I, pp. 230–2. Compare Woolf's 'For we think back through our mothers if we are women. It is useless to go to the great men writers for help, however much one may go to them for pleasure' (*A Room of One's Own*, p. 79).

[2] Thomas Johnson, ed., *The Complete Poems of Emily Dickinson* (Boston: Little, Brown, 1960), No. 613.

Finch and Margaret Cavendish, admired the 'wild poetry' of the Brontës, noted that Barrett Browning's verse-novel *Aurora Leigh* had poetic virtues no prose work could rival, and spoke almost with awe of Christina Rossetti's 'complex song'.[3] Why, then, did she feel that 'Judith Shakespeare' was 'caught and tangled', 'denied', suffocated, self-buried, or not yet born? We can begin to find answers to these questions by briefly reviewing some of the ways in which representative male readers and critics have reacted to poetry by representative women like Barrett Browning and Dickinson.

Introducing *The Selected Poems of Emily Dickinson* in 1959, James Reeves quoted 'a friend' as making a statement which expresses the predominant attitude of many male *literati* toward poetry by women even more succinctly than Woolf's story did: 'A friend who is also a literary critic has suggested, not perhaps quite seriously, that "woman poet" is a contradiction in terms.'[4] In other words, from what Woolf would call the 'masculinist' point of view, the very nature of lyric poetry is inherently incompatible with the nature or essence of femaleness. Remarks by other 'masculinist' readers and critics elaborate on the point. In the midst of favorably reviewing the work of his friend Louise Bogan, for instance, Theodore Roethke detailed the various 'charges most frequently levelled against poetry by women'. Though his statement begins by pretending objectivity, it soon becomes clear that he himself is making such accusations.

Two of the [most frequent] charges . . . are lack of range—in subject matter, in emotional tone—and lack of a sense of humor. And one could, in individual instances among writers of real talent, add other aesthetic and moral shortcomings: the spinning out; the embroidering of trivial themes; a concern with the mere surfaces of life—that special province of the feminine talent in prose—hiding from the real agonies of the spirit; refusing to face up to what existence is; lyric or religious posturing; running between the boudoir and the altar; stamping a tiny foot against God or lapsing into a sententiousness that implies the author has re-invented integrity; carrying on excessively about Fate, about time; lamenting the lot of the woman; caterwauling; writing the same poem about fifty times, and so on. . . .[5]

Even a cursory reading of this passage reveals its inconsistency: women are taxed for both triviality and sententiousness, for both silly superficiality and melodramatic 'carrying on' about profound subjects. More significant, however, is the fact that Roethke attacks female poets for doing just what

    [3] See especially 'Aurora Leigh' and 'I am Christina Rossetti' in *The Second Common Reader* (New York: Harcourt Brace, 1932), pp. 182–92 and 214–21.
    [4] Reprinted in Richard B. Sewall, ed., *Emily Dickinson: A Collection of Critical Essays* (Englewood Cliffs, NJ: Prentice-Hall, 1963), p. 120. In fairness to Reeves, we should note that he quotes this statement in order to dispute it.
    [5] Theodore Roethke, 'The Poetry of Louise Bogan', *Selected Prose of Theodore Roethke*, ed. Ralph J. Mills, Jr. (Seattle: University of Washington Press, 1965), pp. 133–4.

male poets do—that is, for writing about God, fate, time, and integrity; for writing obsessively on the same themes or subjects, and so forth. But his language suggests that it is precisely the sex of these literary women that subverts their art. Shaking a Promethean male fist 'against God' is one perfectly reasonable aesthetic strategy, apparently, but stamping a 'tiny' feminine foot is quite another.

Along similar lines, John Crowe Ransom noted without disapproval in a 1956 essay about Emily Dickinson that 'it is common belief among readers (among men readers at least) that the woman poet as a type . . . makes flights into nature rather too easily and upon errands which do not have metaphysical importance enough to justify so radical a strategy'.[6] Elsewhere in the same essay, describing Dickinson as 'a little home-keeping person' he speculated that 'hardly . . . more' than 'one out of seventeen' of her 1,775 poems are destined to become 'public property', and observed that her life 'was a humdrum affair of little distinction', although 'in her Protestant community the gentle spinsters had their assured and useful place in the family circle, they had what was virtually a vocation'.[7] (But how, he seemed to wonder, could someone with so humdrum a social destiny have written great poetry?) Equally concerned with the problematical relationship between Dickinson's poetry and her femaleness—with, that is, what seemed to be an irreconcilable conflict between her 'gentle' spinsterhood and her fierce art—R. P. Blackmur decided in 1937 that 'she was neither a professional poet nor an amateur; she was a private poet who wrote indefatigably, as some women cook or knit. Her gift for words and the cultural predicament of her time drove her to poetry instead of antimacassars'.[8]

Even in 1971, male readers of Dickinson brooded upon this apparent dichotomy of poetry and femininity. John Cody's *After Great Pain* perceptively analyzes the suffering that many of Dickinson's critics and biographers have refused to acknowledge. But his conclusion emphasizes what he too sees as the incompatibility between womanly fulfillment and passionate art.

Had Mrs Dickinson been warm and affectionate, more intelligent, effective, and admirable, Emily Dickinson early in life would probably have identified with her, become domestic, and adopted the conventional woman's role. She would then have become a church member, been active in community affairs, married, and had children. The creative potentiality would of course still have been there, but would she have discovered it? What motivation to write could have replaced the incentive given by suffering and loneliness? If in spite of her wifely and motherly duties, she had still felt the need to express herself in verse, what would her subject matter have been?

---

[6] 'Emily Dickinson: A Poet Restored', in Sewall, p. 92.
[7] Ibid., p. 89.
[8] Quoted in Reeves, p. 119.

Would art have sprung from fulfillment, gratification, and completeness as abundantly as it did from longing, frustration, and deprivation?[9]

Interestingly, these questions restate an apparently very different position taken by Ransom fifteen years earlier: 'Most probably [Dickinson's] poems would not have amounted to much if the author had not finally had her own romance, enabling her to fulfill herself like any other woman.' Though Ransom speaks of the presence and 'fulfillment' of 'romance', while Cody discusses its tormenting absence, neither imagines that poetry itself could possibly constitute a woman's fulfillment. On the contrary, both assume that the art of a woman poet must in some sense arise from 'romantic' feelings (in the popular, sentimental sense), arise either in response to a real romance or as compensation for a missing one.

In view of this critical obsession with womanly 'fulfillment'—clearly a nineteenth-century notion redefined by twentieth-century thinkers for their own purposes—it is not surprising to find out that when poetry by women *has* been praised it has usually been praised for being 'feminine', just as it has been blamed for being deficient in 'femininity'. Elizabeth Barrett Browning, for instance, the most frequently analyzed, criticized, praised, and blamed woman poet of her day, was typically admired 'because of her understanding of the depth, tenderness, and humility of the love which is given by women',[10] and because 'she was a poet in every fibre of her but adorably feminine. . . .'[11] As the 'Shakespeare of her sex',[12] moreover, she was especially respected for being 'pure and lovely' in her 'private life', since 'the lives of women of genius have been so frequently sullied by sin . . . that their intellectual gifts are [usually] a curse rather than a blessing'.[13] Significantly, however, when Barrett Browning attempted unromantic, 'unfeminine' political verse in *Poems Before Congress*, her collection of 1860, at least one critic decided that she had been 'seized with a . . . fit of insanity', explaining that 'to bless and not to curse is a woman's function. . . .'[14]

As this capsule review of *ad feminam* criticism suggests, there is evidently something about lyric poetry by women that invites meditations on female fulfillment or, alternatively, on female insanity. In devising a story for 'Judith Shakespeare', Woolf herself was after all driven to construct a violent plot that ends with her suicidal heroine's burial beneath a bus-stop near the Elephant

---

[9] John Cody, *After Great Pain: The Inner Life of Emily Dickinson* (Cambridge, Mass: The Belknap Press of Harvard University Press, 1971), p. 495.

[10] Gardner B. Taplin, *The Life of Elizabeth Barrett Browning* (New Haven: Yale University Press, 1957), p. 417.

[11] *The Edinburgh Review*, vol. 189 (1899), pp. 420–39.

[12] Samuel B. Holcombe, 'Death of Mrs Browning', *The Southern Literary Messenger*, 33 (1861), pp. 412–17.

[13] *The Christian Examiner*, vol. 72 (1862), pp. 65–88.

[14] 'Poetic Aberrations', *Blackwood's*, vol. 87 (1860), pp. 490–4.

and Castle. Symbolically speaking, Woolf suggests, modern London, with its technological fumes and its patriarchal roar, grows from the grim crossroads where this mythic woman poet lies dead. And as if to reinforce the morbid ferocity of such imagery, Woolf adds that whenever, reading history or listening to gossip, we hear of witches and magical wise women, 'I think we are on the track of . . . a suppressed poet . . . who dashed her brains out on the moor or mopped and mowed about the highways crazed with the torture that her gift had put her to.' For though 'the original [literary] impulse was to poetry', and 'the "supreme head of song" was a poetess', literary women in England and America have almost universally elected to write novels rather than poems for fear of precisely the madness Woolf attributes to Judith Shakespeare. 'Sure the poore woman is a little distracted', she quotes a contemporary of Margaret Cavendish's as remarking: 'Shee could never be soe rediculous else as to venture at writeing books and in verse too, if I should not sleep this fortnight I should not come to that.'[15] In other words, while the woman novelist, safely shut in prose, may fantasize about freedom with a certain impunity (since she constructs purely fictional alternatives to the difficult reality she inhabits), it appears that the woman poet must in some sense become her own heroine, and that in enacting the diabolical role of witch or wise woman she literally or figuratively risks a melodramatic death at the crossroads of tradition and genre, society and art.

Without pretending to exhaust a profoundly controversial subject, we should note here that there are a number of generic differences between novel-writing and verse-writing which do support the kinds of distinctions Woolf's story implies. For one thing, as we noted earlier, novel-writing is a useful (because lucrative) occupation, while poetry, except perhaps for the narrative poetry of Byron and Scott, has traditionally had little monetary value. That novel-writing was and is conceivably an occupation to live by has always, however, caused it to seem less intellectually or spiritually valuable than verse-writing, of all possible literary occupations the one to which European culture has traditionally assigned the highest status. Certainly when Walter Pater in 1868 defined the disinterested ecstasy of art for his contemporaries by noting that 'art comes to you proposing frankly to give nothing but the highest quality to your moments as they pass, and simply for those moments' sake', he was speaking of what he earlier called 'the poetic passion', alluding to works like the Odes of Keats rather than the novels of Thackeray or George Eliot. Verse-writing—the product of mysterious 'inspiration', divine afflatus, bardic ritual—has historically been a holy vocation.[16] Before the nineteenth

---

[15] *A Room*, p. 65.
[16] See Pater, 'Conclusion' to *The Renaissance*, and, for a general discussion of the poet as priest, M. H. Abrams, *Natural Supernaturalism* (New York: Norton, 1971).

century the poet had a nearly priestly role, and 'he' had a wholly priestly role after Romantic thinkers had appropriated the vocabulary of theology for the realm of aesthetics. But if in Western culture women cannot be priests, then how—since poets are priests—can they be poets? The question may sound sophistic, but there is a good deal of evidence that it was and has been consciously or unconsciously asked, by men and women alike, as often as women suffering from 'the poetic passion' have appeared in the antechambers of literature.

As Woolf shows, though, novel-writing is not just a 'lesser' and therefore more suitably female occupation because it is commercial rather than aesthetic, practical rather than priestly. Where novel-writing depends upon reportorial observation, verse-writing has traditionally required aristocratic education. 'Learn . . . for ancient rules a just esteem;/To copy Nature is to copy them', Alexander Pope admonished aspiring critics and (by implication) poets in 1709, noting that 'Nature and Homer' are 'the same'.[17] As if dutifully acquiescing, even the fiery iconoclast Percy Bysshe Shelley assiduously translated Aeschylus and other Greek 'masters'. As Western society defines 'him', the lyric poet must have aesthetic models, must in a sense speak the esoteric language of literary forms. She or he cannot simply record or describe the phenomena of nature and society, for literary theorists have long believed that, in poetry, nature must be mediated through tradition—that is, through an education in 'ancient rules'. But of course, as so many women writers learned with dismay, the traditional classics of Greek and Latin—meaning the distilled Platonic essence of Western literature, history, philosophy—constituted what George Eliot called 'spheres of masculine learning' inalterably closed to women except under the most extraordinary circumstances. Interestingly, only Barrett Browning, of all the major women poets, was enabled—by her invalid seclusion, her sacrifice of ordinary pleasures— seriously to study 'the ancients'. Like Shelley, she translated Aeschylus' *Prometheus Bound*, and she went even further, producing an unusually learned study of the little-known Greek Christian poets. What is most interesting about Barrett Browning's skill as a classicist, however, is the fact that it was barely noticed in her own day and has been almost completely forgotten in ours.

Suzanne Juhasz has recently and persuasively spoken of the 'double bind' of the woman poet,[18] but it seems almost as if there is a sort of triple bind here. On the one hand, the woman poet who learns a 'just esteem' for Homer is ignored or even mocked—as, say, the eighteenth-century 'Blue Stockings' were. On the other hand, the woman poet who does not (because she is not

---

[17] See Pope, 'An Essay on Criticism', Part I, 11, pp. 135–40.
[18] Suzanne Juhasz, *Naked and Fiery Forms: Modern American Poetry by Women. A New Tradition* (New York: Harper & Row, 1976), 'The Double Bind of the Woman Poet', pp. 1–6.

allowed to) study Homer is held in contempt. On the third hand, however, whatever alternative tradition the woman poet attempts to substitute for 'ancient rules' is subtly devalued. Ransom, for instance, asserts that Dickinson's meters, learned from 'her father's hymnbook', are all based upon 'Folk Line, the popular form of verse and the oldest in our language', adding that 'the great classics of this meter are the English ballads and Mother Goose'. Our instinctive sense that this is a backhanded compliment is confirmed when he remarks that 'Folk Line is disadvantageous . . . if it denies to the poet the use of English Pentameter', which is 'the staple of what we may call the studied or "university" poetry, and . . . is capable of containing and formalizing many kinds of substantive content which would be too complex for Folk Line. Emily Dickinson appears never to have tried it.'[19] If we read 'pentameter' here as a substitute for 'ancient rules', then we can see that once again 'woman' and 'poet' are being defined as contradictory terms.

Finally, and perhaps most crucially, where the novel allows—even encourages—just the self-effacing withdrawal society has traditionally fostered in women, the lyric poem is in some sense the utterance of a strong and assertive 'I'. Artists from Shakespeare to Dickinson, Yeats, and T. S. Eliot have of course qualified this 'I', emphasizing, as Eliot does, the 'extinction of personality' involved in a poet's construction of an artful, masklike persona, or insisting, as Dickinson did, that the speaker of poems is a 'supposed person'.[20] But, nevertheless, the central self that speaks or sings a poem must be forcefully defined, whether 'she'/'he' is real or imaginary. If the novelist, therefore, inevitably sees herself from the *outside*, as an object, a character, a small figure in a large pattern, the lyric poet must be continually aware of herself from the *inside*, as a subject, a speaker: she must be, that is, assertive, authoritative, radiant with powerful feelings while at the same time absorbed in her own consciousness—and hence, by definition, profoundly 'unwomanly', even freakish. For the woman poet, in other words, the contradictions between her vocation and her gender might well become insupportable, impelling her to deny one or the other, even (as in the case of 'Judith Shakespeare') driving her to suicide. For, as Woolf puts it, 'who shall measure the heat and violence of the poet's heart when caught and tangled in a woman's body?'

---

[19] Ransom, ibid.; Sewall, pp. 99–100.
[20] See T. S. Eliot, 'Tradition and the Individual Talent', and Emily Dickinson, letter to T. W. Higginson, July 1892, in *The Letters of Emily Dickinson*, Thomas Johnson, ed. (Cambridge, Mass.: The Belknap Press of Harvard University Press, 1958), vol. II, p. 412.

5 *Yeats and Decolonization**

EDWARD SAID

Yeats has now been almost completely assimilated to the canon as well as the discourses of modern English literature, in addition to those of European high modernism. Both of these institutions of course reckon with him as a great modern Irish poet, deeply affiliated and interacting with his native traditions, the historical and political context of his times, and the extraordinarily complex situation of being a poet in Ireland writing in English. Nevertheless, and despite Yeats's obvious and, I would say, settled presence in Ireland, in British culture and literature and in European modernism, he does present another fascinating aspect: that of the indisputably great *national* poet who articulates the experiences, the aspirations, and the vision of a people suffering under the dominion of an off-shore power. From this perspective Yeats is a poet who belongs to a tradition not usually considered his, that of the colonial world ruled by European imperialism now—that is, during the late nineteenth and early twentieth centuries—bringing to a climactic insurrectionary stage, the massive upheaval of anti-imperialist resistance in the colonies, and of metropolitan anti-imperialist opposition that has been called the age of decolonization. If this is not a customary way of interpreting Yeats for those who know a great deal more about him as an Irish European modernist poet of immense stature than I do, then I can only say that he appears to me, and I am sure to many others in the Third World, to belong naturally to the other cultural domain . . . If this also sheds more light on the present status of Yeats's role in post-independence Ireland, then so much the better. . . .

A great deal, but by no means all, of the resistance to imperialism was conducted in the name of nationalism. Nationalism is a word that has been used in all sorts of sloppy and undifferentiated ways, but it still serves quite adequately to identify the mobilizing force that coalesced into resistance against an alien and occupying empire on the part of peoples possessing a common history, religion and a language. Yet for all its success in ridding many countries and territories of colonial overlords, nationalism has remained, in my opinion, a deeply problematic ideological, as well as sociopolitical, enterprise. At some stage in the anti-resistance phase of nationalism there is a sort of dependence between the two sides of the contest, since after all many of the nationalist struggles were led by bourgeoisies that were partly formed and to some degree produced by the colonial power; these are the

* From *Nationalism, Colonialism and Literature*, Field Day Pamphlet No. 15, Field Day Theatre Company Ltd., Derry, 1988, pp. 5–22.

national bourgeoisies of which Fanon[1] spoke so ominously. These bourgeoisies in effect have often replaced the colonial force with a new class-based and ultimately exploitative force; instead of liberation after decolonization one simply gets the old colonial structures replicated in new national terms.

That is one problem with nationalism . . . The other problem is that the cultural horizons of nationalism are fatally limited by the common history of colonizer and colonized assumed by the nationalist movement itself. Imperialism after all is a cooperative venture. Both the master and the slave participate in it, and both grew up in it, albeit unequally. One of the salient traits of modern imperialism is that in most places it set out quite consciously to modernize, develop, instruct and civilize the natives. An entire massive chapter in cultural history across five continents grows up out of it. The annals of schools, missions, universities, scholarly societies, hospitals in Asia, Africa, Latin America, Europe and America, fill its pages, and have had the effect over time of establishing the so-called modernizing trends in the colonial regions, as well as muting or humanizing the harsher aspects of imperialist domination—all of them bridging the gap between imperial center and peripheral territories. In paying respect to it, acknowledging the shared and combined experiences that produced many of us, we must at the same time note how at its center it nevertheless preserved the nineteenth century imperial divide between native and Westerner. The great colonial schools, for example, taught generations of the native bourgeoisie important truths about history, science, culture. And out of that learning process millions grasped the fundamentals of modern life, yet remained subordinate dependants of an authority based elsewhere than in their lives. Since one of the purposes of colonial education was to promote the history of France or Britain, that same education also demoted the native history. . . .

The culmination of this dynamic of dependence is, I said a moment ago, the resurgent nationalism of the various independence movements. Right across the Third World (including Ireland) in the period from World War One and concluding in the 1940s and 50s, new national states appear, all of them declaring their independence from the various European powers whose rule of direct domination had for various reasons come to an end. Nationalism in India, Ireland and Egypt, for example, was rooted in the long-standing struggle for native rights and independence by nationalist parties like the Congress, Sinn Fein, and the Wafd. Similar processes occurred in other parts of Africa and Asia. . . . Nevertheless, there were two distinct political moments during the nationalist revival, each with its own imaginative culture, the second unthinkable both in politics and history without the first.

[1] See Frantz Fanon, *The Wretched of the Earth*, 1965, first published as *Les Damnés de la terre*, 1961. [Ed.]

One was the period of nationalist anti-imperialism; the other, an era of liberationist anti-imperialist resistance that often followed it. The first was a pronounced awareness of European and Western culture *as* imperialism, as a reflexive moment of consciousness that enabled the African, Caribbean, Irish, Latin American or Asian citizen inching toward independence through decolonization to require a theoretical assertion of the end of Europe's cultural claim to guide and/or instruct the non-European or non-mainland individual. Often this was first done as Thomas Hodgkin has argued 'by prophets and priests', among them poets and visionaries, versions perhaps of Hobsbawm's pre-capitalist protest and dissent. The second more openly liberationist moment occurred during a dramatic prolongation after World War Two of the Western imperial mission in various colonial regions, principal among them Algeria, Vietnam, Palestine, Ireland, Guinea, Cuba. Whether in its general statements such as the Indian constitution, or Pan-Arabism and Pan-Africanism, or in its particularist forms such as Pearse's Gaelic or Senghor's *négritude*, the nationalism that formed the initial basis of the second moment stood revealed both as insufficient and yet as an absolutely crucial first step. Out of this paradox comes the idea of liberation, a strong new post-nationalist theme . . . sometimes requiring the propulsive infusion of theory and sometimes armed, insurrectionary militancy to bring it forward clearly, and unmistakably.

Let us look closely at the literature of the first of these moments, that of anti-imperialist resistance. Its literature develops quite consciously out of a desire to distance the native African, Indian, or Irish individual from the British, French or (later) American master. Before this can be done, however, there is a pressing need for the recovery of the land which, because of the presence of the colonizing outsider, is recoverable at first only through the imagination. Now if there is anything that radically distinguishes the imagination of anti-imperialism it is the primacy of the geographical in it. Imperialism after all is an act of geographical violence through which virtually every space in the world is explored, charted, and finally brought under control. For the native, the history of his/her colonial servitude is inaugurated by the loss to an outsider of the local place, whose concrete geographical identity must thereafter be searched for and somehow restored. From what? Not just from foreigners, but also from a whole other agenda whose purpose and processes are controlled elsewhere. . . .

With the new territoriality there comes a whole set of further assertions, recoveries, and identifications; all of them quite literally grounded on this poetically projected base. The search for authenticity, for a more congenial national origin than that provided by colonial history, for a new pantheon of heroes, myths, and religions, these too are enabled by the land. And along with these nationalistic adumbrations of the decolonized identity, there always goes an almost magically inspired, quasi-alchemical re-development of the native language. Yeats is especially interesting here. He shares with Caribbean and some African writers the predicament of a common language with the colonial overlord, and of course he belongs in many important ways to the Protestant Ascendancy whose Irish loyalties, to put it mildly, were confused. There is, I think, a fairly logical progression then from Yeats's early Gaelicism, with its Celtic preoccupations and themes, to his later systematic mythologies as set down in programmatic poems like 'Ego Dominus Tuus' and in the treatise *A Vision*. For Yeats the overlappings he knew existed between his Irish nationalism and the English cultural heritage that both dominated and empowered him as a writer was bound to cause an over-heated tension, and it is the pressure of this urgently political and secular tension that one may speculate caused him to try to resolve it on a 'higher', that is, non-political level. Thus the deeply eccentric and aestheticised histories he produced in *A Vision* and the later quasi-religious poems are elevations of the tension to an extra-wordly level.

In what must stand as the most interesting and brilliant account of Yeats's idea of revolution, Seamus Deane in *Celtic Revivals* [1985] has suggested that Yeats's early and invented Ireland was 'amenable to his imagination . . . [whereas] he ended by finding an Ireland recalcitrant to it'. Whenever Yeats tried to reconcile his occultist views with an actual Ireland—as in 'The Statues'—the results, Deane says correctly, are strained. Because Yeats's Ireland was a revolutionary country, Yeats was able to use Ireland's back-wardness as the source of its radically disturbing, disruptive return to spiritual ideals that had been lost to an over-developed modern Europe. Moreover in such dramatic realities as the Easter 1916 uprising Yeats also saw the breaking of a cycle of endless, perhaps finally meaningless recurrence, as symbolised by the apparently limitless travails of Cuchulain. Deane's theory therefore is that the birth of an Irish national identity coincides for Yeats with the breaking of the cycle, although it also underscores and reinforces the colonialist British attitude of a specific Irish national character. Thus Yeats's return to mysticism and his recourse to fascism, Deane says perceptively, are underlinings of the colonial predicament to be found, for example, in V. S. Naipaul's representations of India, that of a culture indebted to the mother country for its own self and for a sense of 'Englishness' and yet turning towards the colony: 'such a search for a national signature becomes colonial, on account of the different histories of the two islands. The greatest flowering of such a search has been Yeats's poetry.' And Deane goes on to conclude that far from representing an outdated nationalism, Yeats's wilful mysticism and incoherence do embody a revolutionary potential in the poet's insistence 'that Ireland should retain its culture by keeping awake its consciousness of metaphysical questions'. In a world from which the harsh strains of capitalism has removed thought and reflection, a poet who can stimulate a sense of the eternal and of death into consciousness is the true rebel, a figure whose colonial diminishments spur him to a negative apprehension of his society and of 'civilized' modernity.

The final Adornian[2] formulation of Yeats's quandary as it appears to the contemporary critic is of course powerful and it is attractive. Yet might we not suspect it a little of wanting to excuse Yeats's unacceptable and indigestible reactionary politics—his outright fascism, his fantasies of old homes and families, his incoherently occult divagations—by seeking to translate them into an instance of Adorno's 'negative dialectic', thereby rendering Yeats more heroic than a crudely political reading would have suggested? As a small corrective to Deane's conclusion, could we not more accurately see in Yeats a particularly exacerbated example of the *nativist* (e.g. *négritude*) phenomenon, which has flourished elsewhere as a result of the colonial encounter?

Now it is true that the connections are closer between England and Ireland, than between England and India, or France and Senegal. But the imperial relationship is there in all cases. The colonized may have a *sense* of England and France, speak and write in the dominant language even as he or she tries simultaneously to recover a native original, may even act in ways that directly conflict with the over-all interests of his/her people, and still the divide remains. This it seems to me has always been the case in every colonial relationship, because it is the first principle of imperialism that there is a clear-cut and absolute hierarchical distinction between ruler and ruled. Nativism, alas, reinforces the distinction by revaluating the weaker or sub-servient partner. And it has often led to compelling but often demagogic assertions about a native past, history or actuality that seems to stand free not only of the colonizer but of worldly time itself. One sees the drive backwards in such enterprises as Senghor's *négritude*, or in Soyinka's explorations of the African past, or in the Rastafarian movement, or in the Garveyite solution, or all through the Islamic world, the rediscoveries of various unsullied, pre-colonial Muslim essences. . . . to accept nativism is to accept the consequences of imperialism too willingly, to accept the very radical, religious and political divisions imposed on places like Ireland, India, Lebanon, and Palestine by imperialism itself. To leave the historical world for the metaphysics of essences like negritude, Irishness, Islam, and Catholicism is, in a word, to abandon history. Most often this abandonment in the post-imperial setting has led to some sort of millenarianism, if the movement has any sort of mass base, or it has degenerated into small-scale private craziness, or into an

---

[2] That is, derived from the work of Theodor Adorno (1903–60), member of the 'Frankfurt School' of Marxist social scientists, and author of, amongst other influential writings, *Negative Dialectics*, 1973. [Ed.]

unthinking acceptance of stereotypes, myths, animosities and traditions encouraged by imperialism. No one needs to be reminded that such programs are hardly what great resistance movements had imagined as their goals.

The other reason now for tempering the nativist and, in Yeats's case as formulated by Deane, the specifically Irish colonial attitude with a decent admixture of secular skepticism, is of course that nativism is not the only alternative. Here I return to what I said at the outset, that the first moment of resistance to imperialism brought forth all the various nationalist and independence movements that culminated in the large-scale dismantling of the great classical empires, and the birth of many new states throughout the world. The second moment (liberation), however, still continues with us, and its complexities and turbulence in many instances still defy resolution. In this phase, imperialism courses on, as it were, belatedly and in different forms perhaps, but the relationship of domination continues. Even though there was an Irish Free State by the end of his life Yeats in fact partially belonged to this second moment; the evidence for it is his sustained anti-British sentiment. And we know from the experiences of numerous colonial regions— Algeria, Vietnam, Cuba, Palestine, South Africa, and others—that the struggle for release continued. It is in this phase that I would like to suggest that *liberation*, and not nationalist independence, is the new alternative, liberation which by its very nature involves, in Fanon's words, a transformation of social consciousness beyond national consciousness. . . .

Yeats is very much the same as other poets resisting imperialism, in his insistence on a new narrative for his people, his anger at the schemes for partition (and enthusiasm for its felt opposite, the requirement of wholeness), the celebration and commemoration of violence in bringing about a new order, and the sinuous inter-weaving of loyalty and betrayal in the nationalist setting. Yeats's direct association with Parnell and O'Leary, with the Abbey Theatre, with the Easter Uprising, bring to his poetry what R. P. Blackmur, borrowing from Jung, calls 'the terrible ambiguity of an immediate experience'. . . .

One feels in reading poems like 'Nineteen Hundred and Nineteen' or 'Easter 1916', and 'September 1913', not just the disappointments of life commanded by 'the greasy till' or the violence of roads and horses, of 'weasels fighting in a hole', but also of a terrible new beauty that changes utterly the old political and moral landscape. Like all the poets of decolonization Yeats struggles to announce the contours of an 'imagined' or ideal community, crystallized not only by its sense of itself but also of its enemy. Imagined community, Benedict Anderson's fine phrase for emergent nationalism,[3] is apt here as I have used it, so long as we are not obliged to accept his

---

[3] Benedict Anderson, *Imagined Communities: Reflections on the Origins and Spread of Nationalism*, 1983. [Ed.]

mistakenly linear periodizations of unofficial and official nationalism. In the cultural discourses of decolonization, a great many languages, histories, forms circulate. As Barbara Harlow has shown in *Resistance Literature*, there are spiritual autobiographies, poems of protest, prison memoirs, didactic dramas of deliverance, but in them all is a sense of the instability of time, which has to be made and re-made by the people and its leaders. The shifts in Yeats's accounts of his great cycles invoke this instability, as does the easy commerce in his poetry between popular and formal speech, folk tale, and learned writing. The disquiet of what T. S. Eliot called the 'cunning history, [and] contrived corridors' of time—the wrong turns, the overlap, the senseless repetition, the occasionally glorious moment—furnish Yeats, as they do all the poets of decolonization, with stern martial accents, heroism, and the grinding persistence of 'the uncontrollable mystery on the bestial floor'. . . .

It is interesting that Yeats has often been cited in recent years as someone whose poetry warned of nationalist excesses. He is quoted without attribution, for example, in Gary Sick's book (*All Fall Down*) on the Carter administration's handling of the Iranian hostage crisis 1979–81; and I can distinctly recall that the New York *Times* correspondent in Beirut in 1975–6, James Markham, quotes the same passages from 'The Second Coming' in a piece he did about the onset of the Lebanese civil war in 1977. 'Things fall apart; the centre cannot hold' is one phrase. The other is 'The best lack all conviction, while the worst/Are full of passionate intensity'. Sick and Markham both write as Americans frightened of the revolutionary tide sweeping through a Third World once contained by Western power. Their use of Yeats is minatory: remain orderly, or you're doomed to a frenzy you cannot control. As to how, in an inflamed colonial situation, the colonized are supposed to remain orderly and civilized—given that the colonial order has long since profited the oppressor and has long since been discredited in the eyes of the colonized—neither Sick nor Markham tells us. They simply assume that Yeats, in any event, is on our side, *against* the revolution. It's as if both men could never have thought to take the current disorder back to the colonial intervention itself, which is what Chinua Achebe does in 1958, in his great novel *Things Fall Apart*.

The point, I believe, is that Yeats is at his most powerful precisely as he imagines and renders that very moment itself. His greatest decolonizing works quite literally conceive of the birth of violence, or the violent birth of change, as in 'Leda and the Swan', instants at which there is a blinding flash of simultaneity presented to his colonial eyes—the girl's rape, and alongside that, the question 'did she put on his knowledge with his power/Before the indifferent beak could let her drop?' Yeats situates himself at that juncture where the violence of change is unarguable, but where the results of the violence beseech necessary, if not always sufficient, reason. More precisely,

Yeats's greatest theme in the poetry that culminates in *The Tower* is, so far as decolonization is concerned, how to reconcile the inevitable violence of the colonial conflict with the everyday politics of an ongoing national struggle, and also with the power of each of the various parties in the colonial conflict, with the discourse of reason, of persuasion, of organization, with the require-ments of poetry. Yeats's prophetic perception that at some point violence cannot be enough and that the strategies of politics and reason must come into play is, to my knowledge, the first important announcement in the context of decolonization of the need to balance violent force with an exigent political and organizational process. Fanon's assertion, almost half a century later than Yeats, that liberation cannot be accomplished simply by seizing power (though he says, 'Even the wisest man grows tense with some sort of violence'), underlines the importance of Yeats's insight. That neither Yeats nor Fanon offers a prescription for undertaking the transition from direct force to a period *after* decolonization when a new political order achieves moral hegemony, is part of the difficulty we live with today in Ireland, Asia, Africa, the Caribbean, Latin America and the Middle East.

II *Interpretation*

These critics are all concerned in different but related ways with what is sometimes called 'hermeneutics', after the Greek for interpretation, originally applied to scriptural studies—just as the term 'canon' is derived from a notion of which biblical texts are accepted as the divine Word. Interpreting texts, like interpreting the world, proceeds on the basis of long philosophical traditions, which can quickly lead to complex and allusive arguments.

Lionel Trilling's influential account of 'Freud and Literature', although superseded in complexity and subtlety by later proponents of psychoanalytic interpretations of texts, introduces the basic point: what is the relationship of the artist/ writer's mind to the created work, and what are the implications of this for discovering its meaning? He argues that psychoanalysis cannot determine the 'true meaning' of a work of art, because there is no 'single meaning'. E. D. Hirsch argues that a distinction has to be made between the 'meaning' of a text and its possible 'interpretations': the text, he says, exists objectively and can have its meaning explained; interpretation follows from that. Stanley Fish, taking the Variorum *(i.e. complete scholarly) text of Milton as his starting-point, takes issue with Hirsch's view that 'meaning' resides in a text, and develops his notion of 'interpretive communities' to explain how people come to agree about meanings in texts.*

But the possibility that this raises, the 'disappearance' of the text as an independent entity, worries Robert Scholes, who claims that 'linguistic codes' make texts more than marks on the page. Finally, Hans Robert Jauss, one of the best-known exponents of a formidably learned German school of criticism known as 'reception theory', places the whole discussion in another perspective, relating the issues of interpretation, literary history, and the formation of a 'canon' by arguing for a completely new 'paradigm' or framework of understanding.

1 *Freud and Literature**

LIONEL TRILLING

The Freudian psychology is the only systematic account of the human mind which, in point of subtlety and complexity, of interest and tragic power,

* From Lionel Trilling, *The Liberal Imagination*, Penguin Books, Harmondsworth, Middlesex, 1970, pp. 50–2, 57–65; first publ. 1940, revised 1947.

deserves to stand beside the chaotic mass of psychological insights which literature has accumulated through the centuries. To pass from the reading of a great literary work to a treatise of academic psychology is to pass from one order of perception to another, but the human nature of the Freudian psychology is exactly the stuff upon which the poet has always exercised his art. It is therefore not surprising that the psychoanalytical theory has had a great effect upon literature. Yet the relationship is reciprocal, and the effect of Freud upon literature has been no greater than the effect of literature upon Freud. When, on the occasion of the celebration of his seventieth birthday, Freud was greeted as the 'discoverer of the unconscious', he corrected the speaker and disclaimed the title. 'The poets and philosophers before me discovered the unconscious,' he said. 'What I discovered was the scientific method by which the unconscious can be studied.' . . .

What is it that Freud added that the tendency of literature itself would not have developed without him? If we were looking for a writer who showed the Freudian influence, Proust would perhaps come to mind as readily as anyone else; the very title of his novel, in French more than in English, suggests an enterprise of psychoanalysis and scarcely less so does his method—the investigation of sleep, of sexual deviation, of the way of association, the almost obsessive interest in metaphor; at these and at many other points the 'influence' might be shown. Yet I believe it is true that Proust did not read Freud. Or again, exegesis of *The Waste Land* often reads remarkably like the psychoanalytic interpretation of a dream, yet we know that Eliot's methods were prepared for him not by Freud but by other poets.

Nevertheless, it is of course true that Freud's influence on literature has been very great. Much of it is so pervasive that its extent is scarcely to be determined; in one form or another, frequently in perversions or absurd simplifications, it has been infused into our life and become a component of our culture of which it is now hard to be specifically aware. In biography its first effect was sensational but not fortunate. The early Freudian biographers were for the most part Guildensterns who seemed to know the pipes but could not pluck out the heart of the mystery, and the same condemnation applies to the early Freudian critics. But in recent years, with the acclimatization to psychoanalysis and the increased sense of its refinements and complexity, criticism has derived from the Freudian system much that is of great value, most notably the licence and the injunction to read the work of literature with a lively sense of its latent and ambiguous meanings, as if it were, as indeed it is, a being no less alive and contradictory than the man who created it. And this new response to the literary work has had a corrective effect upon our conception of literary biography. The literary critic or biographer who makes use of the Freudian theory is no less threatened by the dangers of theoretical systematization than he was in the early days, but he is likely to be more aware of these dangers; and I think it is true to say that now the motive of his interpretation is not that of exposing the secret shame of the writer and limiting the meaning of his work, but, on the contrary, that of finding grounds for sympathy with the writer and for increasing the possible significances of the work . . .

I started by saying that Freud's ideas could tell us something about art, but so far I have done little more than try to show that Freud's very conception of art is inadequate. Perhaps, then, the suggestiveness lies in the application of the analytic method to specific works of art or to the artist himself? I do not think so, and it is only fair to say that Freud himself was aware both of the limits and the limitations of psychoanalysis in art, even though he does not always in practice submit to the former or admit the latter.

Freud has, for example, no desire to encroach upon the artist's autonomy; he does not wish us to read his monograph on Leonardo and then say of the *Madonna of the Rocks* that it is a fine example of homosexual, autoerotic painting. If he asserts that in investigation the 'psychiatrist cannot yield to the author', he immediately insists that the 'author cannot yield to the psychiatrist', and he warns the latter not to 'coarsen everything' by using for all human manifestations the 'substantially useless and awkward terms' of clinical procedure. He admits, even while asserting that the sense of beauty probably derives from sexual feeling, that psychoanalysis 'has less to say about beauty than about most other things'. He confesses to a theoretical indifference to the form of art and restricts himself to its content. Tone, feeling, style, and the modification that part makes upon part he does not consider. 'The layman', he says,

may expect perhaps too much from analysis . . . for it must be admitted that it throws no light upon the two problems which probably interest him the most. It can do nothing toward elucidating the nature of the artistic gift, nor can it explain the means by which the artist works—artistic technique.

What, then, does Freud believe that the analytical method can do? Two things: explain the 'inner meanings' of the work of art and explain the temperament of the artist as man.

A famous example of the method is the attempt to solve the 'problem' of *Hamlet* as suggested by Freud and as carried out by Dr Ernest Jones, his early and distinguished follower. Dr Jones's monograph is a work of painstaking scholarship and of really masterly ingenuity. The research undertakes not only the clearing up of the mystery of Hamlet's character, but also the discovery of 'the clue to much of the deeper workings of Shakespeare's mind'. Part of the mystery in question is of course why Hamlet, after he had so definitely resolved to do so, did not avenge upon his hated uncle his father's death. But there is another mystery to the play—what Freud calls 'the mystery of its effect', its magical appeal that draws so much interest toward it. Recalling the many failures to solve the riddle of the play's charm, he wonders if we are to be driven to the conclusion 'that its magical appeal rests solely upon the impressive thoughts in it and the splendour of its language'. Freud believes that we can find a source of power beyond this.

We remember that Freud has told us that the meaning of a dream is its intention, and we may assume that the meaning of a drama is its intention, too. The Jones research undertakes to discover what it was that Shakespeare intended to say about Hamlet. It finds that the intention was wrapped by the author in a dreamlike obscurity because it touched so deeply both his personal life and the moral life of the world; what Shakespeare intended to say is that Hamlet cannot act because he is incapacitated by the guilt he feels at his unconscious attachment to his mother. There is, I think, nothing to be quarrelled with in the statement that there is an Oedipus situation in *Hamlet*; and if psychoanalysis has indeed added a new point of interest to the play, that is to its credit. . . .

It is not here a question of the validity of the evidence, though that is of course important. We must rather object to the conclusions of Freud and Dr Jones on the ground that their proponents do not have an adequate conception of what an artistic meaning is. There is no single meaning to any work of art; this is true not merely because it is better that it should be true, that is, because it makes art a richer thing, but because historical and personal experience show it to be true. Changes in historical context and in personal mood change the meaning of a work and indicate to us that artistic understanding is not a question of fact but of value. Even if the author's intention were, as it cannot be, precisely determinable, the meaning of a work cannot lie in the author's intention alone. It must also lie in its effect. We can say of a volcanic eruption on an inhabited island that it 'means terrible suffering', but if the island is uninhabited or easily evacuated it means something else. In short, the audience partly determines the meaning of the work. But although Freud sees something of this when he says that in addition to the author's intention we must take into account the mystery of *Hamlet's* effect, he nevertheless goes on to speak as if, historically, *Hamlet's* effect had been single and brought about solely by the 'magical' power of the Oedipus motive to which, unconsciously, we so violently respond. Yet there was, we know, a period when *Hamlet* was relatively in eclipse, and it has always been scandalously true of the French, a people not without filial feeling, that they have been somewhat indifferent to the 'magical appeal' of *Hamlet*.

I do not think that anything I have said about the inadequacies of the Freudian method of interpretation limits the number of ways we can deal with a work of art. Bacon remarked that experiment may twist nature on the rack to wring out its secrets, and criticism may use any instruments upon a work of art to find its meanings. The elements of art are not limited to the world of art. They reach into life, and whatever extraneous knowledge of them we gain —for example, by research into the historical context of the work—may quicken our feelings for the work itself and even enter legitimately into those feelings. Then, too, anything we may learn about the artist himself may be enriching and legitimate. But one research into the mind of the artist is simply not practicable, however legitimate it may theoretically be. That is, the investigation of his unconscious intention as it exists apart from the work itself. Criticism understands that the artist's statement of his conscious intention, though it is sometimes useful, cannot finally determine meaning. How much less can we know from his unconscious intention considered as something apart from the whole work? Surely very little that can be called conclusive or scientific. For, as Freud himself points out, we are not in a position to question the artist; we must apply the technique of dream analysis to his symbols, but, as Freud says with some heat, those people do not understand his theory who think that a dream may be interpreted without the dreamer's free association with the multitudinous details of his dream. . . .

I should be sorry if it appeared that I am trying to say that psychoanalysis can have nothing to do with literature. I am sure that the opposite is so. For example, the whole notion of rich ambiguity in literature, of the interplay between the apparent meaning and the latent—not 'hidden'—meaning, has been reinforced by the Freudian concepts, perhaps even received its first impetus from them. Of late years the more perceptive psychoanalysts have surrendered the early pretensions of their teachers to deal 'scientifically' with literature. That is all to the good, and when a study as modest and precise as Dr Franz Alexander's essay on *Henry IV* comes along, an essay which pretends not to 'solve' but only to illuminate the subject, we have something worth having. Dr Alexander undertakes nothing more than to say that in the development of Prince Hal we see the classic struggle of the ego to come to normal adjustment, beginning with the rebellion against the father, going on to the conquest of the super-ego (Hotspur, with his rigid notions of honour and glory), then to the conquests of the *id* (Falstaff, with his anarchic self-indulgence), then to the identification with the father (the crown scene) and the assumption of mature responsibility. An analysis of this sort is not momentous and not exclusive of other meanings; perhaps it does no more than point up and formulate what we all have already seen. It has the tact to *accept* the play and does not, like Dr Jones's study of *Hamlet*, search for a 'hidden motive' and a 'deeper working', which implies that there is a reality to which the play stands in the relation that a dream stands to the wish that generates it and from which it is separable; it is this reality, this 'deeper working', which, according to Dr Jones, produced the play. But *Hamlet* is not merely the product of Shakespeare's thought, it is the very instrument of his thought, and if meaning is intention, Shakespeare did not intend the Oedipus motive or anything less than *Hamlet*; if meaning is effect then it is *Hamlet* which affects us, not the Oedipus motive. *Coriolanus* also deals, and very terribly, with the Oedipus motive, but the effect of the one drama is very different from the effect of the other.

If, then, we can accept neither Freud's conception of the place of art in life nor his application of the analytical method, what is it that he contributes to our understanding of art or to its practice? In my opinion, what he contributes outweighs his errors; it is of the greatest importance, and it lies in no specific statement that he makes about art but is, rather, implicit in his whole conception of the mind.

For, of all mental systems, the Freudian psychology is the one which makes poetry indigenous to the very constitution of the mind. Indeed, the mind, as Freud sees it, is in the greater part of its tendency exactly a poetry-making organ. This puts the case too strongly, no doubt, for it seems to make the workings of the unconscious mind equivalent to poetry itself, forgetting that between the unconscious mind and the finished poem there supervene the social intention and the formal control of the conscious mind. Yet the statement has at least the virtue of counterbalancing the belief, so commonly expressed or implied, that the very opposite is true, and that poetry is a kind of beneficent aberration of the mind's right course.

Freud has not merely naturalized poetry; he has discovered its status as a pioneer settler, and he sees it as a method of thought. Often enough he tries to show how, as a method of thought, it is unreliable and ineffective for conquering reality; yet he himself is forced to use it in the very shaping of his own science, as when he speaks of the topography of the mind and tells us with a kind of defiant apology that the metaphors of space relationship which he is using are really most inexact since the mind is not a thing of space at all, but that there is no other way of conceiving the difficult idea except by metaphor. In the eighteenth century Vico spoke of the metaphorical, imagistic language of the early stages of culture; it was left to Freud to discover how, in a scientific age, we still feel and think in figurative formations, and to create, what psychoanalysis is, a science of tropes, of metaphor and its variants, synecdoche and metonymy.

Freud showed, too, how the mind, in one of its parts, could work without logic, yet not without that directing purpose, that control of intent from which, perhaps it might be said, logic springs. For the unconscious mind works without the syntactical conjunctions which are logic's essence. It recognizes no *because*, no *therefore*, no *but*; such ideas as similarity, agreement, and community are expressed in dreams imagistically by compressing the elements into a unity. The unconscious mind in its struggle with the conscious always turns from the general to the concrete and finds the tangible trifle more congenial than the large abstraction. Freud discovered in the very organization of the mind those mechanisms by which art makes its effects, such devices as the condensations of meanings and the displacement of accent. . . .

2 *The Babel of Interpretations**

E. D. HIRSCH, JR.

How can a consensus be reached with regard to a text's meaning when every known interpretation of every text has always been different in some respect from every other interpretation of the text? The standard answer to this question is that every interpretation is partial. No single interpretation can possibly exhaust the meanings of a text. Therefore, to the extent that different interpretations bring into relief different aspects of textual meaning, the diversity of interpretations should be welcomed; they all contribute to understanding. The more interpretations one knows, the fuller will be one's understanding.

I am not suggesting that this answer is inadequate in every respect. In fact, I shall try to describe more precisely how different interpretations can and do support one another and how they can deepen our understanding. The answer is inadequate only in so far as it fails to account for the distinction between compatible and incompatible interpretations. The answer seems to assume that all 'plausible' or 'respectable' interpretations are compatible merely because they are all capable of being confirmed by the text. However, not all plausible interpretations are compatible. An interpretation of *Hamlet* which views the hero as a dilatory intellectual is not compatible with one that views him as a forceful man of action thwarted by circumstances. Both interpretations are plausible, and perhaps both are incorrect, but they are not compatible. Nor would their incompatibility be removed by concluding that both traits are present in Hamlet's character. That compromise would represent a third interpretation distinct from and incompatible with each of the other two. Interpretive disagreements do exist, and they are not always partial or trivial disagreements.

But the fact that all interpretations are different warrants neither the

* From E. D. Hirsch, Jr., *Validity and Interpretation*, Yale University Press, 1967, pp. 128–33, 134–9.

sanguine belief that all plausible interpretations are helpful and compatible nor the hopeless proposition that all interpretations are personal, temporal, and incommensurable. The apparent babel of interpretations leads to tender-mindedness or despair only if we fail to discriminate between the kinds of differences which interpretations exhibit. All interpretations are indeed different in some respect or other, but not all different interpretations are disparate or incompatible. For example, two interpretations could be different in a vast number of ways—the subjects they treat, the vocabulary in which they are written, the purposes they are designed to serve—yet might nevertheless refer to an identical construction of meaning. On the other hand, two interpretations might be highly similar in vocabulary and purpose but might nevertheless refer to two quite different constructions of meaning. Only the second kind of difference ought properly to be at issue, and in that case we should speak not of different but of disparate interpretations.

This distinction between the meaning of an interpretation and the construction of meaning to which the interpretation refers is one of the most venerable in hermeneutic theory. Ernesti called it the distinction between the art of understanding and the art of explaining—the *subtilitas intelligendi* and the *subtilitas explicandi*.[1] In normal usage both of these functions are embraced flaccidly by the single term 'interpretation', but clarity would be served if we limited that word to the *subtilitas explicandi*—the explanation of meaning—and delimited the *subtilitas intelligendi* by the term 'understanding'.

It is obvious that understanding is prior to and different from interpretation. Anyone who has written a commentary on a text has been aware that he could adopt a number of quite different strategies to convey his understanding and, furthermore, that the strategy he does adopt depends upon his audience and his purposes quite as much as it depends upon his understanding of the text. On the other hand, every reader of interpretations has noticed that he accepts some of them and rejects others and, furthermore, that even when he finds himself in agreement with an interpretation its effect upon him is not always simply to confirm his original conception. Sometimes, it is true, an interpretation merely 'deepens' his understanding, but sometimes it may genuinely 'alter' his understanding. These two functions illustrate very well the distinction between different and disparate interpretations. When a commentary deepens our understanding of a text, we do not experience any sense of conflict with our previous ideas. The new commentary does indeed lay out implications we had not thought of explicitly, but it does not alter our controlling conception of the text's meaning. We find ourselves in agreement from the beginning, and we admire the subtlety with which the interpreter brings out implications we had missed or had only dimly perceived. But this

[1] J. A. Ernesti, *Institutio Interpretis Novi Testamenti* (Leipzig, 1761), Chap. 1, Sec. 4.

'deepening' effect, instead of changing our original understanding, emphatically confirms it and makes us more certain of its rightness. The unnoticed
implications laid out by the interpreter belong to the type of meaning we had
already construed. On the other hand, when we read a commentary that
alters our understanding, we are convinced by an argument (covert or open)
that shows our original construction to be wrong in some respect. Instead of
being comforted by a further confirmation, we are compelled to change,
qualify, adjust our original view. The two functions of 'deepening' and
'altering' are quite distinct and correspond to the two ways in which interpretations differ. A very brief and elliptical commentary might be in complete
agreement with a long and 'inclusive' one, since both could refer to precisely
the same controlling conception of meaning. In that case the interpretations
would be different but not disparate.

In the final chapter I shall consider the problem of discriminating between
disparate interpretations, and also the corollary problem of deciding which of
them is most likely to be right. However, here it is more important to
emphasize the fact that two different interpretations are not necessarily
disparate, for all interpretations are different, and if no two of them could be
identified, then there could be no discipline of interpretation. Of course, any
two interpretations will always be concerned with different sorts and ranges
of implications, but they will not necessarily differ in their conception of the
implications they treat in common or in the importance they allot to those
implications with respect to the controlling purposes and emphases of the
text. Two interpretations that differ in this way can refer to an absolutely
identical meaning. How is this possible? Is it not imprecise to overlook the
subtle variations in meaning suggested by subtle variations in written
commentaries? Is it not the case that meaning can never break away
completely from the categories that an interpreter happens to use?

I have already suggested that the art of interpreting and the art of
understanding are separate functions, too often confused. Two interpreters
might, after all, use different strategies and categories to convey the same
conception of meaning, but the exigencies of written commentary do not
account for all the differences among interpretations. Some of these differences are owing to the fact that interpreters notice and emphasize different
aspects of meaning—even on the level of understanding. In such a case is it
possible or reasonable to assert that their interpretations refer to the same
construction of meaning? Even if their interpretations were broadly compatible, is it not far-fetched to assert that they are ultimately identical? What they
say is always different, but is it not also true that what they *see* is always
different? Is not the babel of interpretations still, after all, a babel?

These questions touch on the same group of problems that had to be faced
in dealing with the reproducibility of meaning and with the psychologistic

conception of meaning. Certainly, it can be reasonably presumed that two interpreters always notice slightly different aspects of meaning even on the level of understanding, but the different aspects might nevertheless be traits belonging to the same type. Similarly, the different meanings which different readers of a text might notice can refer to precisely the same type—which is to say, to the same meaning. This principle is constantly being exemplified in visual experience. When two observers look at a building from different standpoints, they each see quite different aspects of the building, yet, remarkably enough, both observers see the same whole building. They may not even be looking at the same sides, yet each of them imagines (vaguely or explicitly) the unseen sides—otherwise, they would not conceive the object as a building. Thus, while the explicit components of vision are in each case different, what those components refer to may be absolutely identical. A similar phenomenon occurs when one interpreter notices or emphasizes traits that are different from those noticed by another. The explicit components of meaning are different, yet the reference is to a whole meaning, not a partial one, and this object of reference may be the same for both interpreters. That is why a brief and elliptical comment on a text can be in complete agreement with a detailed exegesis. Their mutual compatibility is not based on their incompleteness or partiality, but quite the contrary on the identity of the whole meaning to which they refer. . . .

Of course, the main purpose of textual commentary is often not to make the meaning of a text understood by others, but rather to indicate its value, to judge its importance, to describe its bearings on present or past situations, to exploit it in support of an argument, or to use it as a source of biographical and historical knowledge. These legitimate concerns of textual commentary, and many similar ones, belong to the domain of criticism. Clarity requires that this function—that of criticism—should be distinguished from interpretation. In ordinary speech it is convenient to lump these several functions—understanding, interpretation, judgment, and criticism—under the term 'criticism', and certainly, in practice, these functions are so entangled and codependent that a separation could seem artificial. But the same might be said of many codependent aspects of reality—light and heat, form and content, color and extension. The fact that the functions of criticism are entangled together does not necessitate an imitative confusion of thought. Understanding, interpretation, judgment, and criticism are distinct functions with distinct requirements and aims. That they are always copresent in any written commentary and that they always influence one another are facts that must be reckoned with in this chapter. . . .

UNDERSTANDING, INTERPRETATION, AND HISTORY

The definitive proof that understanding requires an active construction of meaning and is not simply given by the text is the obvious fact that no one can understand an utterance who does not know the language in which it is composed. This would seem to be trivial, but trivial truths can imply far from trivial conclusions. It implies, first of all, that understanding is autonomous, that it occurs entirely within the terms and properties of the text's own language and the shared realities which that language embraces. To understand an utterance it is, in fact, not just desirable but absolutely unavoidable that we understand it in its own terms. We could not possibly recast a text's meanings in different terms unless we had already understood the text in its own. Every speaker and every interpreter must have mastered the convention systems and the shared meaning associations presupposed by a linguistic utterance.

The mastery of these necessary conventions (required for any construction of meaning from linguistic signs) may be called the philological presuppositions of all understanding. Here the word 'philological' is to be taken in the older, broader sense which comprises the whole range of shared realities and conventions—concrete and social, as well as linguistic—which are required in order to construe meaning. Verbal meaning can be construed only on the basis of its own presuppositions, which are not given from some other realm but must be learned and guessed at—a process that is entirely intrinsic to a particular social and linguistic system. The obvious fact that we cannot understand a Greek text when we happen to know only English remains true at the most subtle levels of understanding. One cannot understand meaning without guessing or learning the prerequisites to construing meaning, and since all understanding is 'silent'—that is, cast only in its own terms and not in foreign categories—it follows that all skeptical historicism is founded on a misconception of the nature of understanding.

That is the most important consequence of the 'trivial' point that one has to know the language of a text in order to understand it. The skeptical historicist infers too much from the fact that present-day experiences, categories, and modes of thought are not the same as those of the past. He concludes that we can only understand a text in *our* own terms, but this is a contradictory statement since verbal meaning has to be construed in *its* own terms if it is to be construed at all. Of course, the convention systems under which a text was composed may not in fact be those which we assume when we construe the text, but this has no bearing on the theoretical issue, since no one denies that misunderstanding is not only possible but sometimes, perhaps, unavoidable. The skeptical historicist goes further than this. He argues—to return to our previous analogy—that a native speaker of English has to understand a Greek text in English rather than in Greek. He converts the plausible idea that the mastery of unfamiliar meanings is arduous and uncertain into the idea that we always have to impose our own alien conventions and associations. But this is simply not true. If we do not construe a text in what we rightly or wrongly assume to be its own terms then we do not construe it at all. We do not understand anything that we could subsequently recast in our own terms.[2]

Understanding is silent, interpretation extremely garrulous. Interpretation —the *subtilitas explicandi*—rarely exists in pure form, except in paraphrase or translation. Just as understanding is a *construction* of meaning (not of significance, which I discuss later on), so interpretation is an *explanation* of meaning. However, most commentaries that we call interpretations are concerned with significance as well as meaning. They constantly draw analogies and point out relationships which not only help us to understand meaning but also lead us to perceive values and relevancies. But while interpretations are almost always mixed with criticism they nevertheless always refer to meaning as well, and if the meaning referred to is wrong, the interpretation is wrong too—no matter how valuable it may be in other respects.

If we isolate for a moment the interpretive function of commentaries as distinct from their critical function, we will observe that the art of explaining nearly always involves the task of discussing meaning in terms that are not native to the original text. Of course, this is not constantly true: many good interpreters quote frequently from the original, and one of the best interpretive devices is simply to read a text aloud to an audience. But all interpretations at some point have recourse to categories and conceptions that are not native to the original. A translation or paraphrase tries to render the meaning in new terms; an explanation tries to point to the meaning in new terms. That is why interpretation, like translation, is an art, for the interpreter has to find means of conveying to the uninitiated, in terms familiar to them, those presuppositions and meanings which are equivalent to those in the original meaning. However, different modes of interpretation can, as I have already shown, refer to the very same construction of the original meaning.

The fact that different interpretations can be in agreement throws into perspective the old nostrum that every age must reinterpret the great works of the past. This is a comforting truth to each new generation of critics who earn their bread by reinterpreting, but it is a truth of very limited application.

---

[2] The perspectivism of the radical historicist is not radical enough by half. He forgets that meaning itself is perspective-bound and that, in order to understand verbal meaning from any era including his own, the interpreter has to submit to a double perspective. He preserves his own standpoint and, at the same time, imaginatively realizes the standpoint of the speaker. This is a characteristic of all verbal intercourse.

To the extent that textual commentary functions as interpretation in the strict sense, and not as criticism, the old nostrum simply means that every age requires a different vocabulary and strategy of interpretation.[3] Indeed, each different sort of audience requires a different strategy of interpretation, as all teachers and lecturers are aware. The historicity of all interpretations is an undoubted fact, because the historical givens with which an interpreter must reckon—the language and the concerns of his audience—vary from age to age. However, this by no means implies that the meaning of the text varies from age to age, or that anybody, who has done whatever is required to understand that meaning, understands a different meaning from his predecessors of an earlier age. No doubt Coleridge understood *Hamlet* rather differently from Professor Kittredge.[4] That fact is reflected in their disparate interpretations, but it would be quite wrong to conclude that this disparity was caused merely by the fact that they lived in different periods. It would do both Coleridge and Kittredge an injustice to argue that the times necessitated their manner of understanding, or even that their positions could not be reversed. Both of them would have agreed that at least one of them must be wrong. On the other hand, even if they had entertained the same conception of *Hamlet*, they could not have *written* about the play in the same way. Their purposes, their times, and their audiences were different and so, therefore, were their styles of exposition, their emphases, and their categories. However, the historicity of interpretation is quite distinct from the timelessness of understanding.

All serious students of texts from the past—texts of any genre—are historians. It is not surprising that literary scholars should be particularly sensitive to the formative influence of historical givens and should observe that critics of the past have not only interpreted differently but have understood differently from critics in the present. . . . But these far from surprising possibilities do not have the theoretical importance that is usually attached to them. Not all readers of the same era tend to understand a text in the same way—as we know from our present-day experience. Furthermore, the emphases and categories which characterized the interpretations of a particular time are not the same as the emphases and categories of its understanding. All understanding is necessarily and by nature intrinsic, all interpretation necessarily transient and historical.

---

[3] What is primarily meant by the nostrum is that each new critic or age finds new sorts of significance, new strands of relevance to particular cultural or intellectual contexts. Usually, therefore, it is more descriptive to say that each age must *recriticize* the works of the past in order to keep them alive and ourselves alive to them. As critics we should remind ourselves that we are not perceiving a new work or a new meaning, but a new significance of the work which often could not exist except in our own cultural milieu. That phenomenon in itself proves the relational character of significance.
[4] G. L. Kittredge (1860–1941), Professor of English at Harvard and Shakespearian scholar particularly known for his historical approach to the play, as opposed to Coleridge's 'poetic' approach. [Ed.]

A colleague once pointed out to me that Simone Weil could not have written so brilliantly on the way *The Iliad* discloses the role of brute force in human life if she had not passed through the horrors of Nazism, and, furthermore, that her emphasis on this aspect of *The Iliad* would not have struck a responsive chord in her readers if they had not also witnessed those times. In this observation we can see how closely connected in practice are understanding, interpretation, and criticism, and how necessary it is to distinguish them in theory. Surely Simone Weil's emphasis on the role of force in *The Iliad* brilliantly exploited the experiences she shared with her audience, and probably she did not overemphasize the role of force within Homer's imagination. The element of *criticism* in her commentary was her implication that Homer was right—human life is like that, and we, in this age, know it. The element of *interpretation* in her commentary was her laying out in an ordered way Homer's implications about the role of force in life. But we do not respond to her interpretation just because we live in a violent age; we agree with it because we too have read *The Iliad* and have perceived that same meaning —even if we have not perceived it so explicitly. I cannot imagine any competent reader of any past age who did not implicitly grasp this meaning in *The Iliad*, though I can certainly imagine a time when readers did not feel this meaning to be a comment on life worthy of a special monograph.

If an interpreter exercises tact, he can emphasize any matter or theme he likes without suggesting a false emphasis. A single qualifying comment from time to time, a passing modest disclaimer, or an acknowledgment of the place his theme has in the meaning of the whole will suffice to avoid giving a false impression. It does not matter what one says about a text so long as one understands it and conveys that understanding to a reader. There are no correct 'methods' of interpretation, no uniquely appropriate categories. One does what is necessary to convey an understanding to a particular audience. There are many ways of catching a possum. In his function as an interpreter, the critic's first job is to discover which possum he should catch.

3 *Interpreting the* Variorum*

STANLEY FISH

. . . formal units are always a function of the interpretative model one brings to bear; they are not 'in' the text, and I would make the same argument for intentions. That is, intention is no more embodied 'in' the text than are formal

* From Stanley Fish, *Is There a Text in this Class?*, Harvard University Press, 1980, pp. 164–73, first publ. *Critical Inquiry*, Chicago, 1976.

units; rather an intention, like a formal unit, is made when perceptual or interpretive closure is hazarded; it is verified by an interpretive act, and I would add, it is not verifiable in any other way. This last assertion is too large to be fully considered here, but I can sketch out the argumentative sequence I would follow were I to consider it: intention is known when and only when it is recognized; it is recognized as soon as you decide about it; you decide about it as soon as you make a sense; and you make a sense (or so my model claims) as soon as you can. . . .

This, then, is my thesis: that the form of the reader's experience, formal units, and the structure of intention are one, that they come into view simultaneously, and that therefore the questions of priority and independence do not arise. What does arise is another question: what produces *them?* That is, if intention, form, and the shape of the reader's experience are simply different ways of referring to (different perspectives on) the same interpretive act, what is that act an interpretation *of?* I cannot answer that question, but neither, I would claim, can anyone else, although formalists try to answer it by pointing to patterns and claiming that they are available independently of (prior to) interpretation. These patterns vary according to the procedures that yield them: they may be statistical (number of two-syllable words per hundred words), grammatical (ratio of passive to active constructions, or of right-branching to left-branching sentences, or of anything else); but whatever they are I would argue that they do not lie innocently in the world but are themselves constituted by an interpretive act, even if, as is often the case, that act is unacknowledged. Of course, this is as true of my analyses as it is of anyone else's. In the examples offered here I appropriate the notion 'line ending' and treat it as a fact of nature; and one might conclude that as a fact it is responsible for the reading experience I describe. The truth I think is exactly the reverse: line endings exist by virtue of perceptual strategies rather than the other way around. Historically, the strategy that we know as 'reading (or hearing) poetry' has included paying attention to the line as a unit, but it is precisely that attention which has made the line as a unit (either of print or of aural duration) available. A reader so practiced in paying that attention that he regards the line as a brute fact rather than as a convention will have a great deal of difficulty with concrete poetry; if he overcomes that difficulty, it will not be because he has learned to ignore the line as a unit but because he will have acquired a new set of interpretive strategies (the strategies constitutive of 'concrete poetry reading') in the context of which the line as a unit no longer exists. In short, what is noticed is what has been *made* noticeable, not by a clear and undistorting glass, but by an interpretive strategy.

This may be hard to see when the strategy has become so habitual that the forms it yields seem part of the world. We find it easy to assume that alliteration as an effect depends on a 'fact' that exists independently of any interpretive 'use' one might make of it, the fact that words in proximity begin with the same letter. But it takes only a moment's reflection to realize that the sameness, far from being natural, is enforced by an orthographic convention; that is to say, it is the product of an interpretation. Were we to substitute phonetic conventions for orthographic ones (a 'reform' traditionally urged by purists), the supposedly 'objective' basis for alliteration would disappear because a phonetic transcription would require that we distinguish between the initial sounds of those very words that enter into alliterative relationships; rather than conforming to those relationships, the rules of spelling make them. One might reply that, since alliteration is an aural rather than a visual phenomenon when poetry is heard, we have unmediated access to the physical sounds themselves and hear 'real' similarities. But phonological 'facts' are no more uninterpreted (or less conventional) than the 'facts' of orthography; the distinctive features that make articulation and reception possible are the product of a system of differences that must be *imposed* before it can be recognized; the patterns the ear hears (like the patterns the eye sees) are the patterns its perceptual habits make available.

One can extend this analysis forever, even to the 'facts' of grammar. The history of linguistics is the history of competing paradigms, each of which offers a different account of the constituents of language. Verbs, nouns, cleft sentences, transformations, deep and surface structures, semes, rhemes, tagmemes—now you see them, now you don't, depending on the descriptive apparatus you employ. The critic who confidently rests his analyses on the bedrock of syntactic descriptions is resting on an interpretation; the facts he points to *are* there, but only as a consequence of the interpretive (man-made) model that has called them into being.

The moral is clear: the choice is never between objectivity and interpretation but between an interpretation that is unacknowledged as such and an interpretation that is at least aware of itself. It is this awareness that I am claiming for myself, although in doing so I must give up the claims implicitly made in the first part of this essay. There I argue that a bad (because spatial) model had suppressed what was really happening, but by my own declared principles the notion 'really happening' is just one more interpretation.

INTERPRETIVE COMMUNITIES

It seems then that the price one pays for denying the priority of either forms or intentions is an inability to say how it is that one ever begins. Yet we do begin, and we continue, and because we do there arises an immediate counterobjection to the preceding pages. If interpretive acts are the source of forms rather than the other way around, why isn't it the case that readers are always performing the same acts or a sequence of random acts, and therefore creating the same forms or a random succession of forms? How, in short, does one explain these two 'facts' of reading? (1) The same reader will perform differently when reading two 'different' (the word is in quotation marks because its status is precisely what is at issue) texts; and (2) different readers will perform similarly when reading the 'same' (in quotes for the same reason) text. That is to say, both the stability of interpretation among readers and the variety of interpretation in the career of a single reader would seem to argue for the existence of something independent of and prior to interpretive acts, something which produces them. I will answer this challenge by asserting that both the stability and the variety are functions of interpretive strategies rather than of texts.

Let us suppose that I am reading *Lycidas*. What is it that I am doing? First of all, what I am not doing is 'simply reading', an activity in which I do not believe because it implies the possibility of pure (that is disinterested) perception. Rather, I am proceeding on the basis of (at least) two interpretive decisions: (1) that *Lycidas* is a pastoral and (2) that it was written by Milton. (I should add that the notions 'pastoral' and 'Milton' are also interpretations; that is, they do not stand for a set of indisputable, objective facts; if they did, a great many books would not now be getting written.) Once these decisions have been made (and if I had not made these I would have made others, and they would be consequential in the same way), I am immediately predisposed to perform certain acts, to 'find', by looking for, themes (the relationship between natural processes and the careers of men, the efficacy of poetry or of any other action), to confer significances (on flowers, streams, shepherds, pagan deities), to mark out 'formal' units (the lament, the consolation, the turn, the affirmation of faith, and so on). My disposition to perform these acts (and others; the list is not meant to be exhaustive) constitutes a set of interpretive strategies, which, when they are put into execution, become the large act of reading. That is to say, interpretive strategies are not put into execution after reading (the pure act of perception in which I do not believe); they are the shape of reading, and because they are the shape of reading, they give texts their shape, making them rather than, as it is usually assumed, arising from them. Several important things follow from this account:

1. I did not have to execute this particular set of interpretive strategies because I did not have to make those particular interpretive (pre-reading) decisions. I could have decided, for example, that *Lycidas* was a text in which a set of fantasies and defenses find expression. These decisions would have entailed the assumption of another set of interpretive strategies (perhaps like that put forward by Norman Holland in *The Dynamics of Literary Response*) and the execution of that set would have made another text.

2. I could execute this same set of strategies when presented with texts that did not bear the title (again a notion which is itself an interpretation) *Lycidas*,

A Pastoral Monody. I could decide (it is a decision some have made) that *Adam Bede* is a pastoral written by an author who consciously modeled herself on Milton (still remembering that 'pastoral' and 'Milton' are interpretations, not facts in the public domain); or I could decide, as Empson did,[1] that a great many things not usually considered pastoral were in fact to be so read; and either decision would give rise to a set of interpretive strategies, which, when put into action, would *write* the text I write when reading *Lycidas*. (Are you with me?)

3. A reader other than myself who, when presented with *Lycidas*, proceeds to put into execution a set of interpretive strategies similar to mine (how he could do so is a question I will take up later), will perform the same (or at least a similar) succession of interpretive acts. He and I then might be tempted to say that we agree about the poem (thereby assuming that the poem exists independently of the acts either of us performs); but what we really would agree about is the way to write it.

4. A reader other than myself who, when presented with *Lycidas* (please keep in mind that the status of *Lycidas* is what is at issue), puts into execution a different set of interpretive strategies will perform a different succession of interpretive acts. (I am assuming, it is the article of my faith, that a reader will always execute some set of interpretive strategies and therefore perform some succession of interpretive acts.) One of us might then be tempted to complain to the other that we could not possibly be reading the same poem (literary criticism is full of such complaints) and he would be right; for each of us would be reading the poem he had made.

The large conclusion that follows from these four smaller ones is that the notions of the 'same' or 'different' texts are fictions. If I read *Lycidas* and *The Waste Land* differently (in fact I do not), it will not be because the formal structures of the two poems (to term them such is also an interpretive decision) call forth different interpretive strategies but because my predisposition to execute different interpretive strategies will *produce* different formal structures. That is, the two poems are different because I have decided that they will be. The proof of this is the possibility of doing the reverse (that is why point 2 is so important). That is to say, the answer to the question 'why do different texts give rise to different sequences of interpretive acts?' is that *they don't have to*, an answer which implies strongly that 'they' don't exist. Indeed, it has always been possible to put into action interpretive strategies designed to make all texts one, or to put it more accurately, to be forever making the same text. Augustine urges just such a strategy, for example, in *On Christian Doctrine* where he delivers the 'rule of faith' which is of course a rule of interpretation. It is dazzlingly simple: everything in the Scriptures, and indeed

---

[1] In William Empson, *Some Versions of Pastoral*, 1935. [Ed.]

in the world when it is properly read, points to (bears the meaning of) God's love for us and our answering responsibility to love our fellow creatures for His sake. If only you should come upon something which does not at first seem to bear this meaning, that 'does not literally pertain to virtuous behavior or to the truth of faith', you are then to take it 'to be figurative' and proceed to scrutinize it 'until an interpretation contributing to the reign of charity is produced'. This then is both a stipulation of what meaning there is and a set of directions for finding it, which is of course a set of directions—of interpretive strategies—for making it, that is, for the endless reproduction of the same text. Whatever one may think of this interpretive program, its success and ease of execution are attested to by centuries of Christian exegesis. It is my contention that any interpretive program, any set of interpretive strategies, can have a similar success, although few have been as spectacularly successful as this one. (For some time now, for at least three hundred years, the most successful interpretive program has gone under the name 'ordinary language'.) In our own discipline programs with the same characteristic of always reproducing one text include psychoanalytic criticism, Robertsonianism (always threatening to extend its sway into later and later periods)[2], numerology (a sameness based on the assumption of innumerable fixed differences).

The other challenging question—'why will different readers execute the same interpretive strategy when faced with the "same" text?'—can be handled in the same way. The answer is again that *they don't have to*, and my evidence is the entire history of literary criticism. And again this answer implies that the notion 'same text' is the product of the possession by two or more readers of similar interpretive strategies.

But why should this ever happen? Why should two or more readers ever agree, and why should regular, that is, habitual, differences in the career of a single reader ever occur? What is the explanation on the one hand of the stability of interpretation (at least among certain groups at certain times) and on the other of the orderly variety of interpretation if it is not the stability and variety of texts? The answer to all of these questions is to be found in a notion that has been implicit in my argument, the notion of *interpretive communities*. Interpretive communities are made up of those who share interpretive strategies not for reading (in the conventional sense) but for writing texts, for constituting their properties and assigning their intentions. In other words, these strategies exist prior to the act of reading and therefore determine the shape of what is read rather than, as is usually assumed, the other way round. If it is an article of faith in a particular community that there are a variety of texts, its members will boast a repertoire of strategies for making them. And if a community believes in the existence of only one text, then the single strategy its members employ will be forever writing it. The first community

---

[2] A reference to the American medievalist, D.W. Robertson, Jr.

will accuse the members of the second of being reductive, and they in turn will call their accusers superficial. The assumption in each community will be that the other is not correctly perceiving the 'true text', but the truth will be that each perceives the text (or texts) its interpretive strategies demand and call into being. This, then, is the explanation both for the stability of interpretation among different readers (they belong to the same community) and for the regularity with which a single reader will employ different interpretive strategies and thus make different texts (he belongs to different communities). It also explains why there are disagreements and why they can be debated in a principled way: not because of a stability in texts, but because of a stability in the makeup of interpretive communities and therefore in the opposing positions they make possible. Of course this stability is always temporary (unlike the longed for and timeless stability of the text). Interpretive communities grow larger and decline, and individuals move from one to another; thus, while the alignments are not permanent, they are always there, providing just enough stability for the interpretive battles to go on, and just enough shift and slippage to assure that they will never be settled. The notion of interpretive communities thus stands between an impossible ideal and the fear which leads so many to maintain it. The ideal is of perfect agreement and it would require texts to have a status independent of interpretation. The fear is of interpretive anarchy, but it would only be realized if interpretation (text making) were completely random. It is the fragile but real consolidation of interpretive communities that allows us to talk to one another, but with no hope or fear of ever being able to stop.

In other words interpretive communities are no more stable than texts because interpretive strategies are not natural or universal, but learned. This does not mean that there is a point at which an individual has not yet learned any. The ability to interpret is not acquired; it is constitutive of being human. What is acquired are the ways of interpreting and those same ways can also be forgotten or supplanted, or complicated or dropped from favor ('no one reads that way anymore'). When any of these things happens, there is a corresponding change in texts, not because they are being read differently, but because they are being written differently.

The only stability, then, inheres in the fact (at least in my model) that interpretive strategies are always being deployed, and this means that communication is a much more chancy affair than we are accustomed to think it. For if there are no fixed texts, but only interpretive strategies making them, and if interpretive strategies are not natural, but learned (and are therefore unavailable to a finite description), what is it that utterers (speakers, authors, critics, me, you) do? In the old model utterers are in the business of handing over ready-made or prefabricated meanings. These meanings are said to be encoded, and the code is assumed to be in the world independently of the individuals who are obliged to attach themselves to it (if they do not they run the danger of being declared deviant). In my model, however, meanings are not extracted but made and made not by encoded forms but by interpretive strategies that call forms into being. It follows then that what utterers do is give hearers and readers the opportunity to make meanings (and texts) by inviting them to put into execution a set of strategies. It is presumed that the invitation will be recognized, and that presumption rests on a projection on the part of a speaker or author of the moves *he* would make if confronted by the sounds or marks he is uttering or setting down.

It would seem at first that this account of things simply reintroduces the old objection; for isn't this an admission that there is after all a formal encoding, not perhaps of meanings, but of the directions for making them, for executing interpretive strategies? The answer is that they will only *be* directions to those who already have the interpretive strategies in the first place. Rather than producing interpretive acts, they are the product of one. An author hazards his projection, not because of something 'in' the marks, but because of something he assumes to be in his reader. The very existence of the 'marks' is a function of an interpretive community, for they will be recognized (that is, made) only by its members. Those outside that community will be deploying a different set of interpretive strategies (interpretation cannot be withheld) and will therefore be making different marks.

So once again I have made the text disappear, but unfortunately the problems do not disappear with it. If everyone is continually executing interpretive strategies and in that act constituting texts, intentions, speakers, and authors, how can any one of us know whether or not he is a member of the same interpretive community as any other of us? The answer is that he can't, since any evidence brought forward to support the claim would itself be an interpretation (especially if the 'other' were an author long dead). The only 'proof' of membership is fellowship, the nod of recognition from someone in the same community, someone who says to you what neither of us could ever prove to a third party: 'we know'. I say it to you now, knowing full well that you will agree with me (that is, understand) only if you already agree with me.

4 *Who Cares About the Text?**

ROBERT SCHOLES

My intention here is to offer a corrective critique of the argument made by Fish in *Is There a Text in This Class?* In particular, I shall attack the notion of 'interpretive communities' as vague, inconsistently applied, and unworkable. In the course of this critique I will also sketch out a notion of the literary text and its uses. Before going on the offensive, however, I want to say two things about Stanley Fish and his theory of the text. First, I admire his learning, his ingenuity, and his consummate rhetorical ability. Second, I think that he is right—not just persuasive, but right—up to a point.

In particular, he is right to question the status of texts, pointing out that no text is as simply 'there' as we have sometimes assumed it to be. Interpretation *does* enter the reading process at a very early point. And interpretation is never totally free but always limited by such prior acquisitions as language, generic norms, social patterns, and beliefs. For a simple but fundamental example of this, we have only to look at the Book of Genesis, chapter i: 'And God said, let us make man in our image' (i, 25). The Hebrew word for 'God' in this passage is *Elohim*, the plural of *El*. One could translate the word as a plural—'The Gods'—instead of a singular, and the plural would then agree grammatically with the other plurals, 'us' and 'our', which are in the Hebrew, the Vulgate, and the King James text. Obviously, we cannot introduce 'The Gods' without embarrassment for all monotheistic interpreters of the text. So the word in Judeo-Christian communities will not only be translated as singular but read in Hebrew as singular. This will not prevent some interpreters from saying that the plural is really there and that it signifies the Trinity. Sir Thomas Browne, in *Religio Medici*, described it as an instance of the royal 'we'. Others say that the text bears traces of Mesopotamian polytheism. Still others have argued that this God is androgynous and therefore plural. The point is that to a very real extent one's beliefs will color what one reads. For a monotheist *Elohim* is a singular. What is there, in this instance, depends upon an interpretive stance.

This example will serve to illustrate just how far I am willing to go along with Stanley Fish. I hope it will also serve to indicate where I think we should all part company with him. My view of the interpretive complexities of the passage was based upon its appearance in the King James version and a single reference to the Hebrew text. But suppose I had chosen the modern Anchor version for my text: 'Then God said I will make man in my image, after my likeness.' There are no plurals in this version, *us* and *our* having been replaced

* From Robert Scholes, *Textual Power: Theory and the Teaching of English*, Yale University Press, 1985, pp. 150–6.

by *I* and *my*. To say the very least, this makes the androgynous and polytheistic interpretations more difficult to sustain. Given this particular text, they can hardly even arise. But the very least is all that needs to be said here, for Fish's position is absolutely extreme on this question. He asserts, over and over again, that texts have no properties of their own, that they are always and only what their readers make of them: 'Interpretation is not the art of construing but the art of constructing. Interpreters do not decode poems; they make them.'

Even this might be acceptable if Fish would admit that making a poem from a text is a different activity from making a text in the first place. The issue here is the extent to which a text may be said to guide or offer resistance to the things one makes of it, whether we call these products poems, works, or interpretations. If we think of printed texts only, for the moment, that come to us in the form of inked shapes on pages, is there any significant difference between a page of *Paradise Lost* and a Rorschach blot? At this point one could introduce a straw Fish to answer that question in the negative. But let me instead make the best possible answer that one could make, holding Fish's stated views in this matter.

This answer would say that, yes, there is a difference but it is not in the texts; it is in the ways we interpret them. I can imagine an interpreter so removed from any understanding of English that the text of *Paradise Lost* would carry less significance for him than any Rorschach blot. But I wonder if even an imagination as brilliantly perverse as Fish's could find an interpreter whose language proved to be that in which the Rorschach blot had been encoded, a language in which the blot could be interpreted as seeking to justify the ways of God to men. One can think of it, but even in thinking it one proves the point that it is supposed to deny. There *is* a difference between a text perceived as encoded in a particular language and one that is perceived as not being in any language at all. In fact, to perceive a text *as* a text is to perceive it as being in a language.

Fish might reply that having a language is part of what he means by being in a community of interpreters. But I would answer by pointing out that no language community is congruous with any interpretive community. Christian exegetes, for example, are not confined to any single language, nor are speakers of any single language compelled to be Christian exegetes. Moreover, a text is bound to its language; it exists as a text only in and through its language. It is not so bound to any interpretive community. Nor are perception and belief as constrained by membership in either a linguistic or an interpretive group as Fish maintains. When Wittgenstein said that our world is bounded by our language he did not say that we had no freedom within the boundaries. If you play chess you can only do certain things with the pieces —or you will no longer be playing chess. But those constraints in themselves never tell you what move to make. Language does not speak—any more than the law of gravity falls. Furthermore, language is changed by speech, though gravity is not changed by any act of falling or flying. But enough analogies —let us look more closely at what Fish does mean by an 'interpretive community'.

In the introduction to *Is There a Text in This Class?* Fish says that 'it is interpretive communities, rather than either the text or the reader, that produce meanings and are responsible for the emergence of formal features'. As Fish explains this, we can think and perceive only what our interpretive community allows us to think and perceive. He finds this totalitarian vision completely reassuring. Whatever we think will be right, because we have no choice in this matter. Nor will there be any need to respect the integrity of whatever we are thinking about. The interpretive community will decide for us what is out there and we will duly perceive it. 'Not to worry', says Fish. Not to worry? I remember Mr O'Brien inducting Winston Smith into his interpretive community in *1984*.

Notice what Fish has done. First, he has asserted that readers make texts; then he has shifted his position to say, quite specifically, that meanings are produced by neither text nor reader but by interpretive communities. But he has never made clear what an interpretive community is, how its constituency might be determined, or what could be the source of its awesome power. In practice, he sometimes means simply those who share certain linguistic and cultural information: that is, all those who would understand a certain speech in a certain situation as a request to open the window. At other times he means something like all Christian readers of literary texts. The problem is not just that the size and shape of the 'community' change to suit Fish's needs, though that *is* a problem. A greater difficulty is the putting of such things as the English language and Christian typology on the same plane. One may debate whether *Samson Agonistes* is or is not a Christian poem. But even in order to debate that one must perceive the poem as written in the English language. A Christian reader with no English will not make much of the poem. An English reader with no special Christian interpretive bias can make a good deal of it. The point is that Fish's notion of 'community' will not stand examination. He says that 'a set of interpretive assumptions is always in force'. I would argue that the notion of a single, monolithic *set* of assumptions makes the same totalitarian error that Fish makes in other places. Different, even conflicting, assumptions may preside over any reading of a single text by a single person. It is in fact these very differences—differences *within* the reader, who is never a unified member of a single unified group—it is these very differences that create the space in which the reader exercises a measure of interpretive freedom.

This freedom, however, is most certainly constrained by language. A written text is a set of marks that are as they are only because a certain language was implicated in their composition. A printed text is never only on the page. It is a transaction between what is on the page and the particular linguistic code that originally enabled those marks to carry meaning. This is in fact what distinguishes a written text from a Rorschach blot. Familiarity with a text's linguistic code is assumed by all who discuss the interpretation of literary texts, though some theorists emphasize this and others prefer to ignore it. Fish prefers to ignore it, because any serious consideration of the relationship of both the reader and the writer to language will show that the reader is more constrained than the writer. The reader's choices in 'making' meaning are in fact severely limited by the writer's previous choices of what marks to put on the page. But Fish prefers to ignore this set of constraints in order to emphasize the constraints that can be attributed to membership in an interpretive community.

The notion of interpretive communities, he tells us in his introduction, is now 'central' to his discourse. It explains everything that was dark before. One thing it explains is the status of the reader: 'since the thoughts an individual can think and the mental operations he can perform have their source in some or other interpretive community, he is as much the product of that community (acting as an extension of it) as the meanings it enables him to produce'. The reader is simply a product of 'some or other' interpretive community, and no one can belong to more than one of these communities at a time. 'Members of different communities will disagree', says Fish, and, conversely, those who agree will inevitably be members of the same community. From these premises he draws the truly astonishing conclusion that he has explained 'why there are disagreements and why they can be debated in a principled way'. This conclusion is astonishing because principled debate is precisely what Fish's theory cannot describe. To agree on the principles that govern critical debate—what counts as evidence and so on—would be to accept membership in the same interpretive community. But members of the same interpretive community, by definition, have no disagreements. Therefore, only those who have no disagreements can settle them in a principled way. The only way out of this Catch-22 (or perhaps we ought to call it Fish-22) is to say that accepting the same principles is not the same as belonging to the same interpretive community. But this only raises in more acute form the question of what an interpretive community might actually be.

If the community makes all selves and governs all interpretations, then any difference in behavior must be due to differences in community. ('Members of different communities will disagree.') It follows from this that there must be as many communities as there are different interpretations. This means that the notion of 'interpretive community' in no way coincides with what

Thomas Kuhn would call a paradigm or Michel Foucault an episteme.[1] Nor would it coincide with a discipline like literary criticism or even with a school of criticism like Marxist, Freudian, structuralist, feminist, New Critical, speech-act, stylistic, or what-have-you—for the simple reason that so many interpretive disputes occur *within* each of these schools rather than between them. If an interpretive community is not the same as a critical school, then what is it and where is it? If every different interpretation is the product of a different community, making different assumptions and perceiving a different text, how could one possibly debate or settle such differences? If, as Fish maintains, there can be no *demonstration* in critical debates (because all facts are already interpretations), how can there be debates at all? Fish says that we will have *persuasion* instead of *demonstration*. But I invite him and you to consider just what persuasion without demonstration would be. If there can be no appeal to any facts, even by stipulation, then all that is left is self-interest: the carrot and the stick. How can one have a principled debate with a person who denies the major premise of debate itself: namely, that the issues are to be settled by the evidence presented and the conclusions drawn from it rather than by threatening or bribing the judges? You may think I am being unfair. But Fish honestly admits that his appeal is strictly to self-interest: 'I have been trying to persuade you to believe what I believe because it is in your own best interests as *you* understand them.'

5 *Literary History as a Challenge to Literary Theory**

HANS ROBERT JAUSS

Literary history may be seen as challenging literary theory to take up once again the unresolved dispute between the Marxist and formalist schools. My attempt to bridge the gap between literature and history, between historical and aesthetic approaches, begins at the point at which both schools stop. Their methods understand the literary fact in terms of the circular aesthetic system of production and of representation. In doing so, they deprive literature of a dimension which unalterably belongs to its aesthetic character as

[1] Refers to the philosopher of science, and author of *The Structure of Scientific Revolutions* (1962), where the idea is proposed that what becomes scientific 'fact' depends upon the frame of reference or 'paradigm' brought to the object of understanding at any one time; Foucault's *episteme* has many similarities with this idea (see *The Archaeology of Knowledge*, first Engl. publ. 1972). [Ed.]

* From *New Directions in Literary History*, ed. R. Cohen, Routledge & Kegan Paul, 1974, pp. 11–12, 18, 21–3, 40–1, this essay is a translation by Elizabeth Benzinger of chapters V–XII of *Literaturgeschichte als Provokation der Literaturwissenschaft*, Konstanz, 1967; it forms part of a later published collection of essays, *Literaturgeschichte als Provokation*, Suhrkamp, Frankfurt, 1970.

well as to its social function: its reception and impact. Reader, listener and spectator—in short, the audience—play an extremely limited role in both literary theories. Orthodox Marxist aesthetics treats the reader—if at all—the same way as it does the author; it inquires about his social position or describes his place within the structure of the society. The formalist school needs the reader only as a perceiving subject who follows the directions in the text in order to perceive its form or discover its techniques of procedure. It assumes that the reader has the theoretical knowledge of a philologist sufficiently versed in the tools of literature to be able to reflect on them. The Marxist school, on the other hand, actually equates the spontaneous experience of the reader with the scholarly interest of historical materialism, which seeks to discover relationships between the economic basis of production and the literary work as part of the intellectual superstructure. . . . Neither approach recognizes the true role of the reader to whom the literary work is primarily addressed, a role as unalterable for aesthetic as for historical appreciation.

For the critic who judges a new work, the writer who conceives of his work in light of positive or negative norms of an earlier work and the literary historian who classifies a work in his tradition and explains it historically are also readers before their reflexive relationship to literature can become productive again. In the triangle of author, work and reading public the latter is no passive part, no chain of mere reactions, but even history-making energy. The historical life of a literary work is unthinkable without the active participation of its audience. For it is only through the process of its communication that the work reaches the changing horizon of experience in a continuity in which the continual change occurs from simple reception to critical understanding, from passive to active reception, from recognized aesthetic norms to a new production which surpasses them. The historicity of literature as well as its communicative character presupposes a relation of work, audience and new work which takes the form of a dialogue as well as a process, and which can be understood in the relationship of message and receiver as well as in the relationship of question and answer, problem and solution. The circular system of production and of representation within which the methodology of literary criticism has mainly moved in the past must therefore be widened to include an aesthetics of reception and impact if the problem of understanding the historical sequence of literary works as a continuity of literary history is to find a new solution.

The perspective of the aesthetics of reception mediates between passive reception and active understanding, norm-setting experience and new production. If the history of literature is viewed in this way as a dialogue between work and public, the contrast between its aesthetic and its historical aspects is also continually mediated. Thus the thread from the past appearance to the present experience of a work, which historicism had cut, is tied together.

The relationship of literature and reader has aesthetic as well as historical implications. The aesthetic implication is seen in the fact that the first reception of a work by the reader includes a test of its aesthetic value in comparison with works which he has already read. The obvious historical implication of this is that the appreciation of the first reader will be continued and enriched through further 'receptions' from generation to generation; in this way the historical significance of a work will be determined and its aesthetic value revealed. In this process of the history of reception, which the literary historian can only escape at the price of ignoring his own principles of comprehension and judgment, the repossession of past works occurs simultaneously with the continual mediation of past and present art and of traditional evaluation and current literary attempts. The merit of a literary history based on an aesthetics of reception will depend upon the degree to which it can take an active part in the continual integration of past art by aesthetic experience. This demands on the one hand—in opposition to the objectivism of positivist literary history—a conscious attempt to establish canons, which, on the other hand—in opposition to the classicism of the study of traditions —presupposes a critical review if not destruction of the traditional literary canon. The criterion for establishing such a canon and the ever necessary retelling of literary history is clearly set out by the aesthetics of reception. The step from the history of the reception of the individual work to the history of literature has to lead us to see and in turn to present the historical sequence of works in the way in which they determine and clarify our present literary experience[1] . . . .

I

If literary history is to be rejuvenated, the prejudices of historical objectivism must be removed and the traditional approach to literature must be replaced by an aesthetics of reception and impact. The historical relevance of literature is not based on an organization of literary works which is established *post factum*[2] but on the reader's past experience of the 'literary data'. This relationship creates a dialogue that is the first condition for a literary history. For the literary historian must first become a reader again himself before he can understand and classify a work; in other words, before he can justify his own evaluation in light of his present position in the historical progression of readers.

[1] W. Benjamin (1931) formulated a corresponding idea: 'For it is not a question of showing the written works in relation to their time but of presenting the time which knows them—that is our time —in the time when they originated. Thus literature becomes an organon of history and the task of literary history is to make it this—and not to make it the material of history' (*Angelus Novus*, Frankfurt, 1966, p. 456).

[2] Latin: 'after the fact'. [Ed.]

R. G. Collingwood's criticism of the prevailing ideology of objectivity in history—'History is nothing but the re-enactment of past thought in the historian's mind'[3]—is even more valid for literary history. For the positivistic view of history as the 'objective' description of a series of events in an isolated past neglects the artistic quality as well as the specific historical relevance of literature. A literary work is not an object which stands by itself and which offers the same face to each reader in each period. It is not a monument which reveals its timeless essence in a monologue. It is much more like an orchestration which strikes ever new chords among its readers and which frees the text from the substance of the words and makes it meaningful for the time: 'words which must, at the same time that they speak to him, create an interlocutor capable of listening'.[4] A literary work must be understood as creating a dialogue, and philological scholarship has to be founded on a continuous re-reading of texts, not on mere facts. Philological scholarship is continuously dependent upon interpretation, which must have as its goal, along with learning about the object, the reflection upon and description of the perfection of this knowledge as an impulse to new understanding.

History of literature is a process of aesthetic reception and production which takes place in realization of literary texts on the part of the receptive reader, the reflective critic and the author in his continued creativity. The continuously growing 'literary data' which appear in the conventional literary histories are merely left over from this process; they are only the collected and classified past and therefore not history at all, but pseudohistory. Anyone who considers such literary data as history confuses the eventful character of a work of art with that of historical matter-of-factness. *Perceval* by Chrétien de Troyes, a literary event, is not historical in the same sense as the Third Crusade, which was occurring at the same time. It is not a 'fact' which could be explained as caused by a series of situational preconditions and motives, by the intent of an historical action as it can be reconstructed, and by the necessary and secondary results of this deed as an eventful turning point. The historical context in which a literary work appears is not a factual, independent series of events which exists apart from the reader. *Perceval* becomes a literary event only for the reader who reads this last work of Chrétien in light of his earlier works and who recognizes its individuality in comparison with these and other works which he has already read, so that he gains a new criterion for evaluating works. In contrast to a political event, a literary event has no lasting results which succeeding generations cannot avoid. It can continue to have an effect only if future generations still respond

---

[3] *The Idea of History* (New York and Oxford, 1956), p. 228.
[4] This view of the dialogue-like nature of a literary work of art is found in . . . a tradition of literary aesthetics which is still alive in France and to which I am especially indebted; it finally goes back to a famous sentence in Valéry's poetics, 'C'est l'exécution du poème qui est le poème.'

to it or rediscover it—if there are readers who take up the work of the past again or authors who want to imitate, outdo, or refute it. The organization of literature according to events is primarily integrated in the artistic standards of contemporary and succeeding readers, critics, and authors. Whether it is possible to comprehend and present the history of literature in its specific historicity depends on whether these standards can be objectified.

II

The analysis of the literary experience of the reader avoids the threatening pitfalls of psychology if it describes the response and the impact of a work within the definable frame of reference of the reader's expectations: this frame of reference for each work develops in the historical moment of its appearance from a previous understanding of the genre, from the form and themes of already familiar works, and from the contrast between poetic and practical language.

My thesis is opposed to a widespread skepticism that doubts that an analysis of the aesthetic impact can approach the meaning of a work of art or can produce at best more than a plain sociology of artistic taste. René Wellek directs such doubts against the literary theory of I. A. Richards. Wellek argues that neither the individual consciousness, since it is immediate and personal, nor a collective consciousness, as J. Mukarovsky assumes the effect of an art work to be, can be determined by empirical means.[5] Roman Jakobson wanted to replace the 'collective consciousness' by a 'collective ideology'. This he thought of as a system of values which exists for each literary work as *langue* and which becomes *parole* for the respondent—although incompletely and never as a whole.[6] This theory, it is true, limits the subjectivity of the impact, but it leaves open the question of which data can be used to interpret the impact of a unique work on a certain public and to incorporate it into a system of values. In the meantime there are empirical means which had never been thought of before—literary data which give for each work a specific attitude of the audience (an attitude that precedes the psychological reaction as well as the subjective understanding of the individual reader). As in the case of every experience, the first literary experience of a previously unknown work demands a 'previous knowledge which is an element of experience itself and which makes it possible that anything new we come across may also be read, as it were, in some context of experience'.[7]

[5] R. Wellek, 'The Theory of Literary History', *Études dédiées au quatrième Congrès de linguistes*, Travaux du Cercle Linguistique de Prague (Prague, 1936), p. 179.
[6] In *Slovo a slovenost*, I, 192, cited by Wellek, 'The Theory of Literary History', pp. 179 ff.
[7] G. Buck, *Lernen und Erfahrung* (Stuttgart, 1967), p. 56, who refers here to Husserl (*Erfahrung und Urteil*, esp. §8) but goes farther than Husserl in a lucid description of negativity in the process of experience, which is of importance for the horizon structure of aesthetic experience.

A literary work, even if it seems new, does not appear as something absolutely new in an informational vacuum, but predisposes its readers to a very definite type of reception by textual strategies, overt and covert signals, familiar characteristics or implicit allusions. It awakens memories of the familiar, stirs particular emotions in the reader and with its 'beginning' arouses expectations for the 'middle and end', which can then be continued intact, changed, re-oriented or even ironically fulfilled in the course of reading according to certain rules of the genre or type of text. The psychical process in the assimilation of a text on the primary horizon of aesthetic experience is by no means only a random succession of merely subjective impressions, but the carrying out of certain directions in a process of directed perception which can be comprehended from the motivations which constitute it and the signals which set it off and which can be described linguistically. If, along with W. D. Stempel, one considers the previous horizon of expectations of a text as paradigmatic isotopy, which is transferred to an immanent syntactical horizon of expectations to the degree to which the message grows, the process of reception becomes describable in the expansion of a semiological procedure which arises between the development and the correction of the system.[8] A corresponding process of continuous horizon setting and horizon changing also determines the relation of the individual text to the succession of texts which form the genre. The new text evokes for the reader (listener) the horizon of expectations and rules familiar from earlier texts, which are then varied, corrected, changed or just reproduced. Variation and correction determine the scope, alteration and reproduction of the borders and structure of the genre. The interpretative reception of a text always presupposes the context of experience of aesthetic perception. The question of the subjectivity of the interpretation and the taste of different readers or levels of readers can be asked significantly only after it has been decided which transsubjective horizon of understanding determines the impact of the text. . . .

III

If the horizon of expectations of a work is reconstructed in this way, it is possible to determine its artistic nature by the nature and degree of its effect on a given audience. If the 'aesthetic distance' is considered as the distance between the given horizon of expectations and the appearance of a new work, whose reception results in a 'horizon change' because it negates familiar experience or articulates an experience for the first time, this aesthetic distance can be measured historically in the spectrum of the reaction of the

[8] W. D. Stempel, 'Pour une description des genres littéraires', in *Actes du XIIe congrès internat. de linguistique Romane* (Bucharest, 1968).
'Paradigmatic isotopy' means, roughly speaking, 'a patterning of different kinds of things'. [Ed.]

audience and the judgment of criticism (spontaneous success, rejection or shock, scattered approval, gradual or later understanding). . . .

A literary sensation from the year 1857 may serve as an example of this. In this year two novels were published: Flaubert's *Madame Bovary*, which has since achieved world-wide fame, and *Fanny* by his friend Feydeau, which is forgotten today. Although Flaubert's novel brought with it a trial for obscenity, *Madame Bovary* was at first overshadowed by Feydeau's novel: *Fanny* had thirteen editions in one year and success the likes of which Paris had not seen since Chateaubriand's *Atala*. As far as theme is concerned, both novels fulfilled the expectations of the new audience, which—according to Baudelaire's analysis—had rejected anything romantic and scorned grand as well as naive passion. They treated a trivial subject—adultery—the one in a bourgeois and the other in a provincial milieu. Both authors understood how to give a sensational twist to the conventional, rigid triangle which in the erotic scenes surpassed the customary details. They presented the worn-out theme of jealousy in a new light by reversing the expected relationship of the three classic roles. Feydeau has the youthful lover of the 'femme de trente ans'[9] becoming jealous of his lover's husband, although he has already reached the goal of his desires, and perishing over this tormenting situation; Flaubert provides the adulteries of the doctor's wife in the provinces . . . with a surprising ending, so that the ridiculous figure of the deceived Charles Bovary takes on noble traits at the end. In official criticism of the time there are voices which reject *Fanny* as well as *Madame Bovary* as a product of the new school of 'réalisme', which they accuse of denying all ideals and attacking the ideas on which the order of the society in the Second Empire was based. The horizon of expectations of the public of 1857, here only sketched in, which did not expect anything great in the way of novels after the death of Balzac, explains the differing success of the two novels only when the question of the effect of their narrative form is posed. Flaubert's innovation in form, his principle of 'impersonal telling' (*impassibilité*, which Barbey d'Aurevilly attacked with this comparison: if a story-telling machine could be made of English steel, it would function the same as Monsieur Flaubert[10]), must have shocked the same audience which was offered the exciting contents of *Fanny* in the personable tone of a confessional novel. It could also have found in Feydeau's descriptions popular ideals and frustrations of the level of society which sets the style, and it could delight unrestrainedly in the lascivious main scene in which Fanny (without knowing that her lover is watching from the balcony) seduces her husband—for their moral indignation was forestalled by the reaction of the unfortunate witness. However, as

---

[9] French: literally 'woman of thirty', but understood as 'of a certain age', i.e. middle-aged. [Ed.]

[10] For these and other contemporary verdicts see H. R. Jauss, 'Die beiden Fassungen von Flauberts "Education Sentimentale"', *Heidelberger Jahrbücher*, II (1958), pp. 96–116, esp. 97.

Madame Bovary, which was understood at first only by a small circle of knowledgeable readers and called a turning point in the history of the novel, became a world-wide success, the group of readers who were formed by this book sanctioned the new canon of expectations, which made the weaknesses of Feydeau—his flowery style, his modish effects, his lyrical confessional clichés—unbearable and relegated *Fanny* to the class of bestsellers of yesterday.

I V

The reconstruction of the horizon of expectations, on the basis of which a work in the past was created and received, enables us to find the questions to which the text originally answered and thereby to discover how the reader of that day viewed and understood the work. This approach corrects the usually unrecognized values of a classical concept of art or of an interpretation that seeks to modernize, and it avoids the recourse to a general spirit of the age, which involves circular reasoning. It brings out the hermeneutic difference between past and present ways of understanding a work, points up the history of its reception—providing both approaches—and thereby challenges as platonizing dogma the apparently self-evident dictum of philological metaphysics that literature is timelessly present and that it has objective meaning, determined once and for all and directly open to the interpreter at any time. . . .

Thus a literary work with an unusual aesthetic form can shatter the expectations of its reader and at the same time confront him with a question which cannot be answered by religiously or publicly sanctioned morals. Instead of further examples, a word of reminder is in order here: it was not Bertolt Brecht but the Enlightenment which first proclaimed the competitive relationship between literature and canonized morals. Friedrich Schiller bears witness to this when he makes this express claim in regard to bourgeois drama: 'the rules of the stage begin where the realm of worldly laws ends'.[11] The literary work can also—and in the history of literature this possibility characterizes the most recent period of modernity—reverse the relationship of question and answer and in an artistic medium confront the reader with a new 'opaque' reality which can no longer be understood from the previous horizon of expectations. Thus the newest form of the novel, the much discussed *nouveau roman*, is a form of modern art which—according to Edgar Wind's formulation—presents the paradoxical case 'that the solution is provided, the problem, however, is given up in order that the solution can be understood as the solution'.[12] Here the reader is excluded from the position of

[11] *Die Schaubühne als eine moralische Anstalt betrachtet*, Säkular-Ausgabe, XI, 99.
[12] 'Zur Systematik der künstlerischen Probleme', *Jahrbuch für Asthetik* (1925), 440.

the immediate audience and placed in the position of an uninitiated third person, who in the face of a still meaningless reality must himself find the question which will enable him to discover the perception of the world and the interpersonal problem to which the work's answer is directed.

It follows from all of this that the specific achievement of literature in society can be found only when the function of literature is not understood as one of imitation. If one looks at the moments in history when literary works toppled the taboos of the prevailing morality or offered the reader new solutions for the moral casuistry of his life which later would be sanctioned by the consensus of all readers in a society, a little-studied area of research opens for the literary historian. The chasm between literature and history, between aesthetic and historical knowledge, can be bridged if literary history does not simply once again describe literary works as a reflection of the process of general history, but rather discovers in the course of 'literary evolution' that truly socially formative function which belongs to literature as it competes with other arts and social forces in the emancipation of man from his natural, religious, and social ties.

If the literary critic is willing to overcome his lack of historical sense for the sake of this task, then it can provide an answer to the questions, why and to what ends one can still—or again—study literary history.

III *Literature and Commitment*

In the preceding section, Hans Robert Jauss called for attention to literature's 'socially formative function' as a way towards a new system of interpretations. Thus do scholars and professional critics find their way back to concerns which have long dominated the debate among writers, from Virginia Woolf, Jean-Paul Sartre to Italo Calvino. Only Theodor Adorno—a member of the 'Frankfurt School' of Marxists forced into exile by the Nazis—can be considered a critic in that sense. And yet, as the range and brilliance (as well as density) of his argument shows, he was as much aware of the implications for modern artists (like Schoenberg) and writers (like Brecht, whom he discusses at length) of the larger movements of history, politics, and society as, say, Sartre. Indeed, he takes Sartre's What is Literature?, written under the immediate pressures of the Liberation of France, as his starting-point and touchstone.

Sartre's analysis of the situation of the writer (as he calls it) has proved a lasting provocation to writers asking the same questions about what they should do, as writers, in conditions of extremity, of explicit oppression. Woolf's comparatively modest and quiet request for what a writer who happens to be a woman requires to be a writer, under any conditions, tellingly demonstrates how implicit repression operates. These extracts span the pre-World War II, the immediately post-war, and the recent, 'postmodernist' period—although Calvino, a postmodern novelist, echoes an earlier idea of writers needing to 'give a voice to whatever is without a voice', before going on to the more characteristically contemporary call for literature to be aware of its 'constructed', fictive nature.

Politics, Calvino argues, could well do with a similar awareness of itself, so as to 'distrust itself'. This sophistication might seem something of a luxury to the more openly 'committed' writers, such as Sartre, or Adorno (although Adorno's 'dialectic' allows him to commend formal experimentation); certainly Sartre's scrutiny of the problems facing the black American Richard Wright suggests some of the limitations of a commitment to mere 'style'. But the debate remains open, as we shall see in Part Two—especially in the sections on 'Literature and Ideology', 'New Writings in English', and 'Literature and History'.

I *To Cambridge Women**

VIRGINIA WOOLF

Here am I asking why women did not write poetry in the Elizabethan age, and I am not sure how they were educated; whether they were taught to write; whether they had sitting-rooms to themselves; how many women had children before they were twenty-one; what, in short, they did from eight in the morning till eight at night. They had no money evidently; according to Professor Trevelyan[1] they were married whether they liked it or not before they were out of the nursery, at fifteen or sixteen very likely. It would have been extremely odd, even upon this showing, had one of them suddenly written the plays of Shakespeare, I concluded, and I thought of that old gentleman, who is dead now, but was a bishop, I think, who declared that it was impossible for any woman, past, present, or to come, to have the genius of Shakespeare. He wrote to the papers about it. He also told a lady who applied to him for information that cats do not as a matter of fact go to heaven, though they have, he added, souls of a sort. How much thinking those old gentlemen used to save one! How the borders of ignorance shrank back at their approach! Cats do not go to heaven. Women cannot write the plays of Shakespeare.

Be that as it may, I could not help thinking, as I looked at the works of Shakespeare on the shelf, that the bishop was right at least in this; it would have been impossible, completely and entirely, for any woman to have written the plays of Shakespeare in the age of Shakespeare. Let me imagine, since facts are so hard to come by, what would have happened had Shakespeare had a wonderfully gifted sister, called Judith, let us say. Shakespeare himself went, very probably,—his mother was an heiress—to the grammar school, where he may have learnt Latin—Ovid, Virgil and Horace—and the elements of grammar and logic. He was, it is well known, a wild boy who poached rabbits, perhaps shot a deer, and had, rather sooner than he should have done, to marry a woman in the neighbourhood, who bore him a child rather quicker than was right. That escapade sent him to seek his fortune in London. He had, it seemed, a taste for the theatre; he began by holding horses at the stage door. Very soon he got work in the theatre, became a successful actor, and lived at the hub of the universe, meeting everybody, knowing everybody, practising his art on the boards, exercising his wits in the streets,

---

* From two lectures to women students at Cambridge, 1928, reprinted in Virginia Woolf, *A Room of One's Own*, The Hogarth Press, London, 1929, pp. 69–74, 110–18.

[1] Author of standard *History of England*, G. M. Trevelyan was Regius Professor of Modern History at Cambridge 1927–40. [Ed.]

and even getting access to the palace of the queen. Meanwhile his extraordinarily gifted sister, let us suppose, remained at home. She was as adventurous, as imaginative, as agog to see the world as he was. But she was not
sent to school. She had no chance of learning grammar and logic, let alone
of reading Horace and Virgil. She picked up a book now and then, one of her
brother's perhaps, and read a few pages. But then her parents came in and
told her to mend the stockings or mind the stew and not moon about with
books and papers. They would have spoken sharply but kindly, for they were
substantial people who knew the conditions of life for a woman and loved
their daughter—indeed, more likely than not she was the apple of her father's
eye. Perhaps she scribbled some pages up in an apple loft on the sly, but was
careful to hide them or set fire to them. Soon, however, before she was out
of her teens, she was to be betrothed to the son of a neighbouring wool-
stapler. She cried out that marriage was hateful to her, and for that she was
severely beaten by her father. Then he ceased to scold her. He begged her
instead not to hurt him, not to shame him in this matter of her marriage. He
would give her a chain of beads or a fine petticoat, he said; and there were
tears in his eyes. How could she disobey him? How could she break his heart?
The force of her own gift alone drove her to it. She made up a small parcel
of her belongings, let herself down by a rope one summer's night and took the
road to London. She was not seventeen. The birds that sang in the hedge were
not more musical than she was. She had the quickest fancy, a gift like her
brother's, for the tune of words. Like him, she had a taste for the theatre. She
stood at the stage door; she wanted to act, she said. Men laughed in her face.
The manager—a fat, loose-lipped man—guffawed. He bellowed something
about poodles dancing and women acting—no woman, he said, could
possibly be an actress. He hinted—you can imagine what. She could get no
training in her craft. Could she even seek her dinner in a tavern or roam the
streets at midnight? Yet her genius was for fiction and lusted to feed abundantly upon the lives of men and women and the study of their ways. At last
—for she was very young, oddly like Shakespeare the poet in her face, with
the same grey eyes and rounded brows—at last Nick Greene the actor-
manager took pity on her; she found herself with child by that gentleman and so
—who shall measure the heat and violence of the poet's heart when caught and
tangled in a woman's body?—killed herself one winter's night and lies buried at
some cross-roads where the omnibuses now stop outside the Elephant and
Castle.

That, more or less, is how the story would run, I think, if a woman in
Shakespeare's day had had Shakespeare's genius. But for my part, I agree
with the deceased bishop, if such he was—it is unthinkable that any woman
in Shakespeare's day should have had Shakespeare's genius. For genius like
Shakespeare's is not born among labouring, uneducated, servile people. It

was not born in England among the Saxons and the Britons. It is not born to-day among the working classes. How, then, could it have been born among women whose work began, according to Professor Trevelyan, almost before they were out of the nursery, who were forced to it by their parents and held to it by all the power of law and custom? Yet genius of a sort must have existed among women as it must have existed among the working classes. Now and again an Emily Brontë or a Robert Burns blazes out and proves its presence. But certainly it never got itself on to paper. When, however, one reads of a witch being ducked, of a woman possessed by devils, of a wise woman selling herbs, or even of a very remarkable man who had a mother, then I think we are on the track of a lost novelist, a suppressed poet, of some mute and inglorious Jane Austen, some Emily Brontë who dashed her brains out on the moor or mopped and mowed about the highways crazed with the torture that her gift had put her to. Indeed, I would venture to guess that Anon, who wrote so many poems without signing them, was often a woman. It was a woman Edward Fitzgerald, I think, suggested who made the ballads and the folk-songs, crooning them to her children, beguiling her spinning with them, or the length of the winter's night. . . .

And since a novel has this correspondence to real life, its values are to some extent those of real life. But it is obvious that the values of women differ very often from the values which have been made by the other sex; naturally, this is so. Yet it is the masculine values that prevail. Speaking crudely, football and sport are 'important'; the worship of fashion, the buying of clothes 'trivial'. And these values are inevitably transferred from life to fiction. This is an important book, the critic assumes, because it deals with war. This is an insignificant book because it deals with the feelings of women in a drawing-room. A scene in a battle-field is more important than a scene in a shop—everywhere and much more subtly the difference of value persists. The whole structure, therefore, of the early nineteenth-century novel was raised, if one was a woman, by a mind which was slightly pulled from the straight, and made to alter its clear vision in deference to external authority. One has only to skim those old forgotten novels and listen to the tone of voice in which they are written to divine that the writer was meeting criticism; she was saying this by way of aggression, or that by way of conciliation. She was admitting that she was 'only a woman', or protesting that she was 'as good as a man'. She met that criticism as her temperament dictated, with docility and diffi-dence, or with anger and emphasis. It does not matter which it was; she was thinking of something other than the thing itself. Down comes her book upon our heads. There was a flaw in the centre of it. And I thought of all the women's novels that lie scattered, like small pock-marked apples in an orchard, about the second-hand book shops in London. It was the flaw in the centre that had rotted them. She had altered her values in deference to the opinion of others.

But how impossible it must have been for them not to budge either to the right or to the left. What genius, what integrity it must have required in face of all that criticism, in the midst of that purely patriarchal society, to hold fast to the thing as they saw it without shrinking. Only Jane Austen did it and Emily Brontë. It is another feather, perhaps the finest, in their caps. They wrote as women write, not as men write. Of all the thousand women who wrote novels then, they alone entirely ignored the perpetual admonitions of the eternal pedagogue—write this, think that. They alone were deaf to that persistent voice, now grumbling, now patronising, now domineering, now grieved, now shocked, now angry, now avuncular, that voice which cannot let women alone, but must be at them, like some too conscientious governess, adjuring them, like Sir Egerton Brydges, to be refined; dragging even into the criticism of poetry criticism of sex;[2] admonishing them, if they would be good and win, as I suppose, some shiny prize, to keep within certain limits which the gentleman in question thinks suitable—'. . . female novelists should only aspire to excellence by courageously acknowledging the limitations of their sex'.[3] That puts the matter in a nutshell, and when I tell you, rather to your surprise, that this sentence was written not in August 1828 but in August 1928, you will agree, I think, that however delightful it is to us now, it represents a vast body of opinion—I am not going to stir those old pools; I take only what chance has floated to my feet—that was far more vigorous and far more vocal a century ago. It would have needed a very stalwart young woman in 1828 to disregard all those snubs and chidings and promises of prizes. One must have been something of a firebrand to say to oneself, Oh, but they can't buy literature too. Literature is open to everybody. I refuse to allow you, Beadle though you are, to turn me off the grass. Lock up your libraries if you like; but there is no gate, no lock, no bolt that you can set upon the freedom of my mind.

But whatever effect discouragement and criticism had upon their writing —and I believe that they had a very great effect—that was unimportant compared with the other difficulty which faced them (I was still considering those early nineteenth-century novelists) when they came to set their thoughts on paper—that is that they had no tradition behind them, or one so short and partial that it was of little help. For we think back through our

---

[2] '[She] has a metaphysical purpose, and that is a dangerous obsession, especially with a woman, for women rarely possess men's healthy love of rhetoric. It is a strange lack in the sex which is in other things more primitive and more materialistic'. *New Criterion*, June, 1928.
[3] 'If, like the reporter, you believe that female novelists should only aspire to excellence by courageously acknowledging the limitations of their sex (Jane Austen [has] demonstrated how gracefully this gesture can be accomplished . . .).' *Life and Letters*, August, 1928.

mothers if we are women. It is useless to go to the great men writers for help, however much one may go to them for pleasure. Lamb, Browne, Thackeray, Newman, Sterne, Dickens, De Quincey—whoever it may be—never helped a woman yet, though she may have learnt a few tricks of them and adapted them to her use. The weight, the pace, the stride of a man's mind are too unlike her own for her to lift anything substantial from him successfully. The ape is too distant to be sedulous. Perhaps the first thing she would find, setting pen to paper, was that there was no common sentence ready for her use. All the great novelists like Thackeray and Dickens and Balzac have written a natural prose, swift but not slovenly, expressive but not precious, taking their own tint without ceasing to be common property. They have based it on the sentence that was current at the time. The sentence that was current at the beginning of the nineteenth century ran something like this perhaps: 'The grandeur of their works was an argument with them, not to stop short, but to proceed. They could have no higher excitement or satisfaction than in the exercise of their art and endless generations of truth and beauty. Success prompts to exertion; and habit facilitates success.' That is a man's sentence; behind it one can see Johnson, Gibbon and the rest. It was a sentence that was unsuited for a woman's use. Charlotte Brontë, with all her splendid gift for prose, stumbled and fell with that clumsy weapon in her hands. George Eliot committed atrocities with it that beggar description. Jane Austen looked at it and laughed at it and devised a perfectly natural, shapely sentence proper for her own use and never departed from it. Thus, with less genius for writing than Charlotte Brontë, she got infinitely more said. Indeed, since freedom and fullness of expression are of the essence of the art, such a lack of tradition, such a scarcity and inadequacy of tools, must have told enormously upon the writing of women. Moreover, a book is not made of sentences laid end to end, but of sentences built, if an image helps, into arcades or domes. And this shape too has been made by men out of their own needs for their own uses. There is no reason to think that the form of the epic or of the poetic play suit a woman any more than the sentence suits her. But all the older forms of literature were hardened and set by the time she became a writer. The novel alone was young enough to be soft in her hands—another reason, perhaps, why she wrote novels. Yet who shall say that even now 'the novel' (I give it inverted commas to mark my sense of the words' inadequacy), who shall say that even this most pliable of all forms is rightly shaped for her use? No doubt we shall find her knocking that into shape for herself when she has the free use of her limbs; and providing some new vehicle, not necessarily in verse, for the poetry in her. For it is the poetry that is still denied outlet. And I went on to ponder how a woman nowadays would write a poetic tragedy in five acts. Would she use verse?—would she not use prose rather?

But these are difficult questions which lie in the twilight of the future. I must leave them, if only because they stimulate me to wander from my subject into trackless forests where I shall be lost and, very likely, devoured by wild beasts. I do not want, and I am sure that you do not want me, to broach that very dismal subject, the future of fiction, so that I will only pause here one moment to draw your attention to the great part which must be played in that future so far as women are concerned by physical conditions. The book has somehow to be adapted to the body, and at a venture one would say that women's books should be shorter, more concentrated, than those of men, and framed so that they do not need long hours of steady and uninterrupted work. For interruptions there will always be. Again, the nerves that feed the brain would seem to differ in men and women, and if you are going to make them work their best and hardest, you must find out what treatment suits them—whether these hours of lectures, for instance, which the monks devised, presumably, hundreds of years ago, suit them—what alterations of work and rest they need, interpreting rest not as doing nothing but as doing something but something that is different; and what should that difference be? All this should be discussed and discovered; all this is part of the question of women and fiction. And yet, I continued, approaching the bookcase again, where shall I find that elaborate study of the psychology of women by a woman? If through their incapacity to play football women are not going to be allowed to practise medicine——

Happily my thoughts were now given another turn.

2 *Writing, Reading, and the Public**

JEAN-PAUL SARTRE

NOTE: Sartre begins his argument by asserting that 'the poet is forbidden to commit himself' by the nature of his medium; but the prose-writer is '*a speaker*', his words are 'first of all not objects but designations for objects' . . . The first question, then, is 'Do you have anything to say?'

To speak is to act; anything which one names is already no longer quite the same; it has lost its innocence.

If you name the behaviour of an individual, you reveal it to him; he sees himself. And since you are at the same time naming it to all others, he knows that he is *seen* at the moment he *sees* himself. The furtive gesture which he forgot while making it, begins to exist beyond all measure, to exist for

---

* From Jean-Paul Sartre, *What is Literature?*, transl. B. Frechtman, Methuen, 1967, pp. 12–15, 49–60; first publ. 1948, in *Les Temps Modernes*.

everybody; it is integrated into the objective mind; it takes on new dimensions; it is retrieved. After that, how can you expect him to act in the same way? Either he will persist in his behaviour out of obstinacy and with full knowledge of what he is doing, or he will give it up. Thus, by speaking, I reveal the situation by my very intention of changing it; I reveal it to myself and to others *in order* to change it. I strike at its very heart, I transfix it, and I display it in full view; at present I dispose of it; with every word I utter, I involve myself a little more in the world, and by the same token I emerge from it a little more, since I go beyond it towards the future.

Thus, the prose-writer is a man who has chosen a certain method of secondary action which we may call action by disclosure. It is therefore permissible to ask him this second question: 'What aspect of the world do you want to disclose? What change do you want to bring into the world by this disclosure?' The 'committed' writer knows that words are action. He knows that to reveal is to change and that one can reveal only by planning to change. He has given up the impossible dream of giving an impartial picture of Society and the human condition. Man is the being towards whom no being can be impartial, not even God. For God, if He existed, would be, as certain mystics have seen Him, in a *situation* in relation to man. And He is also the being Who cannot even see a situation without changing it, for His gaze congeals, destroys, or sculpts, or, as does eternity, changes the object in itself. It is in love, in hate, in anger, in fear, in joy, in indignation, in admiration, in hope, in despair, that man and the world reveal themselves *in their truth*. Doubtless, the committed writer can be mediocre; he can even be conscious of being so; but as one cannot write without the intention of succeeding perfectly, the modesty with which he envisages his work should not divert him from constructing it *as if* it were to have the greatest celebrity. He should never say to himself, 'Bah! I'll be lucky if I have three thousand readers', but rather, 'What would happen if everybody read what I wrote?' . . .

Later on we shall try to determine what the goal of literature may be. But from this point on we may conclude that the writer has chosen to reveal the world and particularly to reveal man to other men so that the latter may assume full responsibility before the object which has been thus laid bare. It is assumed that no one is ignorant of the law because there is a code and because the law is written down; thereafter, you are free to violate it, but you know the risks you run. Similarly, the function of the writer is to act in such a way that nobody can be ignorant of the world and that nobody may say that he is innocent of what it's all about. And since he has once committed himself in the universe of language, he can never again pretend that he cannot speak. Once you enter the universe of meanings, there is nothing you can do to get out of it. Let words organize themselves freely and they will make sentences, and each sentence contains language in its entirety and refers back to the whole universe. Silence itself is defined in relationship to words, as the pause in music receives its meaning from the group of notes round it. This silence is a moment of language; being silent is not being dumb; it is to refuse to speak, and therefore to keep on speaking. Thus, if a writer has chosen to remain silent on any aspect whatever of the world, or, according to an expression which says just what it means, to *pass over* it in silence, one has the right to ask him a third question: 'Why have you spoken of this rather than that, and—since you speak in order to bring about change—why do you want to change this rather than that?' . . .

FOR WHOM DOES ONE WRITE?

At first sight, there doesn't seem to be any doubt: one writes for the universal reader, and we have seen, in effect, that the exigency of the writer is, as a rule, addressed to *all* men. But the preceding descriptions are ideal. As a matter of fact the writer knows that he speaks for freedoms which are swallowed up, masked, and unavailable; and his own freedom is not so pure; he has to clean it. It is dangerously easy to speak too readily about eternal values; eternal values are very, very fleshless. Even freedom, if one considers it *sub specie aeternitatis*,[1] seems to be a withered branch; for, like the sea, there is no end to it. It is nothing else but the movement by which one perpetually uproots and liberates oneself. There is no given freedom. One must win an inner victory over one's passions, one's race, one's class, and one's nation and must conquer other men along with oneself. But what counts in this case is the particular form of the obstacle to surmount, of the resistance to overcome. That is what gives form to freedom in each circumstance. If the writer has chosen. . . to talk drivel, he can speak in fine, rolling periods of that eternal freedom which National Socialism, Stalinist communism, and the capitalist democracies all lay claim to. He won't disturb anybody; he won't address anybody. Everything he asks for is granted him in advance. But it is an abstract dream. Whether he wants to or not, and even if he has his eyes on eternal laurels, the writer is speaking to his contemporaries and brothers of his class and race. . . .

The same with reading: people of the same period and community, who have lived through the same events, who have raised or avoided the same questions, have the same taste in their mouth; they have the same complicity, and there are the same corpses among them. That is why it is not necessary to write so much; there are key-words. If I were to tell an audience of Americans about the German occupation, there would have to be a great deal of analysis and precaution. I would waste twenty pages in dispelling precon- ceptions, prejudices, and legends. Afterwards, I would have to be sure of my

---

[1] Latin: 'in the perspective of eternity'. [Ed.]

position at every step; I would have to look for images and symbols in American history which would enable them to understand ours; I would always have to keep in mind the difference between our old man's pessimism and their childlike optimism. If I were to write about the same subject for Frenchmen, we are *entre nous*.[2] For example, it would be enough to say: 'A concert of German military music in the band-stand of a public garden'; everything is there; a raw spring day, a park in the provinces, men with shaven skulls blowing away at their brasses, blind and deaf passers-by who quicken their steps, two or three sullen-looking listeners under the trees, this useless serenade to France which drifts off into the sky, our shame and our anguish, our anger, and our pride too. Thus, the reader I am addressing is neither Micromégas[3] nor L'Ingénu;[4] nor is he God the Father either. He has not the ignorance of the noble savage to whom everything has to be explained on the basis of principles; he is not a spirit or a *tabula rasa*. Neither has he the omniscience of an angel or of the Eternal Father. I reveal certain aspects of the universe to him; I take advantage of what he knows to attempt to teach him what he does not know. Suspended between total ignorance and omniscience, he has a definite stock of knowledge which varies from moment to moment and which is enough to reveal his *historical* character. In actual fact, he is not an instantaneous consciousness, a pure timeless affirmation of freedom, nor does he soar above history; he is involved in it.

Authors too are historical. And that is precisely the reason why some of them want to escape from history by a leap into eternity. The book, serving as a go-between, establishes an historical contact among the men who are steeped in the same history and who likewise contribute to its making. Writing and reading are two facets of the same historical fact, and the freedom to which the writer invites us is not a pure abstract consciousness of being free. Strictly speaking, it *is not*; it wins itself in an historical situation; each book proposes a concrete liberation on the basis of a particular alienation. Hence, in each one there is an implicit recourse to institutions, customs, certain forms of oppression and conflict, to the wisdom and the folly of the day, to lasting passions and passing stubbornness, to superstitions and recent victories of common sense, to evidence and ignorance, to particular modes of reasoning which the sciences have made fashionable and which are applied in all domains, to hopes, to fears, to habits of sensibility, imagination, and even perception, and finally, to customs and values which have been handed down, to a whole world which the author and the reader have in common. It is this familiar world which the writer animates and penetrates with his freedom. It is on the basis of this world that the reader must bring about his

[2] French: 'among ourselves'. [Ed.]
[3] Hero of a philosophical tale by Voltaire, a kind of Gulliver. [Ed.]
[4] The Innocent. [Ed.]

concrete liberation; it is alienation, situation, and history. It is this world which I must change or preserve for myself and others. For if the immediate aspect of freedom is negativity, we know that it is not a matter of the abstract power of saying no, but of a concrete negativity which retains within itself (and is completely coloured by) what it denies. And since the freedoms of the author and reader seek and affect each other through a world, it can just as well be said that the author's choice of a certain aspect of the world determines the reader and, vice versa, that it is by choosing his reader that the author decides upon his subject. . . .

I shall say that a writer is committed when he tries to achieve the most lucid and the most complete consciousness of being embarked, that is, when he causes the commitment of immediate spontaneity to advance, for himself and others, to the reflective. The writer is, *par excellence*, a mediator and his commitment is to mediation. But, if it is true that we must account for his work on the basis of his condition, it must also be borne in mind that his condition is not only that of a man in general but precisely that of a writer as well. . . .

Let us take the case of the great negro writer, Richard Wright. If we consider only his condition as a *man*, that is, as a Southern 'nigger' transported to the North, we shall at once imagine that he can only write about Negroes or Whites *seen through the eyes of Negroes*. Can one imagine for a moment that he would agree to pass his life in the contemplation of the eternal True, Good, and Beautiful when ninety per cent of the negroes in the South are practically deprived of the right to vote? And if anyone speaks here about the treason of the clerks,[5] I answer that there are no clerks among the oppressed. Clerks are necessarily the parasites of oppressing classes or races. Thus, if an American negro finds that he has a vocation as a writer, he discovers his subject at the same time. He is the man who sees the whites from the outside, who assimilates the white culture from the outside, and each of whose books will show the alienation of the black race within American society. Not objectively, like the realists, but passionately, and in a way that will compromise his reader. But this examination leaves the nature of his work undetermined; he might be a pamphleteer, a blues-writer, or the Jeremiah of the Southern negroes.

If we want to go further, we must consider his public. To whom does Richard Wright address himself? Certainly not to the universal man. The essential characteristic of the notion of the universal man is that he is not involved in any particular age, and that he is no more and no less moved by the lot of the negroes of Louisiana than by that of the Roman slaves in the time of Spartacus. The universal man can think of nothing but universal

5 'Clerks', i.e. intellectuals, from the French 'clercs'. [Ed.]

values. He is a pure and abstract affirmation of the inalienable right of man. But neither can Wright think of intending his books for the white racialists of Virginia or South Carolina whose minds are made up in advance and who will not open them. Nor to the black peasants of the bayous who cannot read. And if he seems to be happy about the reception his books have had in Europe, still it is obvious that at the beginning he had not the slightest idea of writing for the European public. Europe is far away. Its indignation is ineffectual and hypocritical. Not much is to be expected from the nations which have enslaved the Indies, Indo-China, and negro Africa. These considerations are enough to define his readers. He is addressing himself to the cultivated negroes of the North and the white Americans of goodwill (intellectuals, democrats of the left, radicals, CIO[6] workers).

It is not that he is not aiming through them at all men but it is *through them* that he is thus aiming. Just as one can catch a glimpse of eternal freedom at the horizon of the historical and concrete freedom which it pursues, so the human race is at the horizon of the concrete and historical group of its readers. The illiterate negro peasants and the Southern planters represent a margin of abstract possibilities around its real public. After all, an illiterate may learn to read. *Black Boy* may fall into the hands of the most stubborn of negrophobes and may open his eyes. This merely means that every human project exceeds its actual limits and extends itself step by step to the infinite.

Now, it is to be noted that there is a fracture at the very heart of this *actual public*. For Wright, the negro readers represent the subjective. The same childhood, the same difficulties, the same complexes: a mere hint is enough for them; they understand with their hearts. In trying to become clear about his own personal situation, he clarifies theirs for them. He mediates, names, and shows them the life they lead from day to day in its immediacy, the life they suffer without finding words to formulate their sufferings. He is their conscience, and the movement by which he raises himself from the immediate to the reflective recapturing of his condition is that of his whole race. But whatever the goodwill of the white readers may be, for a negro author they represent the *Other*. They have not lived through what he has lived through. They can understand the negro's condition only by an extreme stretch of the imagination and by relying upon analogies which at any moment may deceive them. On the other hand, Wright does not completely know them. It is only from without that he conceives their proud security and that tranquil certainty, common to all white Aryans, that the world is white and that they own it. The words he puts down on paper have not the same context for whites as for negroes. They must be chosen by guesswork, since he does not know what resonances they will set up in those strange minds. And when he

[6] Abbreviation for the Congress of Industrial Organizations.

speaks to them, their very aim is changed. It is a matter of implicating them and making them take stock of their responsibilities. He must make them indignant and ashamed.

Thus, each of Wright's works contains what Baudelaire would have called 'a double simultaneous postulation'; each word refers to two contexts; two forces are applied simultaneously to each phrase and determine the incomparable tension of his tale. Had he spoken to the whites alone, he might have turned out to be more prolix, more didactic, and more abusive; to the negroes alone, still more elliptical, more of a confederate, and more elegiac. In the first case, his work might have come close to satire; in the second, to prophetic lamentations. Jeremiah spoke only to the Jews. But Wright, a writer for a split public, has been able both to maintain and go beyond this split. He has made it the pretext for a work of art.

The writer consumes and does not produce, even if he has decided to serve the community's interests with his pen. His works remain gratuitous; thus no price can be set on their value. Their market value is fixed arbitrarily. In some periods he is pensioned and in others he gets a percentage of the sales of the book. But there is no more common measure between the work of the mind and percentage remuneration in modern society than there was between the poem and the royal pension under the old régime. Actually, the writer is not paid; he is fed, well or badly, according to the period. The system cannot work any differently, for his activity is *useless*. It is not at all *useful*; it is sometimes *harmful* for society to become self-conscious. For the fact is that the useful is defined within the framework of an established society and in relationship to institutions, values, and ends which are already fixed. If society sees itself and, in particular, sees itself as *seen*, there is, by virtue of this very fact, a contesting of the established values of the régime. The writer presents it with its image; he calls upon it to assume it or to change itself. At any rate, it changes; it loses the equilibrium which its ignorance had given it; it wavers between shame and cynicism; it practises dishonesty; thus, the writer gives society *a guilty conscience*; he is thereby in a state of perpetual antagonism towards the conservative forces which are maintaining the balance he tends to upset. For the transition to the mediate which can be brought about only by a negation of the immediate is a perpetual revolution.

Only the governing classes can allow themselves the luxury of remunerating so unproductive and dangerous an activity, and if they do so, it is a matter both of tactics and of misapprehension. Misapprehension for the most part: free from material cares, the members of the governing *élite* are sufficiently detached to want to have a reflective knowledge of themselves. They want to retrieve themselves, and they charge the artist with presenting them with their image without realizing that he will then make them assume it. A tactic on the part of some who, having recognized the danger, pension the artist in order to control his destructive power. Thus, the writer is a parasite of the governing *élite*. But, functionally, he moves in opposition to the interests of those who keep him alive. Such is the original conflict which defines his condition.

3 *Commitment**

THEODOR ADORNO

Since Sartre's essay *What is Literature?* there has been less theoretical debate about committed and autonomous literature. Nevertheless, the controversy over commitment remains urgent, so far as anything that merely concerns the life of the mind can be today, as opposed to sheer human survival. Sartre was moved to issue his manifesto because he saw—and he was certainly not the first to do so—works of art displayed side by side in a pantheon of optional edification, decaying into cultural commodities. In such coexistence, they desecrate each other. If a work, without its author necessarily intending it, aims at a supreme effect, it cannot really tolerate a neighbour beside it. This salutary intolerance holds not only for individual works, but also for aesthetic genres or attitudes such as those once symbolized in the now half-forgotten controversy over commitment.

There are two 'positions on objectivity' which are constantly at war with one another, even when intellectual life falsely presents them as at peace. A work of art that is committed strips the magic from a work of art that is content to be a fetish, an idle pastime for those who would like to sleep through the deluge that threatens them, in an apoliticism that is in fact deeply political. For the committed, such works are a distraction from the battle of real interests, in which no one is any longer exempt from the conflict between the two great blocs. The possibility of intellectual life itself depends on this conflict to such an extent that only blind illusion can insist on rights that may be shattered tomorrow. For autonomous works of art, however, such considerations, and the conception of art which underlies them, are themselves the spiritual catastrophe of which the committed keep warning. Once the life of the mind renounces the duty and liberty of its own pure objectification, it has abdicated. Thereafter, works of art merely assimilate themselves to the brute existence against which they protest, in forms so ephemeral (the very charge made against autonomous works by committed writers) that from

* From *Aesthetics and Politics*, trans. Francis MacDonagh, ed. R. Livingstone, P. Anderson, F. Mulhern, New Left Books, 1977, pp. 177–95; first publ. *Noten zur Literatur*, III, Suhrkamp, Frankfurt, 1965.

their first day they belong to the seminars in which they inevitably end. The menacing thrust of the antithesis is a reminder of how precarious the position of art is today. Each of the two alternatives negates itself with the other. Committed art, necessarily detached as art from reality, cancels the distance between the two. 'Art for art's sake' denies by its absolute claims that ineradicable connection with reality which is the polemical *a priori* of the attempt to make art autonomous from the real. Between these two poles the tension in which art has lived in every age till now is dissolved.

Contemporary literature itself suggests doubts as to the omnipotence of these alternatives. For it is not yet so completely subjugated to the course of the world as to constitute rival fronts. The Sartrean goats and the Valéryan[1] sheep will not be separated. Even if politically motivated, commitment in itself remains politically polyvalent so long as it is not reduced to propaganda, whose pliancy mocks any commitment by the subject. On the other hand, its opposite, known in Russian catechisms as formalism, is not decried only by Soviet officials or libertarian existentialists; even 'vanguard' critics themselves frequently accuse so-called abstract texts of a lack of provocation and social aggressivity. Conversely, Sartre cannot praise Picasso's *Guernica* too highly; yet he could hardly be convicted of formalist sympathies in music or painting. He restricts his notion of commitment to literature because of its conceptual character: 'The writer deals with meanings'.[2] Of course, but not only with them. If no word which enters a literary work ever wholly frees itself from its meaning in ordinary speech, so no literary work, not even the traditional novel, leaves these meanings unaltered, as they were outside it. Even an ordinary 'was', in a report of something that was not, acquires a new formal quality from the fact that it was not so. The same process occurs in the higher levels of meaning of a work, all the way up to what once used to be called its 'Idea'. The special position that Sartre accords to literature must also be suspect to anyone who does not unconditionally subsume diverse aesthetic genres under a superior universal concept. The rudiments of external meanings are the irreducibly non-artistic elements in art. Its formal principle lies not in them, but in the dialectic of both moments—which accomplishes the transformation of meanings within it. The distinction between artist and *littérateur* is shallow: but it is true that the object of any aesthetic philosophy, even as understood by Sartre, is not the publicistic aspect of art. Still less is it the 'message' of a work. The latter oscillates unhappily between the subjective intentions of the artist and the demands of an objectively explicit metaphysical meaning. . . .

In aesthetic theory, 'commitment' should be distinguished from 'tendency'.

---

[1] From Paul Valéry (1871–1945), Symbolist poet and advocate of ironic detachment rather than Sartrean engagement. [Ed.]

[2] Jean-Paul Sartre, *What is Literature?*, London, 1967, p. 4.

Committed art in the proper sense is not intended to generate ameliorative measures, legislative acts or practical institutions—like earlier propagandist plays against syphilis, duels, abortion laws or borstals—but to work at the level of fundamental attitudes. For Sartre its task is to awaken the free choice of the agent which makes authentic existence possible at all, as opposed to the neutrality of the spectator. But what gives commitment its aesthetic advantage over tendentiousness also renders the content to which the artist commits himself inherently ambiguous. In Sartre the notion of choice—originally a Kierkegaardian category—is heir to the Christian doctrine 'He who is not with me is against me', but now voided of any concrete theological content. What remains is merely the abstract authority of a choice enjoined, with no regard for the fact that the very possibility of choosing depends on what can be chosen. . . . His plays are . . . bad models of his own existentialism, because they display in their respect for truth the whole administered universe which his philosophy ignores: the lesson we learn from them is one of unfreedom. Sartre's theatre of ideas sabotages the aims of his categories. This is not a specific shortcoming of his plays. It is not the office of art to spotlight alternatives, but to resist by its form alone the course of the world, which permanently puts a pistol to men's heads. In fact, as soon as committed works of art do instigate decisions at their own level, the decisions themselves become interchangeable. Because of this ambiguity, Sartre has with great candour confessed that he expects no real changes in the world from literature—a scepticism which reflects the historical mutations both of society and of the practical function of literature since the days of Voltaire. The principle of commitment thus slides towards the proclivities of the author, in keeping with the extreme subjectivism of Sartre's philosophy, which for all its materialist undertones, still echoes German speculative idealism. In his literary theory the work of art becomes an appeal to subjects, because it is itself nothing other than a declaration by a subject of his own choice or failure to choose.

Sartre will not allow that every work of art, at its very inception, confronts the writer, however free he may be, with objective demands of composition. His intention becomes simply one element among them. Sartre's question, 'Why write?', and his solution of it in a 'deeper choice', are invalid because the author's motivations are irrelevant to the finished work, the literary product. Sartre himself is not so far from this view when he notes that the stature of works increases, the less they remain attached to the empirical person who created them . . . Sartre therefore does not want to situate commitment at the level of the intention of the writer, but at that of his humanity itself. This determination, however, is so generic that commitment ceases to be distinct from any other form of human action or attitude. The point, says Sartre, is that the writer commits himself in the present, '*dans le présent*'; but since he in any case cannot escape it, his commitment to it cannot indicate a programme. . . .

. . . however sublime, thoughts can never be much more than one of the materials for art. Sartre's plays are vehicles for the author's ideas, which have been left behind in the race of aesthetic forms. They operate with traditional plots, exalted by an unshaken faith in meanings which can be transferred from art to reality. But the theses they illustrate, or where possible state, misuse the emotions which Sartre's own drama aims to express, by making them examples. They thereby disavow themselves. . . .

Brecht, in some of his plays, such as the dramatization of Gorky's *The Mother* or *The Measures Taken*, bluntly glorifies the Party. But at times, at least according to his theoretical writings, he too wanted to educate spectators to a new attitude that would be distanced, thoughtful, experimental, the reverse of illusory empathy and identification. In tendency to abstraction, his plays after *Saint Joan* trump those of Sartre. The difference is that Brecht, more consistent than Sartre and a greater artist, made this abstraction into the formal principle of his art, as a didactic poetics that eliminates the traditional concept of dramatic character altogether. He realized that the surface of social life, the sphere of consumption, which includes the psychologically motivated actions of individuals, conceals the essence of society—which, as the law of exchange, is itself abstract. Brecht rejected aesthetic individuation as an ideology. He therefore sought to translate the true hideousness of society into theatrical appearance, by dragging it straight out of its camouflage. The people on his stage shrink before our eyes into the agents of social processes and functions, which indirectly and unknowingly they are in empirical reality. Brecht no longer postulates, like Sartre, an identity between living individuals and the essence of society, let alone any absolute sovereignty of the subject. Nevertheless, the process of aesthetic reduction that he pursues for the sake of political truth, in fact gets in its way. For this truth involves innumerable mediations, which Brecht disdains. What is artistically legitimate as alienating infantilism—Brecht's first plays came from the same milieu as Dada—becomes merely infantile when it starts to claim theoretical or social validity. Brecht wanted to reveal in images the inner nature of capitalism. In this sense his aim was indeed what he disguised it as against Stalinist terror—realistic. He would have refused to deprive social essence of meaning by taking it as it appeared, imageless and blind, in a single crippled life. But this burdened him with the obligation of ensuring that what he intended to make unequivocally clear was theoretically correct. His art, however, refused to accept this *quid pro quo*: it both presents itself as didactic, and claims aesthetic dispensation from responsibility for the accuracy of what it teaches.

Criticism of Brecht cannot overlook the fact that he did not—for objective reasons beyond the power of his own creations—fulfil the norm he set himself as if it were a means to salvation. *Saint Joan* was the central work of his dialectical theatre. (*The Good Woman of Szechuan* is a variation of it in reverse: where Joan assists evil by the immediacy of her goodness, Shen Te, who wills the good, must become evil.) The play is set in a Chicago half-way between the Wild West fables of *Mahagonny* and economic facts. But the more pre-occupied Brecht becomes with information, and the less he looks for images, the more he misses the essence of capitalism which the parable is supposed to present. . . .

Brecht's comedy of the resistible rise of the great dictator *Arturo Ui* exposes the subjective nullity and pretence of a fascist leader in a harsh and accurate light. However, the deconstruction of leaders, as with all individuals in Brecht, is extended into a reconstruction of the social and economic nexus in which the dictator acts. Instead of a conspiracy of the wealthy and powerful, we are given a trivial gangster organization, the cabbage trust. The true horror of fascism is conjured away; it is no longer a slow end-product of the concentration of social power, but mere hazard, like an accident or a crime. This conclusion is dictated by the exigencies of agitation: adversaries must be diminished. . . . The group which engineered the seizure of power in Germany was also certainly a gang. But the problem is that such elective affinities are not extra-territorial: they are rooted within society itself. That is why the buffoonery of fascism, evoked by Chaplin as well, was at the same time also its ultimate horror. If this is suppressed, and a few sorry exploiters of greengrocers are mocked, where key positions of economic power are actually at issue, the attack misfires. *The Great Dictator* loses all satirical force and becomes obscene when a Jewish girl can hit a line of storm-troopers on the head with a pan without being torn to pieces. For the sake of political commitment, political reality is trivialized: which then reduces the political effect.

Sartre's frank doubt whether *Guernica* 'won a single supporter for the Spanish cause' certainly also applies to Brecht's didactic drama. . . . The trappings of epic drama recall the American phrase 'preaching to the converted'. The primacy of lesson over pure form, which Brecht intended to achieve, became a formal device itself. . . . The substance of Brecht's artistic work was the didactic play as an artistic principle. His method, to make immediately apparent events into phenomena alien to the spectator, was also a medium of formal construction rather than a contribution to practical efficacy. It is true that Brecht never spoke as sceptically as Sartre about the social effects of art. But, as an astute and experienced man of the world, he can scarcely have been wholly convinced of them. He once calmly wrote that, to be honest, the theatre was more important to him than any changes in the world it might promote. Yet the artistic principle of simplification not only purged politics of the illusory distinctions projected by subjective reflection into social objectivity, as Brecht intended, but it also falsified the very objectivity which didactic drama laboured to distil. If we take Brecht at his word and make politics the criterion by which to judge his committed theatre, then politics proves his theatre untrue. . . .

Contemporary literary Germany is anxious to distinguish Brecht the artist from Brecht the politician. The major writer must be saved for the West . . . There is truth in this to the extent that both Brecht's artistic force, and his devious and uncontrollable intelligence, went well beyond the official credos and prescribed aesthetics of the People's Democracies. All the same, Brecht must be defended against this defence of him. His work, with its often patent weaknesses, would not have had such power, if it were not saturated with politics. Even its most questionable creations, such as *The Measures Taken*, generate an immediate awareness that issues of the utmost seriousness are at stake. To this extent Brecht's claim that he used his theatre to make men think was justified. It is futile to try to separate the beauties, real or imaginary, of his works from their political intentions. The task of immanent criticism, which alone is dialectical, is rather to synthesize assessment of the validity of his forms with that of his politics. Sartre's chapter 'Why write?' contains the undeniable statement that: 'Nobody can suppose for a moment that it is possible to write a good novel in praise of anti-semitism'.[3] Nor could one be written in praise of the Moscow Trials, even if such praise were bestowed before Stalin actually had Zinoviev and Bukharin murdered.[4] The political falsehood stains the aesthetic form. Where Brecht distorts the real social problems discussed in his epic drama in order to prove a thesis, the whole structure and foundation of the play itself crumbles. *Mother Courage* is an illustrated primer intended to reduce to absurdity Montecuccoli's dictum that war feeds on war.[5] The camp follower who uses the Thirty Years' War to make a life for her children thereby becomes responsible for their ruin. But in the play this responsibility follows rigorously neither from the fact of the war itself nor from the individual behaviour of the petty profiteer; if Mother Courage had not been absent at the critical moment, the disaster would not have happened, and the fact that she has to be absent to earn some money, remains completely generic in relation to the action. The picture-book technique which Brecht needs to spell out his thesis prevents him from proving it. . . . But Brecht needed the old lawless days as an image of his own, precisely because he saw clearly that the society of his own age could no

[3] *What is Literature?*, p. 46.

[4] Reference to *The Measures Taken*, written in 1930, which contained an implicit justification in advance of the Moscow Trials. Zinoviev and Bukharin were condemned in 1938.

[5] From *Memories of War* by the Austrian general Raimondo, Count of Montecuccoli (1609–80), active in the Thirty Years' War. [Ed.]

longer be directly comprehended in terms of people and things. His attempt to reconstruct the reality of society thus led to a false social model and then to dramatic implausibility. Bad politics becomes bad art, and vice-versa. But the less works have to proclaim what they cannot completely believe themselves, the more telling they become in their own right; and the less they need a surplus of meaning beyond what they are. For the rest, the interested parties in every camp would probably be as successful in surviving wars today as they have always been. . . .

Even Brecht's best work was infected by the deceptions of his commitment. Its language shows how far the underlying poetic subject and its message have moved apart. In an attempt to bridge the gap, Brecht affected the diction of the oppressed. But the doctrine he advocated needs the language of the intellectual. The homeliness and simplicity of his tone is thus a fiction. It betrays itself both by signs of exaggeration and by stylized regression to archaic or provincial forms of expression. It can often be importunate, and ears which have not let themselves be deprived of their native sensitivity cannot help hearing that they are being talked into something. It is a usurpation and almost a contempt for victims to speak like this, as if the author were one of them. All roles may be played, except that of the worker. The gravest charge against commitment is that even right intentions go wrong when they are noticed, and still more so, when they then try to conceal themselves. . . .

I have no wish to soften the saying that to write lyric poetry after Auschwitz is barbaric; it expresses in negative form the impulse which inspires committed literature. The question asked by a character in Sartre's play *Morts Sans Sépulture*,[6] 'Is there any meaning in life when men exist who beat people until the bones break in their bodies?', is also the question whether any art now has a right to exist; whether intellectual regression is not inherent in the concept of committed literature because of the regression of society. . . . Yet this suffering, what Hegel called consciousness of adversity, also demands the continued existence of art while it prohibits it; it is now virtually in art alone that suffering can still find its own voice, consolation, without immediately being betrayed by it. The most important artists of the age have realized this. The uncompromising radicalism of their works, the very features defamed as formalism, give them a terrifying power, absent from helpless poems to the victims of our time. But even Schoenberg's *Survivor of Warsaw* remains trapped in the aporia to which, autonomous figuration of heteronomy raised to the intensity of hell, it totally surrenders. There is something embarrassing in Schoenberg's composition—not what arouses anger in Germany, the fact that it prevents people from repressing from memory what they at all costs want to repress—but the way in which, by turning suffering into images,

[6] 1946: *Men Without Shadows* in English. [Ed.]

harsh and uncompromising though they are, it wounds the shame we feel in the presence of the victims. For these victims are used to create something, works of art, that are thrown to the consumption of a world which destroyed them. The so-called artistic representation of the sheer physical pain of people beaten to the ground by rifle-butts contains, however remotely, the power to elicit enjoyment out of it. The moral of this art, not to forget for a single instant, slithers into the abyss of its opposite. The aesthetic principle of stylization, and even the solemn prayer of the chorus, make an unthinkable fate appear to have had some meaning; it is transfigured, something of its horror is removed. This alone does an injustice to the victims; yet no art which tried to evade them could confront the claims of justice. Even the sound of despair pays its tribute to a hideous affirmation. Works of less than the highest rank are also willingly absorbed as contributions to clearing up the past. When genocide becomes part of the cultural heritage in the themes of committed literature, it becomes easier to continue to play along with the culture which gave birth to murder.

There is one nearly invariable characteristic of such literature. It is that it implies, purposely or not, that even in so-called extreme situations, indeed in them most of all, humanity flourishes. Sometimes this develops into a dismal metaphysic which does its best to work up atrocities into 'limiting situations' which it then accepts to the extent that they reveal authenticity in men. In such a homely existential atmosphere the distinction between executioners and victims becomes blurred; both, after all, are equally suspended above the possibility of nothingness, which of course is generally not quite so uncomfortable for the executioners.

Today, the adherents of a philosophy which has since degenerated into a mere ideological sport, fulminate in pre-1933 fashion against artistic distortion, deformation and perversion of life, as though authors, by faithfully reflecting atrocities, were responsible for what they revolt against. The best example of this attitude, still prevalent among the silent majority in Germany, is the following story about Picasso. An officer of the Nazi occupation forces visited the painter in his studio and, pointing to *Guernica*, asked: 'Did you do that?' Picasso is said to have answered, 'No, you did'. Autonomous works of art too, like this painting, firmly negate empirical reality, destroy the destroyer, that which merely exists and, by merely existing, endlessly reiterates guilt. It is none other than Sartre who has seen the connection between the autonomy of a work and an intention which is not conferred upon it but is its own gesture towards reality. 'The work of art', he has written, '*does not have* an end; there we agree with Kant. But the reason is that it *is* an end. The Kantian formula does not account for the appeal which issues from every painting, every statue, every book.'[7] It only remains to add there is no straightforward relationship between this appeal and the thematic commitment of a work. The uncalculating autonomy of works which avoid popularization and adaptation to the market, involuntarily becomes an attack on them. . . . Works of art that react against empirical reality obey the forces of that reality, which reject intellectual creations and throw them back on themselves. There is no material content, no formal category of artistic creation, however mysteriously transmitted and itself unaware of the process, which did not originate in the empirical reality from which it breaks free.

It is this which constitutes the true relation of art to reality, whose elements are regrouped by its formal laws. Even the *avant-garde* abstraction which provokes the indignation of philistines, and which has nothing in common with conceptual or logical abstraction, is a reflex response to the abstraction of the law which objectively dominates society. This could be shown in Beckett's works. These enjoy what is today the only form of respectable fame: everyone shudders at them, and yet no-one can persuade himself that these eccentric plays and novels are not about what everyone knows but no one will admit. Philosophical apologists may laud his works as sketches from an anthropology. But they deal with a highly concrete historical reality: the abdication of the subject. Beckett's *Ecce Homo*[8] is what human beings have become. As though with eyes drained of tears, they stare silently out of his sentences. The spell they cast, which also binds them, is lifted by being reflected in them. However, the minimal promise of happiness they contain, which refuses to be traded for comfort, cannot be had for a price less than total dislocation, to the point of worldlessness. Here every commitment to the world must be abandoned to satisfy the ideal of the committed work of art —that polemical alienation which Brecht as a theorist invented, and as an artist practised less and less as he committed himself more firmly to the role of a friend of mankind. This paradox, which might be charged with sophistry, can be supported without much philosophy by the simplest experience: Kafka's prose and Beckett's plays, or the truly monstrous novel *The Unnameable*, have an effect by comparison with which officially committed works look like pantomimes. Kafka and Beckett arouse the fear which existentialism merely talks about. By dismantling appearance, they explode from within the art which committed proclamation subjugates from without, and hence only in appearance. The inescapability of their work compels the change of attitude which committed works merely demand. He over whom Kafka's wheels have passed, has lost for ever both any peace with the world and any chance of consoling himself with the judgment that the way of the world is bad; the

[7] *What is Literature?*, p. 34.
[8] Latin: 'behold the man', the words of Pilate often used as a tag for portraits of Christ crowned with thorns. [Ed.]

element of ratification which lurks in resigned admission of the dominance of evil is burnt away. . . .

Today the curmudgeons whom no bombs could shake out of their complacency have allied themselves with the philistines who rage against the alleged incomprehensibility of the new art. The underlying impulse of these attacks is petty-bourgeois hatred of sex, the common ground of Western moralists and ideologists of Socialist Realism. No moral terror can prevent the side the work of art shows its beholder from giving him pleasure, even if only in the formal fact of temporary freedom from the compulsion of practical goals. Thomas Mann called this quality of art 'high spirits', a notion intolerable to people with morals. Brecht himself, who was not without ascetic traits—which reappear transmuted in the resistance of any great autonomous art to consumption—rightly ridiculed culinary art; but he was much too intelligent not to know that pleasure can never be completely ignored in the total aesthetic effect, no matter how relentless the work. The primacy of the aesthetic object as pure refiguration does not smuggle consumption, and thus false harmony, in again through the back door. Although the moment of pleasure, even when it is extirpated from the effect of a work, constantly returns to it, the principle that governs autonomous works of art is not the totality of their effects but their own inherent structure. They are knowledge as non-conceptual objects. This is the source of their nobility. It is not something of which they have to persuade men, because it has been given into their hands. This is why today autonomous rather than committed art should be encouraged in Germany. Committed works all too readily credit themselves with every noble value, and then manipulate them at their ease. Under fascism too, no atrocity was perpetrated without a moral veneer. Those who trumpet their ethics and humanity in Germany today are merely waiting for a chance to persecute those whom their rules condemn, and to exercise the same inhumanity in practice of which they accuse modern art in theory. In Germany, commitment often means bleating what everyone is already saying or at least secretly wants to hear. The notion of a 'message' in art, even when politically radical, already contains an accommodation to the world: the stance of the lecturer conceals a clandestine entente with the listeners, who could only be rescued from deception by refusing it. . . .

As eminently constructed and produced objects, works of art, including literary ones, point to a practice from which they abstain: the creation of a just life. This mediation is not a compromise between commitment and autonomy, nor a sort of mixture of advanced formal elements with an intellectual content inspired by genuinely or supposedly progressive politics. The content of works of art is never the amount of intellect pumped into them: if anything, it is the opposite.

Nevertheless, an emphasis on autonomous works is itself socio-political in nature. The feigning of a true politics here and now, the freezing of historical relations which nowhere seem ready to melt, oblige the mind to go where it need not degrade itself. Today every phenomenon of culture, even if a model of integrity, is liable to be suffocated in the cultivation of kitsch. Yet paradoxically in the same epoch it is to works of art that has fallen the burden of wordlessly asserting what is barred to politics. Sartre himself has expressed this truth in a passage which does credit to his honesty.[9] This is not a time for political art, but politics has migrated into autonomous art, and nowhere more so than where it seems to be politically dead. . . . Paul Klee too has a place in any debate about committed and autonomous art; for his work, *écriture par excellence*, had its roots in literature and would not have been what it was without them—or if it had not consumed them. During the First World War or shortly after, Klee drew cartoons of Kaiser Wilhelm as an inhuman iron-eater. Later, in 1920, these became—the development can be shown quite clearly—the *Angelus Novus*, the angel of the machine, who, though he no longer bears any emblem of caricature or commitment, flies far beyond both. The machine angel's enigmatic eyes force the onlooker to try *to* decide whether he is announcing the culmination of disaster or salvation hidden within it. But, as Walter Benjamin, who owned the drawing, said, he is the angel who does not give, but takes.[10]

4 *Right and Wrong Political Uses of Literature**

ITALO CALVINO

. . . society today demands that the writer raise his voice if he wants to be heard, propose ideas that will have impact on the public, push all his instinctive reactions to extremes. But even the most sensational and explosive statements pass over the heads of readers. All is as nothing, like the sound of the wind. Any comment appears no more than a shake of the head, as at a naughty boy. Everyone knows that words are only words, and produce no friction with the world around us: they involve no danger either for the reader or the writer. In the ocean of words, printed or broadcast, the words of the poet or writer are swallowed up.

This is the paradox of the power of literature: it seems that only when it is persecuted does it show its true powers, challenging authority, whereas in our

---

[9] See Jean-Paul Sartre, *L'Existentialisme est un Humanisme*, Paris, 1946, p. 105.
[10] See the Benjamin extract in Section XI below. [Ed.]

* From Italo Calvino, *The Uses of Literature: Essays*, transl. Patrick Creagh, Harcourt Brace Jovanovich, San Diego, New York, and London, 1986, pp. 95–100; first given as a lecture at Amhurst College, 25 Feb. 1976, in English.

permissive society it feels that it is being used merely to create the occasional pleasing contrast to the general ballooning of verbiage. (And yet, should we be so mad as to complain about it? Would to God that even dictators realized that the best method of freeing themselves from the dangers of the written word is to treat it as counting for nothing!)

In the first place, we have to remember that wherever writers are persecuted it means not only that literature is persecuted, but also that there is a ban on many other kinds of discussion and thought (and political thought in the forefront). Fiction, poetry, and literary criticism in such, countries acquire unusual political specific gravity, insofar as they give a voice to all those who are deprived of one. We who live in a state of literary freedom are aware that this freedom implies a society on the move, in which a lot of things are changing (whether for better or worse is another problem); in this case, too, what is in question is the relationship between the message of literature and society, or, more precisely, between the message and the possible creation of a society to receive it. This is the rapport that counts, not the one with political authority, now that those in government cannot claim to hold the reins of society, either in the democracies or in the authoritarian regimes of right or left. Literature is one of a society's instruments of self-awareness—certainly not the only one, but nonetheless an essential instrument, because its origins are connected with the origins of various types of knowledge, various codes, various forms of critical thought.

In a word, what I think is that there are two wrong ways of thinking of a possible political use for literature. The first is to claim that literature should voice a truth already possessed by politics; that is, to believe that the sum of political values is the primary thing, to which literature must simply adapt itself. This opinion implies a notion of literature as ornamental and superfluous, but it also implies a notion of politics as fixed and self-confident: an idea that would be catastrophic. I think that such a pedagogical function for politics could only be imagined at the level of bad literature and bad politics.

The other mistaken way is to see literature as an assortment of eternal human sentiments, as the truth of a human language that politics tends to overlook, and that therefore has to be called to mind from time to time. This concept apparently leaves more room for literature, but in practice it assigns it the task of confirming what is already known, or maybe of provoking in a naïve and rudimentary way, by means of the youthful pleasures of freshness and spontaneity. Behind this way of thinking is the notion of a set of established values that literature is responsible for preserving, the classical and immobile idea of literature as the depository of a given truth. If it agrees to take on this role, literature confines itself to a function of consolation, preservation, and regression—a function that I believe does more harm than good.

Does this mean that all political uses of literature are wrong? No, I believe that just as there are two wrong uses, there are also two right ones.

Literature is necessary to politics above all when it gives a voice to whatever is without a voice, when it gives a name to what as yet has no name, especially to what the language of politics excludes or attempts to exclude. I mean aspects, situations, and languages both of the outer and of the inner world, the tendencies repressed both in individuals and in society. Literature is like an ear that can hear things beyond the understanding of the language of politics; it is like an eye that can see beyond the color spectrum perceived by politics. Simply because of the solitary individualism of his work, the writer may happen to explore areas that no one has explored before, within himself or outside, and to make discoveries that sooner or later turn out to be vital areas of collective awareness.

This is still a very indirect, undeliberate, and fortuitous use for literature. The writer follows his own road, and chance or social and psychological factors lead him to discover something that may become important for political and social action as well. It is the responsibility of the socio-political observer not to leave anything to chance, and to apply his own method to the business of literature in such a way as not to allow anything to escape him.

But there is also, I think, another sort of influence that literature can exert, perhaps not more direct but certainly more intentional on the part of the writer. This is the ability to impose patterns of language, of vision, of imagination, of mental effort, of the correlation of facts, and in short the creation (and by creation I mean selection and organization) of a model of values that is at the same time aesthetic and ethical, essential to any plan of action, especially in political life.

So it comes about that, having excluded political education from the functions of literature, I find myself stating that I do believe in a type of education by means of literature; a type of education that can yield results only if it is difficult and indirect, if it implies the arduous attainment of literary stringency.

Any result attained by literature, as long as it is stringent and rigorous, may be considered firm ground for all practical activities for anyone who aspires to the construction of a mental order solid and complex enough to contain the disorder of the world within itself; for anyone aiming to establish a method subtle and flexible enough to be the same thing as an absence of any method whatever.

I have spoken of two right uses, but now I can discern a third, which is connected to the critical manner in which literature regards itself. If at one time literature was regarded as a mirror held up to the world, or as the direct expression of feelings, now we can no longer neglect the fact that books are made of words, of signs, of methods of construction. We can never forget that what books communicate often remains unknown even to the author himself, that books often say something different from what they set out to say, that in any book there is a part that is the author's and a part that is a collective and anonymous work.

This kind of awareness does not influence literature alone: it can also be useful to politics, enabling that science to discover how much of it is no more than verbal construction, myth, literary *topos*.[1] Politics, like literature, must above all know itself and distrust itself.

As a final observation, I should like to add that if it is impossible today for anyone to feel innocent, if in whatever we do or say we can discover a hidden motive—that of a white man, or a male, or the possessor of a certain income, or a member of a given economic system, or a sufferer from a certain neurosis —this should not induce in us either a universal sense of guilt or an attitude of universal accusation.

When we become aware of our disease or of our hidden motives, we have already begun to get the better of them. What matters is the way in which we accept our motives and live through the ensuing crisis. This is the only chance we have of becoming different from the way we are—that is, the only way of starting to invent a new way of being.

[1] Greek: theme, topic. [Ed.]

PART TWO
Themes and Issues

I *Form and Genre*

The first three items in this section elaborate formal methods for analysing Narrative and Drama. In Story and Discourse, *Seymour Chatman draws on Russian and French 'narratology' (Tomashevsky, Todorov, Barthes, Genette), to make a broad distinction between the 'spine' of all story-telling (in whatever medium), and the variety of techniques which provide a tale with its specific 'discourse'—e.g. the type and role of the narrator, the representation of character, the linking of events into a plot. He proposes two kinds of narrative 'event': 'kernels' (which forward the action) and 'satellites' (which add atmosphere, minor descriptive details, and so on).*

Umberto Eco's richly detailed attempt to begin a semiotic analysis of Drama suggests how important a move away from the dominant trend towards narratology in recent decades might become. His views are to some extent countered, if not overtaken, by Martin Esslin, in the extract from The Field of Drama, *in which it is argued that while an actor is, as Eco claims, a sign of a state of mind or feeling or social situation, the audience never forgets that the actor is also a particular human being enacting that sign. This double awareness makes every performance unique. Just how far Esslin could be said to avoid the 'ideological' implications of performances is a moot point (see the extract by John McGrath in section V for a further development of this).*

John Barrell's introductory remarks to Poetry, Language and Politics *criticize the ahistorical assumptions embedded in the traditional method of analysing poetry, the 'practical criticism' of individual poems. His discussion illustrates the current re-emergence of historically oriented approaches to literary texts as a counter to the formalist emphasis derived from semiotics and structuralism.*

1 *Story and Narrative**

SEYMOUR CHATMAN

. . . literary theory is the study of the nature of literature. It is not concerned with the evaluation or description of any particular literary work for its own sake. It is not literary criticism but the study of the *givens* of criticism, the nature of literary objects and their parts. It is, as René Wellek and Austin Warren point out, an 'organon of methods'.[1]

---

* From Seymour Chatman, *Story and Discourse: Narrative Structure in Fiction and Film*, Cornell University Press, 1978, pp. 18–20, 28–9, 30–1, 43–6, 47–8, 53– 7 .

[1] *Theory of Literature*, 3rd ed. (Harmondsworth, Middlesex, 1963), p. 19.

Like modern linguistics, literary theory might well consider a rationalist and deductive approach rather than the usual empiricist one. It should assume that definitions are to be made, not discovered, that the deduction of literary concepts is more testable and hence more persuasive than their induction. Poetics should construct 'a theory of the structure and functioning of literary discourse, a theory which presents a set [*tableau*] of possible literary objects, such that existing literary works appear as particular realized cases'.[2] Aristotle provides a precedent; the *Poetics* is nothing less than a theory of the properties of a certain type of literary discourse. Northrop Frye is outspokenly deductive in *Anatomy of Criticism*. We need not expect actual works to be pure examples of our categories. The categories plot the abstract network upon which individual works find their place. No individual work is a perfect specimen of a genre—novel or comic epic or whatever. All works are more or less mixed in generic character.

To put it another way, genres are constructs or composites of features. The novel and the drama, for example, require features like plot and character, which are not essential to the lyric poem; but all three may utilize the feature of figurative language. Further, works ordinarily mix features in different dosages: both *Pride and Prejudice* and *Mrs Dalloway* contain examples of indirect free style, but the dosage in *Mrs Dalloway* is much larger, making it a qualitatively different kind of novel. We should not be disconcerted by the fact that texts are inevitably mixed; in that respect they resemble most organic objects. It is their general tendencies that form the subject of rational inquiry.

Narrative theory has no critical axe to grind. Its objective is a grid of possibilities, through the establishment of the minimal narrative constitutive features. It plots individual texts on the grid and asks whether their accommodation requires adjustments of the grid. It does not assert that authors should or should not do so-and-so. Rather, it poses a question: What can we say about the way structures like narrative organize themselves? That question raises subsidiary ones: What are the ways in which we recognize the presence or absence of a narrator? What is plot? Character? Setting? Point of view?

ELEMENTS OF A NARRATIVE THEORY

Taking poetics as a rationalist discipline, we may ask, as does the linguist about language: What are the necessary components—and only those—of a narrative? Structuralist theory argues that each narrative has two parts: a story (*histoire*), the content or chain of events (actions, happenings), plus what may be called the existents (characters, items of setting); and a discourse (*discours*), that is, the expression, the means by which the content is com-

---

[2] Tzvetan Todorov, 'Poetique', in *Qu'est-ce que le structuralisme?*, ed. F. Wahl (Paris, 1968).

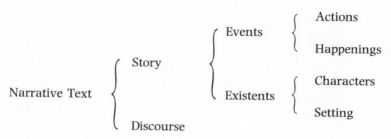

municated. In simple terms, the story is the *what* in a narrative that is depicted, discourse the *how*. The above diagram suggests itself. This kind of distinction has of course been recognized since the *Poetics*. For Aristotle, the imitation of actions in the real world, *praxis*, was seen as forming an argument, *logos*, from which were selected (and possibly rearranged) the units that formed the plot, *mythos*.

The Russian formalists, too, made the distinction, but used only two terms: the 'fable' (*fabula*), or basic story stuff, the sum total of events to be related in the narrative, and, conversely, the 'plot' (*sjužet*), the story as actually told by linking the events together.[3] To formalists, fable is 'the set of events tied together which are communicated to us in the course of the work', or 'what has in effect happened'; plot is 'how the reader becomes aware of what happened', that is, basically, the 'order of the appearance (of the events) in the work itself',[4] whether normal (abc), flashed-back (acb), or begun *in medias res* (bc). . . .

This transposability of the story is the strongest reason for arguing that narratives are indeed structures independent of any medium. . . .

A narrative is a communication; hence, it presupposes two parties, a sender and a receiver. Each party entails three different personages. On the sending end are the real author, the implied author, and the narrator (if any); on the receiving end, the real audience (listener, reader, viewer), the implied audience, and the narratee. . . .

Whether the narrative is experienced through a performance or through a text, the members of the audience must respond with an interpretation: they cannot avoid participating in the transaction. They must fill in gaps with essential or likely events, traits and objects which for various reasons have gone unmentioned. If in one sentence we are told that John got dressed and in the next that he rushed to an airport ticket counter, we surmise that in the

---

[3] Victor Erlich, *Russian Formalism: History, Doctrine*, 2nd ed. (The Hague, 1965), pp. 240–1.
[4] Boris Tomashevsky, *Teorija literatury (Poetika)* (Leningrad, 1925). The relevant section 'Thématique', appears in Todorov, ed., *Théorie de la littérature*, pp. 263–307 and in Lee T. Lemon and Marion J. Reis, ed., *Russian Formalist Criticism: Four Essays* (Lincoln, Neb., 1965), pp. 61–98. The quotations here translate the French text in Todorov, ed., p. 268. The distinction between *fabula* and *sjužet* appears on p. 68 of Lemon and Reis.

interval occurred a number of artistically inessential yet logically necessary events: grabbing his suitcase, walking from the bedroom to the living room and out the front door, then to his car or to the bus or to a taxi, opening the door of the car, getting in, and so on. The audience's capacity to supply plausible details is virtually limitless, as is a geometer's to conceive of an infinity of fractional spaces between two points. Not, of course, that we do so in normal reading. We are speaking only of a logical property of narratives: that they evoke a world of potential plot details, many of which go unmentioned but can be supplied. The same is true of character. We may project any number of additional details about characters on the basis of what is expressly said. If a girl is portrayed as 'blue-eyed', 'blonde', and 'graceful', we assume further that her skin is fair and unblemished, that she speaks with a gentle voice, that her feet are relatively small, and so on. (The facts may be other, but we have to be told so, and our inferential capacity remains undaunted. Indeed, we go on to infer a variety of details to account for the 'discrepancy'.)

Thus there is a special sense in which narratives may be said to select. In non-narrative paintings, selection means the separation of one portion from the rest of the universe. A painter or photographer will frame *this* much imitated nature, and the rest is left beyond the frame. Within that frame the number of details explicitly presented is a stylistic, rather than a general structural question. A Dutch still life painter may include an exact reproduction of minutiae in the set-up before him, down to the smallest dewdrop on a peach, while an Impressionist may dash off a distant pedestrian with a single brush stroke. But a narrative, as the product of a fixed number of statements, can never be totally 'complete', in the way that a photographic reproduction is, since the number of plausible intermediate actions or properties is virtually infinite. In a highly realistic painting, what is shown is determined by what was visible to the painter, and that is a function of his distance from the depicted scene. Scale, then, controls the number of details. But narratives are not restricted by spatial scale and undergo no such control: a visual narrative, a comic strip or movie, can move from close to long shot and return with no effort. And there is a virtually infinite continuum of imaginable details between the incidents, which will not ordinarily be expressed, but which *could* be. The author selects those events he feels are sufficient to elicit the necessary sense of continuum. Normally, the audience is content to accept the main lines and to fill in the interstices with knowledge it has acquired through ordinary living and art experience.

So far we have considered gaps common to all narratives regardless of medium. But there is also a class of indeterminacies—phenomenologists call them Unbestimmtheiten—that arise from the peculiar nature of the medium. The medium may specialize in certain narrative effects and not others. For instance, the cinema can easily—and does routinely—present characters without expressing the contents of their minds. It is usually necessary to infer their thinking from what they overtly say and do. Verbal narrative, on the other hand, finds such a restriction difficult—even Ernest Hemingway, at such pains to avoid directly stating his characters' thoughts and perceptions, sometimes 'slips'. Conversely, verbal narrative may elect not to present some visual aspect, say, a character's clothes. It remains totally *unbestimmt* about them, or describes them in a general way: 'He was dressed in street clothes'. The cinema, however, cannot avoid a rather precise representation of visual detail. It cannot 'say', simply, 'A man came into the room'. He must be dressed in a certain way. In other words clothing, *unbestimmt* in verbal narrative, must be *bestimmt* in a film.

Another restriction on selection and inference is *coherence*. Narrative existents must remain the same from one event to the next. If they do not, some explanation (covert or overt) must occur. If we have a story like 'Peter fell ill. Peter died. Peter was buried', we assume that it is the same Peter in each case. In E. M. Forster's example,[5] 'The king died, and then the queen died of grief', we assume that the queen was in fact the wife of that king. If not, there would have to be some explanation of the queen's death, for example, 'Though she did not know him, she died of the grief she felt for the decay of royal houses'. Some principle of coherence must operate, some sense that the identity of existents is fixed and continuing. Whether or not the events must also be causally linked is not so clear.

The drawing of narrative inferences by the reader is a low-level kind of interpretation. Perhaps it doesn't even deserve the name, since 'interpretation' is so well established as a synonym for 'exegesis' in literary criticism. This narrative filling-in is all too easily forgotten or assumed to be of no interest, a mere reflex action of the reading mind. But to neglect it is a critical mistake, for this kind of inference-drawing differs radically from that required by lyric, expository, and other genres. . . .

The events of a story are traditionally said to constitute an array called 'plot'. Aristotle defined plot (*mythos*) as the 'arrangement of incidents'. Structuralist narrative theory argues that the arrangement is precisely the operation performed by discourse. The events in a story are turned into a plot by its discourse, the modus of presentation. The discourse can be manifested in various media, but it has an internal structure qualitatively different from any one of its possible manifestations. That is, plot, story-as-discoursed, exists at a more general level than any particular objectification, any given movie, novel or whatever. Its order of presentation need not be the same as that of the natural logic of the story. Its function is to emphasize or de-emphasize certain story-events, to interpret some and to leave others to inference, to

[5] In *Aspects of the Novel*, 1927. [Ed.]

show or to tell, to comment or to remain silent, to focus on this or that aspect of an event or character. The author 'can arrange the incidents in a story in a great many ways. He can treat some in detail and barely mention or even omit others, as Sophocles omits everything that happened to Oedipus before the plague in Thebes. He can observe chronological sequence, he can distort it, he can use messengers or flashbacks, and so forth. Each arrangement produces a different plot, and a great many plots can be made from the same story.'[6]

Consider the following mini-plot: (1) Peter fell ill. (2) He died. (3) He had no friends or relatives. (4) Only one person came to his funeral. (These are not meant to represent actual English sentences, but rather units at the abstract level of 'story'; thus a silent movie might express unit one by showing Peter fainting in the street, or lying in bed tossing to and fro.) Statements one, two, and four clearly depict events; they are what I have called 'process statements'. We can display them as dots on a horizontal dimension representing time:

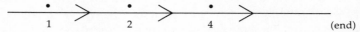

Notice, however, that statement (3) is not of this kind: it is not in the chronological or, better, 'chrono-logical' sequence (the hyphen indicating that we are not merely talking about time, but about the *logic* of time). Indeed, it is not a process statement of an event at all, not something that Peter or someone else did or something that happened, but rather a citation of one of his aspects or qualities, that is, a stasis statement of description. Description must be overtly expressed by language in literary narrative; but in theater or cinema, we simply witness the physical appearance of the actor playing Peter.

But what is an event, in the narrative sense? Events are either *actions* (*acts*) or *happenings*. Both are changes of state. An action is a change of state brought about by an agent or one that affects a patient. If the action is plot-significant, the agent or patient is called a character. Thus the character is narrative—though not necessarily grammatical—subject of the narrative predicate. Our discussion is still at the abstract level of story, quite separate from any particular kind of manifestation. In the linguistic manifestation, at the level of actual English sentence, for example, the character need not be grammatical subject: 'The diamonds were stolen by the thief' or 'The police were informed that some diamonds had been stolen'. In the latter case the character does not even appear in the manifestation; his presence must be inferred.

The principal kinds of actions that a character or other existent can perform are nonverbal physical acts ('John ran down the street'), speeches ('John said,

---

[6] O. B. Hardison, Jr., 'A Commentary on Aristotle's Poetics', *Aristotle's Poetics* (Englewood Cliffs, 1968), p. 123.

"I'm hungry" '; or 'John said that he was hungry'), thoughts (mental verbal articulations, like 'John thought "I must go" ' or 'John thought that he must go'), and feelings, perceptions, and sensations (which are not articulated in words—'John felt uneasy', or 'John saw the car looming ahead'). Narrative theory may use these as primitive terms without prior definition . . .

A happening entails a predication of which the character or other focused existent is narrative object: for example, *The storm cast Peter adrift*. Here again, what is important to a general theory of narrative is not the precise linguistic manifestation but rather the story logic. Thus in 'Peter tried to pull down the sails, but felt the mast give way and the boat caught up by an enormous wave', Peter is the subject of a series of actions at the surface, manifestational level. At the deeper story level he is narrative object, the affected not the effector.

SEQUENCE, CONTINGENCY, CAUSALITY

It has been argued, since Aristotle, that events in narratives are radically correlative, enchaining, entailing. Their sequence, runs the traditional argument, is not simply linear but causative. The causation may be overt, that is, explicit, or covert, implicit.

Consider again E. M. Forster's example (slightly altered for present purposes). Forster argues that 'The king died and then the queen died' is only a 'story' (in the sense of a 'mere chronicle'); 'The king died and then the queen died of grief' is a 'plot', because it adds causation. But the interesting thing is that our minds inveterately seek structure, and they will provide it if necessary. Unless otherwise instructed, readers will tend to assume that even 'The king died and the queen died' presents a causal link, that the king's death has something to do with the queen's. We do so in the same spirit in which we seek coherence in the visual field, that is, we are inherently disposed to turn raw sensation into perception. So one may argue that pure 'chronicle' is difficult to achieve. 'The king died and then the queen died' and 'The king died and then the queen died of grief' differ narratively only in degrees of explicitness at the surface level; at the deeper structural level the causal element is present in both. The reader 'understands' or supplies it; he infers that the king's death is the cause of the queen's. 'Because' is inferred through ordinary presumptions about the world, including the purposive character of speech.

In classical narratives, events occur in distributions: they are linked to each other as cause to effect, effects in turn causing other effects, until the final effect. And even if two events seem not obviously interrelated, we infer that they may be, on some larger principle that we will discover later. . . .

A narrative without a plot is a logical impossibility. It is not that there is no plot, but rather that the plot is not an intricate puzzle, that its events are 'of no great importance', that 'nothing changes'. In the traditional narrative of resolution, there is a sense of problem-solving, of things being worked out in some way, of a kind of ratiocinative or emotional teleology. Roland Barthes uses the term 'hermeneutic' to describe this function, which 'articulate[s] in various ways a question, its response and the variety of chance events which can either formulate the question or delay its answer'. 'What will happen?' is the basic question. In the modern plot of revelation, however, the emphasis is elsewhere; the function of the discourse is not to answer that question nor even to pose it. Early on we gather that things will stay pretty much the same. It is not that events are resolved (happily or tragically), but rather that a state of affairs is revealed. Thus a strong sense of temporal order is more significant in resolved than in revealed plots. Development in the first instance is an unraveling; in the second, a displaying. Revelatory plots tend to be strongly character-oriented, concerned with the infinite detailing of existents, as events are reduced to a relatively minor, illustrative role. Whether Elizabeth Bennet marries is a crucial matter, but not whether Clarissa Dalloway spends her time shopping or writing letters or daydreaming, since any one of these or other actions would correctly reveal her character and plight. . . .

KERNELS AND SATELLITES

Narrative events have not only a logic of connection, but a logic of *hierarchy*. Some are more important than others. In the classical narrative, only major events are part of the chain or armature of contingency. Minor events have a different structure. According to Barthes, each such major event—which I call *kernel*, translating his *noyau*—is part of the hermeneutic code; it advances the plot by raising and satisfying questions.[7] Kernels are narrative moments that give rise to cruxes in the direction taken by events. They are nodes or hinges in the structure, branching points which force a movement into one of two (or more) possible paths. Achilles can give up his girl or refuse; Huck Finn can remain at home or set off down the river; Lambert Strether can advise Chad to remain in Paris or to return; Miss Emily can pay the taxes or send the collector packing; and so on. Kernels cannot be deleted without destroying the narrative logic. In the classical narrative text, proper interpretation of events at any given point is a function of the ability to follow these ongoing selections, to see later kernels as consequences of earlier.

---

[7] See Roland Barthes, *S/Z*, transl. R. Miller, 1975, first publ. Paris, 1970. [Ed.]

begin

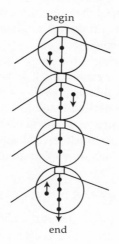

end

A minor plot event—a *satellite*[8]—is not crucial in this sense. It can be deleted without disturbing the logic of the plot, though its omission will, of course, impoverish the narrative aesthetically. Satellites entail no choice, but are solely the workings-out of the choices made at the kernels. They necessarily imply the existence of kernels, but not vice versa. Their function is that of filling in, elaborating, completing the kernel; they form the flesh on the skeleton. The kernel-skeleton theoretically allows limitless elaboration. Any action can be subdivided into a myriad of parts, and those parts into subparts. Satellites need not occur in the immediate proximity of kernels, again because discourse is not equivalent to story. They may precede or follow the kernels, even at a distance. But since events and existents, story and discourse, operate at a deep structural level and independent of medium, one does not look for their precincts in the actual words (or images or whatever) of a given text. They can only be discussed in the analyst's metalanguage, which is a paraphrase (another manifestation) of the narrative.

A convenient diagram to illustrate the relations of kernels and satellites is the one [above]. The kernels are the squares at the top of each circle. The circle is the complete narrative block. Kernels are connected by a vertical line to indicate the main direction of the story-logic; oblique lines indicate possible but unfollowed narrative paths. Dots are satellites; those on the vertical lines

---

[8] This term translates the French structuralist *catalyse*. The English equivalent 'catalyst' would suggest that the cause-and-effect enchainment could not occur *without* its supervention, but the satellite is always logically expendable: Todorov's translation of Tomashevsky's term for kernel is *motif associé*, and for satellite *motif libre* (*Théorie de la littérature*, p. 270). I find the latter misleading since it is precisely the case that satellites depend upon kernels and are tied to them in important ways. Barthes abandons without explanation the *noyau-catalyse* distinction in *S/Z*, though such a distinction seems implicit in his manner of listing the events of 'Sarrasine'.

follow the normal sequencing of the story; those outside the lines, with arrows attached, are anticipatory or retrospective of later or earlier kernels (depending upon which way the arrow points).

Such distinctions in structural narrative theory have been criticized as merely terminological and mechanical: it is said that they 'add nothing, enhance no reading', at best 'merely provide a cumbersome way of explaining what we all do, in the act of normal reading, with unconscious felicity'.[9] But theory is not criticism. Its purpose is not to offer new or enhanced readings of works, but precisely to 'explain what we all do in the act of normal reading, with unconscious felicity'. Such an explanation is not to be despised. . . .

STORIES AND ANTISTORIES

One of the most interesting things about the above diagram of kernels is the way it highlights the difference between classical and one kind of modernist narrative. If the classical narrative is a network (or 'enchainment') of kernels affording avenues of choice only one of which is possible, the *antistory* may be defined as an attack on this convention which treats all choices as equally valid.

Jorge Luis Borges has beautifully described and illustrated the logic of this kind of antistory in 'The Garden of Forking Paths'. The title refers to a novel of that name by a writer named Ts'ui Pên, whose method is described by a British sinologist to the narrator, a Chinese spy who is about to murder him. The sinologist says:

My attention was caught by the sentence, 'I leave to various future times, but not to all, my garden of forking paths.' I had no sooner read this, than I understood. . . . The phrase 'to various future times, but not to all' suggested the image of bifurcating in time, not in space. Rereading the whole work confirmed this theory. In all fiction, when a man is faced with alternatives he chooses one at the expense of the others. In the almost unfathomable Ts'ui Pên, he chooses—simultaneously—all of them. He thus *creates* various futures, various times which start others that will in their turn branch out and bifurcate in other times. This is the cause of the contradictions in the novel.

Fang, let us say, has a secret. A stranger knocks at his door. Fang makes up his mind to kill him. Naturally there are various possible outcomes. Fang can kill the intruder, the intruder can kill Fang, both can be saved, both can die and so on and so on. In Ts'ui Pên's work, all the possible solutions occur, each one being the point of departure

---

[9] Frank Kermode, 'Literature and Linguistics', *The Listener*, December 2, 1971, pp. 769–70. An answer is provided by Jonathan Culler, 'The Linguistic Basis of Structuralism', in David Robey, ed. *Structuralism: An Introduction; Wolfson College Lectures 1972* (Oxford, 1973), who cites Barthes: 'Distinguishing between a criticism which attempts to assign meanings to works, and a "science" of literature or "poetics", he [Barthes] argues that the latter must be a study of the conditions of meaning' (p. 31). These conditions do not give an interpretation but describe the logic according to which interpretations are reached.

for other bifurcations. Sometimes the pathways of this labyrinth converge. For example, you come to this house; but in other possible pasts you are my enemy; in others my friend.[10]

In a genuine sense such texts may be called 'antinarratives', since what they call into question is, precisely, narrative logic, that one thing leads to one and only one other, the second to a third and so on to the finale. But it is incorrect to say that they are without plot, for clearly they depend for their effect on the presupposition of the traditional narrative line of choice.

2 *Semiotics of Theatrical Performance**

UMBERTO ECO

Semiotics can be conceived of either as a unified theoretical approach to the great variety of systems of signification and communication, and in this sense it constitutes a metalinguistic discourse dealing with any of its objects by means of homogeneous categories, or it can be conceived as a description of those various systems insisting on their mutual differences, their specific structural properties, their idiosyncrasies—from verbal language to gestures, from visual images to body positions, from musical sounds to fashions. It shows a wide range of 'languages' ruled by different conventions and laws. It can investigate those various domains either at the elementary level of their consecutive units (such as words, color spots, physical formants of sounds, geometrical or topological shapes) or at the more complex level of texts and discourses—that is, narrative structures, figures of speech and so on.

What, then, are the specific object and the starting level of a semiotics of theatre, since theatre is, among the various arts, the one in which the whole of human experience is co-involved . . . in which human bodies, artifacts, music, literary expressions (and therefore literature, painting, music, architecture and so on) are in play at the same moment? Tadeusz Kowzan, one of the leading theatre semioticians of the present time (the author of *Littérature et spectacle*, Mouton, 1975) has isolated thirteen sign systems at work in a theatrical performance: words, voice inflection, facial mimicry, gesture, body movement, make-up, headdress, costume, accessory, stage design, lighting, music, and noise. Every one of these systems has a logic in itself, and I am not sure that the list is complete. Kowzan, like many others, has rightly pointed out that the object of theatrical semiotics is the performance, or the *mise-en-scène*, not the literary text. But other authors have considered the text as the

---

[10] Translated by Anthony Kerrigan.

* From *The Drama Review*, vol. XXI, No. 1, New York, Mar. 1977, pp. 108–13, 116–17.

'deep structure' of the performance, trying to find in it all the seminal elements of the *mise-en-scène*. Others . . . have studied the elementary structure of dramatic action, or *les situations dramatiques*, therefore merging research in theatre with research of narrative structures—the forerunner of this approach has been, without any doubt, Aristotle. I could continue to list many researchers and different approaches, but you might get the impression that the semiotics of theatre is nothing but an arithmetic sum of the semiotic analyses of other forms of communication.

However the first duty of a new (or old) theory is not only to isolate its own object but also to do it in a more essential way than before. What we ask a theory for, is to give us back an old object illuminated by a new light in order to realize that only from that point of view the object can be really understood. Is semiotics able to do that? I am not sure of it. Semiotics is a very young discipline, only two thousand years old, and it has a terrific task to perform, since nearly everything seems to fall under its headings.

One of its main temptations is to start straight away from the most complex phenomena, instead of rediscovering the most basic features of a given 'language'. Among the various semiotic disciplines, only their older sister (or mother?), linguistics, has demonstrated enough wisdom and prudence to avoid, at its first steps, the analysis of texts. It started with phonemes, words and phrases (and only now is trying to elaborate a transphrastic linguistics, or a theory of texts). But if you look, for instance, at the various attempts in the semiotics of literature, of painting or of architecture, you may detect a sort of 'parvenu' complex. It seems that many literary semioticians would feel ashamed to study *Little Red Riding Hood* instead of *Paradise Lost* . . .

The same is true with a semiotics of theatrical performance. In order to try to formulate it, we should begin with a positively naive attitude, assuming that we do not know what Molière did, who Samuel Beckett was, how Stanislavsky made somebody feel himself to be an apple or how Bertolt Brecht made an apple appear to be a piece of criticism of capitalist society.

Let me start with an example proposed (without thinking of theatre) by the founding father of American semiotics, C. S. Peirce. He once wondered what kind of sign could have been defined by a drunkard exposed in a public place by the Salvation Army in order to advertise the advantages of temperance. He did not answer this question. I shall do it now. Tentatively. . . . Even though trying to keep a naive attitude, we cannot eliminate some background knowledge. We have read not only Aristotle but also Francis Ferguson, Etienne Souriau, Peter Szondi, Umberto Eco and Woody Allen. We know Sophocles, Gilbert and Sullivan, and *King Lear*, *I Love Lucy* and *En attendant Godot* and *A Chorus Line*, *Phèdre* and *No, No Nanette*, *Murder in the Cathedral* and *Let My People Come* and *The Jew of Malta* and *Oh Calcutta!* Therefore we immediately suspect that in that sudden epiphany of intoxication lies the basic mystery of (theatrical) performance.

As soon as he has been put on the platform and shown to the audience, the drunken man has lost his original nature of 'real' body among real bodies. He is no more a world object among world objects—he has become a semiotic device; he is now a *sign*. A sign, according to Peirce, is something that stands to somebody for something else in some respect or capacity—a physical presence referring back to something absent. What is our drunken man referring back to? To a drunken man. But not to *the* drunk who he is, but to *a* drunk. The present drunk—insofar as he is the member of a class—is referring us back to the class of which he is a member. He *stands for* the category he belongs to. There is no difference, in principle, between our intoxicated character and the word 'drunk'.

Apparently this drunk stands for the equivalent expression, 'There is a drunken man', but things are not that simple. The physical presence of the human body along with its characteristics could stand either for the phrase, 'There is a drunken man in this precise place and in this precise moment', or for the one 'Once upon a time there was a drunken man'; it could also mean, 'There are many drunken men in the world'. As a matter of fact, in the example I am giving, and according to Peirce's suggestion, the third alternative is the case. To interpret this physical presence in one or in another sense is a matter of convention, and a more sophisticated theatrical performance would establish this convention by means of other semiotic media—for instance, words. But at the point we are, our tipsy-sign is open to any interpretation: he stands for all the existing drunken men in our real world and in every possible world. he is an open expression (or sign-vehicle) referring back to an open range of possible contents.

Nevertheless, there is a way in which this presence is different from the presence of a word or of a picture. It has not been actively produced (as one produces a word or draws an image)—it has been *picked up* among the existing physical bodies and it has been shown or *ostended*. It is the result of a particular mode of sign production. Ostension has been studied by medieval logicians, by Wittgenstein, by contemporary theorists of theatre (for instance, the Czech, Ivo Osolsobe). Ostension is one of the various ways of signifying, consisting in de-realizing a given object in order to make it stand for an entire class. But ostension is, at the same time, the most basic instance of performance.

You ask me, 'How should I be dressed for the party this evening?' If I answer by showing my tie framed by my jacket and say, 'Like this, more or less', I am signifying by ostension. My tie does not mean my actual tie but your possible tie (which can be of a different stuff and color) and I am 'performing' by representing to you the you of this evening. I am prescribing to you how you should look this evening. With this simple gesture I am doing something that is theatre at its best, since I not only tell you something, but I am offering to you a model, giving you an order or a suggestion, outlining a utopia or a feasible project. I am not only picturing a given behavior, I am in fact eliciting a behavior, emphasizing a duty, mirroring your future. . . . By picturing your future way of dressing (through my present one) I have, however, added the verbal expression 'more or less'. My performance, which was eminently visual and behavioral, has been accompanied by a verbal metalinguistic message establishing some criteria of pertinence. 'More or less' signified 'making an abstraction from the particular stuff, color and size of *my* tie'. It was a rather important device; it helped you to de-realize the object that was *standing for* something else. It was reducing the pertinent features of the vehicle I used to signify 'tie' to you, in order to make it able to signify all the possible ties you can think of.

The same happens with our intoxicated man. It is not necessary that he have a specific face, a specific eye color, a moustache or a beard, a jacket or a sweater. It is, however, necessary (or at least I think so) that his nose be red or violet; his eyes dimmed by a liquid obtuseness; his hair, his moustache or his beard ruffled and dirty; his clothes splashed with mud, sagging and worn-out. I am thinking of the typical Bowery character but when I think of him, I am ready to make abstractions from many features, provided that some essential characteristics are conserved and emphasized. The list of these characteristics is established by a social code, a sort of iconographic convention. The very moment our sergeant of the Salvation Army has chosen the *right* drunk, he has made recourse to a socialized knowledge. His choice has been semiotically oriented. He has been looking for the right man just as one looks for the right word.

Nevertheless, there is something that distinguishes our drunkard from a word. A word is a sign, but it does not conceal its sign-quality. We conventionally accept that through words someone speaks about reality, but we do not confuse words with things (except in cases of mental illness). When speaking, we are conscious that something impalpable (*flatus vocis*) stands for something presumably palpable (except in cases of lying). But not every sign-system follows the same rules as the others. In the case of our elementary model of mise-en-scène, the drunk is a sign, but he is a sign that pretends not to be such. The drunkard is playing a double game: in order to be accepted as a sign, he has to be recognized as a 'real' spatio-temporal event, a real human body. In theatre, there is a 'square semiosis'. With words, a phonic object stands for other objects made with different stuff. In the mise-en-scène an object, first recognized as a real object, is then assumed as a sign in order to refer back to another object (or to a class of objects) whose constitutive stuff is the same as that of the representing object.

I stress this point because it makes evident a crucial semiotic question: that is, the difference between the so-called *natural* and artificial signs. Everybody agrees on the fact that words or pictures are signs insofar as they are intentionally produced by human beings in order to communicate. But many semioticians wonder whether medical symptoms, animal imprints or unintentional body movements are to be considered as signs. Undoubtedly the trace of a cat's paw on the ground means that an animal (namely a cat) has passed there. Undoubtedly if I stagger, it 'means' that I have drunk a little more than is due. But can one consider those events as signs? Is there a difference between signification by means of intentional and artificial devices ruled by a convention (such as words or road signals) and signification as inferred from natural and unintentional events such as symptoms and imprints?

The semiotic approach of Peirce is, in my view, the most powerful because it proposes a unified set of definitions able to take into account both species of signs. Both are instances of something standing for something else on the basis of previous learning (or convention), and I agree with Charles Morris when he says that,

something is a sign only because it is interpreted as a sign of something by some interpreter. . . . Semiotics then is not concerned with the study of a particular kind of object but with ordinary objects insofar (and only insofar) as they participate in semiosis.

I think that this is a paramount definition of the semiosis of mise-en-scène, since it is hard to distinguish, in such a framework, artificial signs from natural ones. What is a Chinese pot upon a table in a set design? A natural object? An artificial device? Is it representing something else?

Our drunk is representing drunkenness. His red nose has been selected as a natural unintentional event able to intentionally (the intention belongs to the Salvation Army, not to him) represent the devastating effects of intemperance. But what about his teeth? There is no specific convention establishing that an average drunken man lacks his incisors or has a set of black teeth. But if our intoxicated man possesses those characteristics, this would work very well. Insofar as the man becomes a sign, those of his characteristics that are not pertinent to the purposes of representation also acquire a sort of vicarious representative importance. The very moment the audience accepts the convention of the mise-en-scène, every element of that portion of the world that has been framed (put upon the platform) becomes significant. . . .

I should, however, stress that, until now, I have incorrectly put together natural and unintentional signs. I have done it on purpose because it is a kind of confusion frequently made by many semioticians. But we should disambiguate it.

On one hand, I can produce a false natural event, as when I purposely produce a false imprint in order to fool somebody. I can produce a false symptom by painting red spots on my face to pretend I have measles.

On the other hand, I can produce unintentionally what usually is conceived to be intentional (the most typical examples are psychoanalytic slips of the tongue or those common errors that everybody makes when speaking a foreign language), but I also can produce intentionally what is usually believed to be unintentional. For instance, his pronunciation shows that a man is, let me say, a Frenchman speaking English. The choice of English words is an intentional act, the way of pronouncing them, even though semiotically important (it means: 'I am a Frenchman') is unintentional. But what about a fictional character purposefully emitting French-like phonemes in order to mean 'I am French', while he is perfectly all-American—maybe a CIA agent trying to get political information by talking with a French Communist (and without knowing—obviously—that he could get the same information by reading the daily *l'Humanité*)? Is there a difference between an actor who, to pretend having been whipped, draws red lines on his shoulders and another one (a more professional actor more religiously following the principles of realism) who really wounds himself in order to get really bleeding traces?

I have no clear and definite responses for these questions. I only wanted to make clear to what an extent the elementary problems of dramatic fiction are strictly linked with the basic problems of general semiotics.

I think (and I have elaborated this point elsewhere) that the elementary mechanisms of human interaction and the elementary mechanisms of dramatic fiction are the same. This is not a witty idea of mine: from Goffman to Bateson and from the current researches in ethnomethodology to the experiences of a Palo Alto group (think also of Eric Berne's behavioral games models in *Games People Play*) everyday life is viewed as an instance of theatrical performance. This finally explains why esthetics and criticism have always suspected that theatrical performances were instances of everyday life. It is not theatre that is able to imitate life; it is social life that is designed as a continuous performance and, because of this, there is a link between theatre and life. . . .

Once this is said—once the methodological standpoint is accepted that both fiction and living reportage are instances of mise-en-scène—it remains to ask, 'How does a character speak who acts as an element of a mise-en-scène?' Do his words have a univocal meaning? Do they mean one thing only and nothing else?

In 1938, the Soviet folklorist Bogatyrev, in a fundamental paper on signs in theatre, pointed out that signs in theatre are not signs of an object but signs of a sign of an object. He meant that, beyond their immediate denotation, all the objects, behaviors and words used in theatre have an additional *connotative* power. For instance, Bogatyrev suggested that an actor playing a starving man can eat some bread as bread—the actor connoting the idea of starvation, but the bread eaten by him being denotatively bread. But under other circumstances, the fact of eating bread could mean that this starving man eats only a poor food, and therefore the piece of bread not only denotes the class of all possible pieces of bread, but also connotes the idea of poverty.

However, our drunken man does something more than connote drunkenness. In doing so, he is certainly realizing a figure of speech, a metonymy, since he stands for the cause of his physical devastation; he also realizes an antonomasia, since he, individually taken, stands for his whole category—he is the drunken man par excellence. But (according to the example of Peirce) he is also realizing an irony by antonymy. He, the drunk, the victim of alcoholism, stands ironically for his contrary; he celebrates the advantages of temperance. He implicitly says, 'I am so, but I should not be like this, and you should not become like me.' Or, at another level, 'Do you see how beautiful I am? Do you realize what a kind of glorious sample of humanity I am representing here?' But in order to get the irony, we need the right framing: in this case, the standards of the Salvation Army surrounding him.

Since we have approached the rhetorical level, we are obliged to face the ideological one. Our drunken man is no longer a bare presence. He is not even a mere figure of speech. He has become an ideological abstraction: temperance vs. intemperance, virtue vs. vice. Who has said that to drink is bad? Who has said that the spectacle of intoxication has to be interpreted as an ironical warning and not as an invitation to the most orgiastic freedom? Obviously, the social context. The fact that the drunk has been exposed under the standards of the Salvation Army obliges the audience to associate his presence to a whole system of values.

What would have happened if the drunk had been exposed under the standard of a revolutionary movement? Would he still have signified 'vice' or rather 'the responsibility of the system', 'the results of a bad administration', 'the whole starving world'? Once we have accepted that the drunk is also a figure of speech, we must begin to look at him also as an ideological statement. A semiotics of the mise-en-scène is constitutively a semiotics of the production of ideologies.

All these things, this complex rhetorical machinery, are, moreover, made possible by the fact that we are not only looking at a human body standing and moving within a physical space. The body could not stagger if there were not an environing space to give it orientation—up and down, right and left, to stand up, to lie down. Were the bodies two or more, space would establish the possibility of associating a given meaning to their mutual distances. In this way we see how the problems of the mise-en-scène refer back to the problems of many other semiotic phenomena, such as proxemics (the semiotics of spatial distances) or kinesics (the semiotics of gestures and body movements). And we realize that the same semiotic parameters can be applied to the semiotics of theatre, of cinema, of architecture, of painting, of sculpture.

From the idiosyncratic character of the theatrical phenomenon we have arrived at the general problems of semiotics. Nevertheless, theatre has additional features distinguishing it from other forms of art and strictly linking it with everyday conversational interaction—for instance, the audience looking at the drunk can laugh, can insult him and he can react to people's reaction. Theatrical messages are shaped also by the feedback produced from their destination point.

So the semiotics of theatrical performance has shown, during our short and introductory analysis, its own *proprium*, its distinguishing and peculiar features. A human body, along with its conventionally recognizable properties, surrounded by or supplied with a set of objects, inserted within a physical space, stands for something else to a reacting audience. In order to do so, it has been framed within a sort of performative situation that establishes that it has to be taken as a sign. From this moment on, the curtain is raised. From this moment on, anything can happen—Oedipus listens to Krapp's last tape, Godot meets La Cantatrice Chauve, Tartuffe dies on the grave of Juliet, el Cid Campeador throws a cream cake in the face of La Dame aux Camélias.

3   *The Signs of Drama**

MARTIN ESSLIN

ICON, INDEX, SYMBOL

I

Present-day semiotics, as first outlined by Peirce and developed and codified by contemporary semioticians like Roland Barthes, Umberto Eco, Erika Fischer-Lichte, Patrice Pavis, distinguishes three basic types of signs.

The simplest type of sign is the one that is instantly recognisable because it represents what it signifies by a direct image of that object, hence it is named by the Greek work for 'Picture'—*Icon*.

The 'pictures' can be realistic and photographic or highly stylised: the little

* From Martin Esslin, *The Field of Drama*, Methuen, 1987, pp. 43–51, 56–64.

bathtubs, wineglasses and beds in travel guides, the schematised figures in skirts or trousers on lavatory doors, all painted or photographic portraits of personalities that tell us what they looked like: they are all very obvious iconic signs. Iconic signs are, of course, very widespread—the entire artforms of representational painting, sculpture and photography can be regarded as systems of iconic signs. But not all icons are visual. The sound of a car horn in a play is an icon of the sound of a car horn.

All dramatic performance is basically iconic: every moment of dramatic action is a direct visual and aural sign of a fictional or otherwise reproduced reality. All other types of signs that are present in a dramatic performance operate within that basic iconic mimesis. The words of the dialogue, the gestures of the actors are signs of a different type, but they are present within the dramatic performance in the context of an iconic reproduction of their use in the 'reality' that is being 'imitated'.

The gestures we use in real life, and which the actors imitate, belong to another category of signs: signs which point to an object, like the arrows on street signs, or the movement I make when somebody asks me: 'Where is he?' and I point with my finger in the direction of the person concerned. These are called '*index*' signs, or also (when the derivation is from the Greek word for showing) 'deictic' signs. These signs derive their meaning from a relationship of contiguity to the object they depict. Personal pronouns, like 'you' or 'he', are deictic signs. We only know who is meant, if the word is accompanied by a gesture, or clearly alludes to a proper name previously mentioned. This type of sign obviously plays an important part in dramatic performance.

The third principal category of signs comprises those that have, unlike index signs and iconic signs, no immediately recognisable organic relationship to their 'signifieds'. This category of signs is called '*symbol*'. The meaning of symbolic signs derives entirely from convention—an agreement that, for example, the sounds D, O, G, dog, will be recognised as referring to a certain species of animal. Only those individuals who subscribe to this convention or agreement—in this case the speakers of English—will be able to understand the meaning of this arbitrary combination of sounds or letters. Most of our speech consists of such arbitrary symbolic signs. But there are many other symbolic signs in gestures, conventions of costume etc.

Index, icon, symbol—these, then, are the three main types of signs that semioticians distinguish.

Signs in the usual sense are tools deliberately employed to establish communication, tools through which one person, or a group of persons, intends to convey a meaning or message to another person. . . .

But there are also instances of 'meaning' being apprehended by an individual, even when there was and is no-one who intended to convey a message or meaning: events or phenomena that are interpreted to mean something

something without any deliberate intention of communication being involved. . . .

These omnipresent signs that have no conscious originator, but are liable to be perceived as having meaning by those who 'read' them, are what Umberto Eco in his *Theory of Semiotics* calls 'natural signs' (smoke rising can be read as a sign that there is a fire) and 'non-intentional signs' (spontaneous, involuntary human acts or gestures that 'give away' hidden emotions and can be read by an observer). Not being intentional signs and thus not capable of being analysed as a 'language' or 'system' most conventional semiotics regard this category of 'involuntary' signs as outside their proper field.

In drama this category of 'natural' signs that, in the real world, exist without anyone deliberately producing them or intending to convey a message, assumes a special importance: dimming lights on the stage, a shot of the sinking sun on the screen, are deliberately used by the director to tell the audience that night is about to fall. The mimetic representation of a darkening sky has become an iconic sign of evening. Thus, in dramatic performance, what are 'natural' signs without a conscious originator of their message become deliberately produced 'icons'. Yet these icons, in turn, may assume 'symbolic' functions: the darkening sky on the stage may be used by the director as a symbolic sign for the ending of a love affair, or death.

And the art of acting might be described as largely concerned with the deliberate, intentional, 'iconic' use of 'non-intentional', 'involuntary' signs or 'symptoms'. An actor who deliberately blushes on the stage produces an image—an iconic sign—of a person willy-nilly displaying such an 'involuntary' symptom of embarrassment. Indeed, it is part of the craft of acting, to be able to blush, laugh or cry at will.

The fascinatingly paradoxical, complicating factor here, however, is that while actors may produce these signs intentionally by simulating such states as sudden outbursts of crying, growing pale from fear, etc., it also often happens that the actors themselves exhibit these signs not by conscious intention, but involuntarily, spontaneously merely by using their imagination to produce the states of mind concerned, so that they themselves will simply start to blush or tremble or cry without any deliberate effort on their part to exhibit these particular symptoms. . . .

This penumbra of uncertainty and inexactness that springs from the presence of involuntary and unintentional signs, highlights the very special situation of dramatic performance as an object for semiotics. Most iconic signs used in other fields are both deliberately produced and capable of being simply understood, interpreted (or as the jargon puts it: 'decoded') by those for whom they have been intended. A painting of a horse will be read by all and sundry as representing a horse. Even an abstract painting will be perceived as a deliberately ambiguous image, or as a statement about pure form and colour.

Iconic signs, moreover, can be very simplified representations of the objects they signify, and therefore concentrate on a single meaning. The lady on the powder-room door is, in fact, very unlike a real lady; a highly abstract—and conventional—symbol which tells us, unambiguously, no more than that this figure has a skirt while the one opposite has trousers. There are those who argue that we recognise these images because we have *learned* to read them, that they themselves are conventional, almost like hieroglyphs or Chinese ideograms—which indeed, mark the borderline between the iconic and the symbolic type of sign.

Yet in drama, as far as the human characters are concerned, there is no abstraction: there a lady appears and she is a completely concrete lady who is being shown to us as the icon—the iconic sign—for a fictional lady. The director who shows us an actress portraying Juliet or Ophelia is telling us: this is what Juliet or Ophelia looked like. The icon here at least aims at suggesting a complete identity in looks between the 'signifier' (the actress) and the 'signified' (the fictional character).

The same is true of many of the objects we see on the stage, even more so of the world depicted in the photographic reality of filmed or televised drama. . . .

2

The types of sign we have discussed—icon; index; symbol; as well as the 'involuntary' (natural or non-intentional) iconic signs without a deliberate originator—combine, in dramatic performance, in a multitude of different sign systems, or 'languages', each with its own 'grammar' and 'syntax' (although the analogy with verbal languages must always be treated with caution, as each sign system has its own limitations).

For example: there is a 'language' of gestures. Some of our gestures are 'deictic'—pointing fingers, frightened looks; others are 'iconic'—we all instantly recognise the meaning of an embrace, an angry blow etc.; others again are 'symbolic': in oriental theatre the slightest movement of a finger may have a definite meaning which, by age-old convention, the spectators have learned to interpret and understand; in Western drama at certain periods there were also such formalised symbolic gestures: in the melodrama of the nineteenth century, for example, turning the face away and lowering the head had become a symbol of grief—here an iconic representation of what happens when someone is suddenly struck by grief had been formalised, ritualised and made into a conventional symbolic gesture. Many such sign systems, many more than in any other art form, are simultaneously at work in dramatic performance.

Yet we may ask: what is the purpose, what are the benefits to spectators, critics, performers, of analysing the typology of signs and sign systems; why should we want to know what types of signs, what sign systems, are present in a given production and how they interact, combine and contradict each other dialectically?

The simplest answer, it seems to me, is that this is the most practical, down-to-earth approach to the act of communication that every dramatic performance is intended to establish: by analysing what signs and sign systems, in what interaction, are present and at least potentially operating upon the sensibilities of the recipients of the communication—the audience —we should arrive at the most concrete, factual basis for gaining a clear conception of what actually takes place in an artistic event like a play or film, far less airy-fairy and abstract than analyses of the psychology of characters or philosophical implications. These, the psychologies and philosophies, are always implied and well worth enlarging upon, but, surely only after the basic bedrock of what actually took place on stage or screen has been established. . . .

And to know how a given sign operates and what kind of sign it is, how it fits into the ultimate over-all effect that is intended must certainly be useful: when the stage darkens at a certain point, will the spectators be inclined to interpret that as an 'iconic' image of the daylight fading in the evening, or will it be seen as a 'symbolic' sign that the situation of the leading character is becoming gloomier, or perhaps both at the same time: the descent of night becoming a symbol of tragedy or misfortune. A knowledge of the 'grammar' and 'syntax' of the interaction of the different signs and sign systems should thus help the director to attain a higher degree of certainty that he will actually convey the meaning he intended, at least to the majority of the audience.

Similarly a clear awareness of how a performance works, and how and why it perhaps fails to work, based on an analysis of all the means that were brought into play by the originators of the performance, should be of considerable help in the critical discussion of a dramatic performance. A semiotic approach should be able to avoid the mere impressionism that besets much dramatic criticism both by daily reviewers and by academics.

As to the spectator: it could be argued that an audience member should merely sit back and let the performance do its work. This view is widespread, but, surely, it is based on a somewhat naive idea of what art is and how it creates its effects. All art, and the art of drama in particular, is largely based on conventions that must be shared between the artist and his audience and must therefore be an acquired skill that, ultimately, must be learned. Much of this learning process occurs almost spontaneously simply through steady and prolonged exposure to the ruling conventions. But true sophistication, the ability to derive the fullest enjoyment, enlightenment and spiritual experience from art does depend on a form of expertise. . . .

THE ACTOR

I

The actor is the iconic sign *par excellence*: a real human being who has become a sign for a human being.

In a brilliant and provocative essay on 'The Semiotics of Theatrical Performance' in which he sketches out some basic considerations of the problems of such a branch of knowledge, before gracefully neglecting to come to grips with it, Umberto Eco cites C. S. Peirce's speculations about a case in which a human being becomes a sign: a drunkard on a platform outside a Salvation Army meeting house, exposed to illustrate the ravages of drink.

Eco points out that a sign, according to Peirce's definition, is 'something that stands for somebody or something else in some respect or capacity'. The drunken man thus is a sign not for himself but for the general category of 'drunks'. The sign thus might stand for sentences like: 'there is a drunken man here' or 'once upon a time there was a drunken man' or 'there are many drunken men in the world'. The drunken man has been chosen to act as a sign because some features about him (by no means all his characteristics or qualities, but only some, essential for the purpose of 'ostension' [semiotic jargon for 'showing']) make him 'typical'—in other words he is not displayed as himself but as a specimen of a whole class of human beings. In this respect, Eco argues, the choice of this particular drunk by the Salvation Army is analogous to the choice of the right word in formulating a sentence. Except that a word is a sign without physical resemblance or relationship to its referent, whereas

the drunk is a sign, but he is a sign that pretends not to be such. The drunkard is playing a double game: in order to be accepted as a sign, he has to be recognized as a real spatio-temporal event, a real human body. In theatre there is a 'square semiosis'. With words, a phonic object stands for other objects made with different stuff. In the mise-en-scène an object, first recognized as a real object, is then assumed as a sign in order to refer back to another object (or to a class of objects) whose constitutive stuff is the same as that of the representing object.[1]

Eco's use of Peirce's paradigm is most stimulating and raises a number of important issues: it incidentally draws attention to the importance of 'framing'—not only does the platform on which he stands transform the ordinary drunk into a sign, but the fact that it is a Salvation Army platform, instantly recognisable as such, makes the drunk, the victim of alcoholism, to stand 'ironically for his contrary; he celebrates the advantages of temperance'.

But as an analogy for dramatic performance, Eco's example is incomplete

---

[1] See preceding extract by Eco, p. 118. [Ed.]

and misses some of the essential points. For in a true dramatic context the drunkard would not be a real drunkard but an actor deliberately simulating the characteristics (the red nose, the bleary eyes etc.) of the drunkard and the audience would be aware of his *skill* in doing so. Apart from recognising the drunkard as a member of a class of human beings and perhaps understanding the message he represents as a warning against alcohol, they will also appreciate and applaud his 'artistry' in producing that effect (or boo him for failing to do so). Moreover, in a dramatic performance the drunkard would, most likely, not merely be an anonymous presence. He would, almost certainly, be playing an individualised fictitious character and thus function as a sign for a *fictional individual* as well as a member of a class of individuals. So that the semiotic role of the actor in a dramatic event is far more complex than Eco's paradigm suggests.

An actor appearing on the stage or screen is, in the first place, himself, the 'real' person that he is with his physical characteristics, his voice and temperament; he is, secondly, himself, transformed, disguised, by costume, make-up, an assumed voice, a mental attitude derived from the study of an empathy with the fictional character he is playing . . . but, thirdly, and most importantly there is the 'fiction' itself, for which he stands, and which ultimately will emerge in the mind of the individual spectator watching the play or film. That spectator, for example, may well notice that the actress—and the stage figure —that represents Juliet is not outstandingly beautiful or attractive; yet in his imagination he will, having understood that she is *supposed* to be outstandingly beautiful, complete the picture, and 'read' the action as though he was seeing an outstandingly beautiful girl. And that fictional figure, in turn, may, like Eco's drunken man, also stand for a whole category or class of individuals, may assume general human meaning.

This extremely complex state of affairs produces its own, highly suggestive and artistically fascinating ambiguities and inner tensions.

An actor playing Hamlet is a sign for the fictional character of Hamlet with all that fictional person's complex individuality. He may also become in the eyes of some members of the audience a representative of a class of individuals (princes, intellectuals who think too much, sons in love with their mothers, the human predicament itself and a multitude of others), but also, unlike the drunk in Peirce's example cited by Eco, he will retain much of his real personality as the actor he is known to be. The semiosis will here not merely be, as Eco posits it for the drunk, 'squared', it will be 'cubed', for the man here stands for a sign that stands for a man who, in turn, is recognised and valued as the original man that he is. It is the tension between the real actor on the one hand, and the fictional character for whom he functions as an iconic sign on the other, that creates one of the main attractions of drama in performance. The audience never forgets that the iconic function of the actor is playful pretence. The suspension of disbelief in the theatre, the cinema or in front of the television screen does not go so far that the sign is taken for the reality. Indeed, most theories of drama, from the ancient Greeks to Brecht, build on that particular tension. A far greater proportion of audiences go to the theatre or cinema or watch television to see particular actors rather than the fictional characters they signify. The economics of the theatre, cinema and television, with their emphasis on the drawing power of the 'star', are built on that fact.

The actor thus is the essential ingredient around which all drama revolves. There can be, and has been, drama without writers, designers, directors—there can never be drama without actors. Even the marionettes of the puppet or shadow theatre, the moving drawings or model figures of animated film, are actors, iconic signs that stand for people or humanised animals and they have, of course, also the voices of human actors.

The actor, as he stands on the stage, or appears on the screen, moreover is more than a mere sign for a fictional character as conceived by the imagination of a writer. His *personality* itself, the indefinable uniqueness of an individual human being . . . adds additional signifiers to those provided by the inventor of the fiction. . . .

This emphasises the profoundly *erotic* nature of drama. The sheer magnetism of human personality is itself a powerful generator of 'meaning'. When a beautiful woman in the role of, say, Juliet steps onto the stage, her appearance signifies: 'This fictional girl was as beautiful as this; Juliet looked like this!' The whole impact, the whole 'meaning' of the play will turn around that basic fact. . . .

2

The basically erotic nature of the attraction of actors accounts for the immense importance of **casting** in dramatic performance. 'Casting' is one of the most basic semiotic systems that generate its meaning. . . .

In addition to the basic meaning-generating quality of his own personality and erotic magnetism the actor has at his disposal an array of sign systems, which could be grouped as comprising, on the one hand, those derived from the expressive techniques based on the use of his or her body: use of the voice in modulating the text, facial expression, gesture ('kinesics'), and grouping or movement in space ('proxemics') and, on the other hand, those the actor *carries* on his body: make-up and costume.

These systems, of course, constantly inter-act: an actor's costume may well greatly influence his gestures and movement (heavy sleeves may enlarge his gestures, a narrow skirt may influence an actress's walk); make-up obviously influences facial expression, etc.

What must also always be kept in mind in analysing the production of meaning in acting is a basic paradox: the actor himself is an icon—a human being acting as a sign for a human being. But a number of the sign systems he uses may themselves be either iconic, deictic or symbolic, or all three at the same time. Thus a white beard is an *iconic* sign of old age, but may also be intended as a *symbolic* indication of wisdom. A conspicuous wig may be an *icon* of a conceited character, but, at the same time may function as a *deictic* sign to draw the audience's attention to the character (to make him, for example, stand out in a group).

This is true of those sign systems that the actor employs intentionally and with deliberation. In addition, acting raises, in a particularly clear form, as Umberto Eco also stresses, the problem of the so-called 'non-intentional' sign. If someone blushes that is a sign that he is embarrassed, even though he wants to hide the fact. An actor, if he is skilled, should be a master of producing such seemingly involuntary signs, at will, and with deliberation. They are icons of the meaning he wants to express; they contain information that he wants to purvey. But it may well also happen, particularly when the actor has been trained in techniques emphasising empathy with the charac- ter's state of mind, that that state of mind spontaneously finds expression in the form of natural, involuntary signs, such as blushing, without the actor deliberately employing a technique to create a blush on his face. And, indeed, certain schools of acting concentrate on the actor 'living' his role in his imagination with such intensity that these signs will appear spontaneously and without his own conscious intervention. If the emotion of the character is truly felt, the expression of it will spontaneously manifest itself to the audience. . . .

Yet even an actor who has consciously planned every nuance of expres- sion, may display unintended signifiers, which may introduce elements of meaning into a performance that he never planned and of which he remains unaware. For example: he may hesitate, when the character is to be fluent, fail to blush when he should do so, or blush when he is not to blush. Or he may simply be too old for his role (by having been 'miscast') and will thus convey—at least to some members of the audience—information that he is very far from wanting to provide. While some of these unintended elements may simply be due to incompetence or lack of artistic talent, it must always be remembered that every performance, however brilliant and competent its originators, is bound to carry an aura of such unintended overtones. . . .

In analysing the process of acting it is useful to be aware of the nature and function of the interplay of the sign systems at the actor's command.

In the **vocal interpretation** of the text, for instance, there is the difference between a purely iconic—naturalistic or realistic—delivery which aims at as accurate a reproduction of natural speech as possible on the one hand, and the more 'declamatory' styles in which the raising or lowering of the pitch, the quickening or slowing of the tempo, the use of 'vibrato', a deep voice for serious and a light voice for playful subject-matter, have fixed symbolic meanings.

The same is true of **facial expression** where the spectrum also extends from the reproduction of natural expression (from the simulated 'non-intentional' sign as an icon of the emotion) at one end, to, at the other, the highly formalised artistry of, for example, oriental styles of theatre, where the raising of an eyebrow, the twitching of the corners of the mouth have definite conventional symbolic meanings.

Such symbolic elements are even more evident in the sphere of **gesture** and **movement** . . . in such styles as Japanese Noh and Kabuki, Chinese classical opera or Indian Kathakali. . . .

The spectator of drama must have something of the talents of that archetypal semiotician, Sherlock Holmes, who was able to discover the most copious and accurate information from the scars on the face and the minutest elements in the dress of any person he met. The tiniest details in the appearance of a character, the cut of his garments, the colour of his complexion, the specks of dirt on his clothes contain an enormous amount of information, and thus play an important part in the delineation of character on the stage, but even more so on the screen, where close-ups can draw attention to the smallest significant elements. In drama originating from wholly different cultures—Indian or Japanese films for example—Western audiences unfamiliar with their codes are often at a loss to understand the characters. Yet it must always be kept in mind that this decoding process is only partially conscious: many members of the audience will tend to react instinctively to the 'general impression' produced by the confluence of a multitude of subliminally perceived characteristics, from the cut of the garments to the mud on the character's shoes (as indeed we react to people we meet in 'real' life).

4 *Close Reading**

JOHN BARRELL

I

What is it that makes the study of English literature a 'discipline'? The most usual answer to that question, over the last half-century or so, has begun by claiming that students of English literature acquire a specific skill, with its own rules and procedures: the skill of close critical reading, or 'practical

* From John Barrell, Introduction, *Poetry, Language and Politics*, Manchester University Press, 1988.

.criticism'. The notion that to grasp the meaning of a text it is necessary to pay close attention to the detail of its articulation is not, of course, unique to the study of English—it is no less crucial to the study of philosophy. But for the student of philosophy, the practice of close critical reading has been performed with a rather different end in view. It has been undertaken in order to arrive at the fullest possible understanding of the argument of a philosophical text, how it holds together, where it falls apart. The close reading undertaken by students of English has been predicated on a different notion of how a text has meaning, or, more usually, on the belief that a 'literary' text has meaning of a different kind from the meaning of other types of texts.

The meaning of a literary text, according to the advocate of practical criticism, is not to be looked for, primarily, in the argument it develops; a literary text is not primarily concerned to develop an argument. It is concerned to represent an 'experience', actual or fictional—a complex of event, feeling, perception, reflection. It does not represent this experience by any simple process of narration or description of the kind that can be summarised or paraphrased in words other than the words of the text, as the argument of a work of philosophy can be. A literary text, and pre-eminently a poem, employs all the resources of language—imagery and other figurative devices, ambiguity, the patterning of sound by rhythm, rhyme, alliteration and so on —in such a way as makes them the signifiers of that experience as much as is its merely paraphrasable meaning. Its meaning is to be discovered no more in what it says than in how it says it, and a competent close reading will be one which describes the text so as to show that the 'what' and 'how' are inseparable, and cannot be conceived of in isolation from each other; or, if they can, that is an indication that the text is 'flawed', that it fails to be fully 'literary'. Thus practical criticism is more than merely a skill: to read a text well is to arrive at a statement of its value. Just as, in the work itself, form and content are inseparable, so in a properly critical close reading, to describe a text is also to evaluate it.

Implicit, and sometimes explicit, in these notions of close reading and of the literary—and I am concerned in what follows with practical criticism not as an articulated approach or method, but as, precisely, a *practice*, developed in practical teaching situations—is the belief that language is thoroughly referential: words have meaning because they refer to something, the world and our experience of it, that is beyond and prior to language. The world we experience is not understood as constructed by language; it is already there, and words name it, describe it more or less accurately. This belief seems to make it possible to speak not only of the value of a text, but of its truth to experience, either to what might be an 'actual' experience represented in the text, or to the fictional experience it represents, whose validity is dependent on its being somehow like actual experience, and so 'rooted' in it. There is of course an evident difficulty in making this kind of judgment, for we can have access to the experience the text refers to only through the text itself, so that it must somehow be claimed that the words of a text can do two things at once. On the one hand, they represent, with more or less success, an experience of the world, whether actual or rooted in the actual; on the other, they enable us first to intuit the 'real' nature of the experience, and then to judge the adequacy of the representation to the reality.

The question of how words can do both these things is answered, or managed rather, by understanding the relations of the real and the representation in the same terms as the relations of form and content are understood. That is to say, insofar as it seems possible to claim of a text that its meaning inheres indivisibly in its form *and* content, it is assumed that the text is an indivisible whole in which the representation of an experience is fully adequate to the reality of it; insofar as the text fails to embody its content fully in its form, the representation is inadequate to the reality. Thus to judge the text's 'truth to experience' is, after all, the same thing as to judge its value. The 'real', ostensibly outside the text and enabling us to evaluate the text's truth, is in fact located, though this is not acknowledged, only inside the text, as a product of the internal relations of form and content.

To make this location of the real within the text more secure and also more invisible, it has been necessary to insist that close critical reading should not be unduly concerned to understand the literary text in relation to the specific historical moment of its production. The meaning of a text, and still less its value, does not depend to any important extent on anything 'external' to it: on when it was written, for example, or whom it addressed, or on what was the function of any particular literary activity—writing epic poems, reading novels—at any particular period or for any particular kind of reader. The meaning of individual words, it is acknowledged, might change with time, and the competent practical critic will need to be aware of semantic changes. A thorough acquaintance with the literary tradition is also necessary, to enable a reader to judge how far a text is held within, and how far it transcends, the conventions of literary expression, and to judge also the degree of 'influence' one writer has over another. Such issues have a bearing on the originality, and so on the 'authenticity' of the text; on whether it is a 'firsthand' account of experience. But otherwise, the process of judging truth and value is a process to be conducted with reference only to the text itself, which contains almost all the information necessary to enable that judgment to be made. If a literary text is true and valuable, it has always been so, and always will be. Its qualities inhere within its language, within the relation between its form and content.

Now it goes without saying that there are a number of works of literature which have almost consistently been found of value since the time they were produced. But the criteria in terms of which they have been found valuable have certainly changed a good deal through history, and they did not usually bear much similarity to the criteria of value embodied in twentieth-century practical criticism. This seems to suggest that earlier readers of different periods may have had different notions of what literary texts meant and how they meant—different from each other, and different from critics of this century. To say that a text has always been regarded as valuable is not therefore in itself to say anything specific about the intrinsic nature of the text or of its language. Furthermore, practical criticism often attributes a permanent value to texts which have previously been largely ignored, and denies such value to texts which have hitherto enjoyed almost continual esteem. Issues like these might have led advocates of the practice to reflect on the historically-specific nature of the practice itself—to ask what it is about their own historical situation that has encouraged them to develop the specific criteria of value embodied in practical criticism.

If they have not done so, this is because to acknowledge that those criteria are historically-specific would of course be to acknowledge that the critical judgments they produce are equally so. They have chosen instead to assume the universality of those judgments by assuming a notion of what it is to be 'fully human', a notion in which the idea of the 'fully literary' is metaphysically and morally grounded. To be fully human is to take on a universal identity, and a permanent one which has not changed throughout the whole of history, and it is to our 'full humanity' that literary texts are claimed to be primarily addressed. If a truthful and valuable work of literature has only occasionally been valued in the past, that is because contingent cultural factors have usually made its potential audience unreceptive to the particular kind of address it makes to that humanity. No such merely contingent factors, however, prevent competent modern readers from appreciating the universal and permanent value of works of literature, and for two reasons. They assume, though without quite saying so, that they have a critical method which makes the intrinsic qualities of a text entirely visible, and that, by virtue of this method, they are able to discover exactly what it means to be fully human; they have found a method of distinguishing the essential from the merely contingent. They can thus lay claim even to the gift of prophecy, for their understanding of why certain texts have 'survived' from the past enables them to predict which will survive into the future. It is, in the last analysis, on these beliefs and assumptions that the authority of practical criticism is based.

So what version of full humanity is produced by this notion of close critical reading? We can begin to answer this question by pointing out that the refusal of the historically-specific nature of the writing of literary texts, and of the method and criteria by which they are now to be read and judged, is also a refusal of the political. Competent readers are those who recognise that their political affiliations, and more generally their shifting political situations as defined in particular by class and gender, are somehow contingent to their identity as readers. How could it be otherwise? For if each separate reader approaches a literary text from within her or his own political situation and allegiances, each will focus on different features of the text as important ('what it means for me'), and all will arrive at different judgments of its truth and value. Their different interpretations and judgments will not speak simply of the text itself, for they will not be based simply on the text's intrinsic qualities.

A similar notion of competence, as something above and beyond the political, is applied to writers. The definition of what is properly a literary text, and the belief in the pre-eminent value of literary over other kinds of texts, are based in part on the claim that the former aim at the resolution of conflicting constructions of experience, or, where that is impossible—some oppositions, it is acknowledged, are irresoluble—at the balance of opposing constructions. These notions of resolution and balance also in part account for the high valuation accorded to instances of ambiguity by practical criticism, for the ambiguous word or construction has seemed to be the epitome of an idea of literary expression as the resolution or balance of oppositions, one which cannot unambiguously be attributed either to the area of form or to that of content. And in a more general sense, the indivisibility of form and content in a literary text, and that associated idea of balance, have been taken as signs of the text's 'control' over the oppositions it thus resolves. Conversely, when an imbalance of form and content is detected, this is a sign of the writer's failure of control (often described as a failure of 'maturity') which is in turn the sign of a failure to subordinate her or his particular situation (gender and class specific, defined by a personal psychological history) to the universal and transcendent position of the fully human.

The judgment that a text fails to achieve a properly literary matching of form and content seems to be based on the feeling that the content has been bent to fit the form, or that the form has been wrenched out of shape to fit the content. But it is hard to know on what such feelings would be based, because, rather as in the question of the adequacy of representation to reality, we would have to believe we can intuit what the content would have been before it was embodied in the text, or what the form was that has been distorted to fit the content. In practice, an unfavourable judgment of the text as 'unbalanced' tends to mean one of two things: that the content is too urgent, emotional, partisan, 'raw', to find adequate embodiment in literary form; or the form is too limp, or too mechanically unresponsive to the energy or subtlety of the content to embody it adequately. A properly balanced text, on the other hand, should be, it emerges, a place rather like a court of law or a dinner-table, where voices should never be raised above a certain register, and where no utterance should be diffident or repetitious. The balance that the text should achieve, which was originally validated and witnessed by the matching of form and content, returns now as what validates and bears witness to that matching.

The notion of balance, as something which proceeds from a position beyond the political, is in fact a thoroughly political notion. That position, a middle point between and above all merely partial and particular situations, bears a close resemblance to a certain ideal construction of the situation of the middle-class—neither aristocratic nor vulgar, neither reactionary nor progressive. And similarly, the balance and resolution which literary texts seek to achieve bear a close resemblance to the political balance which, in England especially, was both cause and effect of the increasing power of the middle class, and which has made the notion of 'balance' itself a term of value with a crucial function in middle-class ideology, underwriting the political authority of 'consensus', or the 'middle ground', by representing as irrational extremism whatever cannot, or whatever refuses to be, gathered into the middle ground. If working-class writers fail to manifest the control necessary to the production of a properly literary text—if the 'tone' of their writings is 'awkward' or 'strident', and so apparently betrays their failure fully to have internalised the linguistic manners of the middle class—then this is evidently the result of their failure to transcend their particular class situation. If middle-class writers fail to exhibit control, this is also the result of a failure to transcend the circumstances of their lives, but their membership of a particular class is not among these.

The universal, the fully human position, from which properly literary texts, and properly literary criticism, can be produced, is also a masculine position. Masculinity cannot of course serve the mediating function between two given opposites that can be served by the position of the middle-class between the aristocratic and the vulgar. So in this case one half of the opposition is elevated into the neutral and therefore, by implication, the 'balanced' position; and the notion that men are generally more 'balanced' than women has no doubt helped to construct the competent writer and reader as masculine. Thus if women writers speak with an uncontrolled 'shrillness' of tone, for example, this is the sign of a failure to transcend their femininity—but no male writer ever lost control of his text through a failure to transcend his masculinity.

In short, the ideology of control, of balance, of unity, primarily as these are believed to be evinced by the mutual inherence of form and content, and the identification of these with the essential and the universal—both require that working-class writers and readers alike, and female writers and readers, should regard their class and gender as contingent to, as irrelevant to, their identity as writers and readers. The evidence of their success in doing so will be that the texts and the readings they produce will not be distinguishable from those ideally produced by middle-class men. Such men, whatever *individual* disabilities they might have to overcome to occupy the position from which creative or critical activity—properly impersonal, literary, and universal—can proceed, are handicapped by no such *generic* disabilities as class and gender. We can become competent close readers, according to these critical principles or assumptions, only insofar as we can identify with a 'universal' identity which turns out to be a thoroughly particular and specific identity, masculine, middle-class, and suspicious equally of reaction and of progress.

II

The sketch I have offered of what I believe to be the politics of traditional practical criticism, as it was taught to me and as it has been taught for decades in English universities, is no more than that—a sketch, and an inadequate one, of the ethos of an institutionalised classroom practice. It is not offered as an account of practical criticism as it was differently defined and instantiated by its most influential exponents, I. A. Richards, for example, or Empson, or Leavis, or (in its American manifestation as the 'new criticism') Cleanth Brooks. And even as a sketch of a teaching practice, it leaves out much that would need to be included in a more worked-up account. It ignores the detail of different practices within the general one. It makes connections between the various assumptions that underlie that general practice in a way that its most committed practitioners would certainly contest, and in doing so it attributes a theoretical, if not a very logical, coherence to a practice which is self-consciously untheoretical and antitheoretical. And because the politics of that practice, and the notion of what it is to be human that lies concealed within it, is never very fully articulated by its practitioners, practical criticism has always been able to remain a very broad church, and it would be hard to find an actual, individual teacher whose practice has ever fully matched the account I have offered.

II *Modernism*

These extracts illustrate the continuing thrust towards formalism of 'modernist' writing, and its critical discussion. At the same time, they offer a critique. Paul Valéry's 'Remarks on Poetry' provide a central statement of the difference between the language of poetry and prose (drawn on earlier by Jean-Paul Sartre, section III): the first is conceived of as 'dancing', the second as 'walking'. But modernist writing in both genres shows language in the mode of 'dancing': poems conceived as autotelic and self-referential, and novels aspiring to an equivalent condition.

The extract from the French structuralist Gérard Genette's widely influential Narrative Discourse *explores the handling of 'time' in narrative from Homer to (in the main) Proust. The latter's* A la recherche du temps perdu *helps Genette propose a subtle and detailed way of analysing modernist narrative, showing how it draws on 'traditional sources of literary narration' only to transcend them.*

In 'Towards a Semiotics of Literature', Robert Scholes develops a sustained critique of the dominant conception of 'the poetic' proposed by Roman Jakobson's well-known 'Closing Statement: Linguistics and Poetics' (1958), which he summarizes. Scholes defines the 'literary' so as to insist upon the communicative function of poems and novels, in contrast with the implicit, Kantian assumption of non-utilitarian purposelessness of Valéry's 'dancing' analogy. Georg Lukács' account of 'The Ideology of Modernism' provides a different kind of criticism, aimed at the ahistoric and asocial conception of human life of many 'modernist' fictions. Finally, Raymond Williams suggests a 'post-modernist' perspective from which to analyse the cultural formation of 'modernism', linking the development of the European metropolitan centres with the social alienation of writers for whom language no longer functions as a communal and communicative act.

1 *Remarks on Poetry**

PAUL VALÉRY

Language is a complex thing, a combination of properties at once effectively bound and independent by nature and function. A discourse may be logical and full of meaning, though without rhythm and measure; it may be agreeable to the ear and perfectly absurd or meaningless; it may be clear and

* From Paul Valéry, 'Remarks on Poetry', in *Symbolism: An Anthology*, ed. T. G. West, Methuen, 1980, pp. 50–2; first publ. in Paul Valéry 'Propos sur la poésie', *Œuvres complètes*, vol. 1, ed. Hytier, Paris, 1957.

empty, vague and delightful. . . . But in order to be aware of its strange multiplicity, it suffices to enumerate all the sciences created to cater for this diversity, each for exploiting one of its elements. One may study a text in many independent ways, for it is of equal interest to phonetics, semantics, syntax, logic, rhetoric, as well as metrics and etymology.

This, then, is the poet at grips with this all-too-impure, inconstant material, bound to speculate on the sound and sense in turn, to meet the demands not only of harmony, of the musical phrase, but also of various intellectual conditions such as logic, grammar, the poem's subject, all kinds of figures and ornaments, not to mention conventional rules. See what an effort is implied by attempting to bring a discourse to a satisfactory conclusion, for which so many requirements must be miraculously met at the same time.

The uncertain and minute workings of literary art begin here. But this art has two aspects, two fundamental modes which are opposed in their radical state, but which, nevertheless, meet and are linked by a host of intermediate degrees. There is *prose* and there is *verse*. Between them are all the mixtures of the two; but today I shall consider them in their radical states. One might illustrate this opposition of the extremes by exaggerating it somewhat: one might say that the limits of language are *music*, on one hand, and *algebra*, on the other.

I shall make use of a comparison I have used before in order to clarify my thoughts on this subject. One day when I was speaking on the same topic in a foreign city and had just used this comparison, one of my listeners gave me a remarkable quotation, which made me realize that the idea was not new, though it was at least to me.

Here is the quotation. It is an excerpt from a letter from Racan[1] to Chapelain,[2] in which Racan tells us that Malherbe[3] likened prose to walking and poetry to dancing, as I shall do in a moment:

Give whatever name you please to my prose—galant, naïve or playful. I am resolved to observe the precepts of my first master Malherbe, and never to look for number or cadence in my periods, nor for any other ornament than the clarity which can express my thoughts. This good man (Malherbe) compared prose to ordinary walking and poetry to dancing, and he used to say that in the things we are obliged to do we must tolerate some negligence, but in the things we do out of vanity it is ridiculous to be no more than mediocre. The lame and the gouty cannot avoid walking, but nothing obliges them to dance the waltz or the cinquepace.

The comparison which Racan attributes to Malherbe, and which I, for my

---

[1] Honorat de Bueil, Seigneur de Racan (1589–1670). From 1605 a friend and pupil of Malherbe, and an early member of the French Academy. [Ed.]
[2] Jean Chapelain (1595–1674), a founding member of the French Academy, an unsuccessful poet but an influential man of letters. [Ed.]
[3] François de Malherbe (1555–1628) turned against the poetic practices of the Pléiade group, stressing purity of language and adherence to prosodic rules. [Ed.]

part, had easily perceived, is direct. I want to show that it is fruitful. It develops at length with a curious precision. Perhaps it is something more than an apparent likeness.

Walking, like prose, always has a precise object. It is an act directed *toward* some object which we aim to reach. The actual circumstances, the nature of the object, the need I have of it, the impulse of my desire, the state of my body and that of the ground, determine the nature of walking, prescribe its direction, speed and ending. All the properties of walking derive from these instantaneous conditions which combine on each occasion in a *new way*, so that no two strides are exactly alike, and each time there is a special creation, which is each time abolished as though absorbed in the completed act.

Dancing is something quite different. It is without doubt a system of acts which are, at the same time, ends in themselves. Dancing goes nowhere. If it pursues something, it is only an ideal object, a state, a pleasure, the ghost of a flower or some self-centred ecstasy, an extremity of life, a summit, a supreme point of being. . . . As different as dance is from utilitarian movement, this essential though infinitely simple observation should be noted: *that it uses the same limbs, the same organs, bones, muscles and nerves as walking itself.*

Exactly the same is true of poetry which uses the same words, forms and tones as prose.

Thus prose and poetry are distinguished by the difference of certain laws or momentary conventions of movement and function, applied to identical elements and mechanisms. That is why one must avoid thinking of poetry as one does of prose. What is true of one has no meaning in many cases when one seeks it in the other. And this is why (to give an example) it is easy to justify the use of inversions; for these alterations of the customary and, in some ways, elementary order of words in French have been criticized in various periods, very superficially to my mind, for reasons which can be summed up by this unacceptable formula: poetry is prose.

Let us continue a bit with the comparison which can bear further scrutiny. A man is walking. He moves from one place to another along a path which is always the path of least action. Here we note that poetry would be impossible if it were subjected to the rule of the straight line. One is taught: 'Say it is raining if you mean it is raining!' But the object of the poet is not and can never be to let us know that it is raining. There is no need for a poet to tell us to take our umbrella. Look what would happen to Ronsard and Hugo, to the rhythm, images and consonances of the finest verses in the world if poetry were subjected to the 'Say it is raining' system! It is only by a clumsy confusion of genres and circumstance that one can reprove a poet for his indirect expressions and complex forms. One overlooks the fact that poetry implies a decision to change the function of language.

I return to the man walking. When this man has completed his movement, when he has reached the spot, the book, the fruit, the object he desired, this possession immediately cancels his whole act, the effort consumes the cause, the end absorbs the means, and, whatever the ways and means of his act and his step, only the result remains. Once the lame or the gouty, whom Malherbe mentioned, have painfully reached the armchair which was their goal, they are no less seated than the alertest of men who might reach the chair in one sprightly step. The same is true of the use of prose. Once the language I have been using—which has expressed my aim, my desire, my command, my opinion, my request or my answer—fulfils its task, it vanishes almost as soon as it arrives. I sent it off to perish, to be transformed irrevocably in you, and I shall know that I was *understood* by the remarkable fact that my discourse no longer exists. It is entirely and definitively replaced by its *meaning* or at least by a certain meaning, that is, by the images, impulses, reactions or acts of the person to whom one speaks; in short, by an inner modification or reorganization of the person. But one who has not understood preserves and *repeats the words*. The experience is simple. . . .

Thus you see that the perfection of that discourse, whose sole destination is comprehension, consists evidently in the facility with which it is transmuted into a quite different thing, into non-language. If you have understood my words, my words themselves are no longer of any importance to you; they have disappeared from your minds while you possess, none the less, their counterpart, you possess in the form of ideas and relationships the means for restoring the meaning of these remarks, *in a form which may be quite different*.

In other words, in practical or abstract uses of language which is specifically *prose*, the form is not preserved, does not survive understanding, but dissolves in clarity, for it has acted, has made itself understood, has lived.

But the poem, on the contrary, does not die for having been of use; it is expressly made to be reborn from its ashes, perpetually to be again what it has been. . . .

Understood thus, poetry differs radically from all prose: in particular, it is clearly opposed to description and narration of events, which tend to give the illusion of reality, that is, to the novel and the story, when their aim is to impart the power of truth to narratives, portraits, scenes and other representations of real life. This difference even has physical signs which are easily observed. Compare the attitude of the novel reader with that of the poetry reader. They might be the same person but the former differs entirely when he reads one or the other work. Look at the novel reader when he plunges into the imaginary life the book brings him. His body no longer exists. He holds his head in his hands. He is, he moves, he acts and he suffers only in the mind. He is absorbed by what he is devouring; he cannot restrain himself, for some sort of demon urges him on. He wants the continuation and the end, he is prey to a kind of alienation: he participates, triumphs, grows sad, he is no longer himself, he is only a brain separated from its outer forces, that is, given over to its images, passing through a sort of *crisis of credulity*.

The poetry reader is quite different.

If poetry truly acts on someone, it is surely not by dividing him in his nature, by communicating him illusions of a fictitious and purely mental life. Poetry imposes upon him no false reality which requires the submission of the mind and thus the abstention of the body. Poetry must extend over the whole being; it excites the muscular organization with rhythms, delivers or unleashes the verbal faculties and exalts all this activity; poetry orders the depths of our being, for it aims to provoke or reproduce the unity and harmony of the living person, an extraordinary unity which manifests itself when a man is possessed by an intense feeling which leaves none of his powers unaffected.

2   *Order in Narrative**

GÉRARD GENETTE

NARRATIVE TIME?

Narrative is a . . . doubly temporal sequence. . . . There is the time of the thing told and the time of the narrative (the time of the signified and the time of the signifier). This duality not only renders possible all the temporal distortions that are commonplace in narratives (three years of the hero's life summed up in two sentences of a novel or in a few shots of a 'frequentative' montage in film, etc.). More basically, it invites us to consider that one of the functions of narrative is to invent one time scheme in terms of another time scheme.[1]

The temporal duality so sharply emphasized here, and referred to by German theoreticians as the opposition between *erzählte Zeit* (story time) and *Erzählzeit* (narrative time),[2] is a typical characteristic not only of cinematic narrative but also of oral narrative, at all its levels of aesthetic elaboration, including the fully 'literary' level of epic recitation or dramatic narration (the narrative of Théramène,[3] for example). It is less relevant perhaps in other forms of narrative expression, such as the *roman-photo*[4] or the comic strip (or

---

* From Gérard Genette, *Narrative Discourse*, transl. Jane Lewin, Basil Blackwell, Oxford, 1986, pp. 33–40, 48–50, 61, 66–8, 78–9, 83–5; first publ. 'Discours du récit', in Genette, *Figures III*, du Seuil, Paris, 1972.

[1] Christian Metz, *Film Language: A Semiotics of the Cinema*, trans. Michael Taylor (New York, 1974), p. 18. [Translator's note: I have altered this translation slightly so as to align its terms with the terms used throughout this book.]

[2] See Gunther Müller, 'Erzählzeit und erzählte Zeit', *Festschrift für P. Kluckhohn und Hermann Schneider*, 1948; reprinted in *Morphologische Poetik* (Tübingen, 1968).

[3] A character in Racine's *Phèdre*, proverbial for his narration of Hippolytus' death. [Translator]

[4] Magazine with love stories told in photographs. [Translator]

a pictorial strip, like the predella of Urbino, or an embroidered strip, like the 'tapestry' of Queen Matilda), which, while making up sequences of images and thus requiring a successive or diachronic reading, also lend themselves to, and even invite, a kind of global and synchronic look—or at least a look whose direction is no longer determined by the sequence of images. The status of written literary narrative in this respect is even more difficult to establish. Like the oral or cinematic narrative, it can only be 'consumed', and therefore actualized, in a *time* that is obviously reading time, and even if the sequentiality of its components can be undermined by a capricious, repetitive, or selective reading, that undermining nonetheless stops short of perfect analexia: one can run a film backwards, image by image, but one cannot read a text backwards, letter by letter, or even word by word, or even sentence by sentence, without its ceasing to be a text. Books are a little more constrained than people sometimes say they are by the celebrated *linearity* of the linguistic signifier, which is easier to deny in theory than eliminate in fact. However, there is no question here of identifying the status of written narrative (literary or not) with that of oral narrative. The temporality of written narrative is to some extent conditional or instrumental; produced in time, like everything else, written narrative exists in space and as space, and the time needed for 'consuming' it is the time needed for *crossing* or *traversing* it, like a road or a field. The narrative text, like every other text, has no other temporality than what it borrows, metonymically, from its own reading.

This state of affairs, we will see below, has certain consequences for our discussion, and at times we will have to correct, or try to correct, the effects of metonymic displacement; but we must first take that displacement for granted, since it forms part of the narrative game, and therefore accept literally the quasi-fiction of *Erzählzeit*, this false time standing in for a true time and to be treated—with the combination of reservation and acquiescence that this involves—as a *pseudo-time*.

Having taken these precautions, we will study relations between the time of the story and the (pseudo-) time of the narrative according to what seem to me to be three essential determinations: connections between the temporal *order* of succession of the events in the story and the pseudo-temporal order of their arrangement in the narrative, which will be the subject of the first chapter; connections between the variable *duration* of these events or story sections and the pseudo-duration (in fact, length of text) of their telling in the narrative—connections, thus, of *speed*—which will be the subject of the second chapter; finally, connections of *frequency*, that is (to limit myself to an approximate formulation), relations between the repetitive capacities of the story and those of the narrative, relations to which the third chapter will be devoted.

ANACHRONIES

To study the temporal order of a narrative is to compare the order in which events or temporal sections are arranged in the narrative discourse with the order of succession these same events or temporal segments have in the story, to the extent that story order is explicitly indicated by the narrative itself or inferable from one or another indirect clue. Obviously this reconstitution is not always possible, and it becomes useless for certain extreme cases like the novels of Robbe-Grillet, where temporal reference is deliberately sabotaged. It is just as obvious that in the classical narrative, on the other hand, reconstitution is most often not only possible, because in those texts narrative discourse never inverts the order of events without saying so, but also necessary, and precisely for the same reason: when a narrative segment begins with an indication like 'Three months earlier . . .' we must take into account both that this scene comes *after* in the narrative, and that it is supposed to have come *before* in the story: each of these, or rather the relationship between them (of contrast or of dissonance), is basic to the narrative text, and suppressing this relationship by eliminating one of its members is not only not sticking to the text, but is quite simply killing it.

Pinpointing and measuring these narrative *anachronies* (as I will call the various types of discordance between the two orderings of story and narrative) implicitly assume the existence of a kind of zero degree that would be a condition of perfect temporal correspondence between narrative and story. This point of reference is more hypothetical than real. Folklore narrative habitually conforms, at least in its major articulations, to chronological order, but our (Western) literary tradition, in contrast, was inaugurated by a characteristic effect of anachrony. In the eighth line of the *Iliad*, the narrator, having evoked the quarrel between Achilles and Agamemnon that he proclaims as the starting point of his narrative (*ex hou de ta prôta*), goes back about ten days to reveal the cause of the quarrel in some 140 retrospective lines (affront to Chryses—Apollo's anger—plague). We know that this beginning *in medias res*, followed by an expository return to an earlier period of time, will become one of the formal topoi of epic, and we also know how faithfully the style of novelistic narration follows in this respect the style of its remote ancestor, even in the heart of the 'realistic' nineteenth century. . . . We will thus not be so foolish as to claim that anachrony is either a rarity or a modern invention. On the contrary, it is one of the traditional resources of literary narration.

Furthermore, if we look a little more closely at the opening lines of the *Iliad* just referred to, we see that their temporal movement is still more complex. Here they are in the translation of Andrew Lang, Walter Leaf, and Ernest Myers:

Sing, goddess, the wrath of Achilles Peleus' son, the ruinous wrath that brought on
the Achaians woes innumerable, and hurled down into Hades many strong souls of
heroes, and gave their bodies to be a prey to dogs and all winged fowls; and so the
counsel of Zeus wrought out its accomplishment from the day when first strife parted
Atreides king of men and noble Achilles.

Who then among the gods set the twain at strife and variance? Even the son of Leto
and of Zeus; for he in anger at the king sent a sore plague upon the host, that the folk
began to perish, because Atreides had done dishonour to Chryses the priest.[5]

Thus, the first narrative subject Homer refers to is the *wrath of Achilles*; the
second is the *miseries of the Greeks*, which are in fact its consequence; but the
third is the *quarrel between Achilles and Agamemnon*, which is its immediate
cause and thus precedes it; then, continuing to go back explicitly from cause
to cause: the *plague*, cause of the quarrel, and finally the *affront to Chryses*,
cause of the plague. The five constituent elements of this opening, which I will
name *A, B, C, D,* and *E* according to the order of their appearance in the
narrative, occupy in the story, respectively, the chronological positions 4, 5,
3, 2, and 1: hence this formula that will synthesize the sequential relationships more or less well: $A4–B5–C3–D2–E1$. We are fairly close to an evenly
retrograde movement.[6]

We must now go into greater detail in our analysis of anachronies. I take
a fairly typical example from *Jean Santeuil*. The situation is one that will
appear in various forms in the *Recherche*: the future has become present but
does not resemble the idea of it that one had in the past. Jean, after several
years, again finds the hotel where Marie Kossichef, whom he once loved, lives,
and compares the impressions he has today with those that he once thought
he would be experiencing today:

Sometimes passing in front of the hotel he remembered the rainy days when he used
to bring his nursemaid that far, on a pilgrimage. But he remembered them without the
melancholy that he then thought he would surely some day savor on feeling that he
no longer loved her. For this melancholy, projected in anticipation prior to the
indifference that lay ahead, came from his love. And this love existed no more.[7]

The temporal analysis of such a text consists first of numbering the sections
according to their change of position in story time. We discover here, in brief,
nine sections divided between two temporal positions that we will designate
2 (*now*) and 1 (*once*), setting aside their iterative nature ('sometimes'). Section

---

[5] Homer, *The Iliad*, trans. Andrew Lang, Walter Leaf, and Ernest Myers (New York: Modern Library,
n.d.), Book I, ll. 1–11. [Translator's note: Genette's reference in the text is to the French translation by
Paul Mazon (Paris, 1962).]

[6] And even more so if we take into account the first—non-narrative—section, in the present tense
of the narrating instance, which thus comes at the last possible moment: 'Sing, goddess'.

[7] Marcel Proust, *Jean Santeuil*, Pléiade ed., p. 674. [Translator's note: the rendering given in the
English edition—trans. Gerard Hopkins (New York, 1956), p. 496—is very free; for purposes of
Genette's analysis, I have used a literal translation of my own.]

A goes in position 2 ('Sometimes passing in front of the hotel he remembered'), *B* in position 1 ('the rainy days when he used to bring his nursemaid that far, on a pilgrimage'), *C* in 2 ('But he remembered them without'), *D* in 1 ('the melancholy that he then thought'), *E* in 2 ('he would surely some day savor on feeling that he no longer loved her'), *F* in 1 ('For this melancholy, projected in anticipation'), *G* in 2 ('prior to the indifference that lay ahead'), *H* in 1 ('came from his love'), *I* in 2 ('And this love existed no more'). The formula of temporal positions, then, is as follows:

$$A2-B1-C2-D1-E2-F1-G2-H1-I2,$$

thus, a perfect zigzag. We will observe in passing that on a first reading the difficulty of this text comes from the apparently systematic way in which Proust eliminates the most elementary temporal indicators (once, now), so that the reader must supply them himself in order to know where he is. But simply picking out the positions does not exhaust temporal analysis, even temporal analysis restricted to questions of sequence, and does not allow us to determine the status of the anachronies: we have yet to define the relationships connecting sections to each other.

If we take section *A* as the narrative starting point, and therefore as being in an autonomous position, we can obviously define section *B* as *retrospective*, and this retrospection we may call subjective in the sense that it is adopted by the character himself, with the narrative doing no more than reporting his present thoughts ('he remembered . . .'); *B* is thus temporally subordinate to *A*: it is defined as retrospective *in relation* to *A*. *C* continues with a simple return to the initial position, without subordination. *D* is again retrospective, but this time the retrospection is adopted directly by the text: apparently it is the narrator who mentions the absence of melancholy, even if this absence is noticed by the hero. *E* brings us back to the present, but in a totally different way from *C*, for this time the present is envisaged as emerging from the past and 'from the point of view' of that past: it is not a simple return to the present but an *anticipation* (subjective, obviously) of the present from within the past; *E* is thus subordinated to *D* as *D* is to *C*, whereas *C*, like *A*, was autonomous. *F* brings us again to position 1 (the past), on a higher level than anticipation *E*: simple return again, but return to 1, that is, to a subordinate position. *G* is again an anticipation, but this time an objective one, for the Jean of the earlier time foresaw the end that was to come to his love precisely as, not indifference, but melancholy at loss of love. *H*, like *F*, is a simple return to 1. *I*, finally, is (like *C*) a simple return to 2, that is, to the starting point.

This brief fragment thus offers us in miniature a quite variegated sample of the several possible temporal relationships: subjective and objective retrospections, subjective and objective anticipations, and simple returns to each of these two positions. As the distinction between subjective and objective anachronies is not a matter of temporality but arises from other categories that we will come to in the chapter on mood, we will neutralize it for the moment. Moreover, to avoid the psychological connotations of such terms as 'anticipation' or 'retrospection', which automatically evoke subjective phenomena, we will eliminate these terms most of the time in favor of two others that are more neutral, designating as *prolepsis* any narrative maneuver that consists of narrating or evoking in advance an event that will take place later, designating as *analepsis* any evocation after the fact of an event that took place earlier than the point in the story where we are at any given moment, and reserving the general term *anachrony* to designate all forms of discordance between the two temporal orders of story and narrative (we will see later that these discordances are not entirely limited to analepsis and prolepsis). . . .[8]

An anachrony can reach into the past or the future, either more or less far from the 'present' moment (that is, from the moment in the story when the narrative was interrupted to make room for the anachrony): this temporal distance we will name the anachrony's *reach*. The anachrony itself can also cover a duration of story that is more or less long: we will call this its *extent*. Thus when Homer, in Book XIX of the *Odyssey*, evokes the circumstances long ago in which Ulysses, while an adolescent, received the wound whose scar he still bears when Euryclea is preparing to wash his feet, this analepsis (filling lines 394–466) has a reach of several decades and an extent of a few days. So defined, the status of anachronies seems to be merely a question of more or less, a matter of measurement particular to each occasion, a timekeeper's work lacking theoretical interest. It is, however, possible (and, I claim, useful) to categorize—without too much emphasis—the characteristics of reach and extent with respect to the ways in which they are connected to certain 'higher' moments in the narrative. This categorization applies in basically the same way to the two main classes of anachronies; but for convenience of exposition and to avoid the risk of becoming too abstract, we will first handle analepses exclusively, and broaden our procedure afterward.

ANALEPSES

Every anachrony constitutes, with respect to the narrative into which it is inserted—onto which it is grafted—a narrative that is temporally second,

---

[8] Here begin the problems (and disgraces) of terminology. *Prolepsis* and *analepsis* offer the advantage of being—through their roots—part of a grammatical-rhetorical family some of whose other members will serve us later; on the other hand, we will have to play on the opposition between the root *-lepse* —which in Greek refers to the fact of taking, whence, in narrative, assuming responsibility for and taking on (prolepsis: to take on something in advance; analepsis: to take on something after the event) —and the root *-lipse* (as in *ellipsis* or *paralipsis*) which refers, on the contrary, to the fact of leaving out, passing by without any mention. But no prefix taken from Greek allows us to subsume the antithesis *pro/ana*. Whence our recourse to *anachrony*, which is perfectly clear but lies outside the system, and whose prefix interferes regrettably with *analepsis*. Regrettably, but significantly.

subordinate to the first in a sort of narrative syntax that we met in the analysis we undertook above of a very short fragment from *Jean Santeuil*. We will henceforth call the temporal level of narrative with respect to which anachrony is defined as such, 'first narrative'. Of course—and this we have already verified—the embeddings can be more complex, and an anachrony can assume the role of first narrative with respect to another that it carries; and more generally, with respect to an anachrony the totality of the context can be taken as first narrative. . . .

This distinction is not as useless as it might seem at first sight. In effect, external analepses and internal analepses (or the internal part of mixed analepses) function for purposes of narrative analysis in totally different ways, at least on one point that seems to me essential. External analepses, by the very fact that they are external, never at any moment risk interfering with the first narrative, for their only function is to fill out the first narrative by enlightening the reader on one or another 'antecedent'. This is obviously the case with some of the examples already mentioned, and it is also, and just as typically, the case with *Un amour de Swann* in the *Recherche du temps perdu*. The case is otherwise with internal analepses: since their temporal field is contained within the temporal field of the first narrative, they present an obvious risk of redundancy or collision. . . .

We have seen how the determination of *reach* allowed us to divide analepses into two classes, external and internal, depending on whether the point to which they reach is located outside or inside the temporal field of the first narrative. The mixed class—not, after all, much resorted to—is in fact determined by a characteristic of *extent*, since this class consists of external analepses prolonged to rejoin and pass beyond the starting point of the first narrative. . . .

[In Proust's *Recherche*] the boldest avoidance (even if the boldness is pure negligence) consists of forgetting the analeptic character of a section of narrative and prolonging that section more or less indefinitely on its own account, paying no attention to the point where it rejoins the first narrative. That is what happens in the episode—famous for other reasons—of the grandmother's death. It opens with an obviously analeptic beginning: 'I went upstairs, and found my grandmother not so well. For some time past, without knowing exactly what was wrong, she had been complaining of her health.' Then the narrative that has been opened in the retrospective mood continues uninterruptedly on up to the death, without ever acknowledging and signaling the moment (although indeed necessarily come to and passed beyond) when Marcel, returning from Mme de Villeparisis's, had found his grandmother 'not so well'. We can never, therefore, either locate the grandmother's death exactly in relation to the Villeparisis matinée, or decide where the analepsis ends and the first narrative resumes.[9] The case is obviously the same, but on a very much broader scale, with the analepsis opened in *Noms de pays: le pays*. We have already seen that this analepsis will continue to the last line of the *Recherche* without paying its respects in passing to the moment of the late insomnias, although these were its source in his memory and almost its narrative matrix: another retrospection that is more than complete, with an extent much greater than its reach, and which at an undetermined point in its career is covertly transformed into an anticipation. In his own way —without proclaiming it and probably even without perceiving it—Proust here unsettles the most basic norms of narration, and anticipates the most disconcerting proceedings of the modern novel.

PROLEPSES

Anticipation, or temporal prolepsis, is clearly much less frequent than the inverse figure, at least in the Western narrative tradition—although each of the three great early epics, the *Iliad*, the *Odyssey*, and the *Aeneid*, begins with a sort of anticipatory summary that to a certain extent justifies the formula Todorov applied to Homeric narrative: 'plot of predestination'.[10] The concern with narrative suspense that is characteristic of the 'classical' conception of the novel ('classical' in the broad sense, and whose center of gravity is, rather, in the nineteenth century) does not easily come to terms with such a practice. Neither, moreover, does the traditional fiction of a narrator who must appear more or less to discover the story at the same time that he tells it. Thus we will find very few prolepses in a Balzac, a Dickens, or a Tolstoy, even if the common practice, as we have already seen, of beginning *in medias res* (or yet, I may venture to say, *in ultimas res*), sometimes gives the illusion of it. It goes without saying that a certain load of 'predestination' hangs over the main part of the narrative in *Manon Lescaut* (where we know, even before Des Grieux opens his story, that it ends with a deportation), or a fortiori in *The Death of Ivan Ilych*, which begins with its epilogue.

The 'first-person' narrative lends itself better than any other to anticipation, by the very fact of its avowedly retrospective character, which authorizes the narrator to allude to the future and in particular to his present situation, for these to some extent form part of his role. Robinson Crusoe can tell us almost at the beginning that the lecture his father gave to turn him aside from nautical adventures was 'truly prophetic', even though at the time he had no idea of it, and Rousseau, with the episode of the combs, does not fail to vouch

---

[9] Proust, *Recherche/Remembrance*, Random House edn., transl. Scott-Moncrieff/Mayor, 1934/1970, vol. I, pp. 928–64.
[10] Tzvetan Todorov, *The Poetics of Prose* (Ithaca, NY, and London, 1977), p. 65.

for not only his past innocence but also the vigor of his retrospective indignation: 'In writing this I feel my pulse quicken yet'.[11] Nonetheless, the *Recherche du temps perdu* uses prolepsis to an extent probably unequaled in the whole history of narrative, even autobiographical narrative,[12] and is thus privileged territory for the study of this type of narrative anachrony. . . .

The importance of 'anachronic' narrative in the *Recherche du temps perdu* is obviously connected to the retrospectively synthetic character of Proustian narrative, which is totally present in the narrator's mind at every moment. Ever since the day when the narrator in a trance perceived the unifying significance of his story, he never ceases to hold all of its threads simultaneously, to apprehend simultaneously all of its places and all of its moments, to be capable of establishing a multitude of 'telescopic' relationships amongst them: a ubiquity that is spatial but also temporal, an 'omnitemporality' . . .

But the very ideas of retrospection or anticipation, which ground the narrative categories of analepsis and prolepsis in 'psychology', take for granted a perfectly clear temporal consciousness and unambiguous relationships among present, past, and future. Only because the exposition required it, and at the cost of excessive schematization, have I until now postulated this to have always been so. In fact, the very frequency of interpolations and their reciprocal entanglement often embroil matters in such a way as to leave the 'simple' reader, and even the most determined analyst, sometimes with no way out. To conclude this chapter we shall examine some of these ambiguous structures which bring us to the threshold of *achrony* pure and simple. . . .

These proleptic analepses and analeptic prolepses are so many complex anachronies, and they somewhat disturb our reassuring ideas about retrospection and anticipation. Let us again recall the existence of open analepses (analepses whose conclusion cannot be localized), which therefore necessarily entails the existence of temporally indefinite narrative sections. But we also find in the *Recherche* some events not provided with any temporal reference whatsoever, events that we cannot place at all in relation to the events surrounding them. To be unplaceable they need only be attached not to some other event (which would require the narrative to define them as being earlier or later) but to the (atemporal) commentarial discourse that accompanies them—and we know what place that has in this work. . . . After the scene of the missed introduction to Albertine, in the *Jeunes filles en fleurs*, the narrator offers some reflections on the subjectivity of the feeling of love, then illustrates this theory with the example of a drawing master who had never known the

---

[11] Rousseau, *Confessions*, Pléiade ed., p. 20.

[12] The *Recherche* contains more than twenty proleptic sections of significant length, not counting simple allusions in the course of a sentence. The analepses of like definition are not more numerous, but it is true that they take up, by their extent, the quasi-totality of the text, and that it is atop that first retrospective layer that analepses and prolepses of the second degree are set.

color of the hair of a mistress he had passionately loved and who had left him a daughter ('I never saw her except with a hat on').[13] Here, no inference from the content can help the analyst define the status of an anachrony deprived of every temporal connection, which is an event we must ultimately take to be dateless and ageless: to be an achrony.

Now, it is not only such isolated events that express the narrative's capacity to disengage its arrangement from all dependence, even inverse dependence, on the chronological sequence of the story it tells. The *Recherche* presents, at least in two places, genuine *achronic structures*. . . . Only by naively confusing the narrative's syntagmatic order with the story's temporal order does one imagine, as hurried readers do, that the meeting with the Duchess or the episode of the steeples comes later than the scene at Montjouvain. The truth is that the narrator had the clearest of reasons for grouping together, in defiance of all chronology, events connected by spatial proximity, by climatic identity (the walks to Méséglise always take place in bad weather, those to Guermantes in good weather), or by thematic kinship (the Méséglise way represents the erotic-affective side of the world of childhood, that of Guermantes its aesthetic side); he thus made clear, more than anyone had done before him and better than they had, narrative's capacity for *temporal autonomy*.

3 *Towards a Semiotics of Literature**

ROBERT SCHOLES

Literature of course is a word, not a thing. In casual conversation the word is used in many ways, some of them in conflict with one another. *Literature* may be thought of as true writing vs. false, as beautiful writing vs. useful, as non-true writing vs. true/false writing, and so on. It can be thought of as consisting of a few established generic forms, such as poem, play, and story, with such debatable genres as the essay and the film lurking on the borders. Most departments of literature function with no better concepts than these. . . .

To some extent I sympathize with the traditional muddle here. Often what begins as clarification ends as nonsense, producing categories so exclusive or inclusive that they bring all attempts at systematic thinking about literature into disrepute. And yet, we who study what we call 'literature' cannot help

[13] *Recherche/Remembrance*, Random House edn., transl. Scott-Moncrieff/Mayor, 1934/1970, vol. I, p. 645.

* From Robert Scholes, 'Towards a Semiotics of Literature', in *What Is Literature?*, ed. Paul Hernadi, Indiana University Press, 1978, pp. 231–49; first publ. *Critical Inquiry*, Chicago, 1977.

but desire to understand better what we are doing. My attempt to deal with the problem here is based on the formalist, structuralist, and semiotic tradition of critical thought, but at certain crucial points I shall bend that tradition in what I take to be a necessary direction. Some might even say that I have bent it beyond the breaking point.

The word *literature*, I wish to argue, should be used to designate a certain body of repeatable or recoverable acts of communication. Later on I shall elaborate on the 'certain' part of the definition, which requires the exclusion of some repeatable or recoverable communicative acts from the literary category. But first I must define the other terms in this definition. *Repeatable or recoverable* requires that something called literature have a certain durability. This may take the form of a written text, a recorded utterance, a reel of film, or something transmitted orally, like a saying, joke, myth, or epic poem. In the oral forms, what is recovered is not usually an identical text but a recognizable structure—the 'same' joke or epic poem in different words—but this 'sameness' brings such works within the limits of this definition of literature. A saying or performance which is not recoverable or repeatable, whether a forgotten joke or a lost manuscript, may well have been literary, but it is no longer a part of literature, since literature consists of the body of available performances only.

The word *act* in the definition of literature being proposed here requires that our repeatable or recoverable utterance be a deliberate action on the part of some sentient being. A mistake is not literature. But it can be made literature by someone else's performance of it. Any utterance or human gesture can be made literary by its being deliberately incorporated into another utterance. Any trivial or vulgar bit of speech or gesture may function in a literary way in a story or play, for instance, or even in a Joycean 'epiphany', just as a piece of driftwood or trash may be incorporated in a work of sculpture, or any found object be turned into visual art by an act of selection and display.

Finally, the word *communication* in the definition must be considered. It has been used here because it includes some non-verbal systems of signification as well as the expected verbal forms. A category termed *literature* which excluded theater and film would be embarrassing and awkward for many reasons, among which is the fact that what is recognizably the same work (Henry James's *Washington Square*, for instance) may exist effectively as a printed text, a stage performance, and a film. The word 'communication' may seem to open the way too far to non-verbal forms like mime and dance, which are clearly communicative, and even to all the visual and musical forms of expression. Most music 'communicates' something, as does most visual art, though clearly there is a broad range from representational forms to 'pure' or abstract forms. Here it may be useful to limit the meaning of communication in this definition to utterances that are reasonably susceptible to verbal restatement or paraphrase. Even so, this will be an untidy border—partly because highly iconological and iconographic works of visual art as well as vocal and programmatic music are to some extent literary.

More important at the moment is that part of the definition originally masked by the word *certain*. What quality, you will wish to know, makes any given communicative act a work of literature? I, like any good Prague School structuralist,[1] will answer, in a word, 'literariness'. This response, of course, is logically splendid but entirely meaningless until the new term is given a less tautological semantic coding—which will be our business here. The major contribution of Roman Jakobson to literary study was his deliverance of us all from 'literature' as an absolute category. 'Literariness', he has taught us, is found in all sorts of utterances, some of which are not especially literary. And a 'literary work' is simply one in which literariness is dominant. Obviously, this allows for borderline cases and disputation, but this is undoubtedly an advantage, since 'literature' as an absolute category always provokes disputation anyway, and by making the argument turn on 'literariness', we should at least know what kind of evidence ought to decide such disputes—if (and it is a large 'if') we can define 'literariness' in a satisfactory way.

It may be, of course, that we need not define literariness as an aspect of utterance at all. One might, in fact, overturn the whole problem by doing as Jonathan Culler suggests in *Structuralist Poetics*, regarding literature not as a function of the work itself but as a special way of reading. Culler suggests that the issue ought not to be the literariness of the text but the 'literary competence' of the reader, and that competence is primarily a mastery of generic conventions—a position with which I am in sympathy. But are all conventions literary? Are all texts potential fictions? The problem of literariness will not go away, whether we locate it in the text, the reader, or the system. The solution, I am about to argue, lies in seeing the 'literary' as a quality that transforms all the major functions of an act of communication, including the role of the reader—which brings us back to Roman Jakobson, especially to his 'Closing Statement: Linguistics and Poetics' (in *Style in Language*, ed. Thomas A. Sebeok).

The six features of a communicative act as popularized by Jakobson's analysis are sender, receiver, contact, message, code, and context. In Jakobson's view, a literary utterance may be distinguished from a non-literary utterance by its emphasis on its own formal structure. This emphasis forces us to consider the utterance as a structured object with a certain density or opacity. It is not a transparent vehicle through which our thoughts are directed to some context or action. It is an entity to be contemplated in its own

---

[1] In 1920, Roman Jakobson moved from his native Russia to Prague, where he founded the Prague Linguistic Circle, the source of seminal work in structuralist linguistics and 'poetics'. [Ed.]

right. This formulation is closely related to many other views, such as those of I. A. Richards and the New Critics. It rests ultimately on a Kantian assumption about the purposelessness of esthetic objects.

It is in part a useful formulation, but I find it objectionable for a number of reasons. For one, it applies much better to verse, especially to highly formulaic verse, than to prose fiction or drama. For another, it abandons much that has been gained by seeing literariness as a feature of communication rather than as a mode of a purposeless activity called 'art'. For once this notion of art is allowed into the picture, all those aspects of literature which are cognitive or instructive are found to be impurities. Rather than accept the notion that much (if not all) literature is a kind of failed art, we who have made literary study a central concern in our lives must seek a definition which accounts for this centrality. Seeing literature as a refinement or elaboration of the elements of communication rather than as a vulgarization of the elements of art is the necessary first step in this direction. Jakobson's neat formulation pays too great a price for its neatness. It turns back toward esthetics just when it should continue on with semiotics, and the result is a definition of literariness that excludes many of the most important qualities of all literature, including much poetry. It is time now to move toward a formulation that will yield us a more satisfactory notion of literariness.

Stated as simply as I can put it, we sense literariness in an utterance when any one of the six features of communication loses its simplicity and becomes multiple or duplicitous. Let me illustrate this first with some minimal cases. We are all familiar with what happens when we sense a difference between the maker of an utterance and the speaker of it. We say then that the words are those of a 'persona' of the author, meaning, as the word implies, that the author has donned a mask. Whenever a communicative act encourages us to sense a difference between maker and speaker, our literary competence has been activated. This is true not only in such obvious situations as when we encounter the words of characters in plays or stories, but in essays also, whenever the essayist adopts a tone or role that seems to be a deviation from some anticipated norm. Even in casual conversation, when a speaker adopts a particular tone, register, or dialect for a given occasion, we notice this as a kind of literary behavior. In written prose a device like the ironic presentation of argument in Swift's 'Modest Proposal' is simply an extreme case of this duplicity of the 'sender' of a communication.

Similarly, if the words of an utterance seem not to be aimed directly at us but at someone else, this duplicitous situation is essentially literary. John Stuart Mill emphasized this when he said that poetry is not heard but overheard. It is perhaps unfortunate, but situations of eavesdropping and voyeurism are in part literary—which is no doubt why they figure so prominently in avowed literary texts. The literary competence of readers with respect to this feature of communicative acts is often a matter of imagining the person to whom the utterance is addressed or of perceiving meanings which are not intended for, or not understood by, the ostensible auditor. Every communicative subtlety requires a corresponding subtlety of interpretation.

We are placed in a literary situation also when the contact is not simple. If spoken words are presented to us in writing, for instance, either the writer or the reader must supply the features of oral communication lost in this translation. . . . Sterne, of course, by recording in writing the reading aloud of a written document [in *Tristram Shandy*, vol. ii, ch. 17] makes the situation doubly literary with respect to the contact. Similarly, all descriptions of things normally perceived visually tend toward the literary because they seek to 'translate' what would be a visual contact into a verbal one. The notion that all written documents are 'literature' is based on this process. In fact, the more difference we sense between the verbal contact of print and our normal means of perception of the objects named in any printed text, the more literary the utterance is likely to be. It is therefore probable that all writing contains at least traces of literariness, but we must remember that literariness does not equal literature until it dominates any given utterance.

Duplicity in the form of the message itself, though immensely complicated, is the aspect of literariness which we presently understand best because it has been most carefully studied. Jakobson and Richards and all the Formalists and New Critics have alerted us to the various sound effects and syntactic pattern-ings of verse as well as to the ironies, ambiguities, paradoxes and other duplicitous features of poetic messages. I do not wish to dwell on these features here except to point out that they function not to cut the work off from the world by making it a self-contained object—as so many theoreticians have argued—rather, they function to create a literary tension between the utterance as communicative and externally referential on the one hand—and as incommunicative and self-referential, on the other. . . .

I have saved the most complicated for last: code and context. We can postpone code even further, since all the features we have been considering as literary may be described in terms of conventions or devices that transform ordinary discourse into literary discourse. As for the problem of context, Jakobson himself removes it from the literary sphere, simply saying that an utterance which emphasizes its context is referential, not poetic, and many theoreticians, like Richards, oppose referential to non-referential discourse as a way of describing the difference between utilitarian and esthetic texts. My intention here is to argue for a contrary assumption. And in doing so I must break with a powerful tradition in semiotic studies that runs from Saussure to Barthes and Eco.

The most powerful assumption in French semiotic thought since Saussure has been the notion that a sign does not connect a name and the object it refers to, but consists of a sound-image and a concept, a signifier and a signified. Saussure, as amplified by Foucault, Barthes, and Eco, has taught us to recognize an unbridgeable gap between words and things, signs and referents. The whole notion of 'sign and referent' has been rejected by the French structuralists and their followers as too materialistic and simple-minded. Signs do not refer to things; they signify concepts, and concepts are aspects of thought, not of reality. This elegant and persuasive formulation has certainly provided a useful critique of naïve realism, vulgar materialism, and various other -isms which can be qualified with crippling adjectives. But it hasn't exactly caused the world to turn into a concept. Even semioticians eat and perform their other bodily functions just as if the world existed solidly around them. That language would generate words like 'orgasm' or 'tonsil' without any assistance from non-verbal experience seems to me highly unlikely. In my view, if language really were a closed system, it would be subject, like any other closed system, to increase in entropy. In fact, it is new input into language from non-verbal experience that keeps it from decaying.

To isolate literariness in the context of an utterance we need a terminology that will enable us to recognize different aspects of contextual reference. The terminology I wish to offer is based on three related binary oppositions, or three aspects of a single, ultimate opposition: absent vs. present, semiotic vs. phenomenal, and abstract vs. concrete. A neutral, unliterary context is present, phenomenal, and concrete. That is, the context is present to both sender and receiver of a given message. It is *there*, perceptually available to both of them, as free of semiotic coding as possible, and it is more like a thing than like an idea. For instance, if two people are together in a room, looking through a window, and one says, 'It is raining', the context is concrete, phenomenal, and present. If, however, they open a book and read the words, 'It is raining', the context is still concrete, still potentially phenomenal, and yet, because it is absent, the meaning of the phrase is totally different. The meaning can no longer be directly referred to the rain outside the window, nor to sunshine outside the window if it were sunny. It is raining not in present reality but in a space we have learned to call fictional. To enter fictional space through the medium of words, we must reverse the processes of perception, generating the images, sounds and other perceptual data that would be available through our senses if we were in the presence of the named phenomena.

If the same phrase were to occur in a letter, since the sender and receiver are not present to one another, and therefore not both in the presence of the phenomenon referred to, the phrase would again generate a fictional space, and the more the writer tried to turn the phenomenon of the rain, which only he had perceptual access to, into words, the more concretely that space would be filled and extended. Any elaborate description of the rain would perforce become more literary. (It is worth noting that a 'description' that substituted analytical or 'scientific' categories for the perceptual categories of human observation would be less literary because less concrete. What we mean by 'concrete' is 'description according to our normal modes of perception'. The codes of fiction are tied to our perceptual system as well as to our language.)

If the letter-writer were to begin by describing the rain outside his window and to end his letter by saying, 'When I said it was raining before, and described all that stuff, it wasn't really raining. I made all that up'—and if we were to receive that letter and read it, how would we react? And if he added a postscript in which he asserted that when he said he had 'made up' the rain he was lying . . .? And so on? The message contradicts itself, aggressively reminding us that we have no access to the context. We can never know whether the writer was looking out a real window at a real rain or not. The fictional status of the 'rain' does not depend on the fact or unfact of rain but on the absence of the 'real' context from the reader. Any description we read is a fiction. . . .

A context that is present and phenomenally available does not invite the literary the way an absent context does. In fact, literariness based on a present context is likely to result from some semiotic violation of that context. If one ,of our rain-watchers should say to the other, 'Nice weather we're having', this would instantly be perceived by the other as a simple irony. In fact this transaction would be so instantaneous that the complex process involved might be lost. What happens in such a situation is this: 'A' says, 'Nice weather'. 'B' is aware that the context denies the statement—the phenomenal denies the semiotic. But knowing that 'A' is aware of the actual situation, and that 'A' is aware that 'B' is aware of it, he knows finally that 'A' is referring to a fictional context—where the weather is indeed nice—as a way of signaling his disapproval of the actual phenomenon of this particular rain. It is this complex process of comparing two contexts that allows us to say that the apparent meaning of the phrase is not the real meaning. What we might regard as the 'figure' or trope, irony, is in fact a function of context and cannot be determined from the form of the message alone. Upon examination, other figures that seem to be more purely verbal, like puns and metaphors, will be seen to function by juxtaposition of contrasting contexts rather than at some purely verbal level. Irony, of course, is only the most extreme semiotic violation of present context. Any recoding of the phenomenal will contain some measure of literariness because it changes the contact (as was observed above), and the more such recoding may be recognized as a distortion, the more literary it will seem. . . .

Finally, I wish to make clear that literariness in itself ought not to be confused with value. All plays are literary but not all are equally valuable. And our reasons for valuing a play may have as much to do with its non-literary function as with its literary form. To the extent that a work of literature points toward our experience as living human beings, we may value it for what we call its 'truth' or 'rightness'—which is not a specifically formal quality but a matter of the fit between a message and its existential context. This opens up an area for discussion too large to be considered here. Suffice it to note that literary coding of discourse is a formal strategy, a means of structuring that enables the maker of the discourse to communicate certain kinds of meaning. We may, of course, value some literary utterances mainly for their formal elegance, but we also may value literary utterances for the insight they provide about aspects of existence, and it would be foolish to pretend this is not so simply because such insight does not lend itself to formal codification.

This means, of course, that the student and teacher of literary texts will have to be something of a historian and something of a philosopher if he or she wishes to approach full understanding of the texts—and even something of a person. Many literary works assume experience of life as an aspect of their context shared by writer and reader. Some works refuse to open to us until we are sufficiently mature. Others close as we lose access to some contexts through growing or forgetting. No study of literature can be purely formal, and all attempts to reduce literary study to this level are misguided if not pernicious. To the extent that semiotic studies insist that communication is a matter of purely formal systems, they too may be misguided if not pernicious. Many semioticians would argue that the meaning of any sign or word is purely a function of its place in a paradigmatic system and its use in a syntagmatic situation. But I wish to suggest that meaning is also a function of human experience. For those who have experienced such things as marriage or bereavement the words themselves will signify something different than they will for those who have had no experience of these things —and much of literature is based on attempts to generate semiotic equivalents for experiences that seem to defy duplication in mere signs.

4   *The Ideology of Modernism**

GEORG LUKÁCS

It is in no way surprising that the most influential contemporary school of writing should still be committed to the dogmas of 'modernist' anti-realism.

* From Georg Lukács, *The Meaning of Contemporary Realism*, transl. E. Bone, Merlin Press, 1963, pp. 19–27; first publ. 1957.

It is here that we must begin our investigation if we are to chart the possibilities of a bourgeois realism. We must compare the two main trends in contemporary bourgeois literature, and look at the answers they give to the major ideological and artistic questions of our time.

We shall concentrate on the underlying ideological basis of these trends (ideological in the above-defined, not in the strictly philosophical, sense). What must be avoided at all costs is the approach generally adopted by bourgeois-modernist critics themselves: that exaggerated concern with formal criteria, with questions of style and literary technique. This approach may appear to distinguish sharply between 'modern' and 'traditional' writing (i.e. contemporary writers who adhere to the styles of the last century). In fact it fails to locate the decisive formal problems and turns a blind eye to their inherent dialectic. We are presented with a false polarization which, by exaggerating the importance of stylistic differences, conceals the opposing principles actually underlying and determining contrasting styles. . . .

What determines the style of a given work of art? How does the intention determine the form? (We are concerned here, of course, with the intention realized in the work; it need not coincide with the writer's conscious intention.) The distinctions that concern us are not those between stylistic 'techniques' in the formalistic sense. It is the view of the world, the ideology or *weltanschauung* underlying a writer's work, that counts. And it is the writer's attempt to reproduce this view of the world which constitutes his 'intention' and is the formative principle underlying the style of a given piece of writing. Looked at in this way, style ceases to be a formalistic category. Rather, it is rooted in content; it is the specific form of a specific content.

Content determines form. But there is no content of which Man himself is not the focal point. However various the *données* of literature (a particular experience, a didactic purpose), the basic question is, and will remain: what is Man?

Here is a point of division: if we put the question in abstract, philosophical terms, leaving aside all formal considerations, we arrive—for the realist school—at the traditional Aristotelian dictum (which was also reached by other than purely aesthetic considerations): Man is *zoon politikon*, a social animal. The Aristotelian dictum is applicable to all great realistic literature. Achilles and Werther, Oedipus and Tom Jones, Antigone and Anna Karenina: their individual existence—their *Sein an sich*,· in the Hegelian terminology; their 'ontological being', as a more fashionable terminology has it—cannot be distinguished from their social and historical environment. Their human significance, their specific individuality cannot be separated from the context in which they were created.

The ontological view governing the image of man in the work of leading modernist writers is the exact opposite of this. Man, for these writers, is by nature solitary, asocial, unable to enter into relationships with other human beings. Thomas Wolfe once wrote: 'My view of the world is based on the firm conviction that solitariness is by no means a rare condition, something peculiar to myself or to a few specially solitary human beings, but the inescapable, central fact of human existence.' Man, thus imagined, may establish contact with other individuals, but only in a superficial, accidental manner; only, ontologically speaking, by retrospective reflection. For 'the others', too, are basically solitary, beyond significant human relationship.

This basic solitariness of man must not be confused with that individual solitariness to be found in the literature of traditional realism. In the latter case, we are dealing with a particular situation in which a human being may be placed, due either to his character or to the circumstances of his life. Solitariness may be objectively conditioned, as with Sophocles' Philoctetes, put ashore on the bleak island of Lemnos. Or it may be subjective, the product of inner necessity, as with Tolstoy's Ivan Ilyitsch or Flaubert's Frédéric Moreau in the *Education Sentimentale*. But it is always merely a fragment, a phase, a climax or anticlimax, in the life of the community as a whole. The fate of such individuals is characteristic of certain human types in specific social or historical circumstances. Beside and beyond their solitariness, the common life, the strife and togetherness of other human beings, goes on as before. In a word, their solitariness is a specific social fate, not a universal *condition humaine*.

The latter, of course, is characteristic of the theory and practice of modernism. I would like, in the present study, to spare the reader tedious excursions into philosophy. But I cannot refrain from drawing the reader's attention to Heidegger's description of human existence as a 'thrownness-into-being' (*Geworfenheit ins Dasein*). A more graphic evocation of the ontological solitariness of the individual would be hard to imagine. Man is 'thrown-into-being'. This implies, not merely that man is constitutionally unable to establish relationships with things or persons outside himself; but also that it is impossible to determine theoretically the origin and goal of human existence.

Man, thus conceived, is an ahistorical being. . . . This negation of history takes two different forms in modernist literature. First, the hero is strictly confined within the limits of his own experience. There is not for him—and apparently not for his creator—any pre-existent reality beyond his own self, acting upon him or being acted upon by him. Secondly, the hero himself is without personal history. He is 'thrown-into-the-world': meaninglessly, unfathomably. He does not develop through contact with the world; he neither forms nor is formed by it. The only 'development' in this literature is the gradual revelation of the human condition. Man is now what he has always been and always will be. The narrator, the examining subject, is in motion; the examined reality is static.

Of course, dogmas of this kind are only really viable in philosophical abstraction, and then only with a measure of sophistry. A gifted writer, however extreme his theoretical modernism, will in practice have to compromise with the demands of historicity and of social environment. Joyce uses Dublin, Kafka and Musil the Hapsburg Monarchy, as the locus of their masterpieces. But the locus they lovingly depict is little more than a backcloth; it is not basic to their artistic intention.

This view of human existence has specific literary consequences. Particularly in one category, of primary theoretical and practical importance, to which we must now give our attention: that of *potentiality*. Philosophy distinguishes between *abstract* and *concrete* (in Hegel, 'real') *potentiality*. These two categories, their interrelation and opposition, are rooted in life itself. *Potentiality*—seen abstractly or subjectively—is richer than actual life. Innumerable possibilities for man's development are imaginable, only a small percentage of which will be realized. Modern subjectivism, taking these imagined possibilities for actual complexity of life, oscillates between melancholy and fascination. When the world declines to realize these possibilities, this melancholy becomes tinged with contempt. . . .

How far were those possibilities even concrete or 'real'? Plainly, they existed only in the imagination of the subject, as dreams or day-dreams. Faulkner, in whose work this subjective potentiality plays an important part, was evidently aware that reality must thereby be subjectivized and made to appear arbitrary. Consider this comment of his: 'They were all talking simultaneously, getting flushed and excited, quarrelling, making the unreal into a possibility, then into a probability, then into an irrefutable fact, as human beings do when they put their wishes into words.' The possibilities in a man's mind, the particular pattern, intensity and suggestiveness they assume, will of course be characteristic of that individual. In practice, their number will border on the infinite, even with the most unimaginative individual. It is thus a hopeless undertaking to define the contours of individuality, let alone to come to grips with a man's actual fate, by means of potentiality. The *abstract* character of potentiality is clear from the fact that it cannot determine development—subjective mental states, however permanent or profound, cannot here be decisive. Rather, the development of personality is determined by inherited gifts and qualities; by the factors, external or internal, which further or inhibit their growth.

But in life potentiality can, of course, become reality. Situations arise in which a man is confronted with a choice; and in the act of choice a man's character may reveal itself in a light that surprises even himself. In literature —and particularly in dramatic literature—the denouement often consists in the realization of just such a potentiality, which circumstances have kept from coming to the fore. These potentialities are, then, 'real' or concrete potentialities. The fate of the character depends upon the potentiality in question, even if it should condemn him to a tragic end. In advance, while still a subjective potentiality in the character's mind, there is no way of distinguishing it from the innumerable abstract potentialities in his mind. It may even be buried away so completely that, before the moment of decision, it has never entered his mind even as an abstract potentiality. The subject, after taking his decision, may be unconscious of his own motives. Thus Richard Dudgeon, Shaw's *Devil's Disciple*, having sacrificed himself as Pastor Andersen, confesses: 'I have often asked myself for the motive, but I find no good reason to explain why I acted as I did'.

Yet it is a decision which has altered the direction of his life. Of course, this is an extreme case. But the qualitative leap of the denouement, cancelling and at the same time renewing the continuity of individual consciousness, can never be predicted. The concrete potentiality cannot be isolated from the myriad abstract potentialities. Only actual decision reveals the distinction.

The literature of realism, aiming at a truthful reflection of reality, must demonstrate both the concrete and abstract potentialities of human beings in extreme situations of this kind. A character's concrete potentiality once revealed, his abstract potentialities will appear essentially inauthentic. Moravia, for instance, in his novel *The Indifferent Ones*, describes the young son of a decadent bourgeois family, Michel, who makes up his mind to kill his sister's seducer. While Michel, having made his decision, is planning the murder, a large number of abstract—but highly suggestive—possibilities are laid before us. Unfortunately for Michel the murder is actually carried out; and, from the sordid details of the action, Michel's character emerges as what it is—representative of that background from which, in subjective fantasy, he had imagined he could escape.

Abstract potentiality belongs wholly to the realm of subjectivity; whereas concrete potentiality is concerned with the dialectic between the individual's subjectivity and objective reality. The literary presentation of the latter thus implies a description of actual persons inhabiting a palpable, identifiable world. Only in the interaction of character and environment can the concrete potentiality of a particular individual be singled out from the 'bad infinity' of purely abstract potentialities, and emerge as the determining potentiality of just this individual at just this phase of his development. This principle alone enables the artist to distinguish concrete potentiality from a myriad abstractions.

But the ontology on which the image of man in modernist literature is based invalidates this principle. If the 'human condition'—man as a solitary being, incapable of meaningful relationships—is identified with reality itself, the distinction between abstract and concrete potentiality becomes null and void. The categories tend to merge. Thus Cesare Pavese notes with John Dos

Passos, and his German contemporary, Alfred Döblin, a sharp oscillation between 'superficial *verisme*' and 'abstract Expressionist schematism'. Criticizing Dos Passos, Pavese writes that fictional characters 'ought to be created by deliberate selection and description of individual features'—implying that Dos Passos' characterizations are transferable from one individual to another. He describes the artistic consequences: by exalting man's subjectivity, at the expense of the objective reality of his environment, man's subjectivity itself is impoverished.

The problem, once again, is ideological. This is not to say that the ideology underlying modernist writings is identical in all cases. On the contrary: the ideology exists in extremely various, even contradictory forms. The rejection of narrative objectivity, the surrender to subjectivity, may take the form of Joyce's stream of consciousness, or of Musil's 'active passivity', his 'existence without quality', or of Gide's '*action gratuite*', where abstract potentiality achieves pseudo-realization. As individual character manifests itself in life's moments of decision, so too in literature. If the distinction between abstract and concrete potentiality vanishes, if man's inwardness is identified with an abstract subjectivity, human personality must necessarily disintegrate. . . .

The disintegration of personality is matched by a disintegration of the outer world. In one sense, this is simply a further consequence of our argument. For the identification of abstract and concrete human potentiality rests on the assumption that the objective world is inherently inexplicable. Certain leading modernist writers, attempting a theoretical apology, have admitted this quite frankly. Often this theoretical impossibility of understanding reality is the point of departure, rather than the exaltation of subjectivity. But in any case the connection between the two is plain. The German poet Gottfried Benn, for instance, informs us that 'there is no outer reality, there is only human consciousness, constantly building, modifying, rebuilding new worlds out of its own creativity'. . . .

The negation of outward reality is not always demanded with such theoretical rigour. But it is present in almost all modernist literature. In conversation, Musil once gave as the period of his great novel, 'between 1912 and 1914'. But he was quick to modify this statement by adding: 'I have not, I must insist, written a historical novel. I am not concerned with actual events. . . . Events, anyhow, are interchangeable. I am interested in what is typical, in what one might call the ghostly aspect of reality.' The word 'ghostly' is interesting. It points to a major tendency in modernist literature: the attenuation of actuality. In Kafka, the descriptive detail is of an extraordinary immediacy and authenticity. But Kafka's artistic ingenuity is really directed towards substituting his *angst*-ridden vision of the world for objective reality. The realistic detail is the expression of a ghostly un-reality, of a nightmare world, whose function is to evoke *angst*. . . . A similar attenuation of reality underlies Joyce's stream of consciousness. It is, of course, intensified where the stream of consciousness is itself the medium through which reality is presented. And it is carried *ad absurdum* where the stream of consciousness is that of an abnormal subject or of an idiot—consider the first part of Faulkner's *Sound and Fury* or, a still more extreme case, Beckett's *Molloy*.

Attenuation of reality and dissolution of personality are thus inter-dependent: the stronger the one, the stronger the other. Underlying both is the lack of a consistent view of human nature. Man is reduced to a sequence of unrelated experimental fragments; he is as inexplicable to others as to himself. In Eliot's *Cocktail Party* the psychiatrist, who voices the opinions of the author, describes the phenomenon:

> Ah, but we die to each other daily
> What we know of other people
> Is only our memory of the moments
> During which we knew them. And they have changed since then.
>
> To pretend that they and we are the same
> Is a useful and convenient social convention
> Which must sometimes be broken. We must also remember
> That at every meeting we are meeting a stranger.

The dissolution of personality, originally the unconscious product of the identification of concrete and abstract potentiality, is elevated to a deliberate principle in the light of consciousness.

5 *Modernism and the Metropolis**

RAYMOND WILLIAMS

. . . it is not the general themes of response to the city and its modernity which compose anything that can be properly called Modernism. It is rather the new and specific location of the artists and intellectuals of this movement within the changing cultural milieu of the metropolis.

For a number of social and historical reasons the metropolis of the second half of the nineteenth century and of the first half of the twentieth century moved into a quite new cultural dimension. It was now much more than the very large city, or even the capital city of an important nation. It was the place

* From Raymond Williams, *The Politics of Modernism: Against the New Conformists*, Verso, 1989, pp. 44–7, 32–5.

where new social and economic and cultural relations, beyond both city and nation in their older senses, were beginning to be formed: a distinct historical phase which was in fact to be extended, in the second half of the twentieth century, at least potentially, to the whole world.

In the earliest phases this development had much to do with imperialism: with the magnetic concentration of wealth and power in imperial capitals and the simultaneous cosmopolitan access to a wide variety of subordinate cultures. But it was always more than the orthodox colonial system. Within Europe itself there was a very marked unevenness of development, both within particular countries, where the distances between capitals and provinces widened, socially and culturally, in the uneven developments of industry and agriculture, and of a monetary economy and simple subsistence or market forms. Even more crucial differences emerged between individual countries, which came to compose a new kind of hierarchy, not simply, as in the old terms, of military power, but in terms of development and thence of perceived enlightenment and modernity.

Moreover, both within many capital cities, and especially within the major metropolises, there was at once a complexity and a sophistication of social relations, supplemented in the most important cases—Paris, above all—by exceptional liberties of expression. This complex and open milieu contrasted very sharply with the persistence of traditional social, cultural and intellectual forms in the provinces and in the less developed countries. Again, in what was not only the complexity but the miscellaneity of the metropolis, so different in these respects from traditional cultures and societies beyond it, the whole range of cultural activity could be accommodated.

The metropolis housed the great traditional academies and museums and their orthodoxies; their very proximity and powers of control were both a standard and a challenge. But also, within the new kind of open, complex and mobile society, small groups in any form of divergence or dissent could find some kind of foothold, in ways that would not have been possible if the artists and thinkers composing them had been scattered in more traditional, closed societies. Moreover, within both the miscellaneity of the metropolis—which in the course of capitalist and imperialist development had characteristically attracted a very mixed population, from a variety of social and cultural origins —and its concentration of wealth and thus opportunities of patronage, such groups could hope to attract, indeed to form, new kinds of audience. In the early stages the foothold was usually precarious. There is a radical contrast between these often struggling (and quarrelling and competitive) groups, who between them made what is now generally referred to as 'modern art', and the funded and trading institutions, academic and commercial, which were eventually to generalize and deal in them. The continuity is one of underlying ideology, but there is still a radical difference between the two generations: the struggling innovators and the modernist establishment which consolidated their achievement.

Thus the key cultural factor of the modernist shift is the character of the metropolis: in these general conditions, but then, even more decisively, in its direct effects on form. The most important general element of the innovations in form is the fact of immigration to the metropolis, and it cannot too often be emphasized how many of the major innovators were, in this precise sense, immigrants. At the level of theme, this underlies, in an obvious way, the elements of strangeness and distance, indeed of alienation, which so regularly form part of the repertory. But the decisive aesthetic effect is at a deeper level. Liberated or breaking from their national or provincial cultures, placed in quite new relations to those other native languages or native visual traditions, encountering meanwhile a novel and dynamic common environment from which many of the older forms were obviously distant, the artists and writers and thinkers of this phase found the only community available to them: a community of the medium; of their own practices.

Thus language was perceived quite differently. It was no longer, in the old sense, customary and naturalized, but in many ways arbitrary and conventional. To the immigrants especially, with their new second common language, language was more evident as a medium—a medium that could be shaped and reshaped—than as a social custom. Even within a native language, the new relationships of the metropolis, and the inescapable new uses in newspapers and advertising attuned to it, forced certain productive kinds of strangeness and distance: a new consciousness of conventions and thus of changeable, because now open, conventions. There had long been pressures towards the work of art as artefact and commodity, but these now greatly intensified, and their combined pressures were very complex indeed. The preoccupying visual images and styles of particular cultures did not disappear, any more than the native languages, native tales, the native styles of music and dance, but all were now passed through this crucible of the metropolis, which was in the important cases no mere melting pot but an intense and visually and linguistically exciting process in its own right, from which remarkable new forms emerged.

At the same time, within the very openness and complexity of the metropolis, there was no formed and settled society to which the new kinds of work could be related. The relationships were to the open and complex and dynamic social process itself, and the only accessible form of this practice was an emphasis on the medium: the medium as that which, in an unprecedented way, defined art. Over a wide and diverse range of practice, this emphasis on the medium, and on what can be done in the medium, became dominant. Moreover, alongside the practice, theoretical positions of the same kind, most notably the new linguistics, but also the new aesthetics of significant form and structure, rose to direct, to support, to reinforce and to recommend. So nearly complete was this vast cultural reformation that, at the levels directly concerned—the succeeding metropolitan formations of learning and practice —what had once been defiantly marginal and oppositional became, in its turn, orthodox, although the distance of both from other cultures and peoples remained wide. The key to this persistence is again the social form of the metropolis, for the facts of increasing mobility and social diversity, passing through a continuing dominance of certain metropolitan centres and a related unevenness of all other social and cultural development, led to a major expansion of metropolitan forms of perception, both internal and imposed. Many of the direct forms and media processes of the minority phase of modern art thus became what could be seen as the common currency of majority communication, especially in films (an art form created, in all important respects, by these perceptions) and in advertising.

It is then necessary to explore, in all its complexity of detail, the many variations in this decisive phase of modern practice and theory. But it is also time to explore it with something of its own sense of strangeness and distance, rather than with the comfortable and now internally accommodated forms of its incorporation and naturalization. This means, above all, seeing the imperial and capitalist metropolis as a specific historical form, at different stages: Paris, London, Berlin, New York. It involves looking, from time to time, from outside the metropolis: from the deprived hinterlands, where different forces are moving, and from the poor world which has always been peripheral to the metropolitan systems. This need involve no reduction of the importance of the major artistic and literary works which were shaped within metropolitan perceptions. But one level has certainly to be challenged: the metropolitan interpretation of its own processes as universals. . . .

WHEN WAS MODERNISM?

Determining the process which fixed the moment of Modernism is a matter, as so often, of identifying the machinery of selective tradition. If we are to follow the Romantics' victorious definition of the arts as outriders, heralds, and witnesses of social change, then we may ask why the extraordinary innovations in social realism, the metaphoric control and economy of seeing discovered and refined by Gogol, Flaubert or Dickens from the 1840s on, should not take precedence over the conventionally Modernist names of Proust, Kafka, or Joyce. The earlier novelists, it is widely acknowledged, make the latter work possible; without Dickens, no Joyce. But in excluding the great realists, this version of Modernism refuses to see how they devised and organized a whole vocabulary and its structure of figures of speech with which to grasp the unprecedented social forms of the industrial city. By the same token, in painting, the Impressionists in the 1860s also defined a new vision and a technique to match in their rendering of modern Parisian life, but it is of course only the Post-Impressionists and the Cubists who are situated in the tradition.

The same questions can be put to the rest of the literary canon and the answers will seem as arbitrary: the Symbolist poets of the 1880s are super-annuated by the Imagists, Surrealists, Futurists, Formalists and others from 1910 onwards. In drama, Ibsen and Strindberg are left behind, and Brecht dominates the period from 1920 to 1950. In every case in these oppositions the late-born ideology of modernism selects the later group. In doing so, it aligns the later writers and painters with Freud's discoveries and imputes to them a view of the primacy of the subconscious or unconscious as well as, in both writing and painting, a radical questioning of the processes of represen-tation. The writers are applauded for their denaturalizing of language, their break with the allegedly prior view that language is either a clear, transparent glass or a mirror, and for making abruptly apparent in the very texture of their narratives the problematic status of the author and his authority. As the author appears in the text, so does the painter in the painting. The self-reflexive text assumes the centre of the public and aesthetic stage, and in doing so declaratively repudiates the fixed forms, the settled cultural authority of the academies and their bourgeois taste, and the very necessity of market popularity (such as Dickens's or Manet's).

These are indeed the theoretic contours and specific authors of 'modern-ism', a highly selected version of the modern which then offers to appropriate the whole of modernity. We have only to review the names in the real history to see the open ideologizing which permits the selection. At the same time, there is unquestionably a series of breaks in all arts in the late nineteenth century: breaks, as we noted, with forms (the three-decker novel disappears) and with power, especially as manifested in bourgeois censorship—the artist becomes a dandy or an anticommercial radical, sometimes both.

Any explanation of these changes and their ideological consequences must start from the fact that the late nineteenth century was the occasion for the greatest changes ever seen in the media of cultural production. Photography, cinema, radio, television, reproduction and recording all make their decisive advances during the period identified as Modernist, and it is in response to these that there arise what in the first instance were formed as defensive cultural groupings, rapidly if partially becoming competitively self-promoting. The 1890s were the earliest moment of the movements, the moment at which the manifesto (in the new magazine) became the badge of self-conscious and self-advertising schools. Futurists, Imagists, Surrealists, Cubists, Vorticists, Formalists and Constructivists all variously announced their arrival with a passionate and scornful vision of the new, and as quickly became fissiparous, friendships breaking across the heresies required in order to prevent innovations becoming fixed as orthodoxies.

The movements are the products, at the first historical level, of changes in public media. These media, the technological investment which mobilized them, and the cultural forms which both directed the investment and expressed its preoccupations, arose in the new metropolitan cities, the centres of the also new imperialism, which offered themselves as transnational capitals of an art without frontiers. Paris, Vienna, Berlin, London, New York took on a new silhouette as the eponymous City of Strangers, the most appropriate locale for art made by the restlessly mobile emigré or exile, the internationally antibourgeois artist. From Apollinaire and Joyce to Beckett and Ionesco, writers were continuously moving to Paris, Vienna and Berlin, meeting there exiles from the Revolution coming the other way, bringing with them the manifestos of post-revolutionary formation.

Such endless border-crossing at a time when frontiers were starting to become much more strictly policed and when, with the First World War, the passport was instituted, worked to naturalize the thesis of the *non*-natural status of language. The experience of visual and linguistic strangeness, the broken narrative of the journey and its inevitable accompaniment of transient encounters with characters whose self-presentation was bafflingly unfamiliar, raised to the level of universal myth this intense, singular narrative of unsettlement, homelessness, solitude and impoverished independence: the lonely writer gazing down on the unknowable city from his shabby apartment. The whole commotion is finally and crucially interpreted and ratified by the City of Emigrés and Exiles itself, New York.

But this version of Modernism cannot be seen and grasped in a unified way, whatever the likenesses of its imagery. Modernism thus defined *divides* politically and simply—and not just between specific movements but even *within* them. In remaining anti-bourgeois, its representatives either choose the formerly aristocratic valuation of art as a sacred realm above money and commerce, or the revolutionary doctrines, promulgated since 1848, of art as the liberating vanguard of popular consciousness. Mayakovsky, Picasso, Silone, Brecht are only some examples of those who moved into direct support of Communism, and D'Annunzio, Marinetti, Wyndham Lewis, Ezra Pound of those who moved towards Fascism, leaving Eliot and Yeats in Britain and Ireland to make their muffled, nuanced treaty with Anglo-Catholicism and the celtic twilight.

After Modernism is canonized, however, by the post-war settlement and its accompanying, complicit academic endorsements, there is then the presumption that since Modernism is *here* in this specific phase or period, there is nothing beyond it. The marginal or rejected artists become classics of organized teaching and of travelling exhibitions in the great galleries of the metropolitan cities. 'Modernism' is confined to this highly selective field and denied to everything else in an act of pure ideology, whose first, unconscious irony is that, absurdly, it stops history dead. Modernism being the terminus, everything afterwards is counted out of development. It is *after*; stuck in the post.

The ideological victory of this selection is no doubt to be explained by the relations of production of the artists themselves in the centres of metropolitan dominance, living the experience of rapidly mobile emigrés in the migrant quarters of their cities. They were exiles one of another, at a time when this was still not the more general experience of other artists, located as we would expect them to be, at home, but without the organization and promotion of group and city—simultaneously located *and* divided. The life of the emigré was dominant among the key groups, and they could and did deal with each other. Their self-referentiality, their propinquity and mutual isolation all served to represent the artist as necessarily estranged, and to ratify as canonical the works of radical estrangement. So, to *want* to leave your settlement and settle nowhere like Lawrence or Hemingway, becomes presented, in another ideological move, as a normal condition.

What has quite rapidly happened is that Modernism quickly lost its anti-bourgeois stance, and achieved comfortable integration into the new international capitalism. Its attempt at a universal market, transfrontier and transclass, turned out to be spurious. Its forms lent themselves to cultural competition and the commercial interplay of obsolescence, with its shifts of schools, styles and fashion so essential to the market. The painfully acquired techniques of significant *dis*connection are relocated, with the help of the special insensitivity of the trained and assured technicists, as the merely technical modes of advertising and the commercial cinema. The isolated, estranged images of alienation and loss, the narrative discontinuities, have become the easy iconography of the commercials, and the lonely, bitter, sardonic and sceptical hero takes his ready-made place as star of the thriller.

These heartless formulae sharply remind us that the innovations of what is called Modernism have become the new but fixed forms of our present moment. If we are to break out of the non-historical fixity of *post*-modernism, then we must search out and counterpose an alternative tradition taken from the neglected works left in the wide margin of the century, a tradition which may address itself not to this by now exploitable because quite inhuman rewriting of the past but, for all our sakes, to a modern *future* in which community may be imagined again.

III *Englishness*

The concept of 'Englishness' has become central to a debate about national identity at least partly inspired by the developing challenge to accepted ideas about the study of English Literature. Attempts to define this concept became especially notable at the time that the present position of English studies in British culture was being established—the 1920s and 1930s. The documents gathered here illustrate both the 'construction' of a certain image of 'Englishness'—as in Neville Cardus's reminiscences about cricket, redolent of a society dominated by boys' public schools (i.e., private schools) and the associated idea of a world divided into 'gentlemen and players'; and its gradual undermining by, for example, E. M. Forster, who shows how the 'middle classes' achieved and held on to power through the schooling of young men. George Orwell, a more radical public-school product, takes the debate a stage further. Writing in time of war, he concludes that the nation does form a family, if with the wrong members in charge.

The social historian Asa Briggs offers a less personal approach, considering how attempts to differentiate the English from other nations have fared. He stresses the emergence of 'sub-cultures' within the nation. The last voice is that of Virginia Woolf: ironically, considering her background, but not considering her gender, the most radical. In the extract from Three Guineas *she challenges the whole structure of the masculine establishment which has commandeered the identity of the nation, and proposes that women should form an 'Outsiders' Society' which takes the 'whole world' as its country. What version of 'Englishness' do we start from? This question clearly connects with those raised in the 'End of Empire' section (V); as well as 'ideology' and, of course, 'gender' (sections IV, VII).*

1 *Good Days**

NEVILLE CARDUS

BATSMANSHIP OF MANNERS

In the summer of 1899 a schoolboy walked to the wicket at Lord's to begin a Lancashire innings against Middlesex; with him was Albert Ward. He was a graceful young cricketer, and a little tuft of hair stood up on the crown of

---

* From Neville Cardus, 'Good Days', 1934, reprinted *Good Days*, Rupert Hart-Davis, 1949, pp. 73–6, 89–93.

his head. His flannels seemed soft and billowy. This boy—his name R. H. Spooner—was making his first appearance in county cricket in his summer holidays, fresh from Marlborough. It would be hard to imagine a severer ordeal for anybody; a trial in the sacrosanct air of Lord's, the searching eyes of the pavilion on you, MacLaren your captain, and one of the bowlers against you Albert Trott at his best, spinning and curving and dipping the ball astonishingly.

R. H. Spooner that day made 83, an innings full of strokes that seemed to ripple over the grass, light and lovely as sunshine. Straight from the playing fields of Marlborough he came and conquered—nay, the word conquered is too hard and aggressive for Spooner; he charmed and won our heart and the hearts of all his opponents. 'It were a pleasure to bowl to Maister Spooner', said an old player to me the other day; 'his batting were as nice as he were hisself'. Yes, it was nice; it was the batsmanship of manners. Spooner told us in every one of his drives past cover that he did not come from the hinterland of Lancashire, where cobbled streets sound with the noise of clogs and industry; he played always as though on the elegant lawns of Aigburth; his cricket was 'county' in the social sense of the term. This flavour of equability took the grimness out of a Lancashire and Yorkshire match even; I once saw him score 200 against Hirst, Rhodes, and Haigh, at Bank Holiday time, and he transformed Old Trafford to Canterbury. I'll swear that on that day long ago there were tents and bunting in the breeze of Manchester while Spooner's bat flicked and flashed from morning till evening.

He was the most lyrical of cricketers, and for that reason he had no need to play a long innings to tell us his secret. The only difference between 30 by Spooner and 150 was a matter of external and unessential form or duration; the spirit moved from the very beginning. A rondo by Mozart is just as complete and true as a symphony by him. One daffodil is as precious and delectable as a hundred daffodils. And a single stroke by Spooner had likewise a quality absolute, beyond the need of mensuration or any mathematical means of valuation whatever. If you consider Spooner's average for the whole of his career it will tell you nothing of consequence about his cricket; as well count the words in a poem or the notes in an allegro.

I must suppose that he hit the ball hard, because I remember seeing fieldsmen blowing their hands after they had stopped a stroke by Spooner. And once I sat on the shilling side when Parker, of Gloucestershire, bowled his first ball in county cricket: Spooner pulled it clean over the rails, and it crashed amongst the dust and cinders like an exploding shell. Yet my impression to-day is that Spooner's cricket was all bouquet; I think of it as I think of a rose, because of the perfume, not because of the substantial stuff which went to its making. Never did I see Spooner strike an ugly position, either at the wicket or in the field, where at cover he was the picture of swift, diving elegance.

If I have called his batsmanship that of manners, I do not mean it was ever affected: every innings by Spooner was natural and modest, like the man himself. The poise was a consequence of an instinctive balance of cultured technical parts. What's bred in the bone comes out in an innings; I never saw Spooner bat without seeing, as a background for his skill and beauty, the fields of Marlborough, and all the quiet summertime amenities of school cricket. He was my favourite player when I was a boy—he and Victor Trumper. And with a boy's illogicality I at one and the same time thought him wonderful and yet always in need of my prayers. All the time I watched him—and often I played truant to do so—I said in my heart, 'Please, Lord, don't let Reggie get out; let him score a century'. Sometimes I was more moderate: 'Please, Lord, let Reggie make 95'. I called him 'Reggie' even in my petitions to Providence. Like every delightful cricketer, he seemed at any moment ready to get out; no great batsman has ever been content to keep strictly within the scope of the things that can be done safely. I remember once seeing Spooner begin an innings against Hirst. All round his legs was the notorious Hirst 'trap'—four fieldsmen holding out avaricious hands. And Hirst swerved the ball terrifically across from Spooner's off-stump. And time after time did Spooner flick the swinging ball at his wrists' end through the leg-trap—each stroke a brave and lovely butterfly going into the flame.

Yet he was a sound as well as a brilliant batsman. There is a stupid legend about the batsmen of old. Because they made runs handsomely it is thought in certain places that they were constantly thrusting out the left leg and leaving their stumps exposed to the breaking ball. Not long ago a cricketer actually said to me, 'Yes, Spooner was splendid to watch, but he couldn't abide the googly'. And I said, 'God forgive you for blasphemy'. In September 1912 Spooner made a century against South Africa, and amongst the bowlers were Pegler, Faulkner, and Schwarz. These men have never had superiors as masters of the googly; they were as clever at spinning the ball as anybody to-day. Spooner played them carefully—with his bat, not with his pads. He was superb in his back strokes; he could hit a four from a defensive position. The second line of defence—which is the pads—was known well enough to the batsmen of the Golden Age: Arthur Shrewsbury organised it scientifically. But it was a second and not a first line of defence; Spooner never put his bat ignominiously over his shoulder to any ball and stuck out his legs crudely and ungraciously. The fact that he could achieve a great innings as a boy against Albert Trott is ample retort to the absurd notion that he was ever at a loss against swerve or spin. No bowler who ever lived could give a cricket ball more than Trott's curve and break.

Spooner and MacLaren—has a county possessed two batsmen who could begin an innings with more than their appeal to the imagination? They were as the King and the Prince, or as the eagle and the flashing swallow. Spooner was one of the cricketers who, when I was very young, made me fall in love with the game; I think of his batting now, in middle age, with gratitude. The delight of it all went into my mind, I hope, to stay there, with all the delight that life has given me in various shapes, aspects, and essences. When the form has gone—for it is material and accidental, and therefore perishable—the spirit remains. And Spooner's cricket in spirit was kin with sweet music, and the wind that makes long grasses wave, and the singing of Elisabeth Schumann in Johann Strauss, and the poetry of Herrick. Why do we deny the art of a cricketer, and rank it lower than a vocalist's or a fiddler's? If anybody tells me that R. H. Spooner did not compel a pleasure as aesthetic as any compelled by the most celebrated Italian tenor that ever lived I will write him down a purist and an ass.

GOOD DAYS

JULY 1931

. . . When you have lived in a lovely place until, at the time, you were part of it, and could feel every day the fragrance of it going into the texture of your being, it is hard afterwards not to get a sort of resentment that the place still goes on and exists complete as ever, though you yourself have left it and have not seen it for years. Many a day in recent summers I have sat on a crowded county cricket ground and sent my thoughts far away to the school over the river. And I have seen in fancy the field white with boys playing cricket, hundreds of them, the bat cracking noisily—and I not there. Old William is not there any longer, either. Yet in his day he seemed as permanent at Shastbury as the ancient oak tree near the wooden pavilion. Year after year he came at the springtime and I with him. My first summer at Shastbury happened when I was young enough to retain the boy's hero-worship for great cricketers of the past. I had seen William play for his county in my schooldays, and now I was at Shastbury on a fresh May evening, eager to meet him in the flesh and next day to begin bowling with him in the nets. I remember walking up the hill in the narrow High Street (it is changed nowadays—a noisy habitation of motor-cars). And I remember going into the small house where William was, as he called it, 'lodging'. I introduced myself, and he shook hands with me while still lying on a sofa, his shirt-sleeves rolled up. I wanted him to know that I knew all about the splendour of his first-class cricket, and I spoke of a day at Brighton when he bowled Ranjitsinhji and Fry with consecutive balls on a perfect wicket. He did not remember it, not until I had prompted his memory. Then it all came back to him, and he reflected for a while and said, 'But it were a long time ago'.

When I knew William he did not often talk of his great days at the game; he even seemed to regret that he had given his life entirely to cricket. Once I was writing a letter in the sitting-room we shared, and he watched me carefully. I dashed off my note home in a few seconds. William, when he had to write a letter, gave up a whole evening to it, and took off his coat. He gazed at me as I wrote rapidly. 'By Gow', said he (avoiding what he would have called blasphemy, for he was religious in a simple old-world way), 'By Gow, if I'd 'a' been able to write like that I'd 'a' never wasted my life at a game.'

Then he spoke of the blessings of education, and asserted that his own son, thank the Lord, was doing well in the 'Co-op.', and might some day become a head cashier. Bless you, old William, wherever you may be to-day; it never occurred to you that playing for England at Lord's and Melbourne was achievement proud enough. No; he believed, at the end of his life, in 'education'. One evening, after net practice, we walked into the park of the township and listened to the band. William was moved by the 'Brightly dawns' of Sullivan. He listened intently, and at the closing cadence he said: 'By Gow, that were beautiful. I'd give all my cricket to play music like that.' It was William, as I have written before, who laid his head on his hands one evening at the end of a long afternoon of bowling, and asked, 'What have we done to-day? We've bowled and bowled and bowled—and for what good? We've prodooced nowt.'

He was one of the old school of professional cricketers; I cannot see him in a Morris-Cowley, as any day I can see many contemporary Test match players. And I cannot see him in suède shoes, or any sort of shoes. William wore enormous boots which had some sort of metal protection built into the edge of the heel. You could hear him coming up the street miles away. 'I pays a lot for my boots', he was fond of telling me, 'but they lasts!' I am glad that he loved Shastbury and knew it was a beautiful place. Often he sat with me in term-time under the big tree, at the day's end. He would smoke his pipe and talk about the time of the year and of weather-lore. 'The swallers are high to-night; it'll be fine to-morrow.' Or 'Red at night's a sailor's delight, Red at morning's a sailor's warning.' And something about the oak and the ash and a summer of 'wet and splash'. He was very fond of that one, because the rhymes brought it within his view of poetry. We would sit there on the darkening field until the last red bar in the west had gone. Then we walked home to our room, and William would have his supper, a glass of beer, a chunk of bread, and an onion. As the lamplight fell on his fine old face I used to think of all the sunshine that had burned on it in his lifetime, here and at the other end of the earth.

2 *Notes on the English Character**

E. M. FORSTER

First Note. I had better let the cat out of the bag at once and record my opinion that the character of the English is essentially middle-class. There is a sound historical reason for this, for, since the end of the eighteenth century, the middle classes have been the dominant force in our community. They gained wealth by the Industrial Revolution, political power by the Reform Bill of 1832; they are connected with the rise and organization of the British Empire; they are responsible for the literature of the nineteenth century. Solidity, caution, integrity, efficiency. Lack of imagination, hypocrisy. These qualities characterize the middle classes in every country, but in England they are national characteristics also, because only in England have the middle classes been in power for one hundred and fifty years. Napoleon, in his rude way, called us 'a nation of shopkeepers'. We prefer to call ourselves 'a great commercial nation'—it sounds more dignified—but the two phrases amount to the same. Of course there are other classes: there is an aristocracy, there are the poor. But it is on the middle classes that the eye of the critic rests —just as it rests on the poor in Russia and on the aristocracy in Japan. Russia is symbolized by the peasant or by the factory worker; Japan by the samurai; the national figure of England is Mr Bull with his top hat, his comfortable clothes, his substantial stomach, and his substantial balance at the bank. Saint George may caper on banners and in the speeches of politicians, but it is John Bull who delivers the goods. And even Saint George—if Gibbon is correct—wore a top hat once; he was an army contractor and supplied indifferent bacon. It all amounts to the same in the end.

Second Note. Just as the heart of England is the middle classes, so the heart of the middle classes is the public-school system. This extraordinary institution is local. It does not even exist all over the British Isles. It is unknown in Ireland, almost unknown in Scotland (countries excluded from my survey), and though it may inspire other great institutions—Aligarh, for example, and some of the schools in the United States—it remains unique, because it was created by the Anglo-Saxon middle classes, and can flourish only where they flourish. How perfectly it expresses their character—far better, for instance, than does the university, into which social and spiritual complexities have already entered. With its boarding-houses, its compulsory games, its system of prefects and fagging, its insistence on good form and on *esprit de corps*, it produces a type whose weight is out of all proportion to its numbers.

On leaving his school, the boy either sets to work at once—goes into the

* From E. M. Forster, *Abinger Harvest*, Edward Arnold, 1936, pp. 3–5; first publ. 1920.

army or into business, or emigrates—or else proceeds to the university, and after three or four years there enters some other profession—becomes a barrister, doctor, civil servant, schoolmaster, or journalist. (If through some mishap he does not become a manual worker or an artist.) In all these careers his education, or the absence of it, influences him. Its memories influence him also. Many men look back on their school days as the happiest of their lives. They remember with regret that golden time when life, though hard, was not yet complex; when they all worked together and played together and thought together, so far as they thought at all; when they were taught that school is the world in miniature, and believed that no one can love his country who does not love his school. And they prolong that time as best they can by joining their Old Boys' society; indeed, some of them remain Old Boys and nothing else for the rest of their lives. They attribute all good to the school. They worship it. They quote the remark that 'the battle of Waterloo was won on the playing-fields of Eton'. It is nothing to them that the remark is inapplicable historically and was never made by the Duke of Wellington, and that the Duke of Wellington was an Irishman. They go on quoting it because it expresses their sentiments; they feel that if the Duke of Wellington didn't make it he ought to have, and if he wasn't an Englishman he ought to have been. And they go forth into a world that is not entirely composed of public-school men or even of Anglo-Saxons, but of men who are as various as the sands of the sea; into a world of whose richness and subtlety they have no conception. They go forth into it with well-developed bodies, fairly developed minds, and undeveloped hearts. And it is this undeveloped heart that is largely responsible for the difficulties of Englishmen abroad. An undeveloped heart—not a cold one. The difference is important. . .

For it is not that the Englishman can't feel—it is that he is afraid to feel. He has been taught at his public school that feeling is bad form. He must not express great joy or sorrow, or even open his mouth too wide when he talks —his pipe might fall out if he did. He must bottle up his emotions, or let them out only on a very special occasion.

3 *Memorable Speech**

Of the many definitions of poetry, the simplest is still the best: 'memorable speech'. That is to say, it must move our emotions, or excite our intellect, for only that which is moving or exciting is memorable, and the stimulus is the audible spoken word and cadence, to which in all its power of suggestion and incantation we must surrender, as we do when talking to an intimate friend. We must, in fact, make exactly the opposite kind of mental effort to that we make in grasping other verbal uses, for in the case of the latter the aura of suggestion round every word through which, like the atom radiating lines of force through the whole of space and time, it becomes ultimately a sign for the sum of all possible meanings, must be rigorously suppressed and its meaning confined to a single dictionary one. For this reason the exposition of a scientific theory is easier to read than to hear. No poetry, on the other hand, which when mastered is not better heard than read is good poetry. . . .

Memorable speech then. About what? Birth, death, the Beatific Vision, the abysses of hatred and fear, the awards and miseries of desire, the unjust walking the earth and the just scratching miserably for food like hens, triumphs, earthquakes, deserts of boredom and featureless anxiety, the Golden Age promised or irrevocably past, the gratifications and terrors of childhood, the impact of nature on the adolescent, the despairs and wisdoms of the mature, the sacrificial victim, the descent into Hell, the devouring and the benign mother? Yes, all of these, but not these only. Everything that we remember no matter how trivial: the mark on the wall, the joke at luncheon, word games, these, like the dance of a stoat or the raven's gamble, are equally the subject of poetry.

We shall do poetry a great disservice if we confine it only to the major experiences of life:

> The soldier's pole is fallen,
> Boys and girls are level now with men,
> And there is nothing left remarkable
> Beneath the visiting moon...[1]

A great many people dislike the idea of poetry as they dislike over-earnest people, because they imagine it is always worrying about the eternal verities. Those, in Mr Spender's words, who try to put poetry on a pedestal only

* From W. H. Auden, 'Introduction to "The Poet's Tongue"', (reprinted in *The English Auden: Poems, Essays and Dramatic Writings* 1927–1939, ed. Edward Mendelson, Faber and Faber, 1977, pp. 327–30.

[1] Auden's remembered version of *Antony and Cleopatra*, IV, xv, 65–8. [Ed.]

succeed in putting it on the shelf. Poetry is no better and no worse than human nature; it is profound and shallow, sophisticated and naïve, dull and witty, bawdy and chaste in turn.

In spite of the spread of education and the accessibility of printed matter, there is a gap between what is commonly called 'highbrow' and 'lowbrow' taste, wider perhaps than it has ever been.

The industrial revolution broke up the agricultural communities, with their local conservative cultures, and divided the growing population into two classes: those whether employers or employees who worked and had little leisure, and a small class of shareholders who did no work, had leisure but no responsibilities or roots, and were therefore preoccupied with themselves. Literature has tended therefore to divide into two streams, one providing the first with a compensation and escape, the other the second with a religion and a drug. The Art for Art's sake of the London drawing-rooms of the '90s, and towns like Burnley and Rochdale, are complementary.

Nor has the situation been much improved by the increased leisure and educational opportunities which the population to-day as a whole possess. Were leisure all, the unemployed would have created a second Athens.

Artistic creations may be produced by individuals, and because their work is only appreciated by a few it does not necessarily follow that it is not good; but a universal art can only be the product of a community united in sympathy, sense of worth, and aspiration; and it is improbable that the artist can do his best except in such a society. . . .

The 'average' man says: 'When I get home I want to spend my time with my wife or in the nursery; I want to get out on to the links or go for a spin in the car, not to read poetry. Why should I? I'm quite happy without it.' We must be able to point out to him that whenever, for example, he makes a good joke he is creating poetry, that one of the motives behind poetry is curiosity, the wish to know what we feel and think, and how, as E. M. Forster says, can I know what I think till I see what I say, and that curiosity is the only human passion that can be indulged in for twenty-four hours a day without satiety.

The psychologist maintains that poetry is a neurotic symptom, an attempt to compensate by phantasy for a failure to meet reality. We must tell him that phantasy is only the beginning of writing; that, on the contrary, like psychology, poetry is a struggle to reconcile the unwilling subject and object; in fact, that since psychological truth depends so largely on context, poetry, the parabolic approach, is the only adequate medium for psychology.

The propagandist, whether moral or political, complains that the writer should use his powers over words to persuade people to a particular course of action, instead of fiddling while Rome burns. But poetry is not concerned with telling people what to do, but with extending our knowledge of good and evil, perhaps making the necessity for action more urgent and its nature more clear, but only leading us to the point where it is possible for us to make a rational and moral choice.

In compiling an anthology such considerations must be borne in mind. First, one must overcome the prejudice that poetry is uplift and show that poetry can appeal to every level of consciousness. We do not want to read 'great' poetry all the time, and a good anthology should contain poems for every mood. Secondly, one must disabuse people of the idea that poetry is primarily an escape from reality. We all need escape at times, just as we need food and sleep, and some escape poetry there must always be. One must not let people think either that poetry never enjoys itself, or that it ignores the grimmer aspects of existence. Lastly, one must show those who come to poetry for a message, for calendar thoughts, that they have come to the wrong door, that poetry may illuminate but it will not dictate.

4 *The Lion and the Unicorn**

GEORGE ORWELL

National characteristics are not easy to pin down, and when pinned down they often turn out to be trivialities or seem to have no connection with one another. Spaniards are cruel to animals, Italians can do nothing without making a deafening noise, the Chinese are addicted to gambling. Obviously such things don't matter in themselves. Nevertheless, nothing is causeless, and even the fact that Englishmen have bad teeth can tell one something about the realities of English life.

Here are a couple of generalisations about England that would be accepted by almost all observers. One is that the English are not gifted artistically. They are not as musical as the Germans or Italians, painting and sculpture have never flourished in England as they have in France. Another is that, as Europeans go, the English are not intellectual. They have a horror of abstract thought, they feel no need for any philosophy or systematic 'world-view'. Nor is this because they are 'practical', as they are so fond of claiming for themselves. One has only to look at their methods of town planning and water supply, their obstinate clinging to everything that is out of date and a nuisance, a spelling system that defies analysis and a system of weights and measures that is intelligible only to the compilers of arithmetic books, to see how little they care about mere efficiency. But they have a certain power of

* From George Orwell, 'The Lion and the Unicorn', written 1941, reprinted in *Collected Essays*, Secker & Warburg, 1968, vol. ii, pp. 58–68.

acting without taking thought. Their world-famed hypocrisy—their double-faced attitude towards the Empire, for instance—is bound up with this. Also, in moments of supreme crisis the whole nation can suddenly draw together and act upon a species of instinct, really a code of conduct which is understood by almost everyone, though never formulated. The phrase that Hitler coined for the Germans, 'a sleep-walking people', would have been better applied to the English. Not that there is anything to be proud of in being called a sleep-walker.

But here it is worth noting a minor English trait which is extremely well marked though not often commented on, and that is a love of flowers. This is one of the first things that one notices when one reaches England from abroad, especially if one is coming from southern Europe. Does it not contradict the English indifference to the arts? Not really, because it is found in people who have no aesthetic feelings whatever. What it does link up with, however, is another English characteristic which is so much a part of us that we barely notice it, and that is the addiction to hobbies and spare-time occupations, the *privateness* of English life. We are a nation of flower-lovers, but also a nation of stamp-collectors, pigeon-fanciers, amateur carpenters, coupon-snippers, darts-players, crossword-puzzle fans. All the culture that is most truly native centres round things which even when they are communal are not official—the pub, the football match, the back garden, the fireside and the 'nice cup of tea'. The liberty of the individual is still believed in, almost as in the nineteenth century. But this has nothing to do with economic liberty, the right to exploit others for profit. It is the liberty to have a home of your own, to do what you like in your spare time, to choose your own amusements instead of having them chosen for you from above. The most hateful of all names in an English ear is Nosey Parker. It is obvious, of course, that even this purely private liberty is a lost cause. Like all other modern peoples, the English are in process of being numbered, labelled, conscripted, 'co-ordinated'. But the pull of their impulses is in the other direction, and the kind of regimentation that can be imposed on them will be modified in consequence. No party rallies, no Youth Movements, no coloured shirts, no Jew-baiting or 'spontaneous' demonstrations. No Gestapo either, in all probability.

But in all societies the common people must live to some extent *against* the existing order. The genuinely popular culture of England is something that goes on beneath the surface, unofficially and more or less frowned on by the authorities. One thing one notices if one looks directly at the common people, especially in the big towns, is that they are not puritanical. They are inveterate gamblers, drink as much beer as their wages will permit, are devoted to bawdy jokes, and use probably the foulest language in the world. They have to satisfy these tastes in the face of astonishing, hypocritical laws (licensing laws, lottery acts, etc. etc.) which are designed to interfere with everybody but in practice allow everything to happen. Also, the common people are without definite religious belief, and have been so for centuries. The Anglican Church never had a real hold on them, it was simply a preserve of the landed gentry, and the Nonconformist sects only influenced minorities. And yet they have retained a deep tinge of Christian feeling, while almost forgetting the name of Christ. The power-worship which is the new religion of Europe, and which has infected the English intelligentsia, has never touched the common people. They have never caught up with power politics. The 'realism' which is preached in Japanese and Italian newspapers would horrify them. One can learn a good deal about the spirit of England from the comic coloured postcards that you see in the windows of cheap stationers' shops. These things are a sort of diary upon which the English people have unconsciously recorded themselves. Their old-fashioned outlook, their graded snobberies, their mixture of bawdiness and hypocrisy, their extreme gentleness, their deeply moral attitude to life, are all mirrored there.

The gentleness of the English civilisation is perhaps its most marked characteristic. You notice it the instant you set foot on English soil. It is a land where the bus conductors are good-tempered and the policemen carry no revolvers. In no country inhabited by white men is it easier to shove people off the pavement. And with this goes something that is always written off by European observers as 'decadence' or hypocrisy, the English hatred of war and militarism. It is rooted deep in history, and it is strong in the lower-middle class as well as the working class. Successive wars have shaken it but not destroyed it. Well within living memory it was common for 'the redcoats' to be booed at in the streets and for the landlords of respectable public houses to refuse to allow soldiers on the premises. In peace time, even when there are two million unemployed, it is difficult to fill the ranks of the tiny standing army, which is officered by the county gentry and a specialised stratum of the middle class, and manned by farm labourers and slum proletarians. The mass of the people are without military knowledge or tradition, and their attitude towards war is invariably defensive. No politician could rise to power by promising them conquests or military 'glory', no Hymn of Hate has ever made any appeal to them. In the last war the songs which the soldiers made up and sang of their own accord were not vengeful but humorous and mock-defeatist.[1] The only enemy they ever named was the sergeant-major.

In England all the boasting and flag-wagging, the 'Rule Britannia' stuff, is

---

[1] For example:

> I don't want to join the bloody Army,
> I don't want to go unto the war;
> I want no more to roam,
> I'd rather stay at home,
> Living on the earnings of a whore.

But it was not in that spirit that they fought.

done by small minorities. The patriotism of the common people is not vocal or even conscious. They do not retain among their historical memories the name of a single military victory. English literature, like other literatures, is full of battle-poems, but it is worth noticing that the ones that have won for themselves a kind of popularity are always a tale of disasters and retreats. There is no popular poem about Trafalgar or Waterloo, for instance. Sir John Moore's army at Corunna, fighting a desperate rearguard action before escaping overseas (just like Dunkirk!) has more appeal than a brilliant victory. The most stirring battle-poem in English is about a brigade of cavalry which charged in the wrong direction. And of the last war, the four names which have really engraved themselves on the popular memory are Mons, Ypres, Gallipoli and Passchendaele, every time a disaster. The names of the great battles that finally broke the German armies are simply unknown to the general public.

The reason why the English anti-militarism disgusts foreign observers is that it ignores the existence of the British Empire. It looks like sheer hypocrisy. After all, the English have absorbed a quarter of the earth and held on to it by means of a huge navy. How dare they then turn round and say that war is wicked?

It is quite true that the English are hypocritical about their Empire. In the working class this hypocrisy takes the form of not knowing that the Empire exists. But their dislike of standing armies is a perfect sound instinct. A navy employs comparatively few people, and it is an external weapon which cannot affect home politics directly. Military dictatorships exist everywhere, but there is no such thing as a naval dictatorship. What English people of nearly all classes loathe from the bottom of their hearts is the swaggering officer type, the jingle of spurs and the crash of boots. Decades before Hitler was ever heard of, the word 'Prussian' had much of the same significance in England as 'Nazi' has today. So deep does this feeling go that for a hundred years past the officers of the British army, in peace time, have always worn civilian clothes when off duty.

One rapid but fairly sure guide to the social atmosphere of a country is the parade-step of its army. A military parade is really a kind of ritual dance, something like a ballet, expressing a certain philosophy of life. The goose-step, for instance, is one of the most horrible sights in the world, far more terrifying than a dive-bomber. It is simply an affirmation of naked power; contained in it, quite consciously and intentionally, is the vision of a boot crashing down on a face. Its ugliness is part of its essence, for what it is saying is 'Yes, I *am* ugly, and you daren't laugh at me', like the bully who makes faces at his victim. Why is the goose-step not used in England? There are, heaven knows, plenty of army officers who would be only too glad to introduce some such thing. It is not used because the people in the street would laugh. Beyond a certain point, military display is only possible in countries where the common people dare not laugh at the army. The Italians adopted the goose-step at about the time when Italy passed definitely under German control, and, as one would expect, they do it less well than the Germans. The Vichy government, if it survives, is bound to introduce a stiffer parade-ground discipline into what is left of the French army. In the British army the drill is rigid and complicated, full of memories of the eighteenth century, but without definite swagger; the march is merely a formalised walk. It belongs to a society which is ruled by the sword, no doubt, but a sword which must never be taken out of the scabbard.

And yet the gentleness of English civilisation is mixed up with barbarities and anachronisms. Our criminal law is as out-of-date as the muskets in the Tower. Over against the Nazi Storm Trooper you have got to set that typically English figure, the hanging judge, some gouty old bully with his mind rooted in the nineteenth century, handing out savage sentences. In England people are still hanged by the neck and flogged with the cat o' nine tails. Both of these punishments are obscene as well as cruel, but there has never been any genuinely popular outcry against them. People accept them (and Dartmoor, and Borstal) almost as they accept the weather. They are part of 'the law', which is assumed to be unalterable.

Here one comes upon an all-important English trait: the respect for constitutionalism and legality, the belief in 'the law' as something above the State and above the individual, something which is cruel and stupid, of course, but at any rate *incorruptible*.

It is not that anyone imagines the law to be just. Everyone knows that there is one law for the rich and another for the poor. But no one accepts the implications of this, everyone takes it for granted that the law, such as it is, will be respected, and feels a sense of outrage when it is not. Remarks like 'They can't run me in; I haven't done anything wrong', or 'They can't do that; it's against the law', are part of the atmosphere of England. The professed enemies of society have this feeling as strongly as anyone else. One sees it in prison-books like Wilfred Macartney's *Walls Have Mouths* or Jim Phelan's *Jail Journey*, in the solemn idiocies that take place at the trials of conscientious objectors, in letters to the papers from eminent Marxist professors, pointing out that this or that is a 'miscarriage of British justice'. Everyone believes in his heart that the law can be, ought to be, and, on the whole, will be impartially administered. The totalitarian idea that there is no such thing as law, there is only power, has never taken root. Even the intelligentsia have only accepted it in theory.

An illusion can become a half-truth, a mask can alter the expression of a face. The familiar arguments to the effect that democracy is 'just the same as' or 'just as bad as' totalitarianism never take account of this fact. All such arguments boil down to saying that half a loaf is the same as no bread. In England such concepts as justice, liberty and objective truth are still believed in. They may be illusions, but they are very powerful illusions. The belief in them influences conduct, national life is different because of them. In proof of which, look about you. Where are the rubber truncheons, where is the castor oil? The sword is still in the scabbard, and while it stays there corruption cannot go beyond a certain point. The English electoral system, for instance, is an all but open fraud. In a dozen obvious ways it is gerrymandered in the interest of the moneyed class. But until some deep change has occurred in the public mind, it cannot become *completely* corrupt. You do not arrive at the polling booth to find men with revolvers telling you which way to vote, nor are the votes miscounted, nor is there any direct bribery. Even hypocrisy is a powerful safeguard. The hanging judge, that evil old man in scarlet robe and horse-hair wig, whom nothing short of dynamite will ever teach what century he is living in, but who will at any rate interpret the law according to the books and will in no circumstances take a money bribe, is one of the symbolic figures of England. He is a symbol of the strange mixture of reality and illusion, democracy and privilege, humbug and decency, the subtle network of compromises, by which the nation keeps itself in its familiar shape.

I have spoken all the while of 'the nation', 'England', 'Britain', as though 45 million souls could somehow be treated as a unit. But is not England notoriously two nations, the rich and the poor? Dare one pretend that there is anything in common between people with £100,000 a year and people with £1 a week? And even Welsh and Scottish readers are likely to have been offended because I have used the word 'England' oftener than 'Britain', as though the whole population dwelt in London and the Home Counties and neither north nor west possessed a culture of its own.

One gets a better view of this question if one considers the minor point first. It is quite true that the so-called races of Britain feel themselves to be very different from one another. A Scotsman, for instance, does not thank you if you call him an Englishman. You can see the hesitation we feel on this point by the fact that we call our islands by no less than six different names, England, Britain, Great Britain, the British Isles, the United Kingdom and, in very exalted moments, Albion. Even the differences between north and south England loom large in our own eyes. But somehow these differences fade away the moment that any two Britons are confronted by a European. It is very rare to meet a foreigner, other than an American, who can distinguish between English and Scots or even English and Irish. To a Frenchman, the Breton and the Auvergnat seem very different beings, and the accent of Marseilles is a stock joke in Paris. Yet we speak of 'France' and 'the French', recognising France as an entity, a single civilisation, which in fact it is. So also with ourselves. Looked at from the outside, even the cockney and the York-shireman have a strong family resemblance.

And even the distinction between rich and poor dwindles somewhat when one regards the nation from the outside. There is no question about the inequality of wealth in England. It is grosser than in any European country, and you have only to look down the nearest street to see it. Economically, England is certainly two nations, if not three or four. But at the same time the vast majority of the people *feel* themselves to be a single nation and are conscious of resembling one another more than they resemble foreigners. Patriotism is usually stronger than class-hatred, and always stronger than any kind of internationalism. Except for a brief moment in 1920 (the 'Hands off Russia' movement) the British working class have never thought or acted internationally. For two and a half years they watched their comrades in Spain slowly strangled, and never aided them by even a single strike.[2] But when their own country (the country of Lord Nuffield and Mr Montagu Norman) was in danger, their attitude was very different. At the moment when it seemed likely that England might be invaded, Anthony Eden appealed over the radio for Local Defence Volunteers. He got a quarter of a million men in the first twenty-four hours, and another million in the subsequent month. One has only to compare these figures with, for instance, the number of conscientious objectors to see how vast is the strength of traditional loyalties compared with new ones.

In England patriotism takes different forms in different classes, but it runs like a connecting thread through nearly all of them. Only the Europeanised intelligentsia are really immune to it. As a positive emotion it is stronger in the middle class than in the upper class—the cheap public schools, for instance, are more given to patriotic demonstrations than the expensive ones —but the number of definitely treacherous rich men, the Laval-Quisling type, is probably very small. In the working class patriotism is profound, but it is unconscious. The working man's heart does not leap when he sees a Union Jack. But the famous 'insularity' and 'xenophobia' of the English is far stronger in the working class than in the bourgeoisie. In all countries the poor are more national than the rich, but the English working class are outstand-ing in their abhorrence of foreign habits. Even when they are obliged to live abroad for years they refuse either to accustom themselves to foreign food or to learn foreign languages. Nearly every Englishman of working-class origin considers it effeminate to pronounce a foreign word correctly. During the war of 1914–18 the English working class were in contact with foreigners to an extent that is rarely possible. The sole result was that they brought back a

---

[2] It is true that they aided them to a certain extent with money. Still, the sums raised for the various aid-Spain funds would not equal five per cent of the turnover of the Football Pools during the same period.

hatred of all Europeans, except the Germans, whose courage they admired. In four years on French soil they did not even acquire a liking for wine. The insularity of the English, their refusal to take foreigners seriously, is a folly that has to be paid for very heavily from time to time. But it plays its part in the English mystique, and the intellectuals who have tried to break it down have generally done more harm than good. At bottom it is the same quality in the English character that repels the tourist and keeps out the invader.

Here one comes back to two English characteristics that I pointed out, seemingly rather at random, at the beginning of the last chapter. One is the lack of artistic ability. This is perhaps another way of saying that the English are outside the European culture. For there is one art in which they have shown plenty of talent, namely literature. But this is also the only art that cannot cross frontiers. Literature, especially poetry, and lyric poetry most of all, is a kind of family joke, with little or no value outside its own language-group. Except for Shakespeare, the best English poets are barely known in Europe, even as names. The only poets who are widely read are Byron, who is admired for the wrong reasons, and Oscar Wilde, who is pitied as a victim of English hypocrisy. And linked up with this, though not very obviously, is the lack of philosophical faculty, the absence in nearly all Englishmen of any need for an ordered system of thought or even for the use of logic.

Up to a point, the sense of national unity is a substitute for a 'world-view'. Just because patriotism is all but universal and not even the rich are uninfluenced by it, there can be moments when the whole nation suddenly swings together and does the same thing, like a herd of cattle facing a wolf. There was such a moment, unmistakably, at the time of the disaster in France. After eight months of vaguely wondering what the war was about, the people suddenly knew what they had got to do: first, to get the army away from Dunkirk, and secondly to prevent invasion. It was like the awakening of a giant. Quick! Danger! The Philistines be upon thee, Samson! And then the swift unanimous action—and then, alas, the prompt relapse into sleep. In a divided nation that would have been exactly the moment for a big peace movement to arise. But does this mean that the instinct of the English will always tell them to do the right thing? Not at all, merely that it will tell them to do the same thing. In the 1931 General Election, for instance, we all did the wrong thing in perfect unison. We were as single-minded as the Gadarene swine. But I honestly doubt whether we can say that we were shoved down the slope against our will.

It follows that British democracy is less of a fraud than it sometimes appears. A foreign observer sees only the huge inequality of wealth, the unfair electoral system, the governing-class control over the Press, the radio and education, and concludes that democracy is simply a polite name for dictatorship. But this ignores the considerable agreement that does unfortunately exist between the leaders and the led. However much one may hate to admit it, it is almost certain that between 1931 and 1940 the National Government represented the will of the mass of the people. It tolerated slums, unemployment and a cowardly foreign policy. Yes, but so did public opinion. It was a stagnant period, and its natural leaders were mediocrities.

In spite of the campaigns of a few thousand left-wingers, it is fairly certain that the bulk of the English people were behind Chamberlain's foreign policy. More, it is fairly certain that the same struggle was going on in Chamberlain's mind as in the minds of ordinary people. His opponents professed to see in him a dark and wily schemer, plotting to sell England to Hitler, but it is far likelier that he was merely a stupid old man doing his best according to his very dim lights. It is difficult otherwise to explain the contradictions of his policy, his failure to grasp any of the courses that were open to him. Like the mass of the people, he did not want to pay the price either of peace or of war. And public opinion was behind him all the while, in policies that were completely incompatible with one another. It was behind him when he went to Munich, when he tried to come to an understanding with Russia, when he gave the guarantee to Poland, when he honoured it, and when he prosecuted the war half-heartedly. Only when the results of his policy became apparent did it turn against him; which is to say that it turned against its own lethargy of the past seven years. Thereupon the people picked a leader nearer to their mood, Churchill, who was at any rate able to grasp that wars are not won without fighting. Later, perhaps, they will pick another leader who can grasp that only Socialist nations can fight effectively.

Do I mean by all this that England is a genuine democracy? No, not even a reader of the *Daily Telegraph* could quite swallow that.

England is the most class-ridden country under the sun. It is a land of snobbery and privilege, ruled largely by the old and silly. But in any calculation about it one has got to take into account its emotional unity, the tendency of nearly all its inhabitants to feel alike and act together in moments of supreme crisis. It is the only great country in Europe that is not obliged to drive hundreds of thousands of its nationals into exile or the concentration camp. At this moment, after a year of war, newspapers and pamphlets abusing the Government, praising the enemy and clamouring for surrender are being sold on the streets, almost without interference. And this is less from a respect for freedom of speech than from a simple perception that these things don't matter. It is safe to let a paper like *Peace News* be sold, because it is certain that ninety-five per cent of the population will never want to read it. The nation is bound together by an invisible chain. At any normal time the ruling class will rob, mismanage, sabotage, lead us into the muck; but let popular opinion really make itself heard, let them get a tug from below that they cannot avoid feeling, and it is difficult for them not to respond. The left-wing writers who denounce the whole of the ruling class as 'pro-Fascist' are grossly over-simplifying. Even among the inner clique of politicians who brought us to our present pass, it is doubtful whether there were any *conscious* traitors. The corruption that happens in England is seldom of that kind. Nearly always it is more in the nature of self-deception, of the right hand not knowing what the left hand doeth. And being unconscious, it is limited. One sees this at its most obvious in the English press. Is the English press honest or dishonest? At normal times, it is deeply dishonest. All the papers that matter live off their advertisements, and the advertisers exercise an indirect censorship over news. Yet I do not suppose there is one paper in England that can be straightforwardly bribed with hard cash. In the France of the Third Republic all but a very few of the newspapers could notoriously be bought over the counter like so many pounds of cheese. Public life in England has never been *openly* scandalous. It has not reached the pitch of disintegration at which humbug can be dropped.

England is not the jewelled isle of Shakespeare's much-quoted passage, nor is it the inferno depicted by Dr Goebbels. More than either it resembles a family, a rather stuffy Victorian family, with not many black sheep in it but with all its cupboards bursting with skeletons. It has rich relations who have to be kow-towed to and poor relations who are horribly sat upon, and there is a deep conspiracy of silence about the source of the family income. It is a family in which the young are generally thwarted and most of the power is in the hands of irresponsible uncles and bedridden aunts. Still, it is a family. It has its private language and its common memories, and at the approach of an enemy it closes its ranks. A family with the wrong members in control —that, perhaps, is as near as one can come to describing England in a phrase.

5 *The English: How the Nation Sees Itself**

ASA BRIGGS

'Before you can rectify the disorders of a state', wrote Voltaire, 'you must examine the character of a people'. Examining the character of the English has been a favourite occupation for foreigners, not least for Frenchmen, England's closest neighbours. One of the travellers of the 19th century, Alexis de Tocqueville, was sufficiently different from many of his fellow-countrymen to make the striking claim that so many of his 'thoughts and feelings' were

---

* From Asa Briggs, 'The English: Custom and Character', in *The English World*, ed. R. Blake, Thames & Hudson, 1982, pp. 248–9, 250–1, 255–8.

shared by the English that England had become 'a second native land of the mind' for him. Like many Englishmen, however, he was puzzled by much that he observed. 'I cannot completely understand', he noted, for example, 'how the spirit of association and the spirit of exclusion came to be so highly developed in the same people, and often to be so intimately combined. . . . What better example of association than the union of individuals who form the club? What is more exclusive than the corporate personality it represents? . . . The same applies to almost all civil and political associations.' It certainly applied, in De Tocqueville's view, to what was usually regarded as the most basic of all English institutions—the family. 'See how families divide up when the birds are able to leave the nest.'

For many foreigners and for some Englishmen, such puzzles have pointed to what seemed to be contradictions, contradictions not only of a pluralist society, with a network of voluntary associations, but of a society in depth, where the present could not—and cannot—be explained adequately in terms only of the recent past. In consequence, there has been much talk of 'cant' and 'hypocrisy', at its height when British power was also at its height in the 19th century. It was then, too, that the notion of *perfide Albion* was widely publicized. Even as far as the clubs and associations were concerned, there seemed to be oddities, if not contradictions. The *Royal* Society for the Prevention of Cruelty to Animals (1824) preceded the *National* Society for the Prevention of Cruelty to Children (1889). Inside a London club the Czech writer Karel Čapek observed in 1925 that a man from the Continent gives himself an air of importance by talking, an Englishman by holding his tongue. He also began one of the last chapters in his *Letters from England* with the remark: 'In England I should like to be a cow or a baby.'

Čapek's letters are only one example of a genre which includes books such as Misson's *Memoirs and Observations in his Travels over England* (1719) and Taine's *Notes on England* (1872). By the last quarter of the 18th century, the view—or views, for there was no unanimity of perception—across the Atlantic was as significant as the view—or views—across the Channel. One particularly percipient American observer, the novelist Henry James, studying England from near and from afar, noted how the 'tone of things' was heavier in England than in the United States: 'Manners and modes are more absolute and positive; they seem to swarm and to thicken the atmosphere about you. Morally and physically it is a denser air than ours.' By contrast, James's father was unconvinced that the English were worth much effort, let alone much subtlety. . . .

There is a second relevant genre, the very existence of which disproved the reflections of James (Senior)—anatomies of England by Englishmen themselves, few of which have been expressive of 'self-complacent quietude'. Anthony Sampson's *Anatomy of Britain* (1962), not surprisingly, was more concerned with the malaise and deeper problems of a declining industrial Britain than with its successes and aspirations but, long before Britain was industrialized, Dr John Brown's *An Estimate of the Manners and Principles of the Times* (1752) revealed the same stance—and went through even more editions. 'Honour' was being converted into 'vanity', Brown complained, and Britain was passing through an 'important and alarming crisis' from which it might not recover.

There is a third relevant genre—tours of exploration from London into the provinces which supplement and to some extent qualify the anatomies. The fascination of John Leland's *Itinerary* (1546) has been vividly appraised by A. L. Rowse in his account of 'the Elizabethan discovery of England'; and for later centuries Daniel Defoe's *A Tour through England and Wales* (1724), William Cobbett's *Rural Rides* (1830) and J. B. Priestley's *English Journey* (1934) are equally indispensable. Such books still appear regularly, the latest of them Richard West's *An English Journey* (1981). It cannot be said that any of the authors of these superior travel books are unruffled, or the kind of people who hold their tongues. West is as sure as Cobbett was that an 'old England' is disappearing visually as well as socially—and that a worse England is taking its place.

Three fundamental points that are made in all such books are: first, that despite the geographical smallness of England there is immense variety; second, that there are regional as well as local differences, not only that between north and south, but one equally old between east and west; and third, that—while finding cultural expression—these diversities are influenced by landscape, by weather and, not least, by the distribution of natural resources, including not only coal and iron, which became important to the economy even before the Industrial Revolution, but wood and stone and water. . . .

RANK, DEGREE AND DEFERENCE

. . . Already in the 1830s De Tocqueville had noted that while 'the French wish not to have superiors, the English wish to have inferiors. The Frenchman constantly raises his eyes above him with anxiety. The Englishman lowers his beneath him with satisfaction. On both sides there is pride, but it is understood in a different way.' Even after the fall of land prices and rents in the late 19th century and the great inrush of foreign corn and frozen meats, the sense of superiority associated with land did not completely wither away.

It is not only deference which has often been singled out as an English trait. Another related feature has received equal attention—the Englishman's natural sense of order. As recently as 1955, Geoffrey Gorer in his book *Exploring English Character*, describes the English people as 'among the most peaceful, gentle, courteous and orderly populations that the civilized world has ever seen'. 'Football crowds', he went on by way of illustration, 'are as orderly as church meetings.' Even if the general proposition is still held to stand, the same illustration could not be chosen today. Yet here we return to diversities of attitudes as well as of appearances. The generalization had not always stood before 1955, as Gorer recognized. The English did not enjoy their 1955 reputation in the Middle Ages, in the Tudor period or in the 17th or 18th centuries. There was little evidence of a natural sense of order in the London riots of 1736, 1768 and 1780 which gave London the reputation of being more turbulent than Paris. It seemed, indeed, to Horace Walpole in 1780, that half of London would quickly be 'reduced to ashes'. Populist Protestantism and anti-popery were battle cries then, as they were to be later. For some Englishmen, indeed, the national identity was a Protestant identity and they sought to trace it back, when they were arguing and not marching or burning, to a time long before the Protestant martyrs, to John Wycliffe and the Lollards.

The 1768 riots, however, were accompanied by different cries—those of 'Wilkes and Liberty'—providing a necessary reminder that it is misleading to focus exclusively on English 'deference' and to ignore alternative strains in English society. The age of Wycliffe was also the age of the Peasants' Revolt (1381), and if the Reformation in England produced an Erastian church, proclaiming a philosophy of order, it also produced an energetic and deliberately Nonconformist Puritan movement. The struggles of the 17th century, culminating in the Civil War and the brief Puritan Commonwealth, eventually saw the defeat of the Puritans as the controlling force of the country. Yet the conception of independence was not lost. The chapel as well as the club could unite sociability and exclusiveness, and quite different traditions of independence and community could be nurtured there from the tradition of order transmitted through the parish church. Of course, in 1768 John Wilkes was no Puritan, and the cries of liberty then had little to do with that particular tradition. Yet it was the acceptance or rejection of that tradition which did much to determine attitudes both to the American and French Revolutions. There was always a 'for' and an 'against' in England, just as apparent in 19th- and 20th-century attitudes to empire as in 18th-century attitudes to revolution. . . .

At least from the time of Edmund Burke onwards, historians of different political persuasions have shared 'Whig' perceptions, sometimes tracing back dominant themes to the continuing sense of an island inheritance, sometimes to the first 'mixing of the peoples', and sometimes—this was true long before Burke—to the special dispensation of Providence.

Old and new were thereby interrelated as well as juxtaposed or contrasted. In the process, what is specifically English was isolated in the details of landscapes as much as in the language of documents, with the ordering of different layers of history accounting for present conjunctions. 'Our liberty', wrote Dickens's contemporary T. B. Macaulay, 'is neither Greek nor Roman; but essentially English. It has a character of its own—a character which has taken a tinge from the sentiments of the chivalrous ages, and which accords with the peculiarities of our manners and our insular situation. It has a language, too, of its own, and a language singularly idiosyncratic, full of meaning to ourselves, scarcely intelligible to strangers.' In this century, Herbert Butterfield, who did more than any other historian to draw attention to Whig perceptions of continuity and change, and to their limitations, himself praised the 'Whiggism' inherent in the processes of change. 'Under the Whig system', he wrote in his *The Englishman and his History* (1944), 'reforms have been overdue on many occasions; yet by the passage of time they have been able to come by a more easy and natural route and with less accompaniment of counter-evil; and we have at least been spared that common nemesis of revolutions—the generation of irreconcilable hatreds within the State. And while conflict can be mitigated in this way, the world has had a chance to grow in reasonableness.'

There have been signs in recent years of an increasing challenge to such interpretations of history, reflecting social and cultural as well as economic and political changes of the kind that have made Gorer's 1955 exploration of English character seem out of date; and in such circumstances Voltaire's dictum has in effect been modified to read: 'Before you can rectify the character of a state, you must examine the disorders of a people.' Some recent historians have taken the fact (which so interested De Tocqueville) that the English have not experienced a revolution of the French type to be a failure, not a success, while 'the spirit of exclusion and of association' extolled by him has been felt by others to be a source of economic weakness when it has shown itself in the form of contemporary trade-unionism: so, too, has the process whereby trade unionists have in various ways been 'taken outside the law'. More recently still, the English have been accused by American historians of failing adequately to adapt themselves to industrialism, in spite, or perhaps because, of the fact that they experienced—and generated—the first Industrial Revolution.

Yet as the shapes of history have changed, our own preoccupation with it has been maintained. New generations of social historians may reject the Whig assumptions of earlier historians, but they look for continuities themselves—no longer in the higher echelons of society but now in the history of the 'common people'. As they rewrite English history as 'history from below', they may be just as concerned with traditions of revolt as with traditions of authority. They may be just as anxious to conserve the symbols of the past as other historians. Moreover, their preference for social history—as distinct from other kinds of history, particularly the diplomatic and the military—has strong 19th-century roots. . . .

In the 20th century the last of the explicitly Whig historians, G. M. Trevelyan, Macaulay's nephew, wrote a best-selling *Social History of England* (1941), which ended not with a panegyric of progress, but with a lament for what was lost. 'The modern Englishman', he concluded, 'is fed and clothed better than his ancestor, but his spiritual side, in all that connects him with the beauty of the world, is utterly starved as no people have been starved in the history of the world.' In such circumstances—and they were wartime circumstances, with England in danger—Trevelyan placed his hope less in poetry than in history: and never was the alliance between the Englishman and his history more forcefully demonstrated than in the huge sales of Trevelyan's book.

SPIRITUAL AND MATERIAL COMFORT

To what extent was the modern Englishman fed and clothed better than his ancestor, and how fair was it to describe him as spiritually starved? The second question is more easily dealt with than the first. In 1941, when Trevelyan's *Social History* appeared, print, among many other things, was rationed, and the first edition of his book had to appear in the United States. Yet in the middle of a protracted and perilous war, there was more emphasis on the 'things of the spirit' than there had been during the 1930s. Travel might be restricted—except for people serving in the Forces—but there was no shortage of entertainment, diversionary or uplifting. One new 20th-century invention, broadcasting, had been developed in Britain since 1922 with a high sense of cultural mission (too high for many listeners); while another late 19th-century invention, the cinema, was at the height of its popularity. Adult education, which had a long tradition in England going back before compulsory and institutionalized school education to the struggle of individuals 'to acquire knowledge under difficulties', was booming. There was talk of a musical renaissance comparable to that in Tudor England, and there were war artists, among them Henry Moore, England's greatest sculptor, recording impressions of wars as they had never been recorded in England before.

It is true, of course, that at the deepest level the power of religion was less strong than it had been in previous wars—the historian of religion David Edwards has called ours 'the secular century'—yet at least some Englishmen felt that they were wielding 'the sword of the spirit' and the churches and chapels were often fuller than they had been in peacetime. There was certainly ample rhetoric of the spirit in such speeches as that by General Smuts in 1942 when he claimed that glory had not departed from the land—'that inward glory, that splendour of spirit, which has shone over this land from the soul of its people, and which has been a beacon light to the oppressed and downtrodden peoples in this new martyrdom of man'. Harold Nicolson quoted these words at the end of an anthology, *England*, published in 1944.

This, too, was one of a genre. Both world wars, different though they were in their scale, their modes of warfare and their consequences, have nurtured anthologies. Perhaps the first to be published in the Second World War was *The English Vision* (1939), edited by Herbert Read, which took one of its texts from D. H. Lawrence, a more unexpected contributor than Smuts. 'I really think', Lawrence had written in a letter of 1922, 'that the most living clue of life in us Englishmen is England, and the great mistake we make is in not uniting together in the strength of this real living clue—religious in the most vital sense—uniting together in England and so carrying the vital spark through.' . . .

All attempts to 'unite together' have been in danger of foundering on the rocks of the English system of social stratification, which changed in the early 19th century from a system based on rank, order and degree to a system based on class. The system has often been commented upon by Englishmen and foreigners though, according to Priestley who has condemned it, 'only a foreigner who has spent years in this country could begin to understand what divides one accepted class from another'. In the 19th century it was often emphasized that it was an open system, quite unlike a caste system. In the 20th century it has often been said that it is giving way to a more complex and more nuanced system of status. Yet in both centuries pleas for 'one nation' suggested that there are at least two. The system is frequently accused of holding back economic growth, as much by limiting aspirations as by diversifying standards of living and life styles. At this point psychology is as relevant as economics. As Priestley once more has insisted, it is wrong to think that the system is imposed from the top: it gains its strength from what happens below. 'I can imagine twenty assorted English in a lifeboat beginning to observe, after the first few hours, their necessary class distinctions. I saw it happen among working women bombed out during the war, when almost immediately they sorted themselves out in terms of microscopic class differences invisible to me. But then it is women . . . who have the sharper eye for these distinctions.' It is therefore not strange that social stratification has always been a more carefully studied field in England than any other branch of sociology and that observation and statistical compilation have been given more attention than theory.

This was one of the points made—significantly in the broadcast Reith lectures—by G. M. Carstairs, and subsequently published in book form in 1963 under the title *This Island Now*. This series of lectures, which provided a not too distant but nonetheless necessarily distanced vantage point from our

own time, was sufficiently controversial to provoke popular attack, particularly, and perhaps characteristically, on those sections dealing with the
more open attitudes towards sexual behaviour which Carstairs discovered
among the younger generation. But it is not necessary to accept all his
conclusions to acknowledge the value of his work to historians.

The title of the lectures, drawn from W. H. Auden's 'Look, Stranger, at this
Island Now', catches many echoes. The first chapter pleads for a more
systematic study of national character, recognizing the existence of sub-
cultures, each with a way of life and a system of values which influence the
behaviour of its members. In our single island there are sub-cultures based not
on privilege but on deprivation. There are also groups under threat, like the
middle-middle-class, who 'can no longer identify each other by their clothes
or their accents; and their favourite holiday resorts have been invaded'. The
second and third chapters deal, as Gorer might have done, with early years
and adolescence and, although they touch on continuity and change, favourite themes of historians, they rely on evidence which historians do not always
use. The fourth chapter on the changing role of women deserves historical
underpinning: it concentrates rightly, given the preoccupations of 1962, on
earlier marriage, smaller families and increased expectation of life for women.
The fifth, which has a title derived not from sociology but from literature
—a poem by T. S. Eliot—is for this reason alone in keeping with a tradition:
it is in keeping with a different, if allied tradition, in that it is as much
concerned with 20th-century losses as with 20th-century gains. The last
chapter, on the changing British character (and Carstairs was writing as a
professor at Edinburgh University on the British rather than the English), is
not surprisingly both the most dated and the most controversial today. The
character has continued to change. The 1960s was an exciting decade with
few moorings. But if Carstairs were writing about the present, he might well
pick out other points. It is not likely, however, that he would abandon the
comparative dimension, which is a necessary element in all studies of different
inheritances and different responses.

6 *Woman and Nationalism**

VIRGINIA WOOLF

But this, you will say, if it means anything, can only mean that you, the
daughters of educated men, who have promised us your positive help, refuse

* From Virginia Woolf, *Three Guineas*, first publ. 1938, reprinted 1952, The Hogarth Press,
pp. 192–8.

to join our society in order that you may make another of your own. And what sort of society do you propose to found outside ours, but in co-operation with it, so that we may both work together for our common ends? That is a question which you have every right to ask, and which we must try to answer in order to justify our refusal to sign the form you send. Let us then draw rapidly in outline the kind of society which the daughters of educated men might found and join outside your society but in co-operation with its ends. In the first place, this new society, you will be relieved to learn, would have no honorary treasurer, for it would need no funds. It would have no office, no committee, no secretary; it would call no meetings; it would hold no conferences. If name it must have, it could be called the Outsiders' Society. That is not a resonant name, but it has the advantage that it squares with facts—the facts of history, of law, of biography; even, it may be, with the still hidden facts of our still unknown psychology. It would consist of educated men's daughters working in their own class—how indeed can they work in any other?[1]—and by their own methods for liberty, equality and peace. Their first duty, to which they would bind themselves not by oath, for oaths and ceremonies have no part in a society which must be anonymous and elastic before everything, would be not to fight with arms. This is easy for them to observe, for in fact, as the papers inform us, 'the Army Council have no intention of opening recruiting for any women's corps'.[2] The country ensures it. Next they would refuse in the event of war to make munitions or nurse the wounded. Since in the last war both these activities were mainly discharged by the daughters of working men, the pressure upon them here too would be slight, though probably disagreeable. On the other hand the next duty to which they would pledge themselves is one of considerable difficulty, and calls

[1]   In the nineteenth century much valuable work was done for the working class by educated men's daughters in the only way that was then open to them. But now that some of them at least have received an expensive education, it is arguable that they can work much more effectively by remaining in their own class and using the methods of that class to improve a class which stands much in need of improvement. If on the other hand the educated (as so often happens) renounce the very qualities which education should have bought—reason, tolerance, knowledge—and play at belonging to the working class and adopting its cause, they merely expose that cause to the ridicule of the educated class, and do nothing to improve their own. But the number of books written by the educated about the working class would seem to show that the glamour of the working class and the emotional relief afforded by adopting its cause, are to-day as irresistible to the middle class as the glamour of the aristocracy was twenty years ago (see *A la recherche du temps perdu*). Meanwhile it would be interesting to know what the true-born working man or woman thinks of the playboys and playgirls of the educated class who adopt the working-class cause without sacrificing middle-class capital, or sharing working-class experience. 'The average housewife', according to Mrs Murphy, Home Service Director of the British Commercial Gas Association, 'washed an acre of dirty dishes, a mile of glass and three miles of clothes and scrubbed five miles of floor yearly' (*Daily Telegraph*, September 29th, 1937). For a more detailed account of working-class life, see *Life as We Have Known It*, by Co-operative working women, edited by Margaret Llewelyn Davies. The *Life of Joseph Wright* also gives a remarkable account of working-class life at first hand and not through pro-proletarian spectacles.
[2]   'It was stated yesterday at the War Office that the Army Council have no intention of opening recruiting for any women's corps.' (*The Times*, October 22nd, 1937.) This marks a prime distinction between the sexes. Pacifism is enforced upon women. Men are still allowed liberty of choice.

not only for courage and initiative, but for the special knowledge of the educated man's daughter. It is, briefly, not to incite their brothers to fight, or to dissuade them, but to maintain an attitude of complete indifference. But the attitude expressed by the word 'indifference' is so complex and of such importance that it needs even here further definition. Indifference in the first place must be given a firm footing upon fact. As it is a fact that she cannot understand what instinct compels him, what glory, what interest, what manly satisfaction fighting provides for him—'without war there would be no outlet for the manly qualities which fighting develops'—as fighting thus is a sex characteristic which she cannot share, the counterpart some claim of the maternal instinct which he cannot share, so is it an instinct which she cannot judge. The outsider therefore must leave him free to deal with this instinct by himself, because liberty of opinion must be respected, especially when it is based upon an instinct which is as foreign to her as centuries of tradition and education can make it.[3] This is a fundamental and instinctive distinction upon which indifference may be based. But the outsider will make it her duty not merely to base her indifference upon instinct, but upon reason. When he says, as history proves that he has said, and may say again, 'I am fighting to protect our country' and thus seeks to rouse her patriotic emotion, she will ask herself, 'What does "our country" mean to me an outsider?' To decide this she will analyse the meaning of patriotism in her own case. She will inform herself of the position of her sex and her class in the past. She will inform herself of the amount of land, wealth and property in the possession of her own sex and class in the present—how much of 'England' in fact belongs to her. From the same sources she will inform herself of the legal protection which the law has given her in the past and now gives her. And if he adds that he is fighting to protect her body, she will reflect upon the degree of physical protection that she now enjoys when the words 'Air Raid Precaution' are written on blank walls. And if he says that he is fighting to protect England from foreign rule, she will reflect that for her there are no 'foreigners', since by law she becomes a foreigner if she marries a foreigner. And she will do her best to make this a fact, not by forced fraternity, but by human sympathy. All these facts will convince her reason (to put it in a nutshell) that her sex and class has very little to thank England for in the past; not much to thank England for in the present; while the security of her person in the future is highly dubious. But probably she will have imbibed, even from the governess, some romantic

---

[3] The following quotation shows, however, that if sanctioned the fighting instinct easily develops. 'The eyes deeply sunk into the sockets, the features acute, the amazon keeps herself very straight on the stirrups at the head of her squadron. . . . Five English parlementaries look at this woman with the respectful and a bit restless admiration one feels for a "fauve" of an unknown species . . .' (*The Martyrdom of Madrid*, Inedited Witnesses, by Louis Delaprée, pp. 34–5. Madrid, 1937.)

notion that Englishmen, those fathers and grandfathers whom she sees marching in the picture of history, are 'superior' to the men of other countries. This she will consider it her duty to check by comparing French historians with English; German with French; the testimony of the ruled—the Indians or the Irish, say—with the claims made by their rulers. Still some 'patriotic' emotion, some ingrained belief in the intellectual superiority of her own country over other countries may remain. Then she will compare English painting with French painting; English music with German music; English literature with Greek literature, for translations abound. When all these comparisons have been faithfully made by the use of reason, the outsider will find herself in possession of very good reasons for her indifference. She will find that she has no good reason to ask her brother to fight on her behalf to protect 'our' country. 'Our country', she will say, 'throughout the greater part of its history has treated me as a slave; it has denied me education or any share in its possessions. "Our" country still ceases to be mine if I marry a foreigner. "Our" country denies me the means of protecting myself, forces me to pay others a very large sum annually to protect me, and is so little able, even so, to protect me that Air Raid precautions are written on the wall. Therefore if you insist upon fighting to protect me, or "our" country, let it be understood, soberly and rationally between us, that you are fighting to gratify a sex instinct which I cannot share; to procure benefits which I have not shared and probably will not share; but not to gratify my instincts, or to protect either myself or my country. For,' the outsider will say, 'in fact, as a woman, I have no country. As a woman I want no country. As a woman my country is the whole world.' And if, when reason has said its say, still some obstinate emotion remains, some love of England dropped into a child's ears by the cawing of rooks in an elm tree, by the splash of waves on a beach, or by English voices murmuring nursery rhymes, this drop of pure, if irrational, emotion she will make serve her to give to England first what she desires of peace and freedom for the whole world.

Such then will be the nature of her 'indifference' and from this indifference certain actions must follow. She will bind herself to take no share in patriotic demonstrations; to assent to no form of national self-praise; to make no part of any claque or audience that encourages war; to absent herself from military displays, tournaments, tattoos, prize-givings and all such ceremonies as encourage the desire to impose 'our' civilization or 'our' dominion upon other people. The psychology of private life, moreover, warrants the belief that this use of indifference by the daughters of educated men would help materially to prevent war. For psychology would seem to show that it is far harder for human beings to take action when other people are indifferent and allow them complete freedom of action, than when their actions are made the centre of excited emotion. The small boy struts and trumpets outside the window: implore him to stop; he goes on; say nothing; he stops. That the daughters of educated men then should give their brothers neither the white feather of cowardice nor the red feather of courage, but no feather at all; that they should shut the bright eyes that rain influence, or let those eyes look elsewhere when war is discussed—that is the duty to which outsiders will train themselves in peace before the threat of death inevitably makes reason powerless.

IV Literature and Ideology

The extracts in this section raise questions about the meaning and place of 'ideology' in works of literature. How far are our responses to a 'literary text' affected by our conscious or unconscious knowledge of the author's affiliations to some explicit, implicit, or unformulated but determinable system of beliefs? How far are we aware of the extent to which our own affiliations influence our responses, our understanding? What do we mean by 'we' and 'our', or by 'author' in this context? There are no easy answers to these questions, as the extracts by Pierre Macherey and Roland Barthes prove.

But in the second extract, Terry Eagleton outlines in a clear and accessible way the Marxist theory which is basic to any understanding of how and why the question of ideology arises in the first place. He also shows its applicability to literary studies, involving a lot more than just a sociology of literature, useful as that may be. Eagleton, himself a Marxist, has been an influential but critical mediator of European structuralist and post-structuralist theory within the teaching of literature in British universities, as well as, to a lesser degree, abroad. He goes on to suggest how the work of Pierre Macherey (also represented here) takes the Marxist approach a stage further; by developing the suggestion that there is considerable variation and autonomy between and within ideological forms— themselves only in the last instance determined by the underlying realities of the economic structure of society.

As Eagleton points out, this development is derived from the views of the French Marxist Louis Althusser, none of whose writing is included here, but whose thinking has been of particular importance since the late sixties, when French left-wing intellectuals opened to question the values inherent in the traditional liberal educational system. Althusser redefined ideology as the way we live and express ourselves in our social and cultural practices, rather than the way we think. The arts enjoy a 'relative autonomy' (i.e. from economic determination), whilst at the same time the 'Ideological State Apparatuses' (ISAs) such as the family and the educational system replicate the interests of the dominant ideology. This viewpoint is developed in the joint work of Pierre Macherey and Etienne Balibar represented here.

One of the disadvantages of a post-Althusserian perspective may be the loss of attention to the writer's consciously held commitment to a pressing cause. The extract from Jean-Paul Sartre included here (see also Part One, section III) attempts to correct that imbalance.

1 *Situation of the Writer in 1947**

JEAN-PAUL SARTRE

Most of the radicals are silent. The reason is that the gap has been revealed not between the author and his public—which, after all, would be in the great literary tradition—but between the literary myth and the historical reality.

We started feeling this gap about 1930, quite a while before publishing our first books. It was about this time that most Frenchmen were stupefied on discovering their historical character. They had, of course, learned at school that man plays and wins or loses in the womb of universal history, but they did not apply it to their own case. They thought in a vague sort of way that it was all right for the dead to be historical. The striking thing about lives of the past is that they always unfold *on the eve* of the great events which exceed forecasts, disappoint expectations, upset plans, and bring new light to bear on the years that have gone by. We have here a case of trickery, a perpetual juggling, as if men were all like Charles Bovary[1] who, discovering after his wife's death the letters she had received from her lovers, all at once saw twenty years of conjugal happiness which *had already been lived* slipping away.

In the century of the aeroplane and electricity we did not think that we were exposed to these surprises. It didn't seem to us that we were *on the eve* of anything. On the contrary, we had the vague pride of feeling that it was *the day after* the last disruption of history. Even if we were at times disturbed by German rearmament, we thought that we were moving on a long, straight road and we felt certain that our lifetime would be uniquely woven of individual circumstances and marked by scientific discoveries and happy reforms.

From 1930 on, the world depression, the coming of Nazism, and the events in China opened our eyes. It seemed as if the ground were going to fall from under us, and suddenly, *for us too*, the great historical juggling began. The first years of the great world Peace suddenly had to be regarded as the years between wars. Each sign of promise which we had greeted had to be seen as a threat. Each day we had lived revealed its true face; we had abandoned ourselves to it trustingly and it was leading us to a new war with secret rapidity, with a rigour hidden beneath its nonchalant airs. And our life as an individual which had seemed to depend upon our efforts, our virtues, and our faults, on our good and bad luck, on the good and bad will of a very small number of people, seemed governed down to its minutest details by obscure

* From Jean-Paul Sartre, *What is Literature?*, transl. B. Frechtman, Methuen, 1967, pp. 156–9, 162–7; first publ. 1948, in *Les Temps modernes*.

[1] Husband of the heroine in Flaubert's *Madame Bovary* (1857). [Ed.]

and collective forces, and its most private circumstances seemed to reflect the state of the whole world. All at once we felt ourselves abruptly *situated.*

The detachment which our predecessors were so fond of practising had become impossible. . . .

History flowed in upon us; in everything we touched, in the air we breathed, in the page we read, in the one we wrote; in love itself we discovered, like a taste of history, so to speak, a bitter and ambiguous mixture of the absolute and the transitory. What need had we patiently to construct self-destructive objects since each of the moments of our life was subtly whisked away from us at the very time that we were enjoying it, since each *present* that we lived with gusto, like an absolute, was struck with a secret death, seemed to us to have its meaning outside itself, for other eyes which had not yet seen the light, and, in a way, to be *already past* in its very presence? Besides, what did surrealist destruction, which leaves everything in place, matter to us, when a destruction by sword and fire threatened everything, surrealism included? . . .

With a perverse taste for standardizing the world, they [our predecessors] amused themselves with finding the imprint of capitalism everywhere. We would have found, without any difficulty, a much more obvious uniformity —cannons everywhere. And then, whether travellers or not, in the face of the conflict which threatened our country, we had understood that we were not citizens of the world since we could not make ourselves be Swiss, Swedish, or Portuguese. The destiny of our works themselves was bound to that of a France in danger. Our elders wrote for idle souls, but for the public which we, in our turn, were going to address the holiday was over. It was composed of men of our sort who, like us, were expecting war and death. For these readers without leisure, occupied without respite with a single concern, there was only one fitting subject. It was about their war and their death that we had to write. Brutally reintegrated into history, we had no choice but to produce a literature of a historical character. . . .

Perhaps a day will come when a happy age, looking back at the past, will see in this suffering and shame one of the paths which led to peace. But we were not on the side of history already made. We were, as I have said, *situated* in such a way that every lived minute seemed to us like something irreducible. Therefore, in spite of ourselves, we came to this conclusion, which will seem shocking to lofty souls: Evil cannot be redeemed.

But, on the other hand, most of the resisters, though beaten, burned, blinded, and broken, did not speak. They broke the circle of Evil and reaffirmed the human—for themselves, for us, and for their very torturers. They did it without witness, without help, without hope, often even without faith. For them it was not a matter of believing in man but of wanting to. Everything conspired to discourage them: so many indications everywhere about them, those faces bent over them, that misery within them. Everything concurred in making them believe that they were only insects, that man is the impossible dream of spies and squealers, and that they would awaken as vermin like everybody else.

This man had to be invented with their martyrized flesh, with their hunted thoughts which were already betraying them—invented on the basis of nothing, for nothing, in absolute gratuitousness. For it is within the human that one can distinguish means and ends, values and preferences, but they were still at the creation of the world and they had only to decide in sovereign fashion whether there would be anything more than the reign of the animal within it. They remained silent and man was born of their silence. We knew that every moment of the day, in the four corners of Paris, man was a hundred times destroyed and reaffirmed.

Obsessed as we were by these tortures, a week did not go by that we did not ask ourselves: 'Suppose I were tortured, what would I do?' And this question alone carried us to the very frontiers of ourselves and of the human. We oscillated between the no-man's-land where mankind denies itself and the barren desert from which it surges and creates itself. Those who had immediately preceded us in the world, who had bequeathed us their culture, their wisdom, their customs, and their proverbs, who had built the houses that we lived in and who had marked the roads with the statues of their great men, practised modest virtues and remained in the moderate regions. Their faults never caused them to fall so low that they did not find others beneath them who were more guilty, nor did their merits cause them to rise so high that they did not see other souls above them whose merit was greater. . . . They died with a good conscience and without ever having explored their condition.

Because of this, their writers gave them a literature of *average situations*. But we could no longer find it *natural* to be men when our best friends, if they were taken, could choose only between abjection and heroism, that is, between the two extremes of the human condition, beyond which there is no longer anything. If they were cowards and traitors, all men were above them; if heroic, all men were below them. In the latter case, which was the more frequent, they no longer felt humanity as a limitless milieu. It was a thin flame within them which they alone kept alive. It kept itself going in the silence which they opposed to their executioners. About them was nothing but the great polar night of the inhuman and of unknowingness, which they did not even *see*, which they guessed in the glacial cold which pierced them.

Our fathers always had witnesses and examples available. For these tortured men, there was no longer any. It was Saint-Exupéry who said in the course of a dangerous mission, 'I am my own witness.' The same for all of them; anguish and forlornness and the sweating of blood begin for a man when he can no longer have any other witness than himself. It is then that he drains the cup, that he experiences his human condition to the bitter end. Of course, we are quite far from having all felt this anguish, but it haunted us like a threat and a promise.

Five years. We lived entranced and as we did not take our profession of writer lightly, this state of trance is still reflected in our writings. We have undertaken to create a literature of extreme situations. . . .

Forced by circumstances to discover the pressure of history, as Torricelli discovered atmospheric pressure, and tossed by the cruelty of the time into that forlornness from where we can see our condition as man to the very limit, to the absurd, to the night of unknowingness, we have a task for which we may not be strong enough (this is not the first time that an age, for want of talents, has lacked its art and its philosophy). It is to create a literature which unites and reconciles the metaphysical absolute and the relativity of the historical fact, and which I shall call, for want of a better name, the literature of great circumstances.[2] It is not a question for us of escaping into the eternal or of abdicating in the face of what the unspeakable Mr Zaslavsky calls in *Pravda* the 'historical process'.

The questions which our age puts to us and which remain *our* questions are of another order. How can one make oneself a man in, by, and for history? Is there a possible synthesis between our unique and irreducible consciousness and our relativity; that is, between a dogmatic humanism and a perspectivism? What is the relationship between morality and politics? How, considering our deeper intentions, are we to take up the objective consequences of our acts? We can rigorously attack these problems in the abstract by philosophical reflection. But if we want to live them, to support our thoughts by those fictive and concrete experiences which are what novels are, we have at our disposal the technique which I have already analysed here and whose ends are rigorously opposed to our designs. Specially perfected to relate the events of an individual life within a stable society, it enabled the novelist to record, describe, and explain the weakening, the vections, the involutions, and the slow disorganization of a particular system in the middle of a universe at rest. But from 1940 on, we found ourselves in the midst of a cyclone. If we wished to orient ourselves in it we suddenly found ourselves at grips with a problem of a higher order of complexity, exactly as a quadratic equation is more complex than a linear. It was a matter of describing the relationship of different partial systems to the total system which contains them when both are in movement and the movements condition each other reciprocally.

In the stable world of the pre-war French novel, the author, placed at a gamma point which represented absolute rest, had fixed guide-marks at his

---

[2] What are Camus, Malraux, Koestler, etc., now producing if not a literature of extreme situations?

disposal to determine the movements of his characters. But we, involved in a system in full evolution, could only know relative movements. Whereas our predecessors thought that they could keep themselves outside history and that they had soared to heights from which they could judge events as they really were, circumstances have plunged us into our time. But since we were in it, how could we see it as a whole? Since we were *situated*, the only novels we could dream of were novels of *situation*, without internal narrators or all-knowing witnesses. In short, if we wished to give an account of our age, we had to make the technique of the novel shift from Newtonian mechanics to generalized relativity; we had to people our books with minds that were half lucid and half overcast, some of which we might consider with more sympathy than others, but none of which would have a privileged point of view either upon the event or upon itself. We had to present creatures whose reality would be the tangled and contradictory tissue of each one's evaluations of all the other characters—himself included—and the evaluation by all the others of himself, and who could never decide from within whether the changes of their destinies came from their own efforts, from their own faults, or from the course of the universe.

Finally, we had to leave doubts, expectations, and the unachieved throughout our works, leaving it up to the reader to conjecture for himself by giving him the feeling, without giving him or letting him guess our feeling, that his view of the plot and the characters were merely one among many others.

But, on the other hand, as I have just pointed out, our very historicity reinstated us because from day to day we were living that absolute which it had seemed at first to take away from us. If our plans, our passions, and our acts were explicable and relative from the viewpoint of past history, they again took on in this forlornness the uncertainty and the risks of the present, their irreducible density.

We were not unaware of the fact that a time would come when historians would be able to survey from all angles this stretch of time which we lived feverishly minute by minute, when they would illuminate our past by our future and would decide upon the value of our undertakings by their outcome and upon the sincerity of our intentions by their success. But the irreversibility of our age belonged only to us. We had to save or lose ourselves gropingly in this irreversible time. These events pounced upon us like thieves and we had to do our job in the face of the incomprehensible and the untenable, to bet, to conjecture without evidence, to undertake in uncertainty and persevere without hope. Our age would be explained, but no one could keep it from having been inexplicable to us. No one could remove the bitter taste, the taste it will have had for us alone and which will disappear with us.

2 *Marxist Criticism**

Marxist criticism is not merely a 'sociology of literature', concerned with how novels get published and whether they mention the working class. Its aim is to *explain* the literary work more fully; and this means a sensitive attention to its forms, styles and meanings.[1] But it also means grasping those forms, styles and meanings as the products of a particular history. The painter Henri Matisse once remarked that all art bears the imprint of its historical epoch, but that great art is that in which this imprint is most deeply marked. Most students of literature are taught otherwise: the greatest art is that which timelessly transcends its historical conditions. Marxist criticism has much to say on this issue, but the 'historical' analysis of literature did not of course begin with Marxism. Many thinkers before Marx had tried to account for literary works in terms of the history which produced them; and one of these, the German idealist philosopher G. W. F. Hegel, had a profound influence on Marx's own aesthetic thought. The originality of Marxist criticism, then, lies not in its historical approach to literature, but in its revolutionary understanding of history itself.

BASE AND SUPERSTRUCTURE

The seeds of that revolutionary understanding are planted in a famous passage in Marx and Engels's *The German Ideology* (1845–6):

The production of ideas, concepts and consciousness is first of all directly interwoven with the material intercourse of man, the language of real life. Conceiving, thinking, the spiritual intercourse of men, appear here as the direct efflux of men's material behaviour . . . we do not proceed from what men say, imagine, conceive, nor from men as described, thought of, imagined, conceived, in order to arrive at corporeal man; rather we proceed from the really active man . . . Consciousness does not determine life: life determines consciousness.

A fuller statement of what this means can be found in the Preface to *A Contribution to the Critique of Political Economy* (1859):

In the social production of their life, men enter into definite relations that are indispensable and independent of their will, *relations of production* which correspond to a definite

---

* From Terry Eagleton, *Marxism and Literary Criticism*, Methuen, 1976, pp. 3–7, 9–19.

[1] Much non-Marxist criticism would reject a term like 'explanation', feeling that it violates the 'mystery' of literature. I use it here because I agree with Pierre Macherey, in his *Pour Une Théorie de la Production Littéraire* (Paris, 1966), that the task of the critic is not to 'interpret' but to 'explain'. For Macherey, 'interpretation' of a text means revising or correcting it in accordance with some ideal norm of what it should be; it consists, that is to say, in refusing the text *as it is*. Interpretative criticism merely 'redoubles' the text, modifying and elaborating it for easier consumption.

stage of development of their material productive *forces*. The sum total of these relations of production constitutes the economic structure of society, the real foundation, on which rises a legal and political superstructure and to which correspond definite forms of social consciousness. The mode of production of material life conditions the social, political and intellectual life process in general. It is not the consciousness of men that determines their being, but on the contrary, their social being that determines their consciousness.

The social relations between men, in other words, are bound up with the way they produce their material life. Certain 'productive forces'—say, the organisation of labour in the middle ages—involve the social relations of villein to lord we know as feudalism. At a later stage, the development of new modes of productive organisation is based on a changed set of social relations—this time between the capitalist class who owns those means of production, and the proletarian class whose labour-power the capitalist buys for profit. Taken together, these 'forces' and 'relations' of production form what Marx calls 'the economic structure of society', or what is more commonly known by Marxism as the economic 'base' or 'infrastructure'. From this economic base, in every period, emerges a 'superstructure'—certain forms of law and politics, a certain kind of state, whose essential function is to legitimate the power of the social class which owns the means of economic production. But the superstructure contains more than this: it also consists of certain 'definite forms of social consciousness' (political, religious, ethical, aesthetic and so on), which is what Marxism designates as *ideology*. The function of ideology, also, is to legitimate the power of the ruling class in society; in the last analysis, the dominant ideas of a society are the ideas of its ruling class.[2]

Art, then, is for Marxism part of the 'superstructure' of society. It is (with qualifications we shall make later) part of a society's ideology—an element in that complex structure of social perception which ensures that the situation in which one social class has power over the others is either seen by most members of the society as 'natural', or not seen at all. To understand literature, then, means understanding the total social process of which it is part. As the Russian Marxist critic Georgy Plekhanov put it: 'The social mentality of an age is conditioned by that age's social relations. This is nowhere quite as evident as in the history of art and literature.'[3] Literary works are not mysteriously inspired, or explicable simply in terms of their authors' psychology. They are forms of perception, particular ways of seeing the world; and as such they have a relation to that dominant way of seeing the world which is the 'social mentality' or ideology of an age. That ideology, in turn, is the product of the concrete social relations into which men enter at a particular

---

[2] This, inevitably, is a considerably over-simplified account. For a full analysis, see N. Poulantzas, *Political Power and Social Classes* (London, 1973).
[3] Quoted in the preface to Henri Arvon's *Marxist Aesthetics* (Cornell, 1970).

time and place; it is the way those class-relations are experienced, legitimized and perpetuated. Moreover, men are not free to choose their social relations; they are constrained into them by material necessity—by the nature and stage of development of their mode of economic production.

To understand *King Lear*, *The Dunciad* or *Ulysses* is therefore to do more than interpret their symbolism, study their literary history and add footnotes about sociological facts which enter into them. It is first of all to understand the complex, indirect relations between those works and the ideological worlds they inhabit—relations which emerge not just in 'themes' and 'preoccupations', but in style, rhythm, image, quality and . . . *form*. But we do not understand ideology either unless we grasp the part it plays in the society as a whole—how it consists of a definite, historically relative structure of perception which underpins the power of a particular social class. This is not an easy task, since an ideology is never a simple reflection of a ruling class's ideas; on the contrary, it is always a complex phenomenon, which may incorporate conflicting, even contradictory, views of the world. To understand an ideology, we must analyse the precise relations between different classes in a society; and to do that means grasping where those classes stand in relation to the mode of production. . . .

LITERATURE AND SUPERSTRUCTURE

It would be a mistake to imply that Marxist criticism moves mechanically from 'text' to 'ideology' to 'social relations' to 'productive forces'. It is concerned, rather, with the *unity* of these 'levels' of society. Literature may be part of the superstructure, but it is not merely the passive reflection of the economic base. Engels makes this clear, in a letter to Joseph Bloch in 1890:

According to the materialist conception of history, the determining element in history is *ultimately* the production and reproduction in real life. More than this neither Marx nor I have ever asserted. If therefore somebody twists this into the statement that the economic element is the *only* determining one, he transforms it into a meaningless, abstract and absurd phrase. The economic situation is the basis, but the various elements of the superstructure—political forms of the class struggle and its consequences, constitutions established by the victorious class after a successful battle, etc.—forms of law—and then even the reflexes of all these actual struggles in the brains of the combatants: political, legal, and philosophical theories, religious ideas and their further development into systems of dogma—also exercise their influence upon the course of the historical struggles and in many cases preponderate in determining their *form*.

Engels wants to deny that there is any mechanical, one-to-one correspondence between base and superstructure; elements of the superstructure constantly react back upon and influence the economic base. The materialist theory of history denies that art can *in itself* change the course of history; but it insists that art can be an active element in such change. Indeed, when Marx came to consider the relation between base and superstructure, it was art which he selected as an instance of the complexity and indirectness of that relationship:

In the case of the arts, it is well known that certain periods of their flowering are out of all proportion to the general development of society, hence also to the material foundation, the skeletal structure, as it were, of its organisation. For example, the Greeks compared to the moderns or also Shakespeare. It is even recognised that certain forms of art, e.g. the epic, can no longer be produced in their world epoch-making, classical stature as soon as the production of art, as such, begins; that is, that certain significant forms within the realm of the arts are possible only at an undeveloped stage of artistic development. If this is the case with the relation between different kinds of art within the realm of art, it is already less puzzling that it is the case in the relation of the entire realm to the general development of society. The difficulty consists only in the general formulation of these contradictions. As soon as they have been specified, they are already clarified.[4]

Marx is considering here what he calls 'the unequal relationship of the development of material production . . . to artistic production'. It does not follow that the greatest artistic achievements depend upon the highest development of the productive forces, as the example of the Greeks, who produced major art in an economically undeveloped society, clearly evidences. Certain major artistic forms like the epic are only *possible* in an undeveloped society. Why then, Marx goes on to ask, do we still respond to such forms, given our historical distance from them?:

But the difficulty lies not in understanding that the Greek arts and epic are bound up with certain forms of social development. The difficulty is that they still afford us artistic pleasure and that in a certain respect they count as a norm and as an unattainable model.

Why does Greek art still give us aesthetic pleasure? The answer which Marx goes on to provide has been universally lambasted by unsympathetic commentators as lamely inept:

A man cannot become a child again, or he becomes childish. But does he not find joy in the child's naiveté, and must he himself not strive to reproduce its truth at a higher stage? Does not the true character of each epoch come alive in the nature of its children? Why should not the historic childhood of humanity, its most beautiful unfolding, as a stage never to return, exercise an eternal charm? There are unruly children and precocious children. Many of the old peoples belong in this category. The Greeks were normal children. The charm of their art for us is not in contradiction to the undeveloped stage of society on which it grew. (It) is its result, rather, and is

----

[4] Introduction to the *Grundrisse* (Harmondsworth, 1973).

inextricably bound up, rather, with the fact that the unripe social conditions under which it arose, and could alone rise, can never return.

So our liking for Greek art is a nostalgic lapse back into childhood—a piece of unmaterialist sentimentalism which hostile critics have gladly pounced on. But the passage can only be treated thus if it is rudely ripped from the context to which it belongs—the draft manuscripts of 1857, known today as the *Grundrisse*. Once returned to that context, the meaning becomes instantly apparent. The Greeks, Marx is arguing, were able to produce major art not *in spite of* but *because of* the undeveloped state of their society. In ancient societies, which have not yet undergone the fragmenting 'division of labour' known to capitalism, the overwhelming of 'quality' by 'quantity' which results from commodity-production and the restless, continual development of the productive forces, a certain 'measure' or harmony can be achieved between man and Nature—a harmony precisely dependent upon the *limited* nature of Greek society. . . .

Two questions, then, emerge from Marx's formulations in the *Grundrisse*. The first concerns the relation between 'base' and 'superstructure'; the second concerns our own relation in the present with past art. To take the second question first: how can it be that we moderns still find aesthetic appeal in the cultural products of past, vastly different societies? In a sense, the answer Marx gives is no different from the answer to the question: How is it that we moderns still respond to the exploits of, say, Spartacus? We respond to Spartacus or Greek sculpture because our own history links us to those ancient societies; we find in them an undeveloped phase of the forces which condition us. Moreover, we find in those ancient societies a primitive image of 'measure' between man and Nature which capitalist society necessarily destroys, and which socialist society can reproduce at an incomparably higher level. We ought, in other words, to think of 'history' in wider terms than our own contemporary history. To ask how Dickens relates to history is not just to ask how he relates to Victorian England, for that society was itself the product of a long history which includes men like Shakespeare and Milton. It is a curiously narrowed view of history which defines it merely as the 'contemporary moment' and relegates all else to the 'universal'. One answer to the problem of past and present is suggested by Bertolt Brecht, who argues that 'we need to develop the historical sense . . . into a real sensual delight. When our theatres perform plays of other periods they like to anni-hilate distance, fill in the gap, gloss over the differences. But what comes then of our delight in comparisons, in distance, in dissimilarity—which is at the same time a delight in what is close and proper to ourselves?'[5]

[5]Appendices to the 'Short Organum on the Theatre', in J. Willett (ed.), *Brecht on Theatre: The Development of an Aesthetic* (London, 1964).

The other problem posed by the *Grundrisse* is the relation between base and superstructure. Marx is clear that these two aspects of society do not form a *symmetrical* relationship, dancing a harmonious minuet hand-in-hand throughout history. Each element of a society's superstructure—art, law, politics, religion—has its own tempo of development, its own internal evolution, which is not reducible to a mere expression of the class struggle or the state of the economy. Art, as Trotsky comments, has 'a very high degree of autonomy'; it is not tied in any simple one-to-one way to the mode of production. And yet Marxism claims too that, in the last analysis, art is determined by that mode of production. How are we to explain this apparent discrepancy?

Let us take a concrete literary example. A 'vulgar Marxist' case about T. S. Eliot's *The Waste Land* might be that the poem is directly determined by ideological and economic factors—by the spiritual emptiness and exhaustion of bourgeois ideology which springs from that crisis of imperialist capitalism known as the First World War. This is to explain the poem as an immediate 'reflection' of those conditions; but it clearly fails to take into account a whole series of 'levels' which 'mediate' between the text itself and capitalist economy. It says nothing, for instance, about the social situation of Eliot himself—a writer living an ambiguous relationship with English society, as an 'aristocratic' American expatriate who became a glorified City clerk and yet identified deeply with the conservative-traditionalist, rather than bourgeois-commercialist, elements of English ideology. It says nothing about that ideology's more general forms—nothing of its structure, content, internal complexity, and how all these are produced by the extremely complex class-relations of English society at the time. It is silent about the form and language of *The Waste Land*—about why Eliot, despite his extreme political conservatism, was an *avant-garde* poet who selected certain 'progressive' experimental techniques from the history of literary forms available to him, and on what ideological basis he did this. We learn nothing from this approach about the social conditions which gave rise at the time to certain forms of 'spirituality', part-Christian, part-Buddhist, which the poem draws on; or of what role a certain kind of bourgeois anthropology (Frazer) and bourgeois philosophy (F. H. Bradley's idealism) used by the poem fulfilled in the ideological formation of the period. We are unilluminated about Eliot's social position as an artist, part of a self-consciously erudite, experimental élite with particular modes of publication (the small press, the little magazine) at their disposal; or about the kind of audience which that implied, and its effect on the poem's styles and devices. We remain ignorant about the relation between the poem and the aesthetic theories associated with it—of what role that aesthetic plays in the ideology of the time, and how it shapes the construction of the poem itself.

Any complete understanding of *The Waste Land* would need to take these (and other) factors into account. It is not a matter of *reducing* the poem to the state of contemporary capitalism; but neither is it a matter of introducing so many judicious complications that anything as crude as capitalism may to all intents and purposes be forgotten. On the contrary: all of the elements I have enumerated (the author's class-position, ideological forms and their relation to literary forms, 'spirituality' and philosophy, techniques of literary production, aesthetic theory) are directly relevant to the base/superstructure model. What Marxist criticism looks for is the unique *conjuncture* of these elements which we know as *The Waste Land*.[6] No one of these elements can be conflated with another: each has its own relative independence. *The Waste Land* can indeed be explained as a poem which springs from a crisis of bourgeois ideology, but it has no simple correspondence with that crisis or with the political and economic conditions which produced it. (As a poem, it does not of course *know itself* as a product of a particular ideological crisis, for if it did it would cease to exist. It needs to translate that crisis into 'universal' terms —to grasp it as part of an unchanging human condition, shared alike by ancient Egyptians and modern man.) *The Waste Land's* relation to the real history of its time, then, is highly *mediated*; and in this it is like all works of art.

LITERATURE AND IDEOLOGY

Frederick Engels remarks in *Ludwig Feuerbach and the End of Classical German Philosophy* (1888) that art is far richer and more 'opaque' than political and economic theory because it is less purely ideological. It is important here to grasp the precise meaning for Marxism of 'ideology'. Ideology is not in the first place a set of doctrines; it signifies the way men live out their roles in class-society, the values, ideas and images which tie them to their social functions and so prevent them from a true knowledge of society as a whole. In this sense *The Waste Land* is ideological: it shows a man making sense of his experience in ways that prohibit a true understanding of his society, ways that are consequently false. All art springs from an ideological conception of the world; there is no such thing, Plekhanov comments, as a work of art entirely devoid of ideological content. But Engels' remark suggests that art has a more complex relationship to ideology than law and political theory, which rather more transparently embody the interests of a ruling class. The question, then, is what relationship art has to ideology.

[6] To put the issue in more complex theoretical terms: the influence of the economic ('base' on *The Waste Land* is evident not in a direct way, but in the fact that it is the economic base which in the last instance determines the state of development of each element of the superstructure (religious, philosophical and so on) which went into its making, and moreover determines the structural interrelations between those elements, of which the poem is a particular conjuncture.

This is not an easy question to answer. Two extreme, opposite positions are possible here. One is that literature is *nothing but* ideology in a certain artistic form—that works of literature are just expressions of the ideologies of their time. They are prisoners of 'false consciousness', unable to reach beyond it to arrive at the truth. It is a position characteristic of much 'vulgar Marxist' criticism, which tends to see literary works merely as reflections of dominant ideologies. As such, it is unable to explain, for one thing, why so much literature actually *challenges* the ideological assumptions of its time. The opposite case seizes on the fact that so much literature challenges the ideology it confronts, and makes this part of the definition of literary art itself. Authentic art, as Ernst Fischer argues in his significantly entitled *Art Against Ideology* (1969), always transcends the ideological limits of its time, yielding us insight into the realities which ideology hides from view.

Both of these cases seem to me too simple. A more subtle (although still incomplete) account of the relationship between literature and ideology is provided by the French Marxist theorist Louis Althusser.[7] Althusser argues that art cannot be reduced to ideology: it has, rather, a particular *relationship* to it. Ideology signifies the imaginary ways in which men experience the real world, which is, of course, the kind of experience literature gives us too— what it feels like to live in particular conditions, rather than a conceptual analysis of those conditions. However, art does more than just passively reflect that experience. It is held within ideology, but also manages to distance itself from it, to the point where it permits us to 'feel' and 'perceive' the ideology from which it springs. In doing this, art does not enable us to *know* the truth which ideology conceals, since for Althusser 'knowledge' in the strict sense means *scientific* knowledge—the kind of knowledge of, say, capitalism which Marx's *Capital* rather than Dickens's *Hard Times* allows us. The difference between science and art is not that they deal with different objects, but that they deal with the same objects in different ways. Science gives us conceptual knowledge of a situation; art gives us the experience of that situation, which is equivalent to ideology. But by doing this, it allows us to 'see' the nature of that ideology, and thus begins to move us towards that full understanding of ideology which is scientific knowledge.

How literature can do this is more fully developed by one of Althusser's colleagues, Pierre Macherey. In his *Pour Une Théorie de la Production Littéraire* (1966), Macherey distinguishes between what he terms 'illusion' (meaning, essentially, ideology), and 'fiction'. Illusion—the ordinary ideological experience of men—is the material on which the writer goes to work; but in working on it he transforms it into something different, lends it a shape and structure. It is by giving ideology a determinate form, fixing it within certain

[7] In his 'Letter on Art in reply to André Daspre', in *Lenin and Philosophy* (London, 1971).

fictional limits, that art is able to distance itself from it, thus revealing to us the limits of that ideology. In doing this, Macherey claims, art contributes to our deliverance from the ideological illusion.

I find the comments of both Althusser and Macherey at crucial points ambiguous and obscure; but the relation they propose between literature and ideology is nonetheless deeply suggestive. Ideology, for both critics, is more than an amorphous body of free-floating images and ideas; in any society it has a certain structural coherence. Because it possesses such relative coherence, it can be the object of scientific analysis; and since literary texts 'belong' to ideology, they too can be the object of such scientific analysis. A scientific criticism would seek to explain the literary work in terms of the ideological structure of which it is part, yet which it transforms in its art: it would search out the principle which both ties the work to ideology and distances it from it. The finest Marxist criticism has indeed done precisely that; Macherey's starting-point is Lenin's brilliant analyses of Tolstoy. To do this, however, means grasping the literary work as a *formal* structure; and it is to this question that we can now turn.

3 *The Text Says What it Does Not Say**

PIERRE MACHEREY

For there to be a critical discourse which is more than a superficial and futile *reprise* of the work, the speech stored in the book must be incomplete; because it has not said everything, there remains the possibility of saying something else, *after another fashion*. The recognition of the area of shadow in or around the work is the initial moment of criticism. But we must examine the nature of this shadow: does it denote a true absence, or is it the extension of a half-presence? This can be reformulated in terms of a previous question: Will it be the pillar of an explanation or the pretext for an interpretation?

Initially, we will be inclined to say that criticism, in relation to its object, is its *explication*. What, then, is involved in making-explicit? Explicit is to implicit as explication is to implication: these oppositions derive from the distinction between the manifest and the latent, the discovered and the concealed. That which is formally accounted for, expressed, and even concluded, is explicit: the 'explicit' at the end of a book echoes the 'incipit' at the beginning, and indicates that 'all is (has been) said'. To explicate comes from

* From Pierre Macherey, *A Theory of Literary Production*, transl. G. Wall, Routledge & Kegan Paul, 1978, chs. 14–16, pp. 82–93; first publ. 1966.

explicare: to display and unfold. 'Spread eagle', a heraldic term: one with wings outstretched. And thus the critic, opening the book—whether he intends to find buried treasure there, or whether he wants to see it flying with its own wings—means to give it a different status, or even a different appearance. It might be said that the aim of criticism is to *speak the truth*, a truth not unrelated to the book, but not as the content of its expression. In the book, then, not everything is said, and for everything to be said we must await the critical 'explicit', which may actually be interminable. Nevertheless, although the critical discourse is not spoken by the book, it is in some way the property of the book, constantly alluded to, though never announced openly. What is this silence—an accidental hesitation, or a statutory necessity? Whence the problem: are there books which say what they mean, without being critical books, that is to say, without *depending directly* on other books?

Here we recognise the classic problem of the interpretation of latent meaning. But, in this new instance, the problem tends to take a new form: in fact, the language of the book claims to be a language complete in itself, the source and measure of all 'diction'. The conclusion is inscribed even in its initial moments. Unwinding *within a closed circle*, this language reveals only . . . itself; it has only its *own* content and its *own* limits, and the 'explicit' is imprinted on each of these terms. Yet it is not perfect: under close scrutiny the speech inscribed by the book appears interminable; but it takes this absence of a conclusion as its ending. In the space in which the work unfolds, everything is to be said, and is therefore never said, but this does not suffer being altered by any other discourse, enclosed as it is within the definitive limits which constitute its imperfection. This seems to be the origin of criticism's inability to add anything to the discourse of the work: at most, it might extend the work—either in a reduction or in a pursuit of its discourse.

Yet it remains obvious that although the work is self-sufficient it does not contain or engender its own theory; it does not *know* itself. When the critic speaks he is not repeating, reproducing or remaking it; neither is he illuminating its dark corners, filling its margins with annotation, specifying that which was never specific. When the critical discourse begins from the hypothesis that the work speaks falteringly, it is not with the aim of *completing* it, reducing its deficiencies, as though the book were too small for the space it occupied. We have seen that a knowledge of the work is not elaborated within the work, but supposes a distance between knowledge and its object; to know what the writer is saying, it is not enough to *let him speak*, for his speech is hollow and can never be completed at its own level. Theoretical inquiry rejects the notion of the *space* or *site* of the work. Critical discourse does not attempt to complete the book, for theory begins from that incompleteness which is so radical that it cannot be located.

Thus, the silence of the book is not a lack to be remedied, an inadequacy to be made up for. It is not a temporary silence that could be finally abolished. We must distinguish the necessity of this silence. For example, it can be shown that it is the juxtaposition and conflict of several meanings which produces the radical otherness which shapes the work: this conflict is not resolved or absorbed, but simply *displayed*.

Thus the work cannot speak of the more or less complex opposition which structures it; though it is its expression and embodiment. In its every particle, the work *manifests*, uncovers, what it cannot say. This silence gives it life.

THE SPOKEN AND THE UNSPOKEN

The speech of the book comes from a certain silence, a matter which it endows with form, a ground on which it traces a figure. Thus, the book is not self-sufficient; it is necessarily accompanied by a *certain absence*, without which it would not exist. A knowledge of the book must include a consideration of this absence.

This is why it seems useful and legitimate to ask of every production what it tacitly implies, what it does not say. Either all around or in its wake the explicit requires the implicit: for in order to say anything, there are other things *which must not be said*. Freud relegated this *absence of certain words* to a new place which he was the first to explore, and which he paradoxically *named*: the unconscious. To reach utterance, all speech envelops itself in the unspoken. We must ask why it does not speak of this interdict: can it be identified before one might wish to acknowledge it? There is not even the slightest hint of the absence of what it does not, perhaps cannot, say: the disavowal (*dénégation*) extends even to the act that banished the forbidden term; its absence is unacknowledged.

This moment of absence founds the speech of the work. Silences shape all speech. Banality?

Can we say that this silence is hidden? What is it? A condition of existence —point of departure, methodical beginning—essential foundation—ideal culmination—absolute origin which lends meaning to the endeavour? Means or form of connection?

Can we make this silence speak? What is the unspoken saying? What does it mean? To what extent is dissimulation a way of speaking? Can something that has hidden *itself* be recalled to our presence? Silence as the source of expression. Is what I am really saying what I am not saying? Hence the main risk run by those who would say everything. After all, perhaps the work is not hiding what it does not say; this is simply *missing*.

Yet the unspoken has many other resources: it assigns speech to its exact position, designating its domain. By speech, silence becomes the centre and principle of expression, its vanishing point. Speech eventually has nothing more to tell us: we investigate the silence, for it is the silence that is doing the speaking.

Silence reveals speech—unless it is speech that reveals the silence.

These two methods of explanation by recourse to the latent or concealed are not equivalent: it is the second which allows least value to the latent, since there appears an absence of speech through the absent speech, that is to say, a certain presence which it is enough to extricate. There is agreement to relate speech to its contrary, figure and ground. But there is a reluctance to leave these terms in equilibrium, an urge to resolve them; figure or ground? Here, once again, we encounter all the ambiguities of the notions of origin and creation. The unacknowledged coexistence of the visible and the hidden: the visible is merely the hidden in a different guise. The problem is merely to *pass across* from the one to the other.

The first image is the more profound, in so far as it enables us to recuperate the form of the second without becoming trapped in a mechanical problematic of transition: in being a necessary medium of expression, this ground of silence does not lose its significance. It is not the sole meaning, but that which endows meaning with a meaning: it is this silence which tells us—not just anything, since it exists to say nothing—which informs us of the precise conditions for the appearance of an utterance, and thus its limits, giving its real significance, without, for all that, speaking in its place. The latent is an intermediate means: this does not amount to pushing it into the background; it simply means that the latent is not another meaning which ultimately and miraculously *dispels* the first (manifest) meaning. Thus, we can see that meaning is in the *relation* between the implicit and the explicit, not on one or the other side of that fence: for in the latter case, we should be obliged to choose, in other words, as ever, translation or commentary.

What is important in the work is what it does not say. This is not the same as the careless notation 'what it refuses to say', although that would in itself be interesting: a method might be built on it, with the task of *measuring silences*, whether acknowledged or unacknowledged. But rather than this, what the work *cannot say* is important, because there the elaboration of the utterance is acted out, in a sort of journey to silence.

The basic issue, then, is to know whether we can examine that absence of speech which is the prior condition of all speech.

Insidious Questions: When we are confronted with any manifestation which someone has permitted us to see, we may ask: what is it meant to conceal? What is it meant to draw our attention from? What prejudice does it seek to raise? and again, how far does the subtlety of the dissimulation go? and in what respect is the man mistaken? (*The Dawn of Day*, section 523)

For Nietzsche, these are insidious questions, *Hinterfrage*, questions which come from behind, held in reserve, lying in wait, snares.

'It might be asked': thus Nietzsche inquires, and even before showing how to put questions, he points out the necessity of *asking* questions; for there are several. The object or target of these questions is 'all that a man allows to appear'. Everything: that is to say that the Nietzschean interrogation—which is the precise opposite of an examination, since, as we shall see, it reaches the point of calling itself into question—is of such theoretical generality that we may wonder if it is legitimate to apply it to the specific domain of literary production. What in fact 'becomes visible' is the work, all the works. We shall try to apply this general proposition to a specific domain.

'All that a man allows to appear': obviously the German words say more than the English. *Lassen*: this is both to do, to allow, and to oblige. This word, better than any other, designates the act of literary production. It reveals it —on condition that we do not search there for the shapes of some evocative magic: inspiration, visitation or creation. Production: to show and to reveal. The question 'What does he mean?' proves that it is not a matter of dispossession. Also 'to reveal' is an affirmation rather than a decision: the expression of an active force, which yet does not exclude a certain autonomous actualisation of the visible.

Interrogation penetrates certain actions: 'hiding', 'diverting attention', and, further on, 'cheating'. Obviously, linking all these, there is a single impulse: 'hiding' is to keep from sight; 'diverting attention' is to show without being seen, to prevent what is visible from being seen; which also expresses the image of 'dissimulation': to dissimulate requires action. Therefore everything happens as though the accent had been shifted: the work is revealed to itself and to others on two different levels: it makes visible, and it makes invisible. Not because something has to be hidden in order to show something else; but because attention is diverted from the very thing which is shown. This is the superposition of utterance and statement (*du parler et du dire*): if the author does not always say what he states, he does not necessarily state what he says.

In the text from Nietzsche, then, it is a question of a prejudice, a mystification, a deception. Not by virtue of this or that particular word, but because of speech itself, all speech. A prejudice is that which is not judged in language but before it, but which is nevertheless offered as a judgment. Prejudice, the pseudo-judgment, is the utterance which remains imperceptibly beyond language.

Yet this proposition has two meanings: speech evokes a prejudice as a judgment; but equally, by the *fact of evocation*, it holds it up as a prejudice. It creates an allegory of judgment. And speech exists because it wishes for this

allegory whose appearance it prepares for. This is the portion of the visible and
the invisible, the revealed and the concealed, of language and silence.

Then we arrive at the meaning of the last questions. '*And yet*': we move to
a new level of the systematic order, in what is almost an inversion. It could
be said that there is a question directed at the first questions. This question
which completes the construction of the trap challenges the first question,
setting off the structure of the work and the structure of the criticism of it.

$$\left.\begin{array}{l} \text{utterance} \\[6pt] \text{question 1} \end{array}\right\} \text{question 2}$$

We can then ask to what extent the first question was based on an error:
because this dissimulation applies to everything it must not be thought that
it is total and unlimited. Since it is a relative silence which depends on an even
more silent margin, it is impossible to dissemble the truth of language.

Naturally it is incorrect to see in this equivocation of speech its division into
the spoken and the unspoken; a division which is only possible because it
makes speech depend on a fundamental veracity, a plenitude of expression,
a reflection of the Hegelian dialectic—that dialectic which Nietzsche (like
Marx, an enemy of idols) could only contemplate in its inverted form. . . .

The ordinary critic (the one who stops at the first question) and the author
are equally remote from a true appreciation of the work: but there is another
kind of critic who asks the second question.

The labyrinth of the two questions—a labyrinth in reverse, because it leads
to a way out—endlessly proposes a choice between a false and a true subtlety:
the one views the author from the critic's point of view, as a critic; the other
only judges him when it has taken up position in the expressive veracity of
language, and his language. Torn from the false limits of its empirical
presence, the work then begins to acquire a significance.

THE TWO QUESTIONS

Thus the critical task is not simple: it necessarily implies the superposition of
two questions. To know the work, we must move outside it. Then, in the
second moment, we question the work in its alleged plenitude; not from a
different point of view, a different side—by translating it into a different
language, or by applying a different standard—but not entirely from within,
from what it says and asserts that it says. Conjecturally, the work has its
margins, an area of incompleteness from which we can observe its birth and
its production.

The critical problem will be in the conjunction of the two questions; not in
a choice between them, but in the point from which they appear to become

differentiated. The complexity of the critical problem will be the articulation between the two questions. To grasp this *articulation* is to accept a discontinuity, to establish a discontinuity: the questions are not spontaneously given in their specificity. Initially, the questions must be asked—asked simultaneously, in a way that amounts to allowing them an equal status.

The recognition of this simultaneity, which precludes any notion of priority, is fundamental because it makes possible—from the beginning—an exorcism of the ghosts of aesthetic legality: by the fact that the question which is supposed to inhabit the mind of the writer is not simple, but divided by its reference to another question, the problem to be explicitly resolved will not be merely the realisation of a project according to the rules of validity (beauty) and conformity (fidelity). Even the question of the formal limits imposed on expression will no longer form part of the problem: it will be completely eliminated as a distinct element of the problematic. In so far as a conscious intention to realise a project of writing begins inevitably by taking the form of an ideological imperative—something *to say* (not the acceptance of rules), in other words something that must not be said—it will have to adopt the conditions of the possibility of such an undertaking: the implements, the actual means of this practice; and the rules will play their part in so far as they are *directly* useful.

The real problem is not that of being restricted by rules—or the absence of such a restriction—but the necessity of inventing forms of expression, or merely finding them: not ideal forms, or forms derived from a principle which transcends the enterprise itself, but forms which can be used immediately as the means of expression for a determinate content; likewise, the question of the value of these forms cannot reach beyond this immediate issue. However, these forms do not exist just in the mode of an immediate presence: they can survive beyond the moment of their usefulness, and it will be seen that this poses a very serious problem; they can be revived, in which case they will have undergone a slight but crucial change in value which must be determined. In fact, these forms do not appear instantaneously but at the end of a long history—a history of the elaboration of ideological themes. The history of forms—which will subsequently be designated as *themes*, in the strict sense of the word—corresponds to the history of ideological themes; indeed, they are exactly parallel, as can easily be demonstrated with the history of any idea: that of Robinson Crusoe, for example. The form takes shape or changes in response to new imperatives of the idea: but it is also capable of independent transformations, or of an inertia, which bends the path of ideological history. But, whatever the mode of its realisation, there is always a correspondence, which could thus be considered automatic: refuting the conception of these two histories as the expression of a superficial question—which is not self-sufficient, because it is based on a parallelism—the question of the work. The level of interpretation determined by this parallelism will only acquire meaning from the elucidation of another level, with which it will have a determining relationship: the question of this question.

The investigation into the conditions of the possibility of the work is accomplished in the answer to an explicit question, but it will not be able to seek the conditions of those conditions, nor will it be able to see that this answer constitutes a question. Nevertheless, the second question will necessarily be posed within the first question, or even through it. It is this second question which, for us, defines the space of history: it reveals the work in so far as it entertains a specific but undisguised (which does not mean innocent) relation with history. We must show, through the study of an effort of expression, how it is possible to render visible the conditions of this effort —conditions of which it has no awareness, though this does not mean that it does not apprehend them: the work encounters the question of questions as an obstacle; it is only aware of the conditions which it adopts or utilises. We could account for this latent knowledge (which necessarily exists, since without it the work would be accomplished no further than if the explicit conditions were not realised) by recourse to *the unconscious of the work* (not of the author). But this unconscious does not perform as an understudy—on the contrary, it arises in the interior of the labour itself: there it is at work —nor as an extension of the explicit purpose, since it derives from a completely different principle. Neither is it a question of another consciousness: the consciousness of another or others, or the other consciousness of the same thing. There is no understudy creative-unconscious to the creative pseudo-consciousness: if there is an unconscious it cannot be creative, in so far as it precedes all production as its condition. It is a question of something other than consciousness: what we are seeking is analogous to that relationship which Marx acknowledges when he insists on seeing material relations as being derived from the social infrastructure behind all ideological phenomena, not in order to explain these phenomena as emanations from the infrastructure, which would amount to saying that the ideological is the economic in another form: whence the possibility of reducing the ideological to the economic.

4 *On Literature as an Ideological Form**

ETIENNE BALIBAR AND PIERRE MACHEREY

It is important to 'locate' the production of literary effects historically as part of the ensemble of social practices. For this to be seen dialectically rather than mechanically, it is important to understand that the relationship of 'history' to 'literature' is not like the relationship or 'correspondence' of two 'branches', but concerns the developing forms of an internal contradiction. Literature and history are not each set up externally to each other (not even as the history *of* literature versus social and political history), but are in an intricate and connected relationship, the historical conditions of existence of anything like a literature. Very generally, this internal relationship is what constitutes the definition of literature as an ideological form.

But this definition is significant only in so far as its implications are then developed. Ideological forms, to be sure, are not straightforward systems of 'ideas' and 'discourses', but are manifested through the workings and history of determinate practices in determinate social relations, what Althusser calls the Ideological State Apparatuses (ISA). The objectivity of literary production therefore is inseparable from given social practices in a given ISA. More precisely, we shall see that it is inseparable from a given linguistic practice (there is a 'French' literature because there is a linguistic practice 'French', i.e. a contradictory ensemble making a national tongue), in itself inseparable from an academic or schooling practice which defines both the conditions for the consumption of literature and the very conditions of its production also. By connecting the objective existence of literature to this ensemble of practices, one can define the material anchoring points which make literature an historic and social reality.

First, then, literature is historically constituted in the bourgeois epoch as an ensemble of language—or rather of specific linguistic practices—inserted in a general schooling process so as to provide appropriate fictional effects, thereby reproducing bourgeois ideology as the dominant ideology. Literature submits to a threefold determination: 'linguistic', 'pedagogic', and 'fictive' (*imaginaire*) (we must return to this point, for it involves the question of a recourse to psychoanalysis for an explanation of literary effects). There is a linguistic determinance because the work of literary production depends on the existence of a common language codifying linguistic exchange, both for its material and for its aims—in so much as literature contributes directly to the maintenance of a 'common language'. That it has this starting point is proved

* From Etienne Balibar and Pierre Macherey, 'On Literature as an Ideological Form', transl. Ian MacLeod, John Whitehead, and Ann Wordsworth, in *Untying the Text: A Post-Structuralist Reader*, ed. Robert Young, Routledge & Kegan Paul, 1981, pp. 83–7, 94–5. First publ. 1978.

by the fact that divergences from the common language are not arbitrary but determined. . . . the common language, i.e. the national language, is bound to the political form of 'bourgeois democracy' and is the historical outcome of particular class struggles. Like bourgeois right, its parallel, the common national language is needed to unify a new class domination, thereby universalising it and providing it with progressive forms throughout its epoch. It refers therefore to a social contradiction, perpetually reproduced via the process which surmounts it. What is the basis of this contradiction?

It is the effect of the historic conditions under which the bourgeois class established its political, economic and ideological dominance. To achieve hegemony, it had not only to transform the base, the relations of production, but also radically to transform the superstructure, the ideological formations. This transformation could be called the bourgeois 'cultural revolution' since it involves not only the formation of a new ideology, but its realisation as the dominant ideology, through new ISA and the remoulding of the relationships between the different ISA. This revolutionary transformation, which took more than a century but which was preparing itself for far longer, is characterised by making the school apparatus the means of forcing submission to the dominant ideology—individual submission, but also, and more importantly, the submission of the very ideology of the dominated classes. Therefore in the last analysis, all the ideological contradictions rest on the contradictions of the school apparatus, and become contradictions subordinated to the form of schooling, within the form of schooling itself.

We are beginning to work out the form taken by social contradictions in the schooling apparatus. It can only establish itself through the formal unity of a unique and unifying educational system, the product of this same unity, which is itself formed from the co-existence of two systems or contradictory networks: those which, by following the institutional division of 'levels of teaching' which in France has long served to materialise this contradiction, we could call the apparatus of 'basic education' (*primaire-professionnel*) and that of 'advanced education' (*secondaire-supérieur*).

This division in schooling, which reproduces the social division of a society based on the sale and purchase of individual labour-power, while ensuring the dominance of bourgeois ideology through asserting a specifically national unity, is primarily and throughout based on a linguistic division. Let us be clear: there as well, the unifying form is the essential means of the division and of the contradiction. The linguistic division inherent in schooling is not like the division between different 'languages' observable in certain pre-capitalist social formations—those languages being a 'language of the common people' (dialect, patois or argot), and a 'language of the bourgeoisie' —on the contrary, the division presupposes a common language, and is the contradiction between different practices of the same language. Specifically, it is in and through the educational system that the contradiction is instituted —through the contradiction between the basic language (*français élémentaire*), as taught at primary school, and the literary language (*français littéraire*) reserved for the advanced level of teaching. This is the basis of the contradiction in schooling techniques, particularly between the basic exercise of 'rédaction-narration', a mere training in 'correct' usage and the reporting of 'reality', and the advanced exercise of comprehension, the 'dissertation–explication de textes', so-called 'creative' work which presupposes the incorporation and imitation of literary material. Hence the contradictions in schooling practice, and in ideological practice and in social practice. What thus appears as the basis of literary production is an unequal and contradictory relation to the same ideology, the dominant one. But this contradiction would not exist if the dominant ideology did not have to struggle all the time for its priority.

From this analysis, given in mere outline, there is an essential point to be grasped: the objectivity of literature, i.e. its relation to objective reality by which it is historically determined, is not a relation to an 'object' which it represents, is not representative. Nor is it purely and simply the instrument for using and transforming its immediate material, the linguistic practices determined within the practice of teaching. Precisely because of their contradictions, they cannot be used as simple primary material: thus all use is an intervention, made from a standpoint, a declaration (in a general sense) from within the contradiction and hence a further development of it. So, the objectivity of literature is its necessary place within the determinate processes and reproduction of the contradictory linguistic practices of the common tongue, in which the effectivity of the ideology of bourgeois education is realised.

This siting of the problem abolishes the old idealist question, 'What is literature?', which is not a question about its objective determinance, but a question about its universal essence, human and artistic.[1] It abolishes it because it shows us directly the material function of literature, inserted within a process which literature cannot determine even though it is indispensable to it. If literary production has for its material and specific base the contradictions of linguistic practices in schooling taken up and internalised (through an indefinitely repeated labour of fiction), it is because literature itself is one of the terms of the contradiction whose other term is determinately bound to literature. Dialectically, literature is simultaneously product

[1] Macherey and Balibar are referring here to Sartre's *What is Literature?* (1948). In the 'Red Letters' interview, Macherey adds: 'He was looking for a definition, a theory of what literature *is*, and in my view, this sort of enterprise is really very traditional and not very revolutionary. The question "what is literature?" is as old as the hills; it revives . . . an idealist and conservative aesthetic. If I had a single clear idea when I began my work, it was that we must abandon this kind of question because "what is literature?" is a false problem. Why? Because it is a question which already contains an answer. It implies that literature is *something*, that literature exists as a *thing*, as an eternal and unchangeable thing with an essence.' [Robert Young]

and material condition of the linguistic division in education, term and effect of its own contradictions. Not surprising therefore that the ideology of literature, itself a part of literature, should work ceaselessly to deny this objective base: to represent literature supremely as 'style', as individual genius, conscious or natural, as creativity, etc., as something outside (and above) the process of education, which is merely able to disseminate literature, and to comment on it exhaustively, though with no possibility of finally capturing it. The root of this constitutive repression is the objective status of literature as an historic ideological form, its relation to the class struggle. And the first and last commandment in its ideology is: 'Thou shalt describe all forms of class struggle, save that which determines thine own self.'

By the same token, the question of the relation of literature to the dominant ideology is posed afresh—escaping a confrontation of universal essences, in which many Marxist discussions have been trapped. To see literature as ideologically determined is not—cannot be—to 'reduce' it to moral ideologies or to political, religious, even aesthetic ideologies which are definable outside literature. Nor is it to make ideology the content to which literature brings form—even when there are themes and ideological statements which are more or less perfectly separable. Such a pairing is thoroughly mechanical, and, moreover, serves to corroborate the way in which the ideology of literature by displacement misconstrues its historic determinance. It merely prolongs the endless false dialectic of 'form' and 'content' whereby the artificially imposed terms alternate so that literature is sometimes perceived as content (ideology), sometimes as form ('real' literature). To define literature as a particular ideological form is to pose quite another problem: the specificity of ideological effects produced by literature and the means (techniques) of production. This returns us to the second question involved in the dialectical materialist concept of reflection. . . .

The literary effect is produced as a complex effect, not only, as shown, because its determinant is the imaginary resolution of one contradiction within another, but because the effect produced is simultaneously and inseparably the materiality of the text (the arrangement of sentences), and its status as a 'literary' text, its 'aesthetic' status. That is, it is both a material outcome and a particular ideological effect, or rather the production of a material outcome stamped with a particular ideological effect which marks it ineradicably. It is the status of the text in its characteristics—no matter what the terms, which are only variants: its 'charm', 'beauty', 'truth', 'significance', 'worth', 'profundity', 'style', 'writing', 'art', etc. Finally, it is the status of the text *per se*, quite simply, for in our society only the text is valid in itself, revealer of its true form; equally, all texts once 'written' are valid as 'literary'. This status extends as well to all the historic dissimilar modes of reading texts: the 'free' reading, reading for the pure 'pleasure' of letters, the critical reading giving a more or less theorised, more or less 'scientific' commentary on form and content, meaning, 'style', 'textuality' (revealing neologism!)—and behind all readings, the explication of texts by academics which conditions all the rest.

Therefore, the literary effect is not just produced by a determinate process, but actively inserts itself within the reproduction of other ideological effects: it is not only itself the effect of material causes, but is also an effect on socially determined individuals, constraining them materially to treat literary texts in a certain way. So, ideologically, the literary effect is not just in the domain of 'feeling', 'taste', 'judgment', and hence of aesthetic and literary ideas; it sets up a process itself: the rituals of literary consumption and 'cultural' practice.

That is why it is possible (and necessary) when analysing the literary effect as produced *qua* text and by means of the text, to treat as equivalents the 'reader' and the 'author'. Equivalent too are the 'intentions' of the author —what he expresses whether in the text itself (integrated within the 'surface' narrative) or alongside the text (in his declarations or even in his 'unconscious' motives as sought out by literary psychoanalysis)—and the interpretations, criticism and commentaries evoked from readers, whether sophisticated or not.

It is not important to know whether the interpretation 'really' identifies the author's intention (since the latter is not the cause of literary effects but is one of the effects). Interpretations and commentaries reveal the (literary) aesthetic effect, precisely, in full view. Literariness is what is recognised as such, and it is recognised as such precisely in the time and to the extent that it activates the interpretations, the criticisms and the 'readings'. This way a text can very easily stop being literary or become so under new conditions.

Freud was the first to follow this procedure in his account of the dream-work and more generally in his method of analysing the compromise formations of the unconscious; he defined what must be understood by the 'text' of the dream. He gave no importance to restoring the manifest content of the dream—to a careful isolated reconstruction of the 'real' dream. Or at least he accedes to it only through the intermediary of the 'dream narrative', which is already a transposition through which via condensation, displacement, and dream symbolism, repressed material makes its play. And he posited that the text of the dream was both the object of analysis and explanation simultaneously, through its own contradictions, the means of its own explanation: it is not just the manifest text, the narrative of the dream, but also all the 'free' associations (i.e., as one well knows, the forced associations, imposed by the psychic conflicts of the unconscious), the 'latent thoughts' for which the dream (or symptom) can serve as a pretext and which it arouses.

In the same way, criticism, the discourse of literary ideology, an endless commentary on the 'beauty' and 'truth' of literary texts, is a train of 'free' associations (in actuality forced and predetermined) which develops and realises the ideological effects of a literary text. In a materialist account of the text one must take them not as located above the text, as the beginnings of its explication, but as belonging to the same level as the text, or more precisely to the same level as the 'surface' narrative whether that is figurative, allegorically treating with certain general ideas (as in the novel or autobiography) or straightforwardly 'abstract', non-figurative (as in the moral or political essay). They are the tendential prolongation of this façade. Free from all question of the individuality of the 'writer', the 'reader' or the 'critic', these are the same ideological conflicts, resulting in the last instance from the same historic contradictions, or from their transformations, that produce the form of the text and of its commentaries.

5 *The Death of the Author**

ROLAND BARTHES

In his story *Sarrasine* Balzac, describing a castrato disguised as a woman, writes the following sentence: '*This was woman herself, with her sudden fears, her irrational whims, her instinctive worries, her impetuous boldness, her fussings, and her delicious sensibility.*' Who is speaking thus? Is it the hero of the story bent on remaining ignorant of the castrato hidden beneath the woman? Is it Balzac the individual, furnished by his personal experience with a philosophy of Woman? Is it Balzac the author professing 'literary' ideas on femininity? Is it universal wisdom? Romantic psychology? We shall never know, for the good reason that writing is the destruction of every voice, of every point of origin. Writing is that neutral, composite, oblique space where our subject slips away, the negative where all identity is lost, starting with the very identity of the body writing.

No doubt it has always been that way. As soon as a fact is *narrated* no longer with a view to acting directly on reality but intransitively, that is to say, finally outside of any function other than that of the very practice of the symbol itself, this disconnection occurs, the voice loses its origin, the author enters into his own death, writing begins. The sense of this phenomenon, however, has varied; in ethnographic societies the responsibility for a narrative is never assumed by a person but by a mediator, shaman or relator whose 'performance'—the mastery of the narrative code—may possibly be admired but never his 'genius'. The author is a modern figure, a product of our society insofar as, emerging from the Middle Ages with English empiricism, French rationalism and the personal faith of the Reformation, it discovered the prestige of the individual, of, as it is more nobly put, the 'human person'.

* From Roland Barthes, *Image—Music—Text*, essays selected and translated by Stephen Heath, Fontana/Collins, 1977, pp. 142–8; written in 1968.

It is thus logical that in literature it should be this positivism, the epitome and culmination of capitalist ideology, which has attached the greatest import-ance to the 'person' of the author. The *author* still reigns in histories of literature, biographies of writers, interviews, magazines, as in the very con-sciousness of men of letters anxious to unite their person and their work through diaries and memoirs. The image of literature to be found in ordinary culture is tyrannically centred on the author, his person, his life, his tastes, his passions, while criticism still consists for the most part in saying that Baudelaire's work is the failure of Baudelaire the man, Van Gogh's his madness, Tchaikovsky's his vice. The *explanation* of a work is always sought in the man or woman who produced it, as if it were always in the end, through the more or less transparent allegory of the fiction, the voice of a single person, the *author* 'confiding' in us.

Though the sway of the Author remains powerful (the new criticism[1] has often done no more than consolidate it), it goes without saying that certain writers have long since attempted to loosen it. In France, Mallarmé was doubtless the first to see and to foresee in its full extent the necessity to substitute language itself for the person who until then had been supposed to be its owner. For him, for us too, it is language which speaks, not the author; to write is, through a prerequisite impersonality (not at all to be confused with the castrating objectivity of the realist novelist), to reach that point where only language acts, 'performs', and not 'me'. Mallarmé's entire poetics consists in suppressing the author in the interests of writing (which is, as will be seen, to restore the place of the reader). Valéry, encumbered by a psycho-logy of the Ego, considerably diluted Mallarmé's theory but, his taste for classicism leading him to turn to the lessons of rhetoric, he never stopped calling into question and deriding the Author; he stressed the linguistic and, as it were, 'hazardous' nature of his activity, and throughout his prose works he militated in favour of the essentially verbal condition of literature, in the face of which all recourse to the writer's interiority seemed to him pure superstition. Proust himself, despite the apparently psychological character of what are called his *analyses*, was visibly concerned with the task of inexorably blurring, by an extreme subtilization, the relation between the writer and his characters; by making of the narrator not he who has seen and felt nor even he who is writing, but he who *is going to write* (the young man in the novel —but, in fact, how old is he and who is he?—wants to write but cannot; the novel ends when writing at last becomes possible). Proust gave modern writing its epic. . . . Leaving aside literature itself (such distinctions really becoming invalid), linguistics has recently provided the destruction of the

---

[1]   i.e. the *nouvelle critique* of the mid 1960s in France, not the Anglo-American 'new criticism' of I. A. Richards and William Empson, Cleanth Brooks and R. S. Crane. [Ed.]

Author with a valuable analytical tool by showing that the whole of the enunciation is an empty process, functioning perfectly without there being any need for it to be filled with the person of the interlocutors. Linguistically, the author is never more than the instance writing, just as *I* is nothing other than the instance saying *I*: language knows a 'subject', not a 'person', and this subject, empty outside of the very enunciation which defines it, suffices to make language 'hold together', suffices, that is to say, to exhaust it.

The removal of the Author (one could talk here with Brecht of a veritable 'distancing', the Author diminishing like a figurine at the far end of the literary stage) is not merely an historical fact or an act of writing; it utterly transforms the modern text (or—which is the same thing—the text is henceforth made and read in such a way that at all its levels the author is absent). The temporality is different. The Author, when believed in, is always conceived of as the past of his own book: book and author stand automatically on a single line divided into a *before* and an *after*. The Author is thought to *nourish* the book, which is to say that he exists before it, thinks, suffers, lives for it, is in the same relation of antecedence to his work as a father to his child. In complete contrast, the modern scriptor is born simultaneously with the text, is in no way equipped with a being preceding or exceeding the writing, is not the subject with the book as predicate; there is no other time than that of the enunciation and every text is eternally written *here and now*. The fact is (or, it follows) that *writing* can no longer designate an operation of recording, notation, representation, 'depiction' (as the Classics would say); rather, it designates exactly what linguists, referring to Oxford philosophy, call a performative, a rare verbal form (exclusively given in the first person and in the present tense) in which the enunciation has no other content (contains no other proposition) than the act by which it is uttered—something like the *I declare* of kings or the *I sing* of very ancient poets. Having buried the Author, the modern scriptor can thus no longer believe, as according to the pathetic view of his predecessors, that this hand is too slow for his thought or passion and that consequently, making a law of necessity, he must emphasize this delay and indefinitely 'polish' his form. For him, on the contrary, the hand, cut off from any voice, borne by a pure gesture of inscription (and not of expression), traces a field without origin—or which, at least, has no other origin than language itself, language which ceaselessly calls into question all origins.

We know now that a text is not a line of words releasing a single 'theological' meaning (the 'message' of the Author-God) but a multi-dimensional space in which a variety of writings, none of them original, blend and clash. The text is a tissue of quotations drawn from the innumerable centres of culture. . . . the writer can only imitate a gesture that is always anterior, never original. His only power is to mix writings, to counter the ones with the others, in such a way as never to rest on any one of them. Did he wish to *express himself*, he ought at least to know that the inner 'thing' he thinks to 'translate' is itself only a ready-formed dictionary, its words only explainable through other words, and so on indefinitely . . . Succeeding the Author, the scriptor no longer bears within him passions, humours, feelings, impressions, but rather this immense dictionary from which he draws a writing that can know no halt: life never does more than imitate the book, and the book itself is only a tissue of signs, an imitation that is lost, infinitely deferred.

Once the Author is removed, the claim to decipher a text becomes quite futile. To give a text an Author is to impose a limit on that text, to furnish it with a final signified, to close the writing. Such a conception suits criticism very well, the latter then allotting itself the important task of discovering the Author (or its hypostases: society, history, psyché, liberty) beneath the work: when the Author has been found, the text is 'explained'—victory to the critic. Hence there is no surprise in the fact that, historically, the reign of the Author has also been that of the Critic, nor again in the fact that criticism (be it new) is today undermined along with the Author. In the multiplicity of writing, everything is to be *disentangled*, nothing *deciphered*; the structure can be followed, 'run' (like the thread of a stocking) at every point and at every level, but there is nothing beneath: the space of writing is to be ranged over, not pierced; writing ceaselessly posits meaning ceaselessly to evaporate it, carrying out a systematic exemption of meaning. In precisely this way litera-ture (it would be better from now on to say *writing*), by refusing to assign a 'secret', an ultimate meaning, to the text (and to the world as text), liberates what may be called an anti-theological activity, an activity that is truly revolutionary since to refuse to fix meaning is, in the end, to refuse God and his hypostases—reason, science, law.

Let us come back to the Balzac sentence. No one, no 'person', says it: its source, its voice, is not the true place of the writing, which is reading. Another —very precise—example will help to make this clear: recent research (J.-P. Vernant[2]) has demonstrated the constitutively ambiguous nature of Greek tragedy, its texts being woven from words with double meanings that each character understands unilaterally (this perpetual misunderstanding is exactly the 'tragic'); there is, however, someone who understands each word in its duplicity and who, in addition, hears the very deafness of the characters speaking in front of him—this someone being precisely the reader (or here, the listener). Thus is revealed the total existence of writing: a text is made of multiple writings, drawn from many cultures and entering into mutual relations of dialogue, parody, contestation, but there is one place where this

---

[2] Cf. Jean-Pierre Vernant (with Pierre Vidal-Naquet), *Mythe et tragedie en Grèce ancienne*, Paris, 1972, esp. pp. 19–40, 99–131.

multiplicity is focused and that place is the reader, not, as was hitherto said, the author. The reader is the space on which all the quotations that make up a writing are inscribed without any of them being lost; a text's unity lies not in its origin but in its destination. Yet this destination cannot any longer be personal: the reader is without history, biography, psychology; he is simply that *someone* who holds together in a single field all the traces by which the written text is constituted. Which is why it is derisory to condemn the new writing in the name of a humanism hypocritically turned champion of the reader's rights. Classic criticism has never paid any attention to the reader; for it, the writer is the only person in literature. We are now beginning to let ourselves be fooled no longer by the arrogant antiphrastical[3] recriminations of good society in favour of the very thing it sets aside, ignores, smothers, or destroys; we know that to give writing its future, it is necessary to overthrow the myth: the birth of the reader must be at the cost of the death of the Author.

[3] i.e. using a word in the opposite sense of its usual meaning. [Ed.]

V End of Empire

These items register in different ways the consequences of the perceived decline in British (but also European) imperial power.

Edward Said comes first, because of the central importance for literary and cultural critics involved in this debate of his book, Orientalism. *The first extract defines his use of the term, and the second, 'Orientalism Now', demonstrates how it can then be applied to an analysis of the 'discourses' (literary and historical), by which the East has been, and still is, represented in the West. Sara Suleri's 'reading' of one key literary example of these discourses, E. M. Forster's* A Passage to India, *while indebted to Said's approach, also employs feminist, psychoanalytical, and deconstructionist theories to situate its meanings. Seamus Heaney's reading of three English poets, Ted Hughes, Geoffrey Hill, and Philip Larkin, shows their work as symptomatic of declining English power. John McGrath's 'untheorized' account of how post-war British drama, with few exceptions (such as John Arden), has simply incorporated 'popular' dissent, adds a further dimension.*

McGrath reminds his Cambridge undergraduate audience of his position, as a product of the northern English working class; and of the relevance of such reminders when considering questions of assimilation and marginalization. Heaney is an Irish poet, addressing an American audience, thereby also claiming a special vantage-point. Any analysis of the discourses of power, as Said calls them, has to take into account how and if it can be 'distanced' in this way. Perhaps only then can the impact of Empire on national and regional cultures and sub-cultures be adequately studied.

Clearly all this has an important bearing upon the issue of 'post-colonial' or 'New Writings in English', the subject of the next section.

1 *The Discourse of the Orient**

EDWARD SAID

On a visit to Beirut during the terrible civil war of 1975–1976 a French journalist wrote regretfully of the gutted downtown area that 'it had once seemed to belong to . . . the Orient of Chateaubriand and Nerval'.[1] He was right about the place, of course, especially so far as a European was concerned. The Orient was almost a European invention, and had been since antiquity a place of romance, exotic beings, haunting memories and landscapes, remarkable experiences. Now it was disappearing; in a sense it had happened, its time was over. Perhaps it seemed irrelevant that Orientals themselves had something at stake in the process, that even in the time of Chateaubriand and Nerval Orientals had lived there, and that now it was they who were suffering; the main thing for the European visitor was a European representation of the Orient and its contemporary fate, both of which had a privileged communal significance for the journalist and his French readers.

Americans will not feel quite the same about the Orient, which for them is much more likely to be associated very differently with the Far East (China and Japan, mainly). Unlike the Americans, the French and the British—less so the Germans, Russians, Spanish, Portuguese, Italians, and Swiss—have had a long tradition of what I shall be calling *Orientalism*, a way of coming to terms with the Orient that is based on the Orient's special place in European Western experience. The Orient is not only adjacent to Europe; it is also the place of Europe's greatest and richest and oldest colonies, the source of its civilizations and languages, its cultural contestant, and one of its deepest and most recurring images of the Other. In addition, the Orient has helped to define Europe (or the West) as its contrasting image, idea, personality, experience. Yet none of this Orient is merely imaginative. The Orient is an integral part of European *material* civilization and culture. Orientalism expresses and represents that part culturally and even ideologically as a mode of discourse with supporting institutions, vocabulary, scholarship, imagery, doctrines, even colonial bureaucracies and colonial styles. In contrast, the American understanding of the Orient will seem considerably less dense, although our recent Japanese, Korean, and Indochinese adventures ought now to be creating a more sober, more realistic 'Oriental' awareness. Moreover, the vastly expanded American political and economic role in the Near East (the Middle East) makes great claims on our understanding of that Orient.

It will be clear to the reader. . . that by Orientalism I mean several things, all of them, in my opinion, interdependent. The most readily accepted desig-

* From Edward W. Said, *Orientalism*, Routledge & Kegan Paul, 1978, pp. 1–9, 226–30.

[1] Thierry Desjardins, *Le Martyre du Liban* (Paris: Plon, 1976), p. 14.

nation for Orientalism is an academic one, and indeed the label still serves in a number of academic institutions. Anyone who teaches, writes about, or researches the Orient—and this applies whether the person is an anthropologist, sociologist, historian, or philologist—either in its specific or its general aspects, is an Orientalist, and what he or she does is Orientalism. Compared with *Oriental studies* or *area studies*, it is true that the term *Orientalism* is less preferred by specialists today, both because it is too vague and general and because it connotes the high-handed executive attitude of nineteenth-century and early-twentieth-century European colonialism. Nevertheless books are written and congresses held with 'the Orient' as their main focus, with the Orientalist in his new or old guise as their main authority. The point is that even if it does not survive as it once did, Orientalism lives on academically through its doctrines and theses about the Orient and the Oriental.

Related to this academic tradition, whose fortunes, transmigrations, specializations, and transmissions are in part the subject of this study, is a more general meaning for Orientalism. Orientalism is a style of thought based upon an ontological and epistemological distinction made between 'the Orient' and (most of the time) 'the Occident'. Thus a very large mass of writers, among whom are poets, novelists, philosophers, political theorists, economists, and imperial administrators, have accepted the basic distinction between East and West as the starting point for elaborate theories, epics, novels, social descriptions, and political accounts concerning the Orient, its people, customs, 'mind', destiny, and so on. *This* Orientalism can accommodate Aeschylus, say, and Victor Hugo, Dante and Karl Marx. A little later in this introduction I shall deal with the methodological problems one encounters in so broadly construed a 'field' as this.

The interchange between the academic and the more or less imaginative meanings of Orientalism is a constant one, and since the late eighteenth century there has been a considerable, quite disciplined—perhaps even regulated—traffic between the two. Here I come to the third meaning of Orientalism, which is something more historically and materially defined than either of the other two. Taking the late eighteenth century as a very roughly defined starting point Orientalism can be discussed and analyzed as the corporate institution for dealing with the Orient—dealing with it by making statements about it, authorizing views of it, describing it, by teaching it, settling it, ruling over it: in short, Orientalism as a Western style for dominating, restructuring, and having authority over the Orient. I have found it useful here to employ Michel Foucault's notion of a discourse, as described by him in *The Archaeology of Knowledge* and in *Discipline and Punish*, to identify Orientalism. My contention is that without examining Orientalism as a discourse one cannot possibly understand the enormously systematic discipline by which European culture was able to manage—and even produce —the Orient politically, sociologically, militarily, ideologically, scientifically, and imaginatively during the post-Enlightenment period. Moreover, so authoritative a position did Orientalism have that I believe no one writing, thinking, or acting on the Orient could do so without taking account of the limitations on thought and action imposed by Orientalism. In brief, because of Orientalism the Orient was not (and is not) a free subject of thought or action. This is not to say that Orientalism unilaterally determines what can be said about the Orient, but that it is the whole network of interests inevitably brought to bear on (and therefore always involved in) any occasion when that peculiar entity 'the Orient' is in question. How this happens is what this book tries to demonstrate. It also tries to show that European culture gained in strength and identity by setting itself off against the Orient as a sort of surrogate and even underground self.

Historically and culturally there is a quantitative as well as a qualitative difference between the Franco-British involvement in the Orient and—until the period of American ascendancy after World War II—the involvement of every other European and Atlantic power. To speak of Orientalism therefore is to speak mainly, although not exclusively, of a British and French cultural enterprise, a project whose dimensions take in such disparate realms as the imagination itself, the whole of India and the Levant, the Biblical texts and the Biblical lands, the spice trade, colonial armies and a long tradition of colonial administrators, a formidable scholarly corpus, innumerable Oriental 'experts' and 'hands', an Oriental professorate, a complex array of 'Oriental' ideas (Oriental despotism, Oriental splendor, cruelty, sensuality), many Eastern sects, philosophies, and wisdoms domesticated for local European use—the list can be extended more or less indefinitely. My point is that Orientalism derives from a particular closeness experienced between Britain and France and the Orient, which until the early nineteenth century had really meant only India and the Bible lands. From the beginning of the nineteenth century until the end of World War II France and Britain dominated the Orient and Orientalism; since World War II America has dominated the Orient, and approaches it as France and Britain once did. Out of that closeness, whose dynamic is enormously productive even if it always demonstrates the comparatively greater strength of the Occident (British, French, or American), comes the large body of texts I call Orientalist.

It should be said at once that even with the generous number of books and authors that I examine, there is a much larger number that I simply have had to leave out. My argument, however, depends neither upon an exhaustive catalogue of texts dealing with the Orient nor upon a clearly delimited set of texts, authors, and ideas that together make up the Orientalist canon. I have depended instead upon a different methodological alternative—whose backbone in a sense is the set of historical generalizations I have so far been making in this Introduction—and it is these I want now to discuss in more analytical detail.

I have begun with the assumption that the Orient is not an inert fact of nature. It is not merely *there*, just as the Occident itself is not just *there* either. We must take seriously Vico's great observation that men make their own history, that what they can know is what they have made, and extend it to geography: as both geographical and cultural entities—to say nothing of historical entities—such locales, regions, geographical sectors as 'Orient' and 'Occident' are man-made. Therefore as much as the West itself, the Orient is an idea that has a history and a tradition of thought, imagery, and vocabulary that have given it reality and presence in and for the West. The two geographical entities thus support and to an extent reflect each other.

Having said that, one must go on to state a number of reasonable qualifications. In the first place, it would be wrong to conclude that the Orient was *essentially* an idea, or a creation with no corresponding reality. When Disraeli said in his novel *Tancred* that the East was a career, he meant that to be interested in the East was something bright young Westerners would find to be an all-consuming passion; he should not be interpreted as saying that the East was *only* a career for Westerners. There were—and are—cultures and nations whose location is in the East, and their lives, histories, and customs have a brute reality obviously greater than anything that could be said about them in the West. About that fact this study of Orientalism has very little to contribute, except to acknowledge it tacitly. But the phenomenon of Orientalism as I study it here deals principally, not with a correspondence between Orientalism and Orient, but with the internal consistency of Orientalism and its ideas about the Orient (the East as career) despite or beyond any correspondence, or lack thereof, with a 'real' Orient. My point is that Disraeli's statement about the East refers mainly to that created consistency, that regular constellation of ideas as the pre-eminent thing about the Orient, and not to its mere being, as Wallace Stevens's phrase has it.

A second qualification is that ideas, cultures, and histories cannot seriously be understood or studied without their force, or more precisely their configurations of power, also being studied. To believe that the Orient was created—or, as I call it, 'Orientalized'—and to believe that such things happen simply as a necessity of the imagination, is to be disingenuous. The relationship between Occident and Orient is a relationship of power, of domination, of varying degrees of a complex hegemony, and is quite accurately indicated in the title of K. M. Panikkar's classic *Asia and Western Dominance*.[2] The Orient

---

[2] K. M. Panikkar, *Asia and Western Dominance* (London: George Allen & Unwin, 1959).

was Orientalized not only because it was discovered to be 'Oriental' in all those ways considered commonplace by an average nineteenth-century European, but also because it *could be*—that is, submitted to being—*made* Oriental. There is very little consent to be found, for example, in the fact that Flaubert's encounter with an Egyptian courtesan produced a widely influential model of the Oriental woman; she never spoke of herself, she never represented her emotions, presence, or history. *He* spoke for and represented her. He was foreign, comparatively wealthy, male, and these were historical facts of domination that allowed him not only to possess Kuchuk Hanem physically but to speak for her and tell his readers in what way she was 'typically Oriental'. My argument is that Flaubert's situation of strength in relation to Kuchuk Hanem was not an isolated instance. It fairly stands for the pattern of relative strength between East and West, and the discourse about the Orient that it enabled.

This brings us to a third qualification. One ought never to assume that the structure of Orientalism is nothing more than a structure of lies or of myths which, were the truth about them to be told, would simply blow away. I myself believe that Orientalism is more particularly valuable as a sign of European-Atlantic power over the Orient than it is as a veridic discourse about the Orient (which is what, in its academic or scholarly form, it claims to be). Nevertheless, what we must respect and try to grasp is the sheer knitted-together strength of Orientalist discourse, its very close ties to the enabling socio-economic and political institutions, and its redoubtable durability. After all, any system of ideas that can remain unchanged as teachable wisdom (in academies, books, congresses, universities, foreign-service institutes) from the period of Ernest Renan in the late 1840s until the present in the United States must be something more formidable than a mere collection of lies. Orientalism, therefore, is not an airy European fantasy about the Orient, but a created body of theory and practice in which, for many generations, there has been a considerable material investment. Continued investment made Orientalism, as a system of knowledge about the Orient, an accepted grid for filtering through the Orient into Western consciousness, just as that same investment multiplied—indeed, made truly productive—the statements proliferating out from Orientalism into the general culture.

Gramsci has made the useful analytic distinction between civil and political society in which the former is made up of voluntary (or at least rational and noncoercive) affiliations like schools, families, and unions, the latter of state institutions (the army, the police, the central bureaucracy) whose role in the polity is direct domination. Culture, of course, is to be found operating within civil society, where the influence of ideas, of institutions, and of other persons works not through domination but by what Gramsci calls consent. In any society not totalitarian, then, certain cultural forms predominate over others,

just as certain ideas are more influential than others; the form of this cultural
leadership is what Gramsci has identified as *hegemony*, an indispensable
concept for any understanding of cultural life in the industrial West. It is
hegemony, or rather the result of cultural hegemony at work, that gives
Orientalism the durability and the strength I have been speaking about so far.
Orientalism is never far from what Denys Hay has called the idea of Europe,[3]
a collective notion identifying 'us' Europeans as against all 'those' non-Euro-
peans, and indeed it can be argued that the major component in European
culture is precisely what made that culture hegemonic both in and outside
Europe: the idea of European identity as a superior one in comparison with
all the non-European peoples and cultures. There is in addition the hegemony
of European ideas about the Orient, themselves reiterating European superiority over Oriental backwardness, usually overriding the possibility that a more
independent, or more skeptical, thinker might have had different views on the
matter.

In a quite constant way, Orientalism depends for its strategy on this flexible
positional superiority, which puts the Westerner in a whole series of possible
relationships with the Orient without ever losing him the relative upper hand.
And why should it have been otherwise, especially during the period of
extraordinary European ascendancy from the late Renaissance to the present?
The scientist, the scholar, the missionary, the trader, or the soldier was in, or
thought about, the Orient because he *could be there*, or could think about it,
with very little resistance on the Orient's part. Under the general heading of
knowledge of the Orient, and within the umbrella of Western hegemony over
the Orient during the period from the end of the eighteenth century, there
emerged a complex Orient suitable for study in the academy, for display in the
museum, for reconstruction in the colonial office, for theoretical illustration
in anthropological, biological, linguistic, racial, and historical theses about
mankind and the universe, for instances of economic and sociological theories
of development, revolution, cultural personality, national or religious
character. Additionally, the imaginative examination of things Oriental was
based more or less exclusively upon a sovereign Western consciousness out
of whose unchallenged centrality an Oriental world emerged, first according
to general ideas about who or what was an Oriental, then according to a
detailed logic governed not simply by empirical reality but by a battery of
desires, repressions, investments, and projections. If we can point to great
Orientalist works of genuine scholarship like Silvestre de Sacy's *Chrestomathie
arabe* or Edward William Lane's *Account of the Manners and Customs of the
Modern Egyptians*, we need also to note that Renan's and Gobineau's racial

---

[3] Denys Hay, *Europe: The Emergence of an Idea*, 2nd ed. (Edinburgh: Edinburgh University Press,
1968).

ideas came out of the same impulse, as did a great many Victorian porno-graphic novels (see the analysis by Steven Marcus of 'The Lustful Turk'[4]).

And yet, one must repeatedly ask oneself whether what matters in Oriental-ism is the general group of ideas overriding the mass of material—about which who could deny that they were shot through with doctrines of European superiority, various kinds of racism, imperialism, and the like, dogmatic views of 'the Oriental' as a kind of ideal and unchanging abstrac-tion?—or the much more varied work produced by almost uncountable individual writers, whom one would take up as individual instances of authors dealing with the Orient. In a sense the two alternatives, general and particular, are really two perspectives on the same material: in both instances one would have to deal with pioneers in the field like William Jones, with great artists like Nerval or Flaubert. And why would it not be possible to employ both perspectives together, or one after the other? Isn't there an obvious danger of distortion (of precisely the kind that academic Orientalism has always been prone to) if either too general or too specific a level of description is maintained systematically?

My two fears are distortion and inaccuracy, or rather the kind of inac-curacy produced by too dogmatic a generality and too positivistic a localized focus. In trying to deal with these problems I have tried to deal with three main aspects of my own contemporary reality that seem to me to point the way out of the methodological or perspectival difficulties I have been discuss-ing, difficulties that might force one, in the first instance, into writing a coarse polemic on so unacceptably general a level of description as not to be worth the effort, or in the second instance, into writing so detailed and atomistic a series of analyses as to lose all track of the general lines of force informing the field, giving it its special cogency. How then to recognize individuality and to reconcile it with its intelligent, and by no means passive or merely dictatorial, general and hegemonic context? . . .

ORIENTALISM NOW

As he appears in several poems, in novels like *Kim*, and in too many catch-phrases to be an ironic fiction, Kipling's White Man, as an idea, a persona, a style of being, seems to have served many Britishers while they were abroad. The actual color of their skin set them off dramatically and reassuringly from the sea of natives, but for the Britisher who circulated amongst Indians, Africans, or Arabs there was also the certain knowledge that he belonged to, and could draw upon the empirical and spiritual reserves of, a long tradition of executive responsibility towards the colored races. It was of this tradition,

[4] Steven Marcus, *The Other Victorians: A Study of Sexuality and Pornography in Mid-Nineteenth Century England* (1966; reprint ed., New York: Bantam Books, 1967), pp. 200–19.

its glories and difficulties, that Kipling wrote when he celebrated the 'road'
taken by White Men in the colonies:

> Now, this is the road that the White Men tread
> When they go to clean a land—
> Iron underfoot and the vine overhead
> And the deep on either hand.
> We have trod that road—and a wet and windy road—
> Our chosen star for guide.
> Oh, well for the world when the White Men tread
> Their highway side by side![5]

'Cleaning a land' is best done by White Men in delicate concert with each
other, an allusion to the present dangers of European rivalry in the colonies;
for failing in the attempt to coordinate policy, Kipling's White Men are quite
prepared to go to war: 'Freedom for ourselves and freedom for our sons/And,
failing freedom, War'. Behind the White Man's mask of amiable leadership
there is always the express willingness to use force, to kill and be killed. What
dignifies his mission is some sense of intellectual dedication; he is a White
Man, but not for mere profit, since his 'chosen star' presumably sits far above
earthly gain. Certainly many White Men often wondered what it was they
fought for on that 'wet and windy road', and certainly a great number of them
must have been puzzled as to how the color of their skins gave them superior
ontological status plus great power over much of the inhabited world. Yet in
the end, being a White Man, for Kipling and for those whose perceptions and
rhetoric he influenced, was a self-confirming business. One became a White
Man because one *was* a White Man; more important, 'drinking that cup',
living that unalterable destiny in 'the White Man's day', left one little time for
idle speculation on origins, causes, historical logic.

Being a White Man was therefore an idea and a reality. It involved a
reasoned position towards both the white and the nonwhite worlds. It meant
—in the colonies—speaking in a certain way, behaving according to a code
of regulations, and even feeling certain things and not others. It meant
specific judgments, evaluations, gestures. It was a form of authority before
which nonwhites, and even whites themselves, were expected to bend. In the
institutional forms it took (colonial governments, consular corps, commercial
establishments) it was an agency for the expression, diffusion, and imple-
mentation of policy towards the world, and within this agency, although a
certain personal latitude was allowed, the impersonal communal idea of being
a White Man ruled. Being a White Man, in short, was a very concrete manner
of being-in-the-world, a way of taking hold of reality, language, and thought.
It made a specific style possible.

[5] Rudyard Kipling, *Verse* (Garden City, NY: Doubleday & Co., 1954), p. 280.

Kipling himself could not merely have happened; the same is true of his White Man. Such ideas and their authors emerge out of complex historical and cultural circumstances, at least two of which have much in common with the history of Orientalism in the nineteenth century. One of them is the culturally sanctioned habit of deploying large generalizations by which reality is divided into various collectives: languages, races, types, colors, mentalities, each category being not so much a neutral designation as an evaluative interpretation. Underlying these categories is the rigidly binomial opposition of 'ours' and 'theirs', with the former always encroaching upon the latter (even to the point of making 'theirs' exclusively a function of 'ours'). This opposition was reinforced not only by anthropology, linguistics, and history but also, of course, by the Darwinian theses on survival and natural selection, and—no less decisive—by the rhetoric of high cultural humanism. What gave writers like Renan and Arnold the right to generalities about race was the official character of their formed cultural literacy. 'Our' values were (let us say) liberal, humane, correct; they were supported by the tradition of belles-lettres, informed scholarship, rational inquiry; as Europeans (and white men) 'we' shared in them every time their virtues were extolled. Nevertheless, the human partnerships formed by reiterated cultural values excluded as much as they included. For every idea about 'our' art spoken for by Arnold, Ruskin, Mill, Newman, Carlyle, Renan, Gobineau, or Comte, another link in the chain binding 'us' together was formed while another outsider was banished. Even if this is always the result of such rhetoric, wherever and whenever it occurs, we must remember that for nineteenth-century Europe an imposing edifice of learning and culture was built, so to speak, in the face of actual outsiders (the colonies, the poor, the delinquent), whose role in the culture was to give definition to what *they* were constitutionally unsuited for.[6]

The other circumstance common to the creation of the White Man and Orientalism is the 'field' commanded by each, as well as the sense that such a field entails peculiar modes, even rituals, of behavior, learning, and possession. Only an Occidental could speak of Orientals, for example, just as it was the White Man who could designate and name the coloreds, or nonwhites. Every statement made by Orientalists or White Men (who were usually interchangeable) conveyed a sense of the irreducible distance separating white from colored, or Occidental from Oriental; moreover, behind each statement there resonated the tradition of experience, learning, and education

---

[6] The themes of exclusion and confinement in nineteenth-century culture have played an important role in Michel Foucault's work, most recently in his *Discipline and Punish: The Birth of the Prison* (New York: Pantheon Books, 1977), and *The History of Sexuality*, Volume 1: An Introduction *(New York: Pantheon Books, 1978).*

that kept the Oriental-colored to his position of *object studied by the Occidental-white*, instead of vice versa. Where one was in a position of power—as Cromer[7] was, for example—the Oriental belonged to the system of rule whose principle was simply to make sure that no Oriental was ever allowed to be independent and rule himself. The premise there was that since the Orientals were ignorant of self-government, they had better be kept that way for their own good.

Since the White Man, like the Orientalist, lived very close to the line of tension keeping the coloreds at bay, he felt it incumbent on him readily to define and redefine the domain he surveyed. Passages of narrative description regularly alternate with passages of re-articulated definition and judgment that disrupt the narrative; this is a characteristic style of the writing produced by Oriental experts who operated using Kipling's White Man as a mask. Here is T. E. Lawrence, writing to V. W. Richards in 1918:

. . . the Arab appealed to my imagination. It is the old, old civilisation, which has refined itself clear of household gods, and half the trappings which ours hastens to assume. The gospel of bareness in materials is a good one, and it involves apparently a sort of moral bareness too. They think for the moment, and endeavour to slip through life without turning corners or climbing hills. In part it is a mental and moral fatigue, a race trained out, and to avoid difficulties they have to jettison so much that we think honorable and grave: and yet without in any way sharing their point of view, I think I can understand it enough to look at myself and other foreigners from their direction, and without condemning it. I know I am a stranger to them, and always will be; but I cannot believe them worse, any more than I could change to their ways.[8]

A similar perspective, however different the subject under discussion may seem to be, is found in these remarks by Gertrude Bell:

How many thousand years this state of things has lasted [namely, that Arabs live in 'a state of war'], those who shall read the earliest records of the inner desert will tell us, for it goes back to the first of them, but in all the centuries the Arab has bought no wisdom from experience. He is never safe, and yet he behaves as though security were his daily bread.[9]

To which, as a gloss, we should add her further observation, this time about life in Damascus:

I begin to see dimly what the civilisation of a great Eastern city means, how they live, what they think; and I have got on to terms with them. I believe the fact of my being English is a great help. . . . We have gone up in the world since five years ago. The difference is very marked. I think it is due to the success of our government in Egypt

[7] i.e. Sir Evelyn Baring, Earl of Cromer, from 1883 to 1906 indirect ruler of Egypt as Consul-General then plenipotentiary; influential author and essayist. [Ed.]

[8] *The Letters of T. E. Lawrence of Arabia*, ed. David Garnett (1938; reprint ed., London: Spring Books, 1964), p. 244.

[9] Gertrude Bell, *The Desert and the Sown* (London: William Heinemann, 1907), p. 244.

to a great extent. . . . The defeat of Russia stands for a great deal, and my impression is that the vigorous policy of Lord Curzon in the Persian Gulf and on the India frontier stands for a great deal more. No one who does not know the East can realise how it all hangs together. It is scarcely an exaggeration to say that if the English mission had been turned back from the gates of Kabul, the English tourist would be frowned upon in the streets of Damascus.[10]

In such statements as these, we note immediately that 'the Arab' or 'Arabs' have an aura of apartness, definiteness, and collective self-consistency such as to wipe out any traces of individual Arabs with narratable life histories. What appealed to Lawrence's imagination was the clarity of the Arab, both as an image and as a supposed philosophy (or attitude) towards life: in both cases what Lawrence fastens on is the Arab as if seen from the cleansing perspective of one not an Arab, and one for whom such unselfconscious primitive simplicity as the Arab possesses is something defined by the observer, in this case the White Man. Yet Arab refinement, which in its essentials corresponds to Yeats's visions of Byzantium where

> Flames that no faggot feeds, flint nor steel has lit,
> Nor storm disturbs, flames begotten of flame,
> Where blood-begotten spirits come
> And all complexities of fury leave[11]

is associated with Arab perdurability, as if the Arab had not been subject to the ordinary processes of history. Paradoxically, the Arab seems to Lawrence to have exhausted himself in his very temporal persistence. The enormous age of Arab civilization has thus served to refine the Arab down to his quintessential attributes, and to tire him out morally in the process. What we are left with is Bell's Arab: centuries of experience and no wisdom. As a collective entity, then, the Arab accumulates no existential or even semantical thickness. He remains the same, except for the exhausting refinements mentioned by Lawrence, from one end to the other of 'the records of the inner desert'. We are to assume that if *an* Arab feels joy, if he is sad at the death of his child or parent, if he has a sense of the injustices of political tyranny, then those experiences are necessarily subordinate to the sheer, unadorned, and persistent fact of being an Arab.

---

[10] Gertrude Bell, *From Her Personal Papers, 1889–1914*, ed. Elizabeth Burgoyne (London: Ernest Benn, 1958), p. 204.

[11] William Butler Yeats, 'Byzantium', *The Collected Poems* (New York: Macmillan Co., 1959), p. 244.

2 *The Geography of* A Passage to India*

SARA SULERI

The adventure of twentieth-century narrative in English has engendered an area studies that, in the act of taking India as its subject, transforms the locality of an historic space into a vast introspective question mark. From *A Passage to India* on, 'books about India' have been more accurately books about the representation of India, with each offering variants of the peculiar logic through which a failure of representation becomes transformed into a characteristically Indian failure. In order to examine such acts of representation as a mode of recolonization, I wish to present a reading of Forster's *A Passage to India*, a paradigmatic text of the subterranean desire to replay, in twentieth-century narrative, the increasingly distant history of nineteenth-century domination. The mode is characterized by the desire to contain the intangibilities of the East within a western lucidity, but this gesture of appropriation only partially conceals the obsessive fear that India's fictionality inevitably generates in the writing mind of the West. The symbolic violence of this fear underlies the impulse to empty the area out of history and to represent India as an amorphous state of mind that is only remembered in order for it to be forgotten.

From their titles on, narratives on the Indian theme declare their intentions to name something so vague as to be nearly unnameable, implying that their subject is disturbingly prone to spill into atmospherics rather than remaining fixed in the place to which it belongs. Something is dislocated, and the fictions proceed to develop on precisely those lines. Typically, the narrator is a cartographer, the only locus of rationality in an area of engulfing unreliability, so that ultimately the narrative mind is the only safe terrain the texts provide. India itself, like a Cheshire cat, functions as a dislocated metaphor for an entity that is notoriously remiss in arriving at the appointed place at the correct time. As a consequence, it becomes a space that imposes its unreality on western discourse to the point where the narrative has no option but to redouble on itself, to internalize the symbolic landscape of India in order to make it human. Thus geography is subsumed into the more immediate and familiar territory of the liberal imagination, in the act of recolonizing its vagrant subject with the intricacies of a defined sensibility.

Such is the imagination, of course, that legitimizes a text like *A Passage to India* as a humanely liberal parable for imperialism, and allows a reader like Trilling[1] to interpret the novel's depiction of Eastern action as a metaphor for

* Harold Bloom, ed., *E. M. Forster's A Passage to India: Modern Critical Interpretations*, Chelsea House Publishers, 1987, pp. 107–13.
[1] Refers to Lionel Trilling, *E. M. Forster*, 1944. [Ed.]

the behavior of the West. In other words, the only difference of India inheres in the fact that it is symbolic of something the western mind must learn about itself. The paradigm that Forster establishes is of crucial importance to all subsequent narratives on India, which, with their exquisite caving in upon themselves, embody a response to the difference of India that Forster so effectively literalized. For it is Forster rather than Kipling who initiates the Western narrative of India: a text like *Kim* in fact reinforces the reality of India by seeing it so clearly as the other that the imperial West must know and dominate. *A Passage to India*, on the other hand, represents India as a metaphor of something other than itself, as a certain metaphysical posture that translates into an image of profound unreality. It thus becomes that archetypal novel of modernity that co-opts the space reserved for India in the Western literary imagination, so that all subsequent novels on the Indian theme appear secretly obsessed with the desire to describe exactly what transpired in the Marabar caves.

'How does one interpret another culture', asks Edward Said [in *Covering Islam*], 'unless prior circumstances have made that culture available for interpretation in the first place?' This question, that of the historic availability of India, is certainly not a problem that preoccupies Forster's protagonists, who are far more interested in decoding that which India tells them about their own interpretability. Thus Forster initiates a narrative mode that is perhaps more fraught with violence than the Orientalist code that Said charts, which is that 'imaginative yet drastically polarized geography dividing the world into two unequal parts, the larger, "different" one called the Orient, the other, also known as "our" world, called the Occident'. Where Forster transgresses even an Orientalist decorum is by implying that India is really not other at all, but merely a mode or passageway to endorse the infinite variety that constitutes a reading of the West. To approach the Indian fictions of the modern West is indeed to confront a secret attack on difference, and to reread the text that is *A Passage to India*. For this fiction most clearly delineates the desire to convert unreadability into unreality, and difference into an image of the writing mind's perception of its own ineffability.

Forster, I hope to demonstrate, constructs a symbolic geography that provides western narrative with its most compelling and durable image of India, which is, of course, the figure of India as a hollow, or a cave. It is the desire to know the hollow, but to leave defeated, that informs the dainty ironies of Forster's narrative, for the narrative mind can only empty its defeat upon the landscape, and depart from the area exhausted, but a little lighter. Since Forster, this model has been rehearsed repeatedly, but nowhere as effectively as in the ostensibly nonfictional text, V. S. Naipaul's *An Area of Darkness*. Both fictions share in that Western project which represents India as an empty site that is bounded only by an aura of irrationality. In examining the two narratives as a genealogical unit, I will attempt to chart the development of that amorphous idiom which begins in the novel an Englishman writes about India, but finally gains a nonfictional authority in the work of an Indian writer fully prepared to cite himself as a living emblem of India's inauthenticity.

In my reading, *A Passage to India* and *An Area of Darkness* are remarkably predisposed towards complete alignment. They are not only the two best British novels about India, but constitute parallel texts where the question posed by one is answered by the other. What can happen here? asks Forster: nothing, responds V. S. Naipaul, except history as the act of possible imagination, because there is only me. He thus proceeds to literalize Forster's image of disappointing emptiness by representing himself as the one self-conscious embodiment of India's massive failure to present a cohesive shape. Whereas this failure functions as the atmospherics of *A Passage to India*, in *An Area of Darkness* it becomes as palpable as the excrement that so appalls Naipaul that he must note and describe it each time it comes his way. To the imperial English mind, India can only be represented as a gesture of possible rape; to the post-colonial and equally English mind, India is nothing more than the imbecile act of self-exposure, whose outrage is too literal to allow for even the secrecy of shame.

That the Orient has traditionally been represented as a figure of seduction, duplicity—and, more darkly, rape—is a commonplace that is clearly established by European historical and travel narratives from the seventeenth century on. It takes Forster, however, to carry the rape image to its most finely wrought conclusion. While *A Passage to India* ostensibly centers on an hysteric who believes she has been raped, the course of the narrative suggests that the real outrage lies in the fact that this rude encounter has been withheld from her. India diffuses into emptiness before it completes the seduction it had promised, as though its own formlessness demands that it can be master of only an incomplete performance. Rape becomes, therefore, dangerously synonymous with sexual disappointment: that the novel is traversed by Western travelers invaded by sensations of impotence as long as they remain on Western territory is a crucial index of Forster's obsession with representing India as a figure of both an erotic yet sterile duplicity.

Forster's narrative is found, and founders on, the idiom of a god who neglects to come. In the key scene where the Hindu Godbole sings for the uncomprehending audience of Fielding's Muslim and British guests, he offers the following commentary:

It was a religious song. I placed myself in the position of a milkmaiden. I say to Shri Krishna, 'Come! come to me only'. The god refuses to come. I grow humble and say: 'Do not come to me only. Multiply yourself into a hundred Krishnas. . . . Come, come, come, come, come, come. He neglects to come.' [Chapter vii]

Despite the parodic sentimentality of this version of Hinduism, the passage nonetheless provides Forster with a refrain that he uses to envelop all the inhabitants of India, where the god neglects to come. The structure of the novel images this neglect through its emblematic representation of empty institutions, or buildings that are somewhat wanton in their lack of habitation. *A Passage to India* makes neat architecture of this lack, in that the three sections of the book—'Mosque', 'Caves', and 'Temple'—function primarily as cavities to contain western perceptions of that which is missing from the East. The edifices thus constitute shells into which Forster can uncurl echoes of what first appears to be a humane compassion, but what gradually and more threateningly develops into an exquisite nostalgia for betrayal. While the novel attempts to delineate a Hindu 'type' as opposed to a Muslim 'type' in its portrayal of native characters like Godbole and Aziz, finally the Muslim merely represents a slightly obscene accessibility that is less than authentically Indian, while the Hindu becomes a little too Indian to be true, always teetering on the brink of transfiguration. Both Mosque and Temple, therefore, collaborate and collapse into the emptiness that is the Cave.

How does one traverse a landscape replete with images of Krishna, but where Krishna will not come? Forster's response, of course, is to construct a retreat through a dualistic vocabulary in which India is ultimately reprehensible because it denies the fixity of an object that the narrative subject can pursue and penetrate. Instead, like the self-dissipating echoes in the Marabar caves, it can only be approached as a sexuality that lacks a cleft, or a single certain entry of understanding. Throughout the novel, Forster manipulates the image of landscape as metaphoric of that possible fulfillment which is continually on the verge of emptying into disappointment. Finally, his only mode to chart the symbolic geography he names India is by means of locating a structure that perfectly resonates with its own absence. Here, he invites his readership to join him in the Marabar caves.

Forster approaches the caves with the polite bewilderment of an intelligent tourist guide who wishes to be respectful of an entity that is really not very interesting. The restraint with which the narrative seeks to image the cave's unbeauty is, however, its secret method of attack:

The caves are readily described. A tunnel eight feet long, five feet high, three feet wide, leads to a circular chamber about twenty feet in diameter. This arrangement occurs again and again throughout the group of hills, and this is all, this is a Marabar Cave. Having seen one such cave, having seen two, having seen three, four, fourteen, twenty-four, the visitor returns to Chandrapore uncertain whether he has had an interesting experience or a dull one or any experience at all. He finds it difficult to discuss the caves, or to keep them apart in his mind. . . . Nothing, nothing attaches to them, and their reputation—for they have one—does not depend upon human speech. [Ch. xii]

The crevices that are India, in other words, are completely exposed to description, but are offensively impervious to interpretation, like the obscene echo that so torments Forster's female characters. To the western imagination, the horror of the caves is their lack of metaphoricity and their indifference to experiential time. That they could represent an historical autonomy can only be envisioned as a nightmare, or as a parodic pretension towards meaning. After having named the caves as areas of empty experience, the narrative proceeds to explore the hideous possibility that they may indeed possess strata of significance:

But elsewhere, deeper in the granite, are there certain chambers that have no entrances? Chambers never unsealed since the arrival of the gods. Local report declares that these exceed in number those that can be visited, as the dead exceed the living—four hundred of them, four thousand or million. Nothing is inside them, they were sealed up before the creation of pestilence or treasure; if mankind grew curious and excavated, nothing, nothing would be added to the sum of good or evil. [chapter xii]

To entertain such a possibility, however, as Fielding attempts and fails to entertain Indians and Europeans to tea, merely corroborates the narrative fear that India is only real in prehistory, or when it arrives after the fact of history. In relation to the existing authority of western narrative, India represents the terrifying docility of Cordelia's nothing, and the further obscenity of that word in the face of power, which knows that nothing can come of nothing.

It is therefore a matter of some perplexity that most of Forster's readers still see in *A Passage to India* a dated kindliness towards the 'Indian question', or an imperial allegory in which an unattractive European female falsely accuses an attractive Indian male of rape. In considering Adela Quested, it is difficult to ignore the complicated defences that cause Forster to represent her as a cipher almost as arid as the Marabar caves. For rather than a woman abused or abusive, Adela essentially plays the part of a conduit or a passageway for the aborted eroticism between the European Fielding and the Indian Aziz. That, finally, is the substance of the novel: the narrative is not brought to rest with the melodramatic rape trial and Adela's recantation, but is impelled into a description of the Indian's ugly failure to apprehend a European sensibility, and the seductive qualities of his continuing ignorance. Aziz's Muslim accessibility is made impenetrable by such an ignorance, which allows the novel to conclude with the 'half-kissing' embrace of the two men who know that rape is unavailable, 'not yet', 'not here'. The potential seduction of India is thus perpetuated by the lovely, half-realized slave-boys of Forster's will to power; his revulsion takes the darker shapes of the caves and the empty nothings of Adela Quested's requesting womb.

Finally, what prevents the European and the Indian from completing their embrace is the obliterating presence of the landscape. The European wants the completion of his desire in the present moment, yet the narrative gives the last word to the land's great power to deny and disappear:

But the horses didn't want it—they swerved apart; the earth didn't want it . . . the temples, the tank, the jail, the palace, the birds, the carrion, the Guest House . . . they didn't want it, they said in their hundred voices, 'No, not yet', and the sky said, 'No, not there'. [chapter xxxvii]

With this concluding sentence, even the difference of India is subsumed into a trope for a vacant and inexplicable rejection. It becomes instead an unimaginable space which cannot be inhabited by the present tense, resisting even the European attempt to coax it into metaphoricity.

3 *Englands of the Mind**

SEAMUS HEANEY

One of the most precise and suggestive of T. S. Eliot's critical formulations was his notion of what he called 'the auditory imagination', 'the feeling for syllable and rhythm, penetrating far below the conscious levels of thought and feeling, invigorating every word; sinking to the most primitive and forgotten, returning to the origin and bringing something back', fusing 'the most ancient and the most civilized mentality'. I presume Eliot was thinking here about the cultural depth-charges latent in certain words and rhythms, that binding secret between words in poetry that delights not just the ear but the whole backward and abysm of mind and body; thinking of the energies beating in and between words that the poet brings into half-deliberate play; thinking of the relationship between the word as pure vocable, as articulate noise, and the word as etymological occurrence, as symptom of human history, memory and attachments.

It is in the context of this auditory imagination that I wish to discuss the language of Ted Hughes, Geoffrey Hill and Philip Larkin. All of them return to an origin and bring something back, all three live off the hump of the English poetic achievement, all three, here and now, in England, imply a continuity with another England, there and then. All three are hoarders and shorers of what they take to be the real England. All three treat England as a region—or rather treat their region as England—in different and complementary ways. I believe they are afflicted with a sense of history that was once the peculiar affliction of the poets of other nations who were not

---

* From Seamus Heaney, *Preoccupations: Selected Prose 1968–1978*, Faber, 1980, pp. 150–6, 158–69; from the Beckman Lecture, University of California, Berkeley, May 1976.

themselves natives of England but who spoke the English language. The poets of the mother culture, I feel, are now possessed of that defensive love of their territory which was once shared only by those poets whom we might call colonial—Yeats, MacDiarmid, Carlos Williams. They are aware of their Englishness as deposits in the descending storeys of the literary and historical past. Their very terrain is becoming consciously precious. A desire to preserve indigenous traditions, to keep open the imagination's supply lines to the past, to receive from the stations of Anglo-Saxon confirmations of ancestry, to perceive in the rituals of show Saturdays and race-meetings and seaside outings, of church-going and marriages at Whitsun, and in the necessities that crave expression after the ritual of church-going has passed away, to perceive in these a continuity of communal ways, and a confirmation of an identity which is threatened—all this is signified by their language.

When we examine that language, we find that their three separate voices are guaranteed by three separate foundations which, when combined, represent almost the total resources of the English language itself. Hughes relies on the northern deposits, the pagan Anglo-Saxon and Norse elements, and he draws energy also from a related constellation of primitive myths and world views. The life of his language is a persistence of the stark outline and vitality of Anglo-Saxon that became the Middle English alliterative tradition and then went underground to sustain the folk poetry, the ballads, and the ebullience of Shakespeare and the Elizabethans. Hill is also sustained by the Anglo-Saxon base, but his proper guarantor is that language as modified and amplified by the vocabularies and values of the Mediterranean, by the early medieval Latin influence; his is to a certain extent a scholastic imagination founded on an England that we might describe as Anglo-Romanesque, touched by the polysyllabic light of Christianity but possessed by darker energies which might be acknowledged as barbaric. Larkin then completes the picture, because his proper hinterland is the English language Frenchified and turned humanist by the Norman conquest and the Renaissance, made nimble, melodious and plangent by Chaucer and Spenser, and besomed clean of its inkhornisms and its irrational magics by the eighteenth century.

And their Englands of the mind might be correspondingly characterized. Hughes's is a primeval landscape where stones cry out and horizons endure, where the elements inhabit the mind with a religious force, where the pebble dreams 'it is the foetus of God', 'where the staring angels go through', 'where all the stars bow down', where, with appropriately pre-Socratic force, water lies 'at the bottom of all things/utterly worn out utterly clear'. It is England as King Lear's heath which now becomes a Yorkshire moor where sheep and foxes and hawks persuade 'unaccommodated man' that he is a poor bare forked thing, kinned not in a chain but on a plane of being with the animals themselves. Their monoliths and lintels. The air is menaced by God's voice in the wind, by demonic protean crow-shapes; and the poet is a wanderer among the ruins, cut off by catastrophe from consolation and philosophy. Hill's England, on the other hand, is more hospitable to the human presence. The monoliths make way for the keeps and chantries if also for the beheading block. The heath's loneliness is kept at bay by the natural magic of the grove and the intellectual force of the scholar's cell. The poet is not a wanderer but a clerk or perhaps an illuminator or one of a guild of masters: he is in possession of a history rather than a mythology; he has a learned rather than an oral tradition. There are wars, but there are also dynasties, ideas of inheritance and order, possibilities for the 'true governaunce of England'. His elegies are not laments for the irrevocable dispersal of the *comitatus* and the ring-giver in the hall, but solemn requiems for Plantagenet kings whose murderous wars are set in a great pattern, to be understood only when 'the sea/Across daubed rocks evacuates its dead'. And Larkin's England similarly reflects features from the period that his language is hived off. His trees and flowers and grasses are neither animistic, nor hallowed by half-remembered druidic lore; they are emblems of mutabilitie. Behind them lies the sensibility of the troubadour and courtier. 'Cut grass lies frail;/Brief is the breath/Mown stalks exhale'; his landscape is dominated neither by the untamed heath nor the totemistic architectures of spire and battlement but by the civic prospects, by roofs and gardens and prospects where urban and pastoral visions interact as 'postal districts packed like squares of wheat'. The poet is no longer a bardic remnant nor an initiate in curious learning nor a jealous master of the secrets of a craft; he is a humane and civilized member of the customs service or the civil service or, indeed, the library service. The moon is no longer his white goddess but his poetic property, to be image rather than icon: 'high and preposterous and separate', she watches over unfenced existence, over fulfil-ment's desolate attic, over an England of department stores, canals and floatings of industrial froth, explosions in mines, effigies in churches, secreta-ries in offices; and she hauls tides of life where only one ship is worth celebration, not a Golden Hind or a Victory, but 'black-/Sailed unfamiliar, towing at her back/A huge and birdless silence'.

Hughes's sensibility is pagan in the original sense: he is a haunter of the *pagus*, a heath-dweller, a heathen; he moves by instinct in the thickets beyond the *urbs*; he is neither urban nor urbane. His poetry is as redolent of the lair as it is of the library. The very titles of his books are casts made into the outback of our animal recognitions. *Lupercal*, a word infested with wolfish stinks yet returning to an origin in Shakespeare's *Julius Caesar*: 'You all did see that on the Lupercal/I thrice presented him a kingly crown'. Yet the word passes back through Shakespeare into the Lupercal, a cave below the western corner of the Palatine Hill in Rome; and the Lupercal was also the festival held on 15 February when, after the sacrifice of goats and a dog, youths dressed only in girdles made from the skins of these victims ran about the bounds of the Palatine city, striking those whom they met, especially women, with strips of goatskin. It was a fertility rite, and it was also a ritual beating of the bounds of the city, and in a way Hughes's language is just this also. Its sensuous fetch, its redolence of blood and gland and grass and water, recalled English poetry in the fifties from a too suburban aversion of the attention from the elemental; and the poems beat the bounds of a hidden England in streams and trees, on moors and in byres. Hughes appeared like Poor Tom on the heath, a civilized man tasting and testing the primitive facts; he appeared as *Wodwo*, a nosing wild man of the woods. The volume *Wodwo* appeared in 1967 and carried as its epigraph a quotation from *Gawain and the Green Knight*, and that deliberate affiliation is instructive. Like the art of Gawain, Hughes's art is one of clear outline and inner richness. His diction is consonantal, and it snicks through the air like an efficient blade, marking and carving out fast definite shapes; but within those shapes, mysteries and rituals are hinted at. They are circles within which he conjures up presences.

Hughes's vigour has much to do with this matter of consonants that take the measure of his vowels like calipers, or stud the line like rivets. 'Everything is inheriting everything', as he says in one of his poems, and what he has inherited through Shakespeare and John Webster and Hopkins and Lawrence is something of that primary life of stress which is the quick of the English poetic matter. His consonants are the Norsemen, the Normans, the Round-heads in the world of his vocables, hacking and hedging and hammering down the abundance and luxury and possible lasciviousness of the vowels. . . . Hughes's aspiration in these early poems is to command all the elements, to bring them within the jurisdiction of his authoritarian voice. . . . The thistles are emblems of the Hughes voice as I see it, born of an original vigour, fighting back over the same ground; and it is not insignificant that in this poem Hughes himself imagines the thistles as images of a fundamental speech, uttering itself in gutturals from behind the sloped arms of consonants: [Quotes last nine lines of 'Thistles']. The gutturals of dialects, which Hughes here connects with the Nordic stratum of English speech, he pronounces in another place to be the germinal secret of his own voice. . . . Hughes attempts to make vocal the inner life, the simple being-thereness, 'the substance, nature and consequences in life' of sea, stone, wind and tree. Blake's pebble and tiger are shadowy presences in the background, as are the landscapes of Anglo-Saxon poetry. And the whole thing is founded on rock, that rock which Hughes presented in his autobiographical essay as his birthstone, holding his emergence in place just as his headstone will hold his decease:

This was the *memento mundi* over my birth: my spiritual midwife at the time and my godfather ever since—or one of my godfathers. From my first day it watched. If it couldn't see me direct, a towering gloom over my pram, it watched me through a species of periscope: that is, by infiltrating the very light of my room with its particular shadow. From my home near the bottom of the south-facing slope of the valley, the cliff was both the curtain and the backdrop to existence.

I quote this piece because it links the childhood core with the adult opus, because that rock is the equivalent in his poetic landscape of dialect in his poetic speech. The rock persists, survives, sustains, endures and informs his imagination, just as it is the bedrock of the language upon which Hughes founds his version of survival and endurance.

Stone and rock figure prominently in the world of Geoffrey Hill's poetry also, but Hill's imagination is not content to grant the mineral world the absolute sway that Hughes allows it. He is not the suppliant chanting to the megalith, but rather the mason dressing it. Hill also beats the bounds of an England, his own native West Midlands, beheld as a medieval England facing into the Celtic mysteries of Wales and out towards the military and ecclesiastical splendours of Europe. His *Mercian Hymns* names his territory Mercia, and masks his imagination under the figure of King Offa, builder of Offa's dyke between England and Wales, builder as well as beater of the boundaries. Hill's celebration of Mercia has a double-focus: one a child's-eye view, close to the common earth, the hoard of history, and the other the historian's and scholar's eye, inquisitive of the meaning, bringing time past to bear on time present and vice versa. But the writing itself is by no means abstract and philosophical. Hill addresses the language, as I say, like a mason addressing a block, not unlike his own mason in Hymn XXIV. . . . The mannered rhetoric of these pieces is a kind of verbal architecture, a grave and sturdy English Romanesque. The native undergrowth, both vegetative and verbal, that barbaric scrollwork of fern and ivy, is set against the tympanum and chancel-arch, against the weighty elegance of imperial Latin. . . .

   In fact, we can see the method more clearly if we put the poem in its proper context, which is in the middle of a group of three entitled *Opus Anglicanum* . . . . The entanglement, the interlacing, is now that of embroidery, and this first poem, I suggest, brings together womanly figures from Hill's childhood memory with the ghostly procession of needleworkers from the medieval castles and convents: [Quotes Hymn XXIII]. Again, the liturgical and Latinate of the first paragraph is abraded and rebutted by the literal and local weight of 'scraping their boots free from lime-splodges and phlegm'—the boots being, I take it, the boots of labourers involved in this never-ending *Opus Anglicanum*, from agricultural origins to industrial developments. And in order just to clinch the thing, consider the third piece, where the 'utilitarian iron work' in which his grandmother was involved is contemplated in a perspective that includes medieval embroidress and mason, and a certain 'transcendence' enters the making of wire nails: [Quotes Hymn XXV]. Ruskin's eightieth letter reflects eloquently and plangently on the injustice of the master and servant situation, on the exploitation of labour, on the demeaning work in a nail forge. The Mayor of Birmingham took him to a house where two women were at work, labouring, as he says, with ancient Vulcanian skill:

So wrought they,—the English matron and maid;—so it was their darg to labour from morning to evening—seven to seven—by the furnace side—the winds of summer fanning the blast of it.

He goes on to compute that the woman and the husband earn altogether £55 a year with which to feed and clothe themselves and their six children, to reproach the luxury of the mill-owning class, and to compare the wives of industrialists contemplating Burne Jones's picture of Venus's mirror 'with these, their sisters, who had only, for Venus's mirror, a heap of ashes; compassed about with no forget-me-nots, but with all the forgetfulness in the world'.

It seems to me here that Hill is celebrating his own indomitable Englishry, casting his mind on other days, singing a clan beaten into the clay and ashes, and linking their patience, their sustaining energy, with the glory of England. The 'quick forge', after all, may be what its origin in Shakespeare's *Henry V* declares it to be, 'the quick forge and working house of thought', but it is surely also the 'random grim forge' of Felix Randal, the farrier. The image shifts between various points and embroiders a new *opus anglicanum* in this intended and allusive poem. And the point of the embroidering needle, of course, is *darg*, that chip off the Anglo-Saxon block, meaning 'a day's work, or the task of a day'.

The *Mercian Hymns* show Hill in full command of his voice. Much as the stiff and corbelled rhetoric of earlier work like *Funeral Music* and 'Requiem for the Plantagenet Kings' stands up and will stand up, it is only when this rhetoric becomes a press tightening on and squeezing out of the language the vigour of common speech, the essential Anglo-Saxon juices, it is only then that the poetry attains this final refreshed and refreshing quality: then he has, in the words of another piece, accrued a 'golden and stinking blaze'.

Finally, to come to Larkin, where what accrues in the language is not 'a golden and stinking blaze', not the rank and fermenting composts of philology and history, but the bright senses of words worn clean in literate conversation. In Larkin's language as in his vision of water, 'any angled light . . . congregate[s] endlessly'. There is a gap in Larkin between the perceiver and the thing perceived, a refusal to melt through long perspectives, an obstinate insistence that the poet is neither a race memory nor a myth-kitty nor a mason, but a real man in a real place. The cadences and vocabulary of his poems are tuned to a rational music. It would seem that he has deliberately curtailed his gift for evocation, for resonance, for symbolist *frissons*. He turned from Yeats to Hardy as his master. He never followed the Laurentian success of his early poem 'Wedding Wind' which ends with a kind of biblical swoon, an image of fulfilled lovers 'kneeling like cattle by all generous waters'. He rebukes romantic aspiration and afflatus with a scrupulous meanness. . . . His tongue moves hesitantly, precisely, honestly, among ironies and negatives. He is the poet of rational light, a light that has its own luminous beauty but which has also the effect of exposing clearly the truths which it touches. Larkin speaks neither a dialect nor a pulpit language; there are no 'hectoring large scale verses' in his three books, nor is there the stubbly intimacy of 'oath-edged talk and pipe-smoke' which he nostalgically annotates among the miners. His language would have pleased those Tudor and Augustan guardians who wanted to polish and beautify their speech, to smooth it for art. What we hear is a stripped standard English voice, a voice indeed with a unique break and remorseful tone, but a voice that leads back neither to the thumping beat of Anglo-Saxon nor to the Gregorian chant of the Middle Ages. Its ancestry begins, in fact, when the Middle Ages are turning secular, and plays begin to take their place beside the Mass as a form of communal telling and knowing. . . .

As well as the Cavalier Larkin, there is a late Augustan Larkin, the poet of decorous melancholy moods, of twilit propriety and shadowy melody. His poem about superannuated racehorses, for example, entitled 'At Grass', could well be subtitled, 'An Elegy in a Country Paddock'. Behind the trees where the horses shelter there could well rise the spire of Stoke Poges church; and behind the smooth numbers of wind distressing the tails and manes, there is the donnish exactitude of tresses being *dis*tressed: [Quotes the first three lines of 'At Grass']. And when, at the conclusion of the poem, 'the groom and the groom's boy/With bridles in the evening come', their footsteps surely echo the ploughman homeward plodding his weary way. . . .

He too returns to origins and brings something back, although he does not return to 'roots'. He puts inverted commas round his 'roots', in fact. His childhood, he says, was a forgotten boredom. He sees England from train windows, fleeting past and away. He is urban modern man, the insular Englishman, responding to the tones of his own clan, ill at ease when out of his environment. He is a poet, indeed, of composed and tempered English nationalism, and his voice is the not untrue, not unkind voice of post-war England, where the cloth cap and the royal crown have both lost some of their potent symbolism, and the categorical, socially defining functions of the working-class accent and the aristocratic drawl have almost been eroded. Larkin's tones are mannerly but not exquisite, well-bred but not mealy-mouthed. If his England and his English are not as deep as Hughes's or as solemn as Hill's, they are nevertheless clearly beloved, and during his sojourn in Belfast in the late fifties, he gave thanks, by implication, for the nurture that he receives by living among his own. The speech, the customs, the institutions of England are, in the words of another English poet, domiciled in Ireland, 'wife to his creating thought'. That was Hopkins in Dublin in the 1880s, sensing that his individual talent was being divorced from his tradition. Here is Larkin remembering the domicile in Belfast in the 1950s: [Quotes 'The Importance of Elsewhere']. Larkin's England of the mind is in many ways continuous with the England of Rupert Brooke's 'Grantchester' and Edward Thomas's 'Adelstrop', an England of customs and institutions, industrial and domestic, but also an England whose pastoral hinterland is threatened by the very success of those institutions. Houses and roads and factories mean that a certain England is 'Going, Going' . . . I think that sense of an ending has driven all three of these writers into a kind of piety towards their local origins, has made them look in, rather than up, to England. The loss of imperial power, the failure of economic nerve, the diminished influence of Britain inside Europe, all this has led to a new sense of the shires, a new valuing of the native English experience. Donald Davie, for example, has published a book of poems, with that very title, *The Shires*, which attempts to annex to his imagination by personal memory or historical meditation or literary connections, each shire of England. It is a book at once intimate and exclusive, a topography of love and impatience, and it is yet another symptom that English poets are being forced to explore not just the matter of England, but what is the matter with England. I have simply presumed to share in that exploration through the medium which England has, for better or worse, impressed upon us all, the English language itself.

4 *Behind the Clichés of Contemporary Theatre**

JOHN MCGRATH

I am trying to discuss a more active intervention by the theatre in forming contemporary life and contributing to the future of our society.

I could have called [these lectures] 'Telling the Story'—because that's what theatre does. You go into a space, and some other people use certain devices to tell you a story. Because they have power over you, in a real sense, while you are there, they make a choice, with political implications, as to which story to tell—and how to tell it.

* From John McGrath, *A Good Night Out: Popular Theatre: Audience, Class and Form*, Methuen, 1981, pp. 1–10, 16–17; from the first of a series of lectures given in Cambridge in 1979.

But we go in, watch their story, and come out, changed. If their work is good, and skilfully written, presented and acted, we come out feeling exhilarated: we are more alive for seeing it, more aware of the possibilities of the human race, more fully human ourselves. So far, so wonderfully universal. But this story we watch can have a meaning: a very specific meaning. What if we are black, say, and we go to see some splendidly effective, but completely racist theatre show? What if we are Jewish, and go to see a piece of anti-semitic drama such as one could easily see in Germany in the 1930s? Are we quite so exhilarated? Quite so fully human? Or would we not feel demeaned, excluded from humanity, diminished in our possibilities and a great deal more pessimistic about the future of the human race than when we went in? The meaning, and value, of theatre can clearly change from country to country, group to group, and—significantly—from class to class.

What does this mean then? That not *all* stories are so wonderfully universal? That the political and social values of the play cannot be the same for one audience as they are for another? What a terribly confusing state of affairs!

How can you know where you stand? How can you be suitably academic, objective and withdrawn? How can you make a universally valid *judgement*?

It is next to impossible to take the existence of various different audiences into account, to codify their possible reactions to a piece of theatre, to evaluate a piece of theatre from *within several frameworks*. So what do we do? Well, I'll tell you what most of us do—we take the point of view of a *normal* person —usually that of a well-fed, white, middle-class, sensitive but sophisticated literary critic: and we *universalize* it as *the* response.

The effect of such a practice is to enshrine certain specific values and qualities of a play above others. For example, mystery—or mysteriousness as it so often becomes. How often has this 'all-pervading air of mystery' been praised by critic and academic alike, from Yeats's *Purgatory* down through Beckett to our own cut-price product, Harold Pinter? Mystery, the ingredient that leavens the loaf—or should I say makes the dough rise?

But many audiences don't like mystery, in that sense of playing games with knowledge, and words, and facts. They become impatient, they want to know what the story is meant to be about, what is supposed to have happened. They wish a different order of mystery. But because we have universalized the critical response to 'mystery' that proclaims it as a truly wonderful thing, we now have to dismiss those audiences as philistine, as outside true theatre culture, as—and this is the Arnold Wesker refinement—in need of education. My belief, and the basis of my practice as a writer in the theatre for the last ten years, has been that there *are* indeed different kinds of audiences, with different theatrical values and expectations, and that we have to be very careful before consigning one audience and its values to the critical dustbin. . . . For the time being let me just note that I do not accept the following assumptions:

1. that art is universal, capable of meaning the same to all people;
2. that the more 'universal' it is, the better it is;
3. that the 'audience' for theatre is an idealized white, middle-class, etc., person and that all theatre should be dominated by the tastes and values of such a person;
4. that, therefore, an audience without such an idealized person's values is an inferior audience; and
5. that the so-called 'traditional values' of English literature are now anything other than an indirect cultural expression of the dominance over the whole of Britain of the ruling class of the south-east of England.

To be more specific, I *do* believe that there is a working-class audience for theatre in Britain which makes demands, and which has values, which are different from those enshrined in our idealized middle-class audience. That these values are no less 'valid'—whatever that means—no less rich in potential for a thriving theatre-culture, no thinner in 'traditions' and subtleties than the current dominant theatre-culture, and that these values and demands contain within them the seeds of a new basis for making theatre that could in many ways be more appropriate to the last quarter of the twentieth century than the stuff that presently goes on at the National Theatre, or at the Aldwych.

Having planted the revolutionary suggestion that middle-class theatre is not by definition the only, or even necessarily the best, kind of theatre, I would like to complicate matters further by talking a little about the 'language'—as they say—of theatre.

Why is the question of the 'language' of theatre a problem? First, let us glance at recent cinema criticism. Here we see a fairly clear consensus, whatever may be the opinions about it, on the subject of the 'language' of cinema. The 'language' of cinema includes the text, the *mise-en-scène*, the lighting, the editing, the locations, the performances, the casting, the camera angles, the use of filters, the music, the effects-track, the framing—in short, everything that is communicated by the reels of celluloid which make up the experience of cinema when adequately projected.

Theatre, however, is still discussed as if it were a book. Now I hope I don't need to say that there does exist a huge body of *dramatic literature*, which is rarely performed and whose 'language' is indeed that of words on the page —and it is far from inadequate as a source of immense literary pleasure.

And of course there is no doubt that words constitute a major element in the language of theatre. But I would remind you that words, the text, may well not be a decisive element in theatre. In fact, the sum total of what happens on the stage may not, in extreme circumstances, be decisive, as Mrs Lincoln once remarked.

I must emphasise that the language of theatre is possibly even more extensive than that normally ascribed to cinema. For not only must the text, *mise-en-scène*, lighting, performances, casting, music, effects, placing on the stage all be taken into account in order to arrive at a description of the stage event, but also the nature of the audience, the nature, social, geographical and physical, of the venue, the price of tickets, the availability of tickets, the nature and placing of the pre-publicity, where the nearest pub is, and the relationships between all these considerations themselves and of each with what is happening on stage. For when we discuss theatre, we are discussing a social event, and a very complex social event, with a long history and many elements, each element also having a long and independent history.

To complicate matters further, each occasion of theatre is different, evanescent and impossible to record. Of course this does not reduce us to silence. But what it does do all too often is to reduce the language of theatre that is studied academically to the most easily obtainable—the words. Perhaps that study will include pictures of the set or leading actors, and descriptions of the theatre building, but, above all, it will be concerned with the words said to have been uttered on the stage. You can buy them in a book, they never change, they are convenient objects of study. But words are not the 'language' of theatre, and by exclusively attending to them we reduce, impoverish the event for academic convenience. The act of *creating theatre* has nothing to do with the making of dramatic literature: dramatic literature is what is sometimes left behind when theatre has been and gone. . . . A serious playwright today must work with *all* the elements of the language of the theatrical event—he or she must reinvent theatre every time he or she writes a play: the whole theatre, not just what is said on stage. The simple acceptance of, say, the location of the event, the kind of publicity available, the price of admission and the behaviour of the box office staff as all being someone else's problem, and not areas of personal concern for creative artists means that in effect a great deal of the meaning of the event socially and politically is taken away from the writer. The play itself can completely change its meaning, given the wrong theatre or wrong publicity, or even the wrong ticket prices.

There are elements in the language of the theatre beyond the text, even beyond the production, which are often more decisive, more central to one's experience of the event than the text or the production. I wish to discuss several of these—notably the choice of venue, audience, performers, and the relationship between performer and audience—in later lectures. For the moment, let me declare that the constant reduction of the language of theatre to one of its elements, simply because that is more reproducible, and therefore more convenient for discussion, is not only misleading but dangerous.

Now one of the basic assumptions about the language of theatre, given the practice of 'universalizing' the expectations of the white middle-class sensitive but sophisticated ideal auditor, is that in order to change the meaning or class-orientation of theatre, all you need to do is to change the content of *some* of what happens on the stage.

For example, there is a whole generation of playwrights who began their writing careers at the Royal Court theatre between 1956 and 1966, who have gone on to create what is in fact the current dominant mode of theatre, and who are said to have allowed the voice of the working class into the British theatre for the first time since Shakespeare, or even the Mystery plays. As Martin Esslin puts it: 'plays dealing with lower-class characters speaking a non-standard English and flouting the conventions of the "who's for tennis" school of playwriting could actually become profitable theatrical ventures'.

I should like to devote part of this first lecture to looking at the work done at the Royal Court during that decade, because those years were crucial and formative for what is now the mainstream of British theatre. Various shifts and changes took place at the Court during that time which have become automatic assumptions today.

I shall not attempt a potted history of how the Royal Court was founded, or indeed how it was able to continue—for those who are interested this is quite adequately documented in *Playwrights' Theatre* by Terry Browne. What I am interested in is what is vulgarly called 'Post-Osborne Drama'. It is an appalling phrase, but one not without meaning, since John Osborne was the first of a line of young, 'lower class', native-born and educated, British dramatists whose work was encouraged and presented by the English Stage Company at the Royal Court. This line includes: Michael Hastings, N. F. Simpson, John Arden, Ann Jellicoe, Arnold Wesker, Donald Howarth, Willis Hall, Alun Owen, Christopher Logue, Harold Pinter, Edward Bond, Henry Livings, Charles Wood, Christopher Hampton, Howard Brenton, David Storey, David Halliwell and Joe Orton.

The writing of these playwrights has come to be the dominant way of 'mediating contemporary reality' of our theatre. They, and their imitators on television, radio and film, are the people who tell the story, in the dramatic forms.

In 1956 John Osborne is said to have inaugurated a New Era; Revitalised various things; Heralded a new Dawn; Opened the Doors of the Theatre to this, that and the other—(mostly the northern working class) and 'Given a New Direction' to British theatre. Subsequent to this amazing 'Open Sesame', many more than forty thieves have entered the cave full of gold and treasures and dipped their fingers into the oaken chests. Many another young writer has followed Osborne into the Royal Court or the Aldwych or the National Theatre. They have been served by an array of talented ex-working-class directors and actors, whose ranks are ever growing. Many of these writers, directors and actors have become both rich and successful—one thinks of John Dexter who directed Wesker's plays once, now at the Met in New York; or Albert Finney with his race horses; Tony Richardson in Hollywood, or Osborne himself, a crusty old eccentric in his club, yapping away about the trade unions ruining the country. All very powerful, influential figures.

More important, this particular *kind* of theatre has become equally respectable, conventional and pernicious. It has spread, or its influence and personnel have spread, into the Royal Shakespeare Company, the National Theatre, and almost all the major repertory theatres, into all areas of television and broadcasting, into many home-grown British films, even from time to time into Covent Garden Opera House. It is the Regular Route, one which I followed myself, for the north-country scholarship boy to take from the university into—ultimately—Harry Saltzman's mansion (in Uxbridge), or Sam Spiegel's big yacht steaming out of Monaco harbour into the Mediterranean sunset. How many times, how many eager young writers, actors, directors have taken their talent along to Sloane Square, or the Hampstead Theatre Club, or the Aldwych, or now the Cottesloe segment of the National Theatre complex, feeling a part of history, but more than that a certain loyalty to their own experience, a certain security in being progressive, even socialist if such is their desire, feeling that this kind of theatre is really significant.

Well of course it is, but it is just *what* it signifies that is the question. Its greatest claim to social significance is that it produced a new 'working-class' art, that it somehow stormed the Winter Palace of bourgeois culture and threw out the old regime and turned the place into a temple of workers' art. Of course it did nothing of the kind. What Osborne and his clever director Tony Richardson had achieved was a method of translating some areas of non-middle-class life in Britain into a form of entertainment that could be sold to the middle classes. Similarly with Wesker, John Dexter's contribution as director of the trilogy was to shape the plays, the performances, the design and the overall mood into artefacts that London's trendier fashion-setters could come to and be titillated by. John Arden's *Live Like Pigs*, however, a relatively unmediated piece of raw life, was immensely unpopular, and the theatre nearly empty throughout its short run. *Epitaph for George Dillon*, of course, and *The Entertainer*, with Olivier quickly onto the band wagon, made a lot of money, and transferred to the West End where they made even more money. Then Arden's *Serjeant Musgrave's Dance* came on and drove them all out again, and lost the money. . . .

From even a brief examination of the elements of the 'event' of theatre, we can see clearly that when the 'post-Osborne' British dramatists set out to 'tell the story', to mediate contemporary reality, they were already inflected towards an account that would be acceptable to the middle class. Much as they may have thought that they had introduced the authentic voice of the working class into the theatre, as I'm sure did Wesker, Alun Owen, Edward Bond, Arden and even Pinter, the message that voice was trying to carry was inevitably swamped by the many other tongues of the event.

Let me go back to my original observations about the non-universality of theatre. Although this 'post-Osborne' drama is now the dominant kind of drama in this country, it is not the only kind. While the audiences at the Royal Court were being 'thrilled' by watching actors pretend to be workers actually working, the other traditions of theatre were not dead. The West End went on being the West End, with Robert Morley in comedies about the troubles of businessmen, and *Salad Days*, and *My Fair Lady*. Many variety theatres were still going in 1956, but they were closing down, almost one a week: the cinema had finally taken over. But the variety performers were moving into the working men's clubs, and the social clubs, and still doing summer seasons and panto which flourished. In the late 40s, Joan Littlewood, Gerry Raffles, Ewan MacColl and a few other socialists had formed various companies to tour with socialist plays before working-class audiences, in Scotland, around Manchester and eventually in the Theatre Royal, Stratford, in East London. There were several Unity theatres, mostly amateur, though some for a time professional, which were closely connected with the Communist Party, and which put on agitational and other socialist plays to working-class audiences. In other words, another, different story was being told. Reality was being mediated in several very different ways.

VI New Writings in English

As Marilyn Butler observed in the opening extract of this anthology (Part One, section I), most literature in English today 'does not speak for the official, London-based "nation"'. The reasons for this have been implicit in the discussions of the preceding section, on 'End of Empire'. One result has been to redefine 'English Literature' as 'Literatures in English'. But the most forceful motive for this redefinition has been the phenomenal rise in 'New Writings' from the ex-colonial countries themselves: literary texts whose very appearance on the horizon poses a challenge to 'metropolitan' claims to offer defining evaluations, to offer an exclusive 'canon' for consumption by teachers, students, and readers generally. This rush of 'New Writings' has been accompanied—inevitably—by writings about those writings. The aim here is simply to give you an idea of the range and quality of the critical debates which have arisen; and to indicate some of the liveliest and most important areas of agreement—and disagreement.

The first item is from one of the most radical, outspoken, and influential voices: Frantz Fanon (1925–61), a psychiatrist from Martinique whose experiences during the Algerian war against the French led him to join the national liberation movement and to become its spokesperson. A Marxist, he believed that Marxist analysis should be 'stretched' when 'we have to do with the colonial problem'. This was in The Wretched of the Earth, where he also made the classic statement concerning literature and its cultural role in the period of decolonization excerpted here. He raises all the basic questions, whether or not others agree with his answers.

Chinua Achebe's challenge to misguided 'colonialist criticism' is an elegantly argued case which turns on traditional oral metaphors as a way of authenticating his own particular experiences, and those of his people. More polemical and eclectic, stressing the need for conscious resistance to European literary/cultural norms, Chinweizu and his co-authors ask why 'orature' should not be granted equal status. Elaine Fido's case against the St Lucian poet Derek Walcott suggests how feminist criticism may be deployed in this context, and anticipates the concerns of section VII. Wole Soyinka's approach to drama takes a world perspective, including classical Greek and Yoruba tragedy, by way of arguing an 'anti-ideology' approach to consciousness. The last extract, from The Empire Writes Back, offers a summing up, while taking the discussion beyond the predominantly Afro-Caribbean emphasis of the preceding extracts.

1 *On National Culture*[*]

FRANTZ FANON

I am ready to concede that on the plane of factual being the past existence of an Aztec civilization does not change anything very much in the diet of the Mexican peasant of today. I admit that all the proofs of a wonderful Songhai civilization will not change the fact that today the Songhais are under-fed and illiterate, thrown between sky and water with empty heads and empty eyes. But it has been remarked several times that this passionate search for a national culture which existed before the colonial era finds its legitimate reason in the anxiety shared by native intellectuals to shrink away from that Western culture in which they all risk being swamped. Because they realize they are in danger of losing their lives and thus becoming lost to their people, these men, hot-headed and with anger in their hearts, relentlessly determine to renew contact once more with the oldest and most pre-colonial springs of life of their people.

Let us go farther. Perhaps this passionate research and this anger are kept up or at least directed by the secret hope of discovering beyond the misery of today, beyond self-contempt, resignation and abjuration, some very beautiful and splendid era whose existence rehabilitates us both in regard to ourselves and in regard to others. I have said that I have decided to go farther. Perhaps unconsciously, the native intellectuals, since they could not stand wonder-struck before the history of today's barbarity, decided to go back farther and to delve deeper down; and, let us make no mistake, it was with the greatest delight that they discovered that there was nothing to be ashamed of in the past, but rather dignity, glory and solemnity. The claim to a national culture in the past does not only rehabilitate that nation and serve as a justification for the hope of a future national culture. In the sphere of psycho-affective equilibrium it is responsible for an important change in the native. Perhaps we have not sufficiently demonstrated that colonialism is not simply content to impose its rule upon the present and the future of a dominated country. Colonialism is not satisfied merely with holding a people in its grip and emptying the native's brain of all form and content. By a kind of perverted logic, it turns to the past of the oppressed people, and distorts, disfigures and destroys it. This work of devaluing pre-colonial history takes on a dialectical significance today.

When we consider the efforts made to carry out the cultural estrangement

[*] From Frantz Fanon, 'On National Culture', in *The Wretched of the Earth*, trans. Constance Farrington, Penguin Books, Harmondsworth, Middlesex, 1967, pp. 168–78; first publ. 1961 as *Les Damnés de la terre* by François Marpero, éditeur, with a Preface by Jean-Paul Sartre; from a 'Statement' made at the Second Congress of Black Artists and Writers, Rome, 1959.

so characteristic of the colonial epoch, we realize that nothing has been left to chance and that the total result looked for by colonial domination was indeed to convince the natives that colonialism came to lighten their darkness. The effect consciously sought by colonialism was to drive into the natives' heads the idea that if the settlers were to leave, they would at once fall back into barbarism, degradation and bestiality.

On the unconscious plane, colonialism therefore did not seek to be considered by the native as a gentle, loving mother who protects her child from a hostile environment, but rather as a mother who unceasingly restrains her fundamentally perverse offspring from managing to commit suicide and from giving free rein to its evil instincts. The colonial mother protects her child from itself, from its ego, and from its physiology, its biology and its own unhappiness which is its very essence.

In such a situation the claims of the native intellectual are no luxury but a necessity in any coherent programme. The native intellectual who takes up arms to defend his nation's legitimacy and who wants to bring proofs to bear out that legitimacy, who is willing to strip himself naked to study the history of his body, is obliged to dissect the heart of his people.

Such an examination is not specifically national. The native intellectual who decides to give battle to colonial lies fights on the field of the whole continent. The past is given back its value. Culture, extracted from the past to be displayed in all its splendour, is not necessarily that of his own country. Colonialism, which has not bothered to put too fine a point on its efforts, has never ceased to maintain that the Negro is a savage; and for the colonist, the Negro was neither an Angolan nor a Nigerian, for he simply spoke of 'the Negro'. For colonialism, this vast continent was the haunt of savages, a country riddled with superstitions and fanaticism, destined for contempt, weighed down by the curse of God, a country of cannibals—in short, the Negro's country. Colonialism's condemnation is continental in its scope. The contention by colonialism that the darkest night of humanity lay over pre-colonial history concerns the whole of the African continent. The efforts of the native to rehabilitate himself and to escape from the claws of colonialism are logically inscribed from the same point of view as that of colonialism. . . .

And it is only too true that those who are most responsible for this racialization of thought, or at least for the first movement towards that thought, are and remain those Europeans who have never ceased to set up white culture to fill the gap left by the absence of other cultures. Colonialism did not dream of wasting its time in denying the existence of one national culture after another. Therefore the reply of the colonized peoples will be straight away continental in its breadth. In Africa, the native literature of the last twenty years is not a national literature but a Negro literature. The concept of Negro-ism,[1] for example, was the emotional if not the logical antithesis of that insult which the white man flung at humanity. . . .

The poets of Negro-ism will not stop at the limits of the continent. From America, black voices will take up the hymn with fuller unison. The 'black world' will see the light and Busia from Ghana, Birago Diop from Senegal, Hampaté Ba from the Sudan and Saint-Clair Drake from Chicago will not hesitate to assert the existence of common ties and a motive power that is identical.

The example of the Arab world might equally well be quoted here. We know that the majority of Arab territories have been under colonial domination. Colonialism has made the same effort in these regions to plant deep in the minds of the native population the idea that before the advent of colonialism their history was one which was dominated by barbarism. The struggle for national liberty has been accompanied by a cultural phenomenon known by the name of the awakening of Islam. The passion with which contemporary Arab writers remind their people of the great pages of their history is a reply to the lies told by the occupying power. The great names of Arabic literature and the great past of Arab civilization have been brandished about with the same ardour as those of the African civilizations. . . .

This historical necessity in which the men of African culture find themselves to racialize their claims and to speak more of African culture than of national culture will tend to lead them up a blind alley. Let us take for example the case of the African Cultural Society. This society had been created by African intellectuals who wished to get to know each other and to compare their experiences and the results of their respective research work. The aim of this society was therefore to affirm the existence of an African culture, to evaluate this culture on the plane of distinct nations and to reveal the internal motive forces of each of their national cultures. But at the same time this society fulfilled another need: the need to exist side by side with the European Cultural Society, which threatened to transform itself into a Universal Cultural Society. There was therefore at the bottom of this decision the anxiety to be present at the universal trysting place fully armed, with a culture springing from the very heart of the African continent. Now, this Society will very quickly show its inability to shoulder these different tasks, and will limit itself to exhibitionist demonstrations, while the habitual behaviour of the members of this Society will be confined to showing Europeans that such a thing as African culture exists, and opposing their ideas to those of ostentatious and narcissistic Europeans. We have shown that such an attitude is normal and draws its legitimacy from the lies propagated by men

---

[1] Literal translation of 'Negritude', now commonly accepted French term for the literary-cultural movement fostering an awareness of the black heritage and values; coined by Fanon's compatriot from Martinique, Aimé Césaire, in 1947 in his *Cahier d'un retour au pays natal*. [Ed.]

of Western culture. But the degradation of the aims of this Society will become more marked with the elaboration of the concept of Negro-ism. The African Society will become the cultural society of the black world and will come to include the Negro dispersion, that is to say the tens of thousands of black people spread over the American continents.

The Negroes who live in the United States and in Central or Latin America in fact experience the need to attach themselves to a cultural matrix. Their problem is not fundamentally different from that of the Africans. The whites of America did not mete out to them any different treatment from that of the whites that ruled over the Africans. We have seen that the whites were used to putting all Negroes in the same bag. During the first congress of the African Cultural Society which was held in Paris in 1956, the American Negroes of their own accord considered their problems from the same standpoint as those of their African brothers. Cultured Africans, speaking of African civilizations, decreed that there should be a reasonable status within the state for those who had formerly been slaves. But little by little the American Negroes realized that the essential problems confronting them were not the same as those that confronted the African Negroes. The Negroes of Chicago only resemble the Nigerians or the Tanganyikans in so far as they were all defined in relation to the whites. But once the first comparisons had been made and subjective feelings were assuaged, the American Negroes realized that the objective problems were fundamentally heterogeneous. . . .

Negro-ism therefore finds its first limitation in the phenomena which take account of the formation of the historical character of men. Negro and African-Negro culture broke up into different entities because the men who wished to incarnate these cultures realized that every culture is first and foremost national, and that the problems which kept Richard Wright or Langston Hughes on the alert were fundamentally different from those which might confront Leopold Senghor or Jomo Kenyatta. . . .

Thus we see that the cultural problem as it sometimes exists in colonized countries runs the risk of giving rise to serious ambiguities. The lack of culture of the Negroes, as proclaimed by colonialism, and the inherent barbarity of the Arabs ought logically to lead to the exaltation of cultural manifestations which are not simply national but continental, and extremely racial. In Africa, the movement of men of culture is a movement towards the Negro-African culture or the Arab-Moslem culture. It is not specifically towards a national culture. Culture is becoming more and more cut off from the events of today. . . .

In order to ensure his salvation and to escape from the supremacy of the white man's culture the native feels the need to turn backwards towards his unknown roots and to lose himself at whatever cost in his own barbarous people. Because he feels he is becoming estranged, that is to say because he feels that he is the living haunt of contradictions which run the risk of becoming insurmountable, the native tears himself away from the swamp that may suck him down and accepts everything, decides to take all for granted and confirms everything even though he may lose body and soul. The native finds that he is expected to answer for everything, and to all comers. He not only turns himself into the defender of his people's past; he is willing to be counted as one of them, and henceforward he is even capable of laughing at his past cowardice.

This tearing away, painful and difficult though it may be, is, however, necessary. If it is not accomplished there will be serious psycho-affective injuries and the result will be individuals without an anchor, without a horizon, colourless, stateless, rootless—a race of angels. It will be also quite normal to hear certain natives declare 'I speak as a Senegalese and as a Frenchman . . .'. . . . The intellectual who is Arab and French, or Nigerian and English, when he comes up against the need to take on two nationalities, chooses, if he wants to remain true to himself, the negation of one of these determinations. But most often, since they cannot or will not make a choice, such intellectuals gather together all the historical determining factors which have conditioned them and take up a fundamentally 'universal standpoint'.

This is because the native intellectual has thrown himself greedily upon Western culture. Like adopted children who only stop investigating the new family framework at the moment when a minimum nucleus of security crystallizes in their psyche, the native intellectual will try to make European culture his own. He will not be content to get to know Rabelais and Diderot, Shakespeare and Edgar Allan Poe; he will bind them to his intelligence as closely as possible . . .

But at the moment when the nationalist parties are mobilizing the people in the name of national independence, the native intellectual sometimes spurns these acquisitions which he suddenly feels make him a stranger in his own land. It is always easier to proclaim rejection than actually to reject. The intellectual who through the medium of culture has filtered into Western civilization, who has managed to become part of the body of European culture —in other words who has exchanged his own culture for another—will come to realize that the cultural matrix, which now he wishes to assume since he is anxious to appear original, can hardly supply any figureheads which will bear comparison with those, so many in number and so great in prestige, of the occupying power's civilization. History, of course, though nevertheless written by the Westerners and to serve their purposes, will be able to evaluate from time to time certain periods of the African past. But, standing face to face with his country at the present time, and observing clearly and objectively the events of today throughout the continent which he wants to make his own, the intellectual is terrified by the void, the degradation and the savagery he sees there. Now he feels that he must get away from white culture. He must seek his culture elsewhere, anywhere at all; and if he fails to find the substance of culture of the same grandeur and scope as displayed by the ruling power, the native intellectual will very often fall back upon emotional attitudes and will develop a psychology which is dominated by exceptional sensitivity and susceptibility. . . .

This is sufficient explanation of the style of those native intellectuals who decide to give expression to this phase of consciousness which is in process of being liberated. It is a harsh style, full of images, for the image is the drawbridge which allows unconscious energies to be scattered on the surrounding meadows. It is a vigorous style, alive with rhythms, struck through and through with bursting life; it is full of colour, too, bronzed, sun-baked and violent. This style, which in its time astonished the peoples of the West, has nothing racial about it, in spite of frequent statements to the contrary; it expresses above all a hand-to-hand struggle and it reveals the need that man has to liberate himself from a part of his being which already contained the seeds of decay. . . .

If in the world of poetry this movement reaches unaccustomed heights, the fact remains that in the real world the intellectual often follows up a blind alley. When at the height of his intercourse with his people, whatever they were or whatever they are, the intellectual decides to come down into the common paths of real life, he only brings back from his adventuring formulas which are sterile in the extreme. He sets a high value on the customs, traditions and the appearances of his people; but his inevitable, painful experience only seems to be a banal search for exoticism. The sari becomes sacred, and shoes that come from Paris or Italy are left off in favour of pampooties, while suddenly the language of the ruling power is felt to burn your lips. . . .

If we wanted to trace in the works of native writers the different phases which characterize this evolution we would find spread out before us a panorama on three levels. In the first phase, the native intellectual gives proof that he has assimilated the culture of the occupying power. His writings correspond point by point with those of his opposite numbers in the mother country. His inspiration is European and we can easily link up these works with definite trends in the literature of the mother country. This is the period of unqualified assimilation. . . .

In the second phase we find the native is disturbed; he decides to remember what he is. This period of creative work approximately corresponds to that immersion which we have just described. But since the native is not a part of his people, since he only has exterior relations with his people, he is content to recall their life only. Past happenings of the bygone days of his childhood will be brought up out of the depths of his memory; old legends will be reinterpreted in the light of a borrowed aestheticism and of a conception of the world which was discovered under other skies. . . .

Finally, in the third phase, which is called the fighting phase, the native, after having tried to lose himself in the people and with the people, will on the contrary shake the people. Instead of according the people's lethargy an honoured place in his esteem, he turns himself into an awakener of the people; hence comes a fighting literature, a revolutionary literature, and a national literature. During this phase a great many men and women who up till then would never have thought of producing a literary work, now that they find themselves in exceptional circumstances—in prison, with the Maquis or on the eve of their execution—feel the need to speak to their nation, to compose the sentence which expresses the heart of the people and to become the mouthpiece of a new reality in action.

2 Colonialist Criticism*

CHINUA ACHEBE

The word 'colonialist' may be deemed inappropriate for two reasons. First, it has come to be associated in many minds with that brand of cheap, demagogic and outmoded rhetoric which the distinguished Ghanaian public servant Robert Gardiner no doubt has in mind when he speaks of our tendency to 'intone the colonial litany', implying that the time has come when we must assume responsibility for our problems and our situation in the world and resist the temptation to blame other people. Secondly, it may be said that whatever colonialism may have done in the past, the very fact of a Commonwealth Conference today is sufficient repudiation of it, is indeed a symbol of a new relationship of equality between peoples who were once masters and servants.

Yet in spite of the strength of these arguments one feels the necessity to deal with some basic issues raised by a certain specious criticism which flourishes in African literature today and which derives from the same basic attitude and assumption as colonialism itself and so merits the name 'colonialist'. This attitude and assumption was crystallized in Albert Schweitzer's immortal dictum in the heyday of colonialism: 'The African is indeed my brother, but my junior brother'. The latter-day colonialist critic, equally given to big-brother arrogance, sees the African writer as a somewhat unfinished

* From Chinua Achebe, *Hopes and Impediments: Selected Essays 1965–87*, Heinemann, 1988, pp. 46–58, 60; based on a paper read to the Association for Commonwealth Literature and Language Studies at Makerere University, Uganda, Jan. 1974.

European who with patient guidance will grow up one day and write like every other European, but meanwhile must be humble, must learn all he can and while at it give due credit to his teachers in the form of either direct praise or, even better since praise sometimes goes bad and becomes embarrassing, manifest self-contempt. Because of the tricky nature of this subject, I have chosen to speak not in general terms but wherever possible specifically about my own actual experience. In any case, as anyone who has heard anything at all about me may know already, I do have problems with universality and other concepts of that scope, being very much a down-to-earth person. But I will hope by reference to a few other writers and critics to show that my concerns and anxieties are perhaps not entirely personal.

When my first novel was published in 1958 a very unusual review of it was written by a British woman, Honor Tracy, who is perhaps not so much a critic as a literary journalist. But what she said was so intriguing that I have never forgotten it. If I remember rightly she headlined it 'Three cheers for mere Anarchy!' The burden of the review itself was as follows: These bright Negro barristers (how barristers came into it remains a mystery to me to this day, but I have sometimes woven fantasies about an earnest white woman and an unscrupulous black barrister) who talk so glibly about African culture, how would they like to return to wearing raffia skirts? How would novelist Achebe like to go back to the mindless times of his grandfather instead of holding the modern job he has in broadcasting in Lagos?

I should perhaps point out that colonialist criticism is not always as crude as this but the exaggerated grossness of a particular example may sometimes prove useful in studying the anatomy of the species. There are three principal parts here: Africa's inglorious past (raffia skirts) to which Europe brings the blessing of civilization (Achebe's modern job in Lagos) and for which Africa returns ingratitude (sceptical novels like *Things Fall Apart*).

Before I go on to more advanced varieties I must give one more example of the same kind as Honor Tracy's which on account of its recentness (1970) actually surprised me:

The British administration not only safeguarded women from the worst tyrannies of their masters, it also enabled them to make their long journeys to farm or market without armed guard, secure from the menace of hostile neighbours . . . The Nigerian novelists who have written the charming and bucolic accounts of domestic harmony in African rural communities, are the sons whom the labours of these women educated; the peaceful village of their childhood to which they nostalgically look back was one which had been purged of bloodshed and alcoholism by an ague-ridden district officer and a Scottish mission lassie whose years were cut short by every kind of intestinal parasite.

It is even true to say that one of the most nostalgically convincing of the rural African novelists used as his sourcebook not the memories of his grandfathers but the records of the despised British anthropologists . . . The modern African myth-maker hands down a vision of colonial rule in which the native powers are chivalrously viewed through the eyes of the hard-won liberal tradition of the late Victorian scholar, while the expatriates are shown as schoolboys' blackboard caricatures.[1]

I have quoted this at such length because first of all I am intrigued by Iris Andreski's literary style which recalls so faithfully the sedate prose of the district officer government anthropologist of sixty or seventy years ago—a tribute to her remarkable powers of identification as well as to the durability of colonialist rhetoric. 'Tyrannies of their masters' . . . 'menace of hostile neighbours' . . . 'purged of bloodshed and alcoholism'. But in addition to this Iris Andreski advances the position taken by Honor Tracy in one significant and crucial direction—its claim to a deeper knowledge and a more reliable appraisal of Africa than the educated African writer has shown himself capable of.

To the colonialist mind it was always of the utmost importance to be able to say; 'I know my natives', a claim which implied two things at once: (a) that the native was really quite simple and (b) that understanding him and controlling him went hand in hand—understanding being a pre-condition for control and control constituting adequate proof of understanding. Thus in the heyday of colonialism any serious incident of native unrest, carrying as it did disquieting intimations of slipping control, was an occasion not only for pacification by the soldiers but also (afterwards) for a royal commission of inquiry—a grand name for yet another perfunctory study of native psychology and institutions. Meanwhile a new situation was slowly developing as a handful of natives began to acquire European education and then to challenge Europe's presence and position in their native land with the intellectual weapons of Europe itself. To deal with this phenomenal presumption the colonialist devised two contradictory arguments. He created the 'man of two worlds' theory to prove that no matter how much the native was exposed to European influences he could never truly absorb them; like Prester John[2] he would always discard the mask of civilization when the crucial hour came and reveal his true face. Now, did this mean that the educated native was no different at all from his brothers in the bush? Oh, no! He *was* different; he was worse. . . . Iris Andreski's book is more than old wives' tales, at least in intention. It is clearly inspired by the desire to undercut the educated African witness (the modern myth-maker, she calls him) by appealing direct to the unspoilt woman of the bush who has retained a healthy gratitude for Europe's intervention in Africa. This desire accounts for all that reliance one finds in modern European travellers' tales on the evidence of 'simple natives'—

[1] Iris Andreski, *Old Wives' Tales*, New York, 1971, p. 26.
[2] From the novel (1910) of the same name by the imperial statesman and adventure writer, John Buchan (1875–1940). [Ed.]

houseboys, cooks, drivers, schoolchildren—supposedly more trustworthy than the smart alecs . . .

Most African writers write out of an African experience and of commitment to an African destiny. For them that destiny does not include a future European identity for which the present is but an apprenticeship. And let no one be fooled by the fact that we may write in English for we intend to do unheard of things with it. Already some people are getting worried. This past summer I met one of Australia's leading poets, A. D. Hope, in Canberra, and he said wistfully that the only happy writers today were those writing in small languages like Danish. Why? Because they and their readers understood one another and knew precisely what a word meant when it was used. I had to admit that I hadn't thought of it that way. I had always assumed that the Commonwealth of Nations was a great bonus for a writer, that the English-Speaking Union was a desirable fraternity. But talking with A. D. Hope that evening, I felt somewhat like an illegitimate child face to face with the true son of the house lamenting the excesses of an adventurous and profligate father who had kept a mistress in every port. I felt momentarily nasty and thought of telling A. D. Hope: You ain't seen nothin' yet! But I know he would not have understood. And in any case, there was an important sense in which he was right—that every literature must seek the things that belong unto its peace, must, in other words, speak of a particular place, evolve out of the necessities of its history, past and current, and the aspirations and destiny of its people. . . .

In his book, *The Emergence of African Fiction*, Charles Larson tells us a few revealing things about universality. In a chapter devoted to Lenrie Peters' novel which he finds particularly impressive he speaks of 'its universality, its very limited concern with Africa itself'. Then he goes on to spell it all out:

That it is set in Africa appears to be accidental, for, except for a few comments at the beginning, Peters's story might just as easily take place in the southern part of the United States or in the southern regions of France or Italy. If a few names of characters and places were changed one would indeed feel that this was an American novel. In short, Peters's story is universal.

But Larson is obviously not as foolish as this passage would make him out to be, for he ends it on a note of self-doubt which I find totally disarming. He says:

Or am I deluding myself in considering the work universal? Maybe what I really mean is that *The Second Round* is to a great degree Western and therefore scarcely African at all.[3]

. . . Does it ever occur to these universities to try out their game of

---

[3] Charles Larson, *The Emergence of African Fiction*, Indiana University Press, Indianapolis, 1971, pp. 230, 238.

changing names of characters and places in an American novel, say, a Philip Roth or an Updike, and slotting in African names just to see how it works? But of course it would not occur to them. It would never occur to them to doubt the universality of their own literature. In the nature of things the work of a Western writer is automatically informed by universality. It is only others who must strain to achieve it. . . .

If colonialist criticism were merely irritating one might doubt the justification of devoting a whole essay to it. But strange though it may sound some of its ideas and precepts do exert an influence on our writers, for it is a fact of our contemporary world that Europe's powers of persuasion can be far in excess of the merit and value of her case. . . .

A review of Yambo Ouologuem's *Bound to Violence* (Heinemann Educational Books, London, 1971) by a Philip M. Allen in the *Pan-African Journal* was an excellent example of sophisticated, even brilliant colonialist criticism. . . .

Mr Allen is quite abrupt in dismissing all the 'various polemical factions' and ideologists who have been claiming Ouologuem for their side. Of course they all miss the point,

. . . for Ouologuem isn't writing their novel. He gives us an Africa cured of the pathetic obsession with racial and cultural confrontation and freed from invidious tradition-mongering . . . His book knows no easy antithesis between white and black, western and indigenous, modern and traditional. Its conflicts are those of the universe, not accidents of history.

And in final demonstration of Ouologuem's liberation from the constraint of local models Mr Allen tells us:

Ouologuem does not accept Fanon's idea of liberation, and he calls African unity a theory for dreamers. His Nakem is no more the Mali of Modibo Keita or the continent of Nkrumah than is the golden peace of Emperor Sundiata or the moral parish of Muntu.[4]

Mr Allen's rhetoric does not entirely conceal whose ideological team *he* is playing on, his attitude to Africa, in other words. . . .

That a 'critic' playing on the ideological team of colonialism should feel sick and tired of Africa's 'pathetic obsession with racial and cultural confrontation' should surprise no one. Neither should his enthusiasm for those African works that show 'no easy antithesis between white and black'. But an African who falls for such nonsense, not only in spite of Africa's so very recent history but, even more, in the face of continuing atrocities committed against millions of Africans in their own land by racist minority regimes, deserves a lot of pity. Certainly anyone, white or black, who chooses to see violence as the abiding principle of African civilization is free to do so. But let him not pass himself

[4] Philip Allen, '*Bound to Violence* by Yambo Ouologuem', *Pan-African Journal*, vol. IV, no. 4, New York, Fall 1971, pp. 518–23.

off as a restorer of dignity to Africa, or attempt to make out that he is writing about man and about the state of civilization in general. . . . Perhaps for most ordinary people what Africa needs is a far less complicated act of restoration. The Canadian novelist and critic Margaret Laurence saw this happening already in the way many African writers are interpreting their world, making it

. . . neither idyllic, as the views of some nationalists would have had it, nor barbaric, as the missionaries and European administrators wished and needed to believe.[5]

And in the epilogue to the same book she makes the point even more strongly:

No writer of any quality has viewed the old Africa in an idealized way, but they have tried to regain what is rightly theirs—a past composed of real and vulnerable people, their ancestors, not the figments of missionary and colonialist imaginations.

Ultimately the question of ideological sides which Mr Allen threw in only to dismiss it again with contempt may not be as far-fetched as he thinks. For colonialism itself was built also on an ideology (although its adherents may no longer realize it) which, despite many setbacks, survives into our own day, and indeed is ready again at the end of a quiescent phase of self-doubt for a new resurgence of proselytization, even, as in the past, among its prime victims!

Fortunately, it can no longer hope for the role of unchallenged arbiter in other people's affairs that it once took so much for granted. There are clear signs that critics and readers from those areas of the world where continuing incidents and recent memories of racism, colonialism and other forms of victimization exist will more and more demand to know from their writers just on whose ideological side they are playing. And we writers had better be prepared to reckon with this questioning. For no amount of prestige or laurels of metropolitan reputation would seem large enough to silence or overawe it. Consider, for instance, a recent judgement on V. S. Naipaul by a fellow Caribbean, Ivan Van Sertima:

His brilliancy of wit I do not deny but, in my opinion, he has been overrated by English critics whose sensibilities he insidiously flatters by his stock-in-trade: self-contempt.[6]

. . . One need not accept these judgements in order to see them as signs of things to come.

Meanwhile the seduction of our writers by the blandishments of colonialist criticism is matched by its misdirection of our critics. Thus an intelligent man like Dr Sunday Anozie, the Nigerian scholar and critic, is able to dismiss the high moral and social earnestness sometimes expressed by one of our greatest poets, Christopher Okigbo, as only a mark of underdevelopment. In his book,

[5] Margaret Laurence, *Long Drums and Cannons*, Macmillan, 1968, p. 9.
[6] *Caribbean Writers*, New Beacon, 1968, foreword.

Christopher Okigbo, the most extensive biographical and critical study of the poet to date, Dr Anozie tells us of Okigbo's 'passion for truth' which apparently makes him sometimes too outspoken, makes him the talkative weaverbird 'incapable of whispered secrets'. And he proceeds to offer the following explanation:

No doubt the thrill of actualized prophecy can sometimes lead poets particularly in the young countries to confuse their role with that of seers, and novelists to see themselves as teachers. Whatever the social, psychological, political and economic basis for it in present-day Africa, this interchangeability of role between the creative writer and the prophet appears to be a specific phenomenon of underdevelopment and therefore, like it also, a passing or ephemeral phase.[7]

And he cites the authority of C. M. Bowra in support of his explanation.[8] The fallacy of the argument lies, of course, in its assumption that when you talk about a people's 'level of development' you define their total condition and assign them an indisputable and unambiguous place on mankind's evolutionary ladder; in other words, that you are enabled by the authority of that phrase to account for all their material as well as spiritual circumstance. Show me a people's plumbing, you say, and I can tell you their art.

I should have thought that the very example of the Hebrew poet/prophets which Dr Anozie takes from Bowra to demonstrate underdevelopment and confusion of roles would have been enough to alert him to the folly of his thesis. Or is he seriously suggesting that the poetry of these men—Isaiah, for example—written, it seems, out of a confusion of roles, in an underdeveloped society, is less good than what is written today by poets who are careful to remain within the proper bounds of poetry within developed societies? Personally I should be quite content to wallow in Isaiah's error and write 'For unto us a child is born'.

Incidentally any reader who is at all familiar with some of the arguments that go on around modern African literature will have noticed that in the passage I have just quoted from Dr Anozie he is not only talking about Okigbo but also alluding (with some disapproval) to a paper I read at Leeds University ten years ago which I called 'The Novelist as Teacher'; Anozie thus kills two weaverbirds dexterously with one stone! In his disapproval of what I had to say he follows, of course, in the footsteps of certain Western literary schoolmasters from whom I had already earned many sharp reprimands for that paper, who told me in clear terms that an artist had no business being so earnest.

It seems to me that this matter is of serious and fundamental importance, and must be looked at carefully. Earnestness and its opposite, levity, may be neither good nor bad in themselves but merely appropriate or inappropriate

[7] *Christopher Okigbo*, Evans Brothers, 1970, p. 17.
[8] See Sir C. M. Bowra, *Primitive Song*, (1962) [Ed.]

according to circumstance. I hold, however, and have held from the very moment I began to write, that earnestness *is* appropriate to my situation. Why? I suppose because I have a deep-seated need to alter things within that situation, to find for myself a little more room than has been allowed me in the world. I realize how pompous or even frightening this must sound to delicate sensibilities, but I can't help it.

The missionary who left the comforts of Europe to wander through my primeval forest was extremely earnest. He had to be; he came to change my world. The builders of empire who turned me into a 'British protected person' knew the importance of being earnest; they had that quality of mind which Imperial Rome before them understood so well: *gravitas*. Now, it seems to me pretty obvious that if I desire to change the role and identity fashioned for me by those earnest agents of colonialism I will need to borrow some of their resolve. Certainly I could not hope to do it through self-indulgent levity. . . .

The first nationalists and freedom fighters in the colonies, hardly concerned to oblige their imperial masters, were offensively earnest. They had no choice. They needed to alter the arrangement which kept them and their people out in the rain and the heat of the sun. They fought and won some victories. They changed a few things and seemed to secure certain powers of action over others. But quite quickly the great collusive swindle that was independence showed its true face to us. And we were dismayed; but only momentarily for even in our defeat we had gained something of inestimable value—a baptism of fire. . . .

The colonialist critic, unwilling to accept the validity of sensibilities other than his own, has made particular point of dismissing the African novel. He has written lengthy articles to prove its non-existence largely on the grounds that the novel is a peculiarly Western genre, a fact which would interest us if our ambition was to write 'Western' novels. But, in any case, did not the black people in America, deprived of their own musical instruments, take the trumpet and the trombone and blow them as they had never been blown before, as indeed they were not designed to be blown? And the result, was it not jazz? Is any one going to say that this was a loss to the world or that those first Negro slaves who began to play around with the discarded instruments of their masters should have played waltzes and foxtrots? No! Let every people bring their gifts to the great festival of the world's cultural harvest and mankind will be all the richer for the variety and distinctiveness of the offerings.

My people speak disapprovingly of an outsider whose wailing drowned the grief of the owners of the corpse. One last word to the owners. It is because our own critics have been somewhat hesitant in taking control of our literary criticism (sometimes—let's face it—for the good reason that we will not do the hard work that should equip us) that the task has fallen to others, some of whom (again we must admit) have been excellent and sensitive. And yet most of what remains to be done can best be tackled by ourselves, the owners. If we fall back, can we complain that others are rushing forward? A man who does not lick his lips, can he blame the harmattan for drying them?

3 *Decolonizing African Literature**

CHINWEIZU, ONWUCHEKWA JEMIE AND IHECHUKWU MADUBUIKE

THE AFRICAN NOVEL AND ITS CRITICS

The novel is usually defined as an extended fictional prose narrative whose subject matter is 'man in society'. There are some misleading terms in this usage which need to be rectified if an intelligent and fruitful discussion of the matter is to take place. First, what is misleadingly called 'the novel' is really the European or Western novel. This is implicit in the practice of referring to the European or Western novel as 'the novel', whereas other regional novels are routinely qualified as 'African novel', 'Chinese novel', etc. This behavior has the same misleading and disorienting effect as that which is produced when Western culture insists on calling itself 'civilization' instead of 'Western civilization', conveying the undeserved impression that it had attained a unique situation called 'civilization', and that no other culture in the world had.

Secondly, the term 'man in society' is, strictly speaking, used to mean man in European or Western bourgeois society. It is not used to refer, for instance, to man in Western feudal society, let alone to man in Celtic Britain, Viking Scandinavia, Ainu Japan, or in any African societies before the European incursion.

To correct these misusages, the term 'the novel' should, strictly speaking, be used to stand generically for all extended fictional prose narratives treating of any bourgeois reality (i.e., whose subject matter is man in any bourgeois society), and the term 'European novel' or 'Western novel' should be routinely applied to novels which treat of European or Western bourgeois reality. In this way they can be properly distinguished from their counterparts in other regions which treat of Japanese, Chinese, or African bourgeois realities. Historically, the European bourgeoisie was the first to emerge and so the first to accumulate a substantial body of written extended fictional prose nar-

* From Chinweizu, Onwuchekwa Jemie and Ihechukwu Madubuike, *Toward the Decolonization of African Literature: African Fiction and Poetry and Their Critics*, KPI/Routledge & Kegan Paul, 1985, pp. 18–20, 27–30, 87–91, 256–9; first publ. in Nigeria by Fourth Dimension Publishers, 1980.

ratives treating of a bourgeois reality. But this historical precedence ought not to be used to make the European novel stand for the worldwide genre of which it is only a regional version.

The European novel is said to have evolved in the 18th century, its ancestors being the prose and verse narratives, epics and romances, of the Greco-Roman and medieval eras of Europe. The evolution of the European novel from these forms roughly coincided with the developments in European society usually known as the Renaissance—a process which involved the decline of religion, the rise of science and the secular state, the rise of the notion of man as the center of his universe, the rise of protestantism and its stress on individualism, and the conquest of political power by the European bourgeois class, with a concomitant transition in European governments from feudal monarchies to bourgeois constitutional governments. These changes are reflected in European narrative literature in the decline of kingly, aristocratic, and divine heroes, and in the rise of bourgeois protagonists. Secularization was reflected in the narrowing of the view of human society —the world of the novel—to exclude ghosts, the supernatural, and other fantastic beings. But since bourgeois Europe still adhered to the Christian faith, this secularization did not go so far as to eliminate the Christian God, angels, devils and saints from the world of the European novel. The European novel therefore focused on the interaction of European bourgeois man with his immediate physical environment, human society, and Christian divinities.

Admittedly, in the central tradition of the European bourgeois novel, divinities do not usually appear in their own persons as they did in Greco-Roman and medieval European epics, dramas, romances and tales. Rather, they figure indirectly through their human intermediaries; their presence is transmitted by the priests through baptisms, marriages, communions, confessions and other rites and rituals, and through the fear these priests instill and the influence they exert on the society's ethical opinions and (sometimes) behavior.

Significantly enough, even when African divinities do not appear in their own persons in African novels but, like the official European gods, manifest themselves through their institutions, priests, rites and rituals, the eurocentric critics nevertheless rail against them as an unwelcome intrusion of what they consider 'primitivism' into the enlightened secular court of the novel. Clearly, given the retention of Christian spiritual beings in the European bourgeois view of man in society, there is certainly nothing in a bourgeois world view, other perhaps than European prejudice, that would call for the exclusion of spiritual beings from the world of the novel. European academics may choose to banish ghosts, goblins, fantastic beings, etc. from the world of the European novel; that is their prerogative. But it is not their prerogative to seek to banish them from the world of any non-European novel. In particular, it is not their prerogative to seek to banish them from the world of the African novel when the African bourgeoisie have not banished such beings from their reality. Indeed, it is not the prerogative of any European to banish from or introduce anything into Africa. . . .

The fact that the novel, an extended fictional narrative, treats of bourgeois reality is not sufficient to take it out of the general category to which belong extended fictional narratives that treat of feudal society, slave society, socialist society, or other social formations. In other words, far from being a unique and unprecedented achievement, the novel is merely the bourgeois counterpart of the romances and epics of the feudal and pre-feudal eras. The romance, the heroic epic, and the novel are *equivalent forms* in their respective social formations. Specifically, their equivalence consists in the fact that they are extended, narrated, imaginative constructs which handle or treat of the social reality of the dominant stratum of their respective social formations. Being equivalent forms, the novels of a given nation or region would stand in similar relationships to the romances and epics from earlier eras of that given nation or region.

Thus, for instance, the Chinese or Japanese novel of their respective bourgeois eras would bear the same relationship to the Chinese or Japanese romance or epic of their respective feudal and pre-feudal eras as the European bourgeois novel would bear to the romance and epic of Europe's pre-bourgeois times. By the same token, the pre-colonial equivalents of Africa's bourgeois novel would be found in the extended narratives of pre-colonial Africa, particularly in the epics and romances of that era. By the way, it should be noted that the terms 'epic', 'romance', and 'novel' are merely European terms for some European versions of extended narratives which have their counterparts throughout the world in analogous social formations. One therefore shouldn't, strictly speaking, look for Japanese 'epics' or African 'romances' (that is, not in the European sense of these terms), but rather for the dominant and functionally equivalent forms of extended narrative in feudal Japan or pre-colonial Africa.

These equivalent forms from earlier eras of a given society are the proper antecedents or prototypes of the novel in each society. Wherever a bourgeois class has come into prominence, and has produced novels to reflect its own social realities, such indigenous antecedents have helped to shape the development of its novel. Therefore in the case of the African novel it is important to realize that its indigenous antecedents should be sought in the continent's traditions of extended narrative.

However, even those critics who recognize, in the case of the European tradition, that Europe's extended narratives, both the oral and the written, whether in prose or verse, were the antecedents or prototypes of the European novel, seem reluctant to search in the analogously appropriate area for whatever African antecedents to the African novel there are. Part of their problem in this regard might well derive from the fact that they are unaware of, or turn a blind eye to, Africa's pre-colonial, written, longer narratives. To further compound their blindness, they have, out of various cultural biases, constructed a grand mountain that separates oral and written literatures, and are unable to look beyond that divide. They are therefore unwilling to even entertain the notion that some extended narrative antecedents to the African novel might exist in Africa's oral traditions. If at such moments they had managed to cure themselves of their parochial formal fixation upon the writtenness of narrative texts, they might have remembered that the earliest of their own European narratives, some of them still unsurpassed, were oral long before they were written down, and they might then have been better disposed to look into Africa's oral traditions for some of the African antecedents to the African novel. But in a situation bedevilled by imperialist arrogance, racist bias, a formalist bias against orature, and the unexamined assumption that Africa had no pre-colonial written texts, these glib scholars and critics quite contentedly turn their eyes away from where they ought to look, and in their pompous ignorance roundly declare, as does Roscoe, that

the novel, *as it is known in the West*, precisely *because it is a written form*, has no history whatever in Africa. . . . It is a literary import . . . from Europe . . . It is not, in its nature, an African form . . . It is not a fact of the African past.[1]

Roscoe again misperceives the matter. That the novel, a bourgeois form of extended fictional narrative, has no history in pre-colonial Africa, is not at all because it is a written form. As we have said, there were written literatures in pre-colonial Africa. It is rather because there was no African bourgeoisie in pre-colonial Africa. And even if there had been such a bourgeoisie, its novel would hardly be expected to conform to the characteristics of the Western novel. Africa is simply not the West.

In order to buttress their entrenched prejudices, these scholars and critics seem compelled to make more of the written form itself than is warranted, and seem concomitantly compelled to disparage, without the warrant of examination, the capabilities of the entire oral medium in order to attribute to the influence of that medium whatever features in the African novel they find not to the liking of their European or Europeanized tastes. In examining these mutually supportive and formalist prejudices, that is, their prejudice in favor of the written form and their prejudice against the oral form, let us begin with their prejudice in favor of the written form and evaluate some of the claims that have been made for that form.

---

[1] Adrian Roscoe, *Mother is Gold: A Study in West African Literature*, Cambridge University Press, 1971, p. 75. Italics added by authors.

Roscoe's view on the written form is not unrepresentative. What is remarkable is that such views are shared by otherwise good African scholars and critics. For example, Emmanuel Obiechina tells us:

Literacy is crucial to the emergence of the novel, because the novel is meant to be read by the individual in quiet isolation, and complex narrative is more easily sustained and followed by reading it than by hearing it.[2]

Although it is true that the novel historically has been a written form it is doubtful that some claims made for it on that account cannot also be made for non-written extended narratives. For instance, some epics display all the complexities of character, situation, plot, theme, technique, etc., that are found in the novel. Since these epics were generally written down from the fully developed oral form, it follows that all the complexity found in them was sustained and followed by narrating and listening, during the centuries when they were handed down by word of mouth. Specifically, such epics as the *Iliad*, the *Odyssey*, *Beowulf*, the *Nibelungenlied*, the prose and verse *Eddas*, *Sundiata*, *Mwindo*, *Monzon and the King of Kore*, and *Kambili*, which were orally delivered long before they were written down, all display the complexity of plot, theme, situation, technique, character development, etc. of both the consciously written epics such as the *Divine Comedy*, the *Aeneid*, and *Paradise Lost* (which incidentally were modelled on the oral ones), and of the novel at its most complex and extended, as in *War and Peace*, *Ulysses*, *Remembrance of Things Past*, and *Don Quixote*. These examples would conclusively demonstrate that any claim that a work has to be written in order to be as complex as a novel is at best a prejudice, however fashionable or accepted. In other words, literacy or writing, as such, is not a condition for satisfying those supposedly distinguishing characteristics of the novel. An oral epic or an extended oral narrative, insofar as it has those characteristics which are said to distinguish the novel, and especially those that are alleged to derive from the fact that the novel is a written form, could be designated if not an *oral novel*, then at least a *prototype* of the novel.

It would follow, therefore, that even though it might be demonstrated that the novel, a written bourgeois form, did not exist in Africa before the European invasion, its oral antecedents or prototypes did. . . .

Developments since Joyce, Proust and Kafka, as for instance in the French *nouveau roman*, overwhelmingly demonstrate that the novel is an open form, and that there is no ideal form to which all novels must conform. In particular, we should not be misled by the connotations of the terms 'well-made' or 'pure' into idealizing or strenuously imitating the forms of the 19th-century European bourgeois novel. The forms of the novel are capable

[2] Emmanuel Obiechina, *Culture, Tradition and Society in the West African Novel*, Cambridge University Press, 1975, p. 3.

of change in every direction. In the making of the novel, it is 'morning yet on creation day', to borrow a phrase from Chinua Achebe.[3]

Most of the objections to thematic and ideological matters in the African novel sound like admonitions from imperialist motherhens to their wayward or outright rebellious captive chickens. They cluck: 'Be Universal! Be Universal!' And what they don't consider universal they denounce as anthropological, atavistic, autobiographical, sociological, journalistic, topical ephemera. When they first encountered African novels, eurocentric critics praised their detailed descriptions of African setting and customs as 'quaint', 'exotic', 'fantastic' and 'bewitching'; but now that their nouveau-mania has tired of such material, they denounce it as anthropological data and 'local color'. Those works which they denounce as autobiographical, sociological, journalistic and topical, are usually those works whose subject matter, if handled from an African perspective, cannot but indict the colonial order. For instance, an African brought up under colonialism, when employing autobiographical material in his fiction, would be hard put to avoid an at least implicit criticism of colonialism.

When these critics denounce what they consider didacticism, propaganda, or inconsistency of moral attitude, they usually do so only when these things criticise or militate against European bourgeois values. In their concern with promoting the Western brand of individualism, they denounce as 'situational' those presentations in which some individual does not dominate or wilfully tower over his social environment. And of course they do not want to hear or read 'protest literature' since the protest is, and has to be, overwhelmingly against what the bourgeois order, which is managed from and in the primary interest of the West, is doing to the African.

Furthermore, when some critics complain against 'too many *Things Fall Aparts*', or when some others call for 'an urgent release from the fascination of the past', reminding everyone that the past 'is not a fleshpot for escapist indulgence', they could be said, at least in part, to be urging a moratorium on literary examination of the colonial experience. If their complaint is meant to also imply that African writers should focus exclusively on the modern African state and turn a blind eye to its colonial antecedents, it should be rejected as anti-historical and misleading. We see no reason why all kinds and periods of African experience should not be open to the writer to explore.

To the allied charge that there is a preponderance of autobiographical novels, we ask: why not? Autobiography is a legitimate literary quarry; autobiographical novels are a species of the historical novel. Perhaps what irks the critics who levy this charge is that the Euro-African conflict is the theme of a large part of these autobiographical novels. We should point out

---

[3] See Chinua Achebe, *Morning Yet on Creation Day: Essays*, Heinemann, 1975. [Ed.]

that for those who grew up under colonialism, this conflict is the central event of their environment.

Considering Africa's recent history, it would indeed be surprising if autobiographical novels, and, through them, the Euro-African conflict, did not feature heavily in African literature. Is this charge against an abundance of autobiographical novels not another effort to block examination of colonialism and its impact on African society and individuals? Indeed, other themes should be explored, but that should not require a reduction in the number of works dealing with autobiography or culture conflict. Given our history, we can't have too many autobiographical novels, or too many *Things Fall Aparts*.

Fidel Castro once described the attitudes and interests from which such criticisms emanate:

Novels which attempt to reflect the reality of the world of imperialism's rapacious deeds; the poems aspiring to protest against its enslavement, its interference in life, in thought, in the very bodies of nations and peoples; and the militant arts which in their expression try to capture the forms and content of imperialism's aggression and the constant pressure on every progressive living and breathing thing and on all that is revolutionary, which teaches, which—full of light and conscience, of clarity and beauty—tries to guide men and peoples to better destinies, to the highest summits of life and justice—all these meet imperialism's severest censure.[4]

It is therefore not surprising that the eurocentric critics of the African novel, concerned as they are with keeping upon us the hold of the mythologies of imperialism, choose to ignore new developments within their own traditions, and exhort our novelists to bury themselves in an archaic and vestigial branch of the Western tradition. While our writers do not need, in a sort of reflex reaction to these antediluvian critics, to embark on the wild fads of the contemporary European literary scene, the need for experimentation in creating from different traditions a novel adequate for probing African realities, ought to be acknowledged. . . .

CULTURAL CONTINUITY: THE AFRICAN WRITER AND THE AFRICAN PAST

In contemporary African literature and criticism there have been three dominant attitudes towards the African past: shamefaced rejection; romantic embrace; and realistic appraisal. Those who reject the African past and would have as little to do with it as possible are those who, shamed by imperialist propaganda and misrepresentation, would wish to forget it entirely and to hurry off into a euromodernist African future. Prominent among them are those champions of tigritude, those African neo-Tarzanists who dismiss

---

[4] Fidel Castro, 'The Second Declaration of Havana', 1962, quoted in Jonah Raskin, *The Mythology of Imperialism*, epigraph, Delta Books, New York, 1971.

African literature that deals with the African past as a 'literature of self-worship', a literature of narcissism.[5] Against this school of thought headed by Wole Soyinka, it must be emphasized that since our past has been vilified by imperialism, and since an imperialist education has tried to equip us with all manner of absurd views and reactions to our past, we do need to reclaim and rehabilitate our genuine past, to repossess our true and entire history in order to acquire a secure launching pad into our future. Thus, a concern with our past will never be out of place.

Those African writers and critics who understand the need for us to repossess and rehabilitate our past have approached it with either romanticism or critical realism. In our view, there are excellent grounds for avoiding a romanticization of our past and for according it a critical and realistic appraisal. Most important is the fact that we cannot afford to build on misinformation, and romanticism has a tendency to put misleading glosses upon whatever it gazes upon. In this regard, the romanticism of the negritude school is notorious. But before proceeding to examine this, we should first disentangle three important aspects of negritude and state our attitudes to them.

First, there is its African nationalist consciousness which revolts against European cultural imperialism. As we argued earlier, an active African nationalist consciousness is indispensable to the task of African liberation. For its stand and contributions in this department, African nationalism is indebted to negritude. To its champions we offer our salute!

The second important aspect of negritude is its concern with recapturing for modern literature the technical repertory of traditional African orature. This again is a crucial project in cultural retrieval. Without it, the task of ensuring continuity between traditional and modern African culture would be practically impossible. For its pioneering efforts in this department, African nationalism is again indebted to negritude. To its champions, we also offer our salute!

The third important aspect of negritude is the image of traditional Africa which it has held up to view. This is highly questionable. In reaction to colonial insults the negritude poets generally salve their wounds with extravagant nostalgia for a vaguely conceived past. But ought we to persist in this disservice to our past, and even to our present? Was our past one uninterrupted orgy of sensuality? One boring canvas of idyllic goodness, fraternity and harmony? Were our ancestors a parade of plaster saints who never, among themselves, struck a blow, or hurt a fly, and who suffered all psychic and physical pain gladly and cheerfully, or never suffered at all?

---

[5] 'Tigritude': a derogatory term apparently used by Wole Soyinka in the early sixties to undermine negritude: a tiger, he said, does not need to proclaim its tigritude. [Ed.]

No doubt, at its inception, even this romanticism filled a historic need. It was an understandably extreme reaction, offering blanket praise in retort to Europe's blanket condemnation of Africa. But that mythical portrait of traditional Africa can prove to be a new prison. In the task of decolonization we cannot afford an uncritical glorification of the past. We may brandish our memories of empires of ages ago as shields against Western disparagement, but we also know that before colonialism came there was slavery. Who hunted the slaves? And who sold them for guns, trinkets and gin? And the African attitudes and roles which made that slave trade possible, are they not part of that nostalgic past? Are those attitudes not still with us, poisoning our present? How much of this illusion of purity and sanctity can survive the events of the past two decades? After all, 'When a nigger kicks a nigger/Where is the negritude?' (Madubuike). Even though other parts of the blame belong elsewhere, we cannot deny our own share of the responsibility.

As regards the arts, romanticism of the negritude kind, because it venerates what it considers a gold past, could discourage our use of exemplars from that past as points of contemporary departure. By encouraging the minting of facsimiles, it could imprison the contemporary imagination in a bygone era. As has happened in the plastic arts, especially in the lamentable case of airport art, the romantic minting of facsimiles from a golden past could saddle us with anachronistic imagery, and prevent the evolution of new literary forms out of the old, resulting in a fossilization of forms and a literary stasis.

In contrast, critical realism, because it does not spread a gloss of sanctity on the past, does not extol every aspect of it. It is content to praise what it sees as praiseworthy, and to dispraise what it sees as not praiseworthy. It thereby treats our past like any other valid era of culture. This enables us to see welcome as well as objectionable similarities between our present and our past, and such discrimination and selectivity enables us to adopt desirable features from the arts of our past as we endeavor to anchor our modern culture in our tradition. Because critical realism prevents us from treating exemplars as sacrosanct, it allows for the evolution of new forms through adaptations from the old. When, as in Okigbo's 'Path of Thunder', contemporary events and objects are put into the traditional image matrix and described with traditional terms of rhetoric, the effect is refreshing. We thereby obtain a modernism that has emerged from a clearly African poetic tradition.

Other examples in which aspects of our modern literature have been successfully grafted onto traditional trunks include the following: Tutuola's *Palm-Wine Drinkard*, *My Life in the Bush of Ghosts* and other novels, which are embedded in the Yoruba mythic imagination; Achebe's *Things Fall Apart* and *Arrow of God* which capture, in English, Igbo speech patterns, proverbs and idiom; and Okot p'Bitek's *Song of Lawino*, *Song of Ocol*, *Song of a Prisoner* and *Song of Malaya*, each of which uses authentic African imagery and Acholi rhetorical devices to examine an aspect of the contemporary African condition.[6]

4 Macho Attitudes and Derek Walcott*

ELAINE SAVORY FIDO

'Madeleine, you cannot as a woman know a man' *Malcochon*

In the late-twentieth-century ferment of critical debate, there are many schools which represent particular socio-political directions, such as Marxist, or philosophical theses, such as those of the Phenomenologists, Structuralists *et al.* Feminist criticism, whatever that means at this point, when the term feminist is itself highly debatable and even unacceptable within the community of progressive women,[1] is one more critical direction which reflects a special interest. The collective effect of these differing and often conflicting critical theories/groups has been at least helpful to the realization by some in the Western countries that much of what passes for universal criteria of taste are actually merely culturally and class-dictated opinions. More than that, in Third World critical circles the interconnections between anti-racist and anti-colonialist perspectives and those of the women's movements are beginning to be closely examined. This is nowhere more important than in the work of masculinist male writers in Third World societies who often unthinkingly reflect mass male prejudice/myth about women. We are aware that some of these attitudes are so widespread as to amount to a *cultural* bias in the male culture of a particular society, but they nevertheless receive special reinforcement and endorsement when a talented and mainly effective writer includes them in his major work.

The argument of this paper seeks to demonstrate that not only is the work of Derek Walcott, a deservedly celebrated poet, dramatist and theatre practitioner in the Caribbean, inclusive of strong prejudices about women but that these are often associated with weakening of power in his writing. It seems reasonable to assume, after all, that prejudices, which deflect the individual from exploration and growth, will have that same effect on those areas of

---

[6] See, e.g., Amos Tutuola, *The Palm-Wine Drinkard*, Faber, 1965; Okot p'Bitek, *Song of Lawino*, East African Publishing House, Nairobi, 1966. [Ed.]

* From *Journal of Commonwealth Literature*, Vol. xxi, No. 1, Oxford, 1986, pp. 109–18.

[1] Despite the Caribbean Association for Feminist Research and Action having been formed and having determined feminist in its own terms as someone who is male or female with a commitment to ending the oppression of women, feminist is still a difficult term for many Third World women to accept because of the American/European emphasis which it has long had.

writing which are centred in them. Fortunately, given his attitudes to women, Walcott's creative world is a predominantly male one, in which men have close and important understanding of one another. He also deals with racism, colonialism and the situation of the poor masses with intelligence, anger and originality. But his treatment of women is full of clichés, stereotypes and negativity. I shall seek to show how some of his worst writing is associated with these portraits of women, which sometimes lead him to the brink of losing verbal control, or give rise to a retreat into abstract, conventional terms which prevent any real treatment of the subject.

A good deal of recent thinking about literary activity has focused on the relation between reader and writer through the text, and there is an import-ance now given in a good deal of Third World literary analysis to the issue of clashes between the writer's reality/prejudices and those of the reader.[2] It is no longer possible to deny that certain attitudes expressed in literary works are bound to alienate the reader in unconstructive ways (as opposed to healthy provocation of thought/issues). Racism, class prejudice, sexism and colonialist attitudes are endemic in so many cultures that it might seem unfair to ask that writers control/eliminate them in themselves, but that is indeed the issue as we continue to look to serious art for moral sensitivity and the expansion of our conceptual horizons.

The philosophical position which links aesthetic achievement to moral sensitivity is a bold one, but the British philosopher Hugo Meynell has stated such a case:

. . . good art satisfies characteristically by showing us what it is to experience, to understand, to judge, or to decide . . . Its effect is to militate against those limitations of our consciousness which are due to our physical and social environment. Bad art is to a great extent, when not merely technically incompetent, that which imposes or reinforces such limitations.[3]

He goes on to say that bad art also does not permit the reader to experiment with feeling, sensation and moral judgement. Good art, he suggests, produces a complex state of mind in the reader, a state in which both condemnation and sympathy are *equally* difficult or easy, and responses are therefore highly likely to be thought-provoking, tentative and to therefore lead to further consideration and to resistance to facile opinions. Good art, then, would lead a reader out of the enclosures of perception which she/he has inherited and

---

[2] 'Meaning was not something which all men and women everywhere intuitively shared, and then articulated in their various tongues and scripts: what meaning you were able to articulate depended on what script or speech you shared in the first place.' Terry Eagleton on the Structuralists, *Literary Theory*, Oxford: Basil Blackwell, 1983, p. 107. See also, for an excellent study of the implications of colonialist ideology in creative literature, Abdul JanMohamed, *Manichean Aesthetics: The Politics of Literature in Colonial Africa*, Amhurst, Mass.: Univ. of Mass. Press, 1983.
[3] Hugo Meynell, 'Aesthetic Satisfaction', paper read at the Eighth National Conference of the British Society of Aesthetics in 1973, pp. 7–8.

into exploratory thought. What I suggest in this paper is that relative technical incompetence (or, alternatively, aesthetic limitation, over-control or linguistic evasion) arises out of limitations of perception as much as of the artist's
talent and training. . . . For whatever reason, Walcott's most recent work has
been disappointing.[4] I shall not deal with that, but rather with the serious
implications of the treatment of women in his earlier works.

Walcott's Caribbean region is a place of tension between the sexes. Single
mothers, still very numerous, and often in economic difficulty, are still
somehow perceived often by men as powerful, despite their social and
economic powerlessness. Men talk about women in hostile ways (although
the younger educated man is beginning to respond to the strength of the
women's movement in the region). The degree of female autonomy, leadership and sexual independence which has been forced to develop in many
Caribbean women as a result of male behaviour is not recognised as an
advantage to the region, but as a reason for men to resist change being
advocated by feminists. The good husbands and lovers of the Caribbean are
also too often silent and invisible: the creative literature at present available
for young women to read abounds with portraits of difficult male–female
relations and with stereotypical attitudes towards women, depicting them as
victims of male violence or in other ways as losers or marginal figures.

Walcott's work reflects this world. Some portraits of women will first make
it clear how his vision of women focuses on fear/disgust on the part of the
man. In a poem about Othello and Desdemona, the association of sexuality
and violence is very explicit, interwoven of course in this case with racial
tension. The quality of the writing betrays a failure to hold these elements
together in a creative way. The overblown emotional crudity of the following
passage will serve to illustrate how Walcott can rely upon images from the
world of sexist prejudice and racial myth:

> And yet, whatever fury girded
> on that saffron-sunset turban, moon-shaped sword
> was not his racial, panther-black revenge
> pulsing her chamber with raw musk, its sweat
> but horror of the moon's change,
> of the corruption of an absolute,
> like a white fruit
> pulped ripe by fondling but doubly sweet.[5]

The technical competence is here stretched so taut that it collapses. In the

---

[4] *Midsummer*, London: Faber and Faber, 1984, and *The Fortunate Traveller*, New York: Farrar, Straus and Giroux, 1981, both have a facility with words which is disturbingly superficial. . . . many of the images of woman discussed in my paper reappear: the Muse as woman, Helen, woman used as superficial illustration (. . . 'Lift up that old Greek skirt, and every girl sees what philosophy is about.' *Midsummer*, p. 22), woman as the sea, mother *et al.*
[5] 'Goats and Monkeys', *The Castaway*, London: Cape, 1965, pp. 27–8.

centre of this passage, there is a tension between idealism and disgust which characterizes another portrait of woman's sexuality in *Another Life*. Here a beautiful woman is unfaithful to her husband and although this is indeed an immorality which might justify moral rebuke, Walcott's choice of language once more reveals powerful resentments against a woman less than devoted to her husband, and furthermore sexually adventurous, and insinuates that her son is damaged by her nature.

> Next day her golden face seemed shrunken,
> then, when he ulyseed, she bloomed again. . .
> Dressed in black lace, like an impatient widow,
> I imagined that skin, pomegranate, under silks
> the sheen of water, and that
> sweet-sour smell vixens give off.[6]

This passage presents a tension between woman's loveliness (golden) and her sexual nature (pomegranate skin, sweet-sour smell, vixens) which create a repulsive intimacy with the woman, which is what happens also in the passage on Desdemona and Othello. . . .

In the portrait of Anna, youthful love of the poet-persona in *Another Life*, there is a threatening quality which Edward Baugh has considered:

> I see her stride
> as ruthless as that flax-bright harvester
> Judith, with Holofernes' lantern in her hand.

This too is a kind of idealisation, as Judith by her murder of Holofernes, proved herself a partner and heroine; but the connotations which adhere to her when she is seen from Holofernes' point of view are inescapable, complicating Anna's connotations of simplicity and truth.[7]

This image of Anna as a murderous female (perceived via the freemasonry of maleness rather than through the role she plays in her culture by her action), comes after a description of her sexual energy in a mildly threatening context:

> For one late afternoon, when again she stood
> in the door of a twilight always left ajar,
> when dusk had softened the first bulb
> the colour of the first weak star,
> I asked her, 'Choose',
> the amazed dusk held its breath,
> the earth's pulse staggered,
> she nodded, and that nod
> married earth with lightning . . .

[6] London: Cape, 1973, p. 31.
[7] This entire extract is taken from Edward Baugh, *Derek Walcott: Memory as Vision: Another Life*, London: Longman, 1978, p. 56. See also *Another Life*, p. 89. [Ed.]

I hear that open laugh,
I see her stride . . [8]

The images of Anna here are idealised, romanticized (something of the famous bathos of Hemingway's 'the earth moved' for orgasmic experience in his novel *For Whom the Bell Tolls* lurks in 'the earth's pulse' and the 'amazed dusk'), but there is a sense of the energy of this young woman being part of natural forces which could be hostile to the poet. The fear of strong female sexuality which characterizes patriarchy is present here: Anna is young and innocent but there is that about her which will be powerful, and it is this quality which creates conflict in the poet-persona.

Of all these passages, the first one discussed (from 'Of Goats and Monkeys') is the weakest, from an aesthetic point of view, but all the passages are relatively slack. Both the descriptions of the Captain's wife and Anna have a facile quality, produced in the former by an urgency of tone which disturbs the rhythm of the lines in a breathless hostility couched in nearly abusive language, and in the latter by a choice of conventional 'poetic' words/phrases which seem to evade Anna as much as they describe her, and are woven into a conversational, all too easy, tone. In none of these passages is there that wonderful tightness of rhythm and unorthodoxy of word, image and idea which marks Walcott at his best. It is as if woman has little reality in Walcott's imagination, and that there is little between romanticism on the one hand and appalled rejection on the other in her treatment in his works.

One of the most powerful and revealing descriptions of woman as ideal which he offers comes in his prose essay which prefaces the collection of plays *Dream on Monkey Mountain*:

The last image is of a rain-flushed dawn, after a back-breaking night of filming, in a slowly greying field where the sea-wind is like metal on the cheek. In the litter of the field among tarpaulins, stands a shawled girl caught in that gesture which abstractedly gathers cloth to shoulder, her black hair lightly lifting, the tired pale skin flushed, lost in herself and the breaking camp. She was white, and that no longer mattered. Her stillness annihilated years of anger. His heart thanked her silently from the depth of exhaustion, for she was one of a small army of his dreams. She was a vessel caught at the moment of their Muse, her clear vacancy the question of a poem which is its own answer. She was among the sentries who had watched till dawn.[9]

The elements in this description are important. Once more there is use of conventional images, romantic aspects of woman in conjunction with romanticisms about nature. The woman is white, and Walcott's attitude to that is honest and important: her whiteness is no longer a source of anger because her passivity and service to the poet have absolved her of her colour (but what

8   *Another Life*, pp. 8–9.
9   *Dream on Monkey Mountain and Other Plays*, London: Cape, 1972, p. 39.

images this conjures of the passive, serving white wife being able only through her service to transcend the history of her race's guilt). Here the underlying violence in the Othello–Desdemona poem and the underlying fear of Anna in *Another Life* are explained: woman is ideal if she is an extension of the man's imagination, a servant of his will and a quiescent figure in his world. Let her set out with a stride (like Anna) towards her own goals, and she becomes dangerous. Though the passage from the preface to *Dream* is overwritten and highly removed from the reality of the real woman it describes (who was in fact anything but a merely passive handmaiden of the poet), it does contain some important elements for our study. The woman described is used to aggrandize the poet's (male artist's) need for female support/inspiration for his work, and also is perceived through a romantic distancing. . . .

Walcott's work contains many images of beautiful, desirable women as *passive* creatures who await the male decision/appreciation. But these women are often described in near-cliché, pretty images which belong in popular myths of femininity. Walcott is rarely near to the originality and sturdiness of his portraits of men when he deals with women although he is sometimes negatively innovative, as with the image of the 'spiky cunts'.[10] Often the woman is associated with conventional images like the moon, treated conventionally. The moon and the sea become (as in other poets ambivalent about women, like T. S. Eliot and Christopher Okigbo) convenient ways of showing abstract approval to women. When Walcott wants to describe sexual happiness, he looks for a conventionally pretty word. . . .

. . . in *Another Life*, the moon is a maternal force which, like Anna, is associated with the cosmic power of lightning, but here there is no rejection as a result:

> The moon came to the window and stayed there.
> He was her subject, changing when she changed . . .
> his dun flesh peeled white by her lightning strokes![11]

Walcott's ultimate refinement of woman takes her out of the world altogether:

> I live on the water,
> alone. Without wife and children . . .
>
> Now I require nothing,
> from poetry, but true feeling,
> no pity, no fame, no healing. Silent wife,
> we can sit watching grey water . . .[12]

Woman becomes art, and a certain resolution settles over the poetry.

This whole context of woman as image in Walcott's work contrasts

[10] *The Star-Apple Kingdom*, p. 8.
[11] *Another Life*, p. 6.
[12] *Sea-Grapes*, London: Cape, p. 91.

abruptly with the creations for which he is justifiably known and admired: the male pairs who abound in his work, like Makak and Moustique, or the odd couple of *Pantomime*, and the individual male creations like the Devil in *Tijean* or Afa in *Sea at Dauphin*, or the poet-persona in *Another Life*, are all living beings precisely because they are complex, perceived with tolerance, wryness, compassion and a bold honesty, a blend of realism and romanticism which makes the characterization close to archetype but not in the least unconvincing. The characters seem to absorb their creator's full attention, and ours: their language is subtle, containing a true balance between opposites held together in a creative tension. . . .

In *Dream on Monkey Mountain*, he offers an archetype of the White woman which owes something to Jean Genet's *The Blacks*, and which despite the obvious relevance of a symbol of whiteness being destroyed to release the hero of the play from his own psychic enslavement to self-hate, presents a stage image of justified violence against woman. Man revolts against the tyranny of his own fantasies/desires, choosing to destroy that which he cannot otherwise resist. It is important that this image of white racism is presented as a *woman*, justified object of hate and violence which lies just under the surface of the adoring lover (as we graphically saw in 'Goats and Monkeys', in the portrait of Othello). Clearly, the white woman was not the only oppressor in the slavery-colonial period in the Caribbean, but the White man seems less culpable in Walcott's world, for both the Devil in *Tijean* and the grand failure Harry in *Pantomime* are perceived as human despite their evident capacity for tyranny. Perhaps Walcott only makes allowances for *male* evil, out of the freemasonry of maleness which regardless of race, culture or history, can unite against woman. It is also perhaps important that the White woman predominates as a symbol over the Black woman in Walcott's work, possibly because she is more distant and unknowable as a person (because of the male resistance to reality in woman, and because of racial tensions), and therefore is easier to evade as a reality than a woman of the community with which Walcott predominantly identifies, i.e. the African majority.

Women writers, critics and philosophers are at work at this time trying to undo the damage which has been done to women and to relations between women and men, by the refusal of male society to cope with the reality of woman's resources and strengths. Of course, just as the slave/servant knows the master better than the master can know her/him, so the woman knows male culture better than the man knows hers. Adrienne Rich, the poet and feminist writer, has said that woman must re-see and re-vise: once the ability to see properly is achieved then many things change.

5 Drama and the African World-View*

WOLE SOYINKA

First, let us dispose of some red herrings. The serious divergences between a traditional African approach to drama and the European will not be found in lines of opposition between creative individualism and communal creativity, nor in the level of noise from the auditorium—this being the supposed gauge of audience-participation—at any given performance. They will be found more accurately in what is a recognisable Western cast of mind, a compartmentalising habit of thought which periodically selects aspects of human emotion, phenomenal observations, metaphysical intuitions and even scientific deductions and turns them into separatist myths (or 'truths') sustained by a proliferating superstructure of presentation idioms, analogies and analytical modes. I have evolved a rather elaborate metaphor to describe it; appropriately it is not only mechanistic but represents a period technology which marked yet another phase of Western man's comprehensive world-view.

You must picture a steam-engine which shunts itself between rather closely-spaced suburban stations. At the first station it picks up a ballast of allegory, puffs into the next emitting a smokescreen on the eternal landscape of nature truths. At the next it loads up with a different species of logs which we shall call naturalist timber, puffs into a half-way stop where it fills up with the synthetic fuel of surrealism, from which point yet another holistic world-view is glimpsed and asserted through psychedelic smoke. A new consignment of absurdist coke lures it into the next station from which it departs giving off no smoke at all, and no fire, until it derails briefly along constructivist tracks and is towed back to the starting-point by a neo-classic engine.

This, for us, is the occidental creative rhythm, a series of intellectual spasms which, especially today, appears susceptible even to commercial manipulation. And the difference which we are seeking to define between European and African drama as one of man's formal representation of experience is not simply a difference of style or form, nor is it confined to drama alone. It is representative of the essential differences between two world-views, a difference between one culture whose very artifacts are evidence of a cohesive understanding of irreducible truths and another, whose creative impulses are directed by period dialectics. So, to begin with, we must jettison that fashionable distinction which tends to encapsulate Western drama as a form of esoteric enterprise spied upon by fee-paying strangers, as contrasted with a communal evolution of the dramatic mode of expression, this latter being the African.

* From Wole Soyinka, *Myth, Literature and the African World*, Cambridge University Press, 1976, pp. 37–9, 61–3; from a series of lectures given while Visiting Fellow, Churchill College, Cambridge, 1973.

Of far greater importance is the fact that Western dramatic criticism habitually reflects the abandonment of a belief in culture as defined within man's knowledge of fundamental, unchanging relationships between himself and society and within the larger context of the observable universe.

Let us, by way of a paradigmatic example, take a common theme in traditional mask-drama: a symbolic struggle with chthonic presences, the goal of the conflict being a harmonious resolution for plenitude and the well-being of the community.[1] Any individual within the 'audience' knows better than to add his voice *arbitrarily* even to the most seductive passages of an invocatory song, or to contribute a refrain to the familiar sequence of liturgical exchanges among the protagonists. The moment for choric participation is well-defined, but this does not imply that until such a moment, participation ceases. The so-called audience is itself an integral part of that arena of conflict; it contributes spiritual strength to the protagonist through its choric reality which must first be conjured up and established, defining and investing the arena through offerings and incantations. The drama would be non-existent except within and against this symbolic representation of earth and cosmos, except within this communal compact whose choric essence supplies the collective energy for the challenger of chthonic realms. Overt participation when it comes is channelled through a formalised repertoire of gestures and liturgical responses. The 'spontaneous' participant from within the audience does not permit himself to give vent to a bare impulse or a euphoria which might bring him out as a dissociated entity from within the choric mass. If it does happen, as of course it can, the event is an aberration which may imperil the eudaemonic goals of that representation. The interjector—whose balance of mind is regarded as being temporarily disturbed—is quietly led out and the appropriate (usually unobtrusive) spells are cast to counter the risks of the abnormal event. . . .

Asked recently whether or not I accepted the necessity for a literary ideology, I found myself predictably examining the problem from the inside, that is, from within the consciousness of the artist in the process of creating. It was a familiar question, one which always reappears in multiple guises. My response was—a social vision, yes, but not a literary ideology. Generally the question reflects the preoccupation, neither of the traditional nor the contemporary writer in African society but of the analyst after the event, the critic. An examination of the works of most contemporary writers confirms this. But then, it would be equally false to suggest that contemporary African literature

---

[1] The remarks which follow are based on plays observed *in situ*, that is, on the spot where the performance originates and ends, and at its appropriate time of the year, not itinerant variations on the same theme. The specific play referred to here was a harvest play which took place on a farm-clearing some three miles south of Ihiala in the then Eastern Region of Nigeria, 1961.

'Chthonic': from the Greek: of or relating to the underworld. [Ed.]

is not consciously formulated around certain frameworks of ideological intent. The problem is partly one of terminology and the associations of literary history, mostly European. The danger which a literary ideology poses is the act of consecration—and of course excommunication. Thanks to the tendency of the modern consumer-mind to facilitate digestion by putting in strict categories what are essentially fluid operations of the creative mind upon social and natural phenomena, the formulation of a literary ideology tends to congeal sooner or later into instant capsules which, administered also to the writer, may end by asphyxiating the creative process. Such a methodology of assessment does not permit a non-prejudicial probing of the capsule itself, at least not by the literature which brings it into being or which it later brings into being. Probing, if there is any, is an incestuous activity on its own, at least until the fabrication of a rival concept. It is easy to see that this process can only develop into that in-breeding which offers little objective enlightenment about its nature since its idiom and concepts are not freed from the ideology itself. When the reigning ideology fails finally to retain its false comprehensive adequacy, it is discarded. A new set, inviolable mould is fabricated to contain the current body of literature or to stimulate the next along predetermined patterns.

There may appear to be contrary instances to invalidate the suggestion that literary ideologies are really the conscious formulation of the critic, not the artist. But this contradiction exists only when we take as our frame of reference—which regrettably still seems the automatic thing to do—European literary experience. The idea of literature as an objective existence in itself is a very European idea, and ideologies are very much systems of thought or speculative goals considered desirable for the health of existing institutions (society, ecology, economic life etc.) which are, or have come to be regarded as, ends in themselves. Take the French Surrealist movement: even while paying lip-service to the claims of literature as an expression of an end (the infinity of human experience), the Surrealists laboured, by their obsessive concentration on the ontology of a creative medium (in their case literature) to set the medium apart as an autogenous phenomenon, so cutting it off from the human phenomenon which it is supposed to reflect, or on behalf of which it is supposed to speculate. Perhaps it came from taking far too literally the annunciation of the Gospel—In the beginning was the *Word*. Similar claims for the objective existence of the medium are even more overtly stated in the other arts, painting especially. Since we have no experience of such distortions of objective relationships in African society, it is reasonable to claim that a literary ideology traditionally has had little to do with the actual process of creating that literature. In contemporary times there has been one important exception to this pattern, apart from lesser related efforts which periodically attempt to bring the direction of African writing under a fiat of instant-assimilation poetics.

Some literary ideologies take private hallucinatory forms. Samuel Beckett, for instance, gropes incessantly towards the theatrical statement that can be made in one word, a not-too-distant blood-relation of the chimeric obsessions of the Surrealists. If we leave the lunatic fringe of the literary Unilateral Declaration of Independence, however, we discover that despite its tendency towards narrow schematism, a literary ideology does occasionally achieve coincidence—and so a value expansion—with a social vision. From merely turning the mechanics of creativity into a wilful self-regulating domain, irrespective of the burden of statement, it elevates its sights to a regenerative social goal which makes continuing demands on the nature of that ideological medium and prevents its smug stagnation. Brecht's ideology of theatre and dramatic literature is the most successful example.

6 Post-Colonial Reconstructions: Literature, Meaning, Value*

BILL ASHCROFT, GARETH GRIFFITHS, AND HELEN TIFFIN

Post-colonial theories of literature emerge from a view of language grounded in an assertion of the importance of practice over the code, the importance of the 'variant' over the 'standard'. There is also a sense in which post-colonial writing itself, as well as the systematic indigenous theories, offers a broader, non-Eurocentric perspective on some traditional questions of theory. What kinds of writing 'fit' or could be considered to fit into the category 'literature'; how do texts 'mean'; by what criteria could or should these texts be evaluated; how do they dismantle the process of ascribing 'merit' through critical practice; and how applicable are the universalist assertions of European theory to the growing body of post-European literatures. This perspective does not necessarily exclude conclusions which may be reached within Eurocentric theory, but its very existence questions the circumscribed range of that theory's project.

'LITERATURE'

The interaction of english writing with the older traditions of orature or literature in post-colonial societies, and the emergence of a writing which has

* From Bill Ashcroft, Gareth Griffiths, and Helen Tiffin, *The Empire Writes Back: Theory and Practice in Post-Colonial Literatures*, Routledge New Accents, 1989, pp. 181–5, 187–9.

as a major aim the assertion of social and cultural difference, have radically questioned easy assumptions about the characteristics of the genres we usually employ as structuring and categorizing definitives (novel, lyric, epic, play etc.). Our sense, not only of that which ought to enter the canon, but also of what could be given the name 'literature', has been altered by writers incorporating and adapting traditional forms of imaginative expression to the exigencies of an inherited english language. For example, African literatures, as a result of their interface with traditional oral narratives, have offered a number of alter/native ways of conceiving narrative structure. These have influenced both the structure and features of 'novels' produced in english in that continent, and insisted on the inclusion of many forms of performance art in any effective cross-cultural discussion of the structure and form of narrative. The perspective of cross-cultural literatures has given explicit confirmation to the perception that genres cannot be described by essential characteristics, but by an interweaving of features, a 'family resemblance' which denies the possibility of either essentialism or limitation.

Any writer may extend the 'boundaries' of a genre, but the writer who incorporates forms from other traditions articulates more clearly the constant adjustments we make to our perceptions of what is admitted to the category of 'literature'. Most English literary forms evolved in an historical environment quite alien to the cultures of most post-colonial countries. In one sense, the European forms created a basis on which the indigenous literature in english could develop. But this is more a marriage of convenience than a deep cultural commitment to the received genres. Once writing in english is established as a regular social practice, it begins to adapt itself to the traditional ways of formulating the imaginative arts. The received forms do not remain the authentic centre of this complex of practices, but, in time, become one series of forms among many. Inevitably the sensibilities of individual writers will be influenced by the literary and aesthetic assumptions of their own cultures. More often the use of the local tradition will be quite conscious and deliberate; for example, the use of traditions derived from oral performance art and religious epic in the Indian novel, orature and proverb in West Africa and, in settler colonies, various forms of ritual from indigenous speech, such as the 'yarn' in Australia.

Clearly, wherever they exist, traditional pre-colonial indigenous forms are especially important both in the syncretic practice which develops and as an expression of a renewed sense of identity and self-value in the independence period. Ghanaian poet and novelist Kofi Awoonor, for example, claims that the artist must return to traditional sources for inspiration itself. His work makes full use of traditional forms like the dirge . . . Another traditional form employed by contemporary writers is the song of abuse, which opens with a direct address to the person being abused, develops through a catalogue of his or her vices, particularly those that affect the author, and closes with a declaration of the poet's independence. Clearly, the allowable variations of content in the song of abuse offer wide possibilities for any contemporary African poet writing in english. The purpose of using such traditional forms, for Awoonor, for example, is to knit the existing motifs and forms into an artistic whole so that the artist 'is ultimately restored, to a community sensibility, to a resolution, a restoration of calm and quietude'.[1]

The use of traditional forms has not been limited to short poetic pieces. The first Maori novel, Witi Ihimaera's *Tangi* (1973), a novel 'about' his father's death and the subsequent Maori funeral *tangi*, is in fact a sustained lament incorporating all the traditional oral features of repetition, eulogy, and oratory. The lament transposed into novel form achieves remarkable power as a profound celebration of Maori culture, community, and family life. But it puts particular pressure on received notions of what actually constitutes a novel as well as on the received processes of evaluation. To a western reader, used to the tradition of linear progression, character development, and novel form, this lament could seem tedious, repeating as it does the writer's sense of loss and desolation in a book of circular structure. But such a reaction alerts us immediately to the Eurocentric nature of such an evaluation and the need to incorporate cultural context into any assessment of literary worth.

Ideas of narrative structure area are also altered. Salman Rushdie has made it quite clear that the techniques of the novel *Midnight's Children* reproduce the traditional techniques of the Indian oral narrative tradition. In an interview he says:

Listening to this man (a famous story teller in Baroda) reminded me of the shape of the oral narrative. It's not linear. An oral narrative does not go from the beginning to the middle to the end of the story. It goes in great swoops, it goes in spirals or in loops, it every so often reiterates something that happened earlier to remind you, and then takes you off again, sometimes summarises itself, it frequently digresses off into something that the story teller appears just to have thought of, then it comes back to the main thrust of the narrative . . .

So that's what *Midnight's Children* was, I think, and I think everything about Laurence Sterne, Garcia Marquez, and all that, comes a long way behind that, and that was the thing that I felt when writing it that I was trying to do.[2]

This technique of circling back from the present to the past, of building tale within tale, and persistently delaying climaxes are all features of traditional narration and orature. Witness this account of the narrative technique of the traditional clown-narrator (the 'Vidushka') in the ancient Indian performance art of *Kuttiyattam*:

---

[1] Kofi Awoonor, 'Voyage and the Earth', *New Letters*, 40, no. 1, Autumn, 1973, p. 88.
[2] Rushdie interview, *Kunapipi*, vol. 7, no. 1, 1985, p. 8.

The Vidushka can take all kinds of liberties; in fact he is expected to and encouraged to do so. He can indulge in any kind of extravagance, provided he can come back to the main thread of the narrative without getting lost in his own elaborations. He could turn his narrative into a string of short stories or take one of these stories and lengthen it for hours or days. Thus the oral narrative can easily achieve the length of a novel —if length is a criterion at all.[3]

This oral technique, itself grafted onto the fragments of ancient Sanskrit written texts which form the basis for *Kuttiyattam* performance, illustrates the possibilities of undoing the assumptions of logocentric texts in post-colonial practice. Rushdie can employ similar graftings in the development of the relationship between the narrator and 'listener' (Padma) in *Midnight's Children*. Rushdie assures us that such techniques from orature are consciously part of his writing. Also, of course, there are many literary sources in traditional Indian written narrative we could look to as unconscious influences which are far older than Sterne; for example the fourth century Brhatkatha of Gunadhya.[4] In fact, to anyone familiar with traditional Indian writing and orature it is clear that Rushdie's text is profoundly intertextual with the whole of the Indian narrative tradition.

Post-colonial texts like *Midnight's Children* (or Amos Tutuola's *The Palm-Wine Drinkard* three decades earlier) have been subjected to a schizophrenic form of critical dismissal. On the one hand contemporary nationalist critics dismissed these texts because in their view they only reproduced in a translated or 'plagiarized' form the traditional techniques of narration and so failed the test of 'authenticity'; on the other hand, European critics, out of ignorance, failed entirely to record the debt of these texts to African and Indian traditional forms. What neither position did was to engage with the text as an extreme example of that hybridity which is the primary characteristic of all post-colonial texts, whatever their source.

MEANING

Another question posed by post-colonial literatures is 'Could the *concept* of meaning itself be Eurocentric?' Our understanding of the concrete nature of languages with no written script, for instance, suggests at least the necessity for a greater questioning of the way in which the meanings of words function. But post-colonial writing has provided a distinct approach to the question of meaning because in these texts the 'message event' itself is so important. Whereas the history of European literary theory has been an arena in which the three poles of any meaning exchange—the language, the utterer or writer, and the hearer or reader—have been locked in a gladiatorial contest

[3] A. Paniker, 'The oral narrative tradition in Mayalam', *The Literary Criterion*, vol. 21, no. 2, 1986.
[4] See A. Krishnamoorthy, 'Makings of the Indian Novel', *The Literary Criterion*, vol. 21, nos. 1 and 2, 1986.

over the ownership of meaning, the nature of post-colonial writing has helped to reveal that the situation is not so simple. All three 'functions' of this exchange participate in the 'social' situation of the written text. The insistence of post-colonial critics that writing is a social practice with an indelible social function suggests the possibility that meaning, too, is a social accomplishment characterized by the participation of the writer and reader functions within the 'event' of the particular discourse. . . .

VALUE

Post-colonial literatures, spanning considerably diverse cultural traditions, have revealed with unequivocal clarity that value, like meaning, is not an intrinsic quality but a relation between the object and certain criteria brought to bear upon it. For instance, it is apparent that those people who have a strong link with an oral tradition judge literature quite differently from those who continue a written tradition. The presence of features of African orature in novels which, viewed with European assumptions about novel structure, may look like simple, even imitative reproductions of existing styles, must change our valuation of the text's 'originality' or its 'success'. For example, European critics have generally regarded the Malawian novelist David Rubadiri's *No Bride Price* (1967) as a simple, sociological account and a classic realist text. Yet criticism informed by an understanding of African oral performance and orature has shown how it reflects the pattern of traditional drum narratives which have been built into the structural features of the text. Faced with the vastly different criteria which people from diverse cultures obviously bring to bear upon all matters of judgement, we are presented with clear and extraordinary confirmation of the tenuousness of the notion of 'intrinsic value'.

For Homi Bhabha, the process of evaluation in universalist and nationalist theories, which are overwhelmingly representationalist, becomes a process of establishing a mimetic adequacy. Because such theories propose a predomin-antly mimetic view of the relation between the text and a *given* pre-constituted reality, evaluation becomes the business of establishing the representative 'truth' of the text:

The 'image' must be measured against the 'essential' or 'original' in order to establish its degree of *representativeness*, the correctness of the image. The text is not seen as *productive* of meaning but essentially reflective or expressive.[5]

Consequently it is broadly within these empiricist terms that the discourses of universalist and nationalist criticism circulate and pose the questions of

---

[5] Homi Bhabha, 'Representation and the colonial text; a critical explanation of some forms of mimeticism' in *The Theory of Reading*, ed. Frank Gloversmith, Harvester, Brighton, 1984, p. 100.

colonial difference and discrimination, and this is the essentially limiting factor which initiates their practice.

An 'intrinsic' value, linked as it is with an 'essential' meaning, is crucial to the operation of the universalist conception of the literary. The intrinsic and essential must, by definition, be universal, and of course the universal is the province of the discourse which imposes its criteria. In the evaluation of post-colonial literatures it is the centre which imposes its criteria as universal, and dictates an order in terms of which the cultural margins must always see themselves as disorder and chaos.

VII *Language and Gender*

The extracts in this section represent some of the most significant currents in the thinking that has transformed our understanding of the relation between women and literature in the modern world. Feminist critics have made a massive contribution to the contemporary challenge to the notion of a received literary 'canon', as the earlier extracts by Sandra Gilbert and Susan Gubar (Part One, section I) and Virginia Woolf (Part One, section III and Part Two, section III) suggest. Woolf insisted on the importance of the historical perspective: if women could comprehend what happened to their mothers and grandmothers, they would be on their way to understanding, perhaps changing, their own position. This conviction was shared by Simone de Beauvoir, whose monumental The Second Sex *(1949), published twenty years after Woolf's* A Room of One's Own, *proposed a broader approach. Accompanying her exploration of the role of women in literature by scrutinizing their place in biology, anthropology, religion, and philosophy, her Introduction brings out her central argument: that women's role has been socially constructed, defined in relation to men—who are seen as the 'Absolute', while women are the 'Other'.*

Cora Kaplan's account of 'Language and Gender' is deeply influenced by the philosophically inclined tradition founded by de Beauvoir, although she goes on to draw from the French psychoanalyst Jacques Lacan ways to think about how gender affects our relations with language. As the most prestigious form of language, poetry became a genre whose difficulties for women could only be explained by going beyond literary history, towards the question of sex and gender as distinct concepts. The writing of the French critic Hélène Cixous is also profoundly influenced by psycho-analytic thought: she proclaims the possibility of a feminine writing—écriture feminine—which would break down the barriers excluding women from public speech. Toni Morrison's essay on 'Rootedness' is also concerned with the forces which have excluded women from writing and speech; but, alert to the barriers facing those who are poor, and black, she returns to the lessons of history—the concern of contributors to the next section. Her view of history culminates in a warning, drawn from a consideration of her own novel, Song of Solomon: *if our understanding of the past is exclusive, our future will be impoverished.*

1 *Woman and the Other**

SIMONE DE BEAUVOIR

For a long time I have hesitated to write a book on woman. The subject is irritating, especially to women; and it is not new. Enough ink has been spilled in quarrelling over feminism, and perhaps we should say no more about it. It is still talked about, however, for the voluminous nonsense uttered during the last century seems to have done little to illuminate the problem. After all, is there a problem? And if so, what is it? Are there women, really? Most assuredly the theory of the eternal feminine still has its adherents who will whisper in your ear: 'Even in Russia women still are *women*'; and other erudite persons—sometimes the very same—say with a sigh: 'Woman is losing her way, woman is lost.' One wonders if women still exist, if they will always exist, whether or not it is desirable that they should, what place they occupy in this world, what their place should be. 'What has become of women?' was asked recently in an ephemeral magazine.

But first we must ask: what is a woman? *'Tota mulier in utero'*, says one, 'woman is a womb'. But in speaking of certain women, connoisseurs declare that they are not women, although they are equipped with a uterus like the rest. All agree in recognizing the fact that females exist in the human species; today as always they make up about one half of humanity. And yet we are told that femininity is in danger; we are exhorted to be women, remain women, become women. It would appear, then, that every female human being is not necessarily a woman; to be so considered she must share in that mysterious and threatened reality known as femininity. Is this attribute something secreted by the ovaries? Or is it a Platonic essence, a product of the philosophic imagination? Is a rustling petticoat enough to bring it down to earth? Although some women try zealously to incarnate this essence, it is hardly patentable. It is frequently described in vague and dazzling terms that seem to have been borrowed from the vocabulary of the seers, and indeed in the times of St Thomas it was considered an essence as certainly defined as the somniferous virtue of the poppy.

But conceptualism has lost ground. The biological and social sciences no longer admit the existence of unchangeably fixed entities that determine given characteristics, such as those ascribed to woman, the Jew, or the Negro. Science regards any characteristic as a reaction dependent in part upon a *situation*. If today femininity no longer exists, then it never existed. But does the word *woman*, then, have no specific content? This is stoutly affirmed by those who hold to the philosophy of the enlightenment, of rationalism, of

* From Simone de Beauvoir, 'Introduction', *The Second Sex* (1949), transl. and ed. H. M. Parshley, 1953, reprinted Pan Books, 1988, pp. 13–19, 23–4.

nominalism; women, to them, are merely the human beings arbitrarily designated by the word *woman*. Many American women particularly are prepared to think that there is no longer any place for woman as such; if a backward individual still takes herself for a woman, her friends advise her to be psychoanalysed and thus get rid of this obsession. In regard to a work, *Modern Woman: The Lost Sex*, which in other respects has its irritating features, Dorothy Parker has written: 'I cannot be just to books which treat of woman as woman . . . My idea is that all of us, men as well as women, should be regarded as human beings.' But nominalism is a rather inadequate doctrine, and the anti-feminists have had no trouble in showing that women simply *are not* men. Surely woman is, like man, a human being; but such a declaration is abstract. The fact is that every concrete human being is always a singular, separate individual. To decline to accept such notions as the eternal feminine, the black soul, the Jewish character, is not to deny that Jews, Negroes, women exist today—this denial does not represent a liberation for those concerned, but rather a flight from reality. Some years ago a well-known woman writer refused to permit her portrait to appear in a series of photographs especially devoted to women writers; she wished to be counted among the men. But in order to gain this privilege she made use of her husband's influence! Women who assert that they are men lay claim none the less to masculine consideration and respect. I recall also a young Trotskyite standing on a platform at a boisterous meeting and getting ready to use her fists, in spite of her evident fragility. She was denying her feminine weakness; but it was for love of a militant male whose equal she wished to be. The attitude of defiance of many American women proves that they are haunted by a sense of their femininity. In truth, to go for a walk with one's eyes open is enough to demonstrate that humanity is divided into two classes of individuals whose clothes, faces, bodies, smiles, gaits, interests, and occupations are manifestly different. Perhaps these differences are superficial, perhaps they are destined to disappear. What is certain is that they do most obviously exist.

If her functioning as a female is not enough to define woman, if we decline also to explain her through 'the eternal feminine', and if nevertheless we admit, provisionally, that women do exist, then we must face the question: what is a woman?

To state the question is, to me, to suggest, at once, a preliminary answer. The fact that I ask it is in itself significant. A man would never set out to write a book on the peculiar situation of the human male. But if I wish to define myself, I must first of all say: 'I am a woman'; on this truth must be based all further discussion. A man never begins by presenting himself as an individual of a certain sex; it goes without saying that he is a man. The terms *masculine* and *feminine* are used symmetrically only as a matter of form, as on legal papers. In actuality the relation of the two sexes is not quite like that of two electrical poles, for man represents both the positive and the neutral, as is indicated by the common use of *man* to designate human beings in general; whereas woman represents only the negative, defined by limiting criteria, without reciprocity. In the midst of an abstract discussion it is vexing to hear a man say: 'You think thus and so because you are a woman'; but I know that my only defence is to reply: 'I think thus and so because it is true,' thereby removing my subjective self from the argument. It would be out of the question to reply: 'And you think the contrary because you are a man', for it is understood that the fact of being a man is no peculiarity. A man is in the right in being a man; it is the woman who is in the wrong. It amounts to this: just as for the ancients there was an absolute vertical with reference to which the oblique was defined, so there is an absolute human type, the masculine. Woman has ovaries, a uterus: these peculiarities imprison her in her subjectivity, circumscribe her within the limits of her own nature. It is often said that she thinks with her glands. Man superbly ignores the fact that his anatomy also includes glands, such as the testicles, and that they secrete hormones. He thinks of his body as a direct and normal connection with the world, which he believes he apprehends objectively, whereas he regards the body of woman as a hindrance, a prison, weighed down by everything peculiar to it. 'The female is a female by virtue of a certain *lack* of qualities,' said Aristotle; 'we should regard the female nature as afflicted with a natural defectiveness.' And St Thomas for his part pronounced woman to be an 'imperfect man', an 'incidental' being. This is symbolized in Genesis where Eve is depicted as made from what Bossuet called 'a supernumerary bone' of Adam.

Thus humanity is male and man defines woman not in herself but as relative to him; she is not regarded as an autonomous being. Michelet writes: 'Woman, the relative being . . .' And Benda is most positive in his *Rapport d'Uriel*: 'The body of man makes sense in itself quite apart from that of woman, whereas the latter seems wanting in significance by itself . . . Man can think of himself without woman. She cannot think of herself without man.' And she is simply what man decrees; thus she is called 'the sex', by which is meant that she appears essentially to the male as a sexual being. For him she is sex—absolute sex, no less. She is defined and differentiated with reference to man and not he with reference to her; she is the incidental, the inessential as opposed to the essential. He is the Subject, he is the Absolute —she is the Other.

The category of the *Other* is as primordial as consciousness itself. In the most primitive societies, in the most ancient mythologies, one finds the expression of a duality—that of the Self and the Other. This duality was not originally attached to the division of the sexes; it was not dependent upon any empirical facts. It is revealed in such works as that of Granet on Chinese thought and those of Dumézil on the East Indies and Rome. The feminine element was at first no more involved in such pairs as Varuna-Mitra, Uranus-Zeus, Sun-Moon, and Day-Night than it was in the contrasts between Good and Evil, lucky and unlucky auspices, right and left, God and Lucifer. Otherness is a fundamental category of human thought.

Thus it is that no group ever sets itself up as the One without at once setting up the Other over against itself. If three travellers chance to occupy the same compartment, that is enough to make vaguely hostile 'others' out of all the rest of the passengers on the train. In small-town eyes all persons not belonging to the village are 'strangers' and suspect; to the native of a country all who inhabit other countries are 'foreigners'; Jews are 'different' for the anti-Semite, Negroes are 'inferior' for American racists, aborigines are 'natives' for colonists, proletarians are the 'lower class' for the privileged.

Lévi-Strauss, at the end of a profound work on the various forms of primitive societies, reaches the following conclusion: 'Passage from the state of Nature to the state of Culture is marked by man's ability to view biological relations as a series of contrasts; duality, alternation, opposition, and symmetry, whether under definite or vague forms, constitute not so much phenomena to be explained as fundamental and immediately given data of social reality.'[1] These phenomena would be incomprehensible if in fact human society were simply a *Mitsein* or fellowship based on solidarity and friendliness. Things become clear, on the contrary, if, following Hegel, we find in consciousness itself a fundamental hostility towards every other consciousness; the subject can be posed only in being opposed—he sets himself up as the essential, as opposed to the other, the inessential, the object.

But the other consciousness, the other ego, sets up a reciprocal claim. The native travelling abroad is shocked to find himself in turn regarded as a 'stranger' by the natives of neighbouring countries. As a matter of fact, wars, festivals, trading, treaties, and contests among tribes, nations, and classes tend to deprive the concept *Other* of its absolute sense and to make manifest its relativity; willy-nilly, individuals and groups are forced to realize the reciprocity of their relations. How is it, then, that this reciprocity has not been recognized between the sexes, that one of the contrasting terms is set up as the sole essential, denying any relativity in regard to its correlative and defining the latter as pure otherness? Why is it that women do not dispute male sovereignty? No subject will readily volunteer to become the object, the inessential; it is not the Other who, in defining himself as the Other, establishes the One. The Other is posed as such by the One in defining himself as the One. But if the Other is not to regain the status of being the One, he must

---

[1] See C. Lévi-Strauss, *Les Structures élémentaires de la parenté*.

be submissive enough to accept this alien point of view. Whence comes this submission in the case of woman?

There are, to be sure, other cases in which a certain category has been able to dominate another completely for a time. Very often this privilege depends upon inequality of numbers—the majority imposes its rule upon the minority or persecutes it. But women are not a minority, like the American Negroes or the Jews; there are as many women as men on earth. Again, the two groups concerned have often been originally independent; they may have been formerly unaware of each other's existence, or perhaps they recognized each other's autonomy. But a historical event has resulted in the subjugation of the weaker by the stronger. The scattering of the Jews, the introduction of slavery into America, the conquests of imperialism are examples in point. In these cases the oppressed retained at least the memory of former days; they possessed in common a past, a tradition, sometimes a religion or a culture.

The parallel drawn by Bebel between women and the proletariat is valid in that neither ever formed a minority or a separate collective unit of mankind. And instead of a single historical event it is in both cases a historical development that explains their status as a class and accounts for the membership of *particular individuals* in that class. But proletarians have not always existed, whereas there have always been women. They are women in virtue of their anatomy and physiology. Throughout history they have always been subordinated to men and hence their dependency is not the result of a historical event or a social change—it was not something that *occurred*. The reason why otherness in this case seems to be an absolute is in part that it lacks the contingent or incidental nature of historical facts. A condition brought about at a certain time can be abolished at some other time, as the Negroes of Haiti and others have proved; but it might seem that a natural condition is beyond the possibility of change. In truth, however, the nature of things is no more immutably given, once for all, than is historical reality. If woman seems to be the inessential which never becomes the essential, it is because she herself fails to bring about this change. Proletarians say 'We'; Negroes also. Regarding themselves as subjects, they transform the bourgeois, the whites, into 'others'. But women do not say 'We', except at some congress of feminists or similar formal demonstration; men say 'women', and women use the same word in referring to themselves. They do not authentically assume a subjective attitude. The proletarians have accomplished the revolution in Russia, the Negroes in Haiti, the Indo-Chinese are battling for it in Indo-China; but the women's effort has never been anything more than a symbolic agitation. They have gained only what men have been willing to grant; they have taken nothing, they have only received. . . .

In proving woman's inferiority, the anti-feminists then began to draw not only upon religion, philosophy, and theology, as before, but also upon science

—biology, experimental psychology, etc. At most they were willing to grant 'equality in difference' to the *other* sex. That profitable formula is most significant; it is precisely like the 'equal but separate' formula of the Jim Crow laws aimed at the North American Negroes. As is well known, this so-called equalitarian segregation has resulted only in the most extreme discrimination. The similarity just noted is in no way due to chance, for whether it is a race, a caste, a class, or a sex that is reduced to a position of inferiority, the methods of justification are the same. 'The eternal feminine' corresponds to 'the black soul' and to 'the Jewish character'. True, the Jewish problem is on the whole very different from the other two—to the anti-Semite the Jew is not so much an inferior as he is an enemy for whom there is to be granted no place on earth, for whom annihilation is the fate desired. But there are deep similarities between the situation of woman and that of the Negro. Both are being emancipated today from a like paternalism, and the former master class wishes to 'keep them in their place'—that is, the place chosen for them. In both cases the former masters lavish more or less sincere eulogies, either on the virtues of 'the good Negro' with his dormant, childish, merry soul—the submissive Negro—or on the merits of the woman who is 'truly feminine' —that is, frivolous, infantile, irresponsible—the submissive woman. In both cases the dominant class bases its argument on a state of affairs that it has itself created. As George Bernard Shaw puts it, in substance. 'The American white relegates the black to the rank of shoeshine boy; and he concludes from this that the black is good for nothing but shining shoes.' This vicious circle is met with in all analogous circumstances; when an individual (or a group of individuals) is kept in a situation of inferiority, the fact is that he is inferior. But the significance of the verb to *be* must be rightly understood here; it is in bad faith to give it a static value when it really has the dynamic Hegelian sense of 'to have become'. Yes, women on the whole *are* today inferior to men; that is, their situation affords them fewer possibilities. The question is: should that state of affairs continue?

2 *Language and Gender**

CORA KAPLAN

Poetry is a privileged metalanguage in western patriarchal culture. Although other written forms of high culture—theology, philosophy, political theory,

* From Cora Kaplan, 'Language and Gender', *Sea Changes: Culture and Feminism*, Verso, 1986, pp. 69–72, 79–86.

drama, prose fiction—are also, in part, language about language, in poetry this introverted or doubled relation is thrust at us as the very reason-for-being of the genre. Perhaps because poetry seems, more than any other sort of imaginative writing, to imitate a closed linguistic system it is presented to us as invitingly accessible to our understanding once we have pushed past its formal difficulties. Oddly we still seem to expect poetry to produce universal meanings. The bourgeois novel is comfortably established as a genre produced by and about a particular class, but there is an uneasy feel about the bourgeois poem. Poetry is increasingly written by members of oppressed groups, but its popular appeal is so small in western society today that its shrinking audience may make its elitism or lack of it a non-issue. Its appeal may have diminished in relation to other literary forms but its status and function in high culture continues to be important. This paper examines women's poetry as part of an investigation of women's use of high language, that is, the language, public, political and literary, of patriarchal societies.

A study of women's writing will not get us any closer to an enclosed critical practice, a 'feminist literary criticism'. There can in one sense be no feminist literary criticism, for any new theoretical approach to literature that uses gender difference as an important category involves a profoundly altered view of the relation of both sexes to language, speech, writing and culture. For this reason I have called my paper Language and Gender rather than Women and Poetry, although it grew out of work on a critical anthology of English and American women's poetry that I introduced and edited a few years ago.[1] Some of the problems raised there still seem central to me—the insertion of female centred subject matter into a male literary tradition, the attendant problems of expressing this matter in a formal symbolic language, the contradictions between the romantic notion of the poet as the transcendent speaker of a unified culture and the dependent and oppressed place of women within that culture. New problems have occurred to me as equally important. The difficulty women have in writing seems to me to be linked very closely to the rupture between childhood and adolescence, when, in western societies (and in other cultures as well) public speech is a male privilege and women's speech restricted by custom in mixed sex gatherings, or, if permitted, still characterized by its private nature, an extension of the trivial domestic discourse of women. For male speakers after puberty, the distinction between public and private speech is not made in nearly such a strong way, if at all. Obviously, in the twentieth century and earlier, such distinctions have been challenged and in some cases seem to be broken down, but the distinction is

---

[1] Cora Kaplan, *Salt and Bitter and Good: Three Centuries of English and American Women Poets*. London and New York, 1975.

still made. The prejudice seems persistent and irrational unless we acknowledge that control of high language is a crucial part of the power of dominant
groups, and understand that the refusal of access to public language is one
of the major forms of the oppression of women within a social class as well
as in trans-class situations.

A very high proportion of women's poems are about the right to speak and
write. The desire to write imaginative poetry and prose was and is a demand
for access to and parity within the law and myth-making groups in society.
The decision to storm the walls and occupy the forbidden place is a recognition of the value and importance of high language, and often contradicts
and undercuts a more radical critique in women's poetry of the values
embedded in formal symbolic language itself. To be a woman and a poet
presents many women poets with such a profound split between their social,
sexual identity (their 'human' identity) and their artistic practice that the split
becomes the insistent subject, sometimes overt, often hidden or displaced, of
much women's poetry. . . .

Do men and women in patriarchal societies have different relationships to
the language they speak and write? Statements of such a difference, questions
about its source, persistence and meaning run through western writing since
Greek times. Often buried in that larger subject, the exploration and definition
of gender difference in culture, it becomes a distinct issue when women speak
or write, and men protest, not only or primarily at what they say, but at the
act itself. Recently left feminists have used work on ideology by the French
political philosopher, Louis Althusser, together with the psychoanalytic
theories of Freud and his modern French interpreter, Jacques Lacan, to clarify
their understanding of the construction of femininity.[2] Contemporary work
on ideology in France accepts Freud's theory of the unconscious and is
concerned, among other things, with the construction of the subject in
culture. Language is the most important of all the forms of human communication. Through the acquisition of language we become human and
social beings: the words we speak situate us in our gender and our class.
Through language we come to 'know' who we are. In elaborating and
extending Freud's work, Lacan emphasizes the crucial importance of
language as the signifying practice in and through which the subject is made
into a social being. Social entry into patriarchal culture is made in language,
through speech. Our individual speech does not, therefore, free us in any
simple way from the ideological constraints of our culture since it is through
the forms that articulate those constraints that we speak in the first place. . . .

---

[2] Louis Althusser, 'Ideology and Ideological State Apparatus', and 'Freud and Lacan'; in *Lenin, and
Philosophy and Other Essays*, London, 1971. Jacques Lacan, *Écrits: A Selection*, London, 1977. Jacques
Lacan, *The Four Fundamentals of Psycho-Analysis*, London, 1977. See also *Feminine Sexuality: Jacques
Lacan and the école freudienne*, Juliet Mitchell and Jacqueline Rose, eds., London, 1982.

There is a haunting painting by Odilon Redon of a woman's face in ivory cameo, further enclosed in a green oval mist. A wraithlike madonna, still, and at the same time full of intense activity, she holds two fingers to her lips, and, perhaps, a cupped paw to her ear. The picture is titled *Silence*. Enjoining silence, she is its material image. A speaking silence—image and injunction joined—she is herself spoken, twice spoken we might say—once by the artist who has located *his* silence in a female figure, and once again by the viewer who accepts as natural this abstract identification of woman = silence and the complementary imaging of women's speech as whispered, subvocal, the mere escape of trapped air ... shhhhhhh.

More, her speech seems limited by some function in which she is wrapped as deeply as in the embryonic mist. Mother or nurse, the silence she enjoins and enacts is on behalf of some sleeping other. In enforcing our silence and her own she seems to protect someone else's speech. Her silence and muted speech, as I interpret it, is both chosen and imposed by her acceptance of her femininity. It has none of the illusory freedom of choice that we associate with a taciturn male. It is not the silence of chosen isolation either, for even in a painting significantly without other figures it is an inextricably social silence.

Redon's Madonna trails meanings behind it like the milky way. *Silence* makes a point central to my argument that is perhaps difficult to make with any literary epigraph. Social silence as part of the constitution of female identity—i.e., subjectivity—is a crucial factor in her handling of written language. In an as yet almost unresearched area there is very little evidence to suggest that women's common, everyday speech is in any way less complex than men's and some evidence to suggest that girls not only speak earlier than boys but develop linguistic complexity earlier too. It has been tentatively suggested that although girls are more 'verbal' (whatever that may mean) by the age of eleven or twelve, there is less meaning in their speech, though the phonemic complexity is greater. Robin Lakoff, in *Language and Woman's Place*,[3] does not adduce any particular evidence for her ideas or locate her women speakers in any class, race or locale, but suggests that women do speak a sort of second-class English which is more interrogatory, more full of 'empty' qualifiers ('lovely', 'kind of') and, because vulgarity is censored, is super-genteel and grammatically more correct than men's speech. It is by no means clear that these observations would be true (if at all) of any group of women except perhaps upwardly mobile middle-class white American women, and if true of this group it seems much more likely to be related to a class plus gender instability than to be a particular quality of women's speech. In any case, recent debates over the language of class and of Black English has produced persuasive evidence that a restricted or alterna-

---

[3] Robin Lakoff, *Language and Woman's Place*, New York, 1975.

tive code does not necessarily produce restricted meanings. The variations
that Lakoff lists as being special to women's speech seem very slight when
compared to the variations of grammatical structure in Black English
compared to standard English. Obviously the subject has barely been opened
much less closed, but one might hazard that women speak the language of
their class, caste, or race and that any common variants, which are in any
case never fully observed, do not in themselves limit the meanings their
speech can have. The sanction against female obscenity can have a particular
application in the sanction against the telling of jokes and the use of wit by
women, since dirty jokes are forms of common speech in which the repressed
meanings of early sexual feelings are expressed in tight symbolic narratives.

It is the intra- and trans-class prejudice against women as speakers at all
which seems most likely to erode women's use of 'high' language. This
preference is connected with the patriarchal definition of ideal femininity.
'Silence gives the proper grace to women', Sophocles writes in *Ajax*. Its
contradictions are expressed succinctly in the play, 'The Man who Married a
Dumb Wife'. A famous physician is called in to cure the beautiful mute. He
succeeds, she speaks, and immediately begins to prattle compulsively, until
the husband bitterly regrets his humane gesture. His only wish is to have her
dumb again so that he might love her as before. Women speak on sufferance
in the patriarchal order. Yet although the culture may prefer them to be
silent, they must have the faculty of speech in order that they may be
recognised as human. One reading of the Dumb Wife, whose speech is her
only flaw, is that the physician's alchemy was necessary to reassure the
husband that he had married a human woman, although her unrestrained,
trivial speech destroys his ability to see her as the ideal love object.

Elizabeth Barrett Browning comments bitterly on the prohibition against
women as speakers of public language in her long feminist poem *Aurora Leigh*.
Aurora, who defies society to become a major poet, recounts her education
at the hands of her aunt who was a model of all that was 'womanly':

> I read a score of books on womanhood...— books that boldly assert
> Their right of comprehending husband's talk
> When not too deep, and even of answering
> With pretty 'may it please you', or 'so it is', —
> Their rapid insight and fine aptitude,
> Particular worth and general missionariness,
> As long as they keep quiet by the fire
> And never say 'no' when the world says 'ay', ... their, in brief,
> Potential faculty in everything
> Of abdicating power in it.

Aurora calls 'those years of education' a kind of water torture, 'flood succeeding flood/To drench the incapable throat ...' The imposed silence is described

as intersubjective, a silence whose effort is bent towards 'comprehending husband's talk'.[4] Women writers from the seventeenth century onwards (when women first entered the literary ranks in any numbers) comment in moods which range from abnegation to outright anger on the culture's prohibition against women's writing, often generalizing it to women's speech. They compare their situation to that of 'state prisoners, pen and ink denied' and their suppressed or faulty speech to the child's or the 'lisping boy's'. Emily Dickinson's 'They shut me up in Prose/As when a little Girl/They put me in the Closet — / Because they liked me "still" — '[5] condenses all these metaphors by connecting verbal imprisonment to the real restrictions of female childhood, and adds the point that the language most emphatically denied to women is the most concentrated form of symbolic language — poetry.

The consciousness of the taboo and its weight seemed to press heavily on the women who disobeyed it, and some form of apology, though tinged with irony, occurs in almost all of the women poets, as well as in many prose writers, whether avowed feminists or not, as an urgent perhaps propitiating preface to their speech. In the introduction to the anthology I ascribed this compulsion to an anticipatory response to male prejudice against women writers, and so it was. But it now seems to me that it goes much deeper, and is intimately connected as I have said with the way in which women become social beings in the first place, so that the very condition of their accession to their own subjectivity, to the consciousness of a self which is both personal and public is their unwitting acceptance of the law which limits their speech. This condition places them in a special relation to language which becomes theirs as a consequence of becoming human, and at the same time not theirs as a consequence of becoming female.

The best writing by women about women writing has been about fiction; the weakest about poetry. Fiction, whether gothic, sentimental or realistic, has a narrative structure and gendered characters in which the author can locate and distance her own speech. One might say that the narrative discourse itself provides a sort of third term for the woman author by locating (even, and perhaps especially, in a first person narrative) the loss or absence of power anywhere but in her own voice. If fiction has been the most successful genre for women writers it is not, as has been often suggested, because the novel makes use of the domestic scene, or the life of the feelings, or 'trivial' observation, all those things supposedly close to women's experience, but because its scene is that world of social relations, of intersubjectivity, in which the author can reconcile to some extent her speech and her silence

---

[4] Elizabeth Barrett Browning, *Aurora Leigh and Other Poems*, Cora Kaplan ed., London, 1978, First Book, pp. 51–2.
[5] Kaplan, *Salt and Bitter and Good*, p. 154.

and be the first to explore and expose her bisexuality without the threat of losing her feminine identity.

3 *The Laugh of the Medusa**

HÉLÈNE CIXOUS

I shall speak about women's writing: about *what it will do*. Woman must write her self: must write about women and bring women to writing, from which they have been driven away as violently as from their bodies—for the same reasons, by the same law, with the same fatal goal. Woman must put herself into the text—as into the world and into history—by her own movement.

The future must no longer be determined by the past. I do not deny that the effects of the past are still with us. But I refuse to strengthen them by repeating them, to confer upon them an irremovability the equivalent of destiny, to confuse the biological and the cultural. Anticipation is imperative.

Since these reflections are taking shape in an area just on the point of being discovered, they necessarily bear the mark of our time—a time during which the new breaks away from the old, and, more precisely, the (feminine) new from the old (*la nouvelle de l'ancien*). Thus, as there are no grounds for establishing a discourse, but rather an arid millennial ground to break, what I say has at least two sides and two aims: to break up, to destroy; and to foresee the unforeseeable, to project.

I write this as a woman, toward women. When I say 'woman', I'm speaking of woman in her inevitable struggle against conventional man; and of a universal woman subject who must bring women to their senses and to their meaning in history. But first it must be said that in spite of the enormity of the repression that has kept them in the 'dark'—that dark which people have been trying to make them accept as their attribute—there is, at this time, no general woman, no one typical woman. What they have *in common* I will say. But what strikes me is the infinite richness of their individual constitutions: you can't talk about *a* female sexuality, uniform, homogeneous, classifiable into codes—any more than you can talk about one unconscious resembling another. Women's imaginary is inexhaustible, like music, painting, writing: their stream of phantasms is incredible.

I have been amazed more than once by a description a woman gave me of

* From Hélène Cixous, 'The Laugh of the Medusa', transl. Keith Cohen and Paula Cohen, in *New French Feminisms*, ed. Elaine Marks and Isabelle de Courtivon, Harvester Press, Brighton, 1981, pp. 245–64. Published in *Signs*, Summer 1976. This is a revised version of 'Le rire de la méduse', which appeared in *L'Arc* (1975), pp. 39–54.

a world all her own which she had been secretly haunting since early childhood. A world of searching, the elaboration of a knowledge, on the basis of a systematic experimentation with the bodily functions, a passionate and precise interrogation of her erotogeneity. This practice, extraordinarily rich and inventive, in particular as concerns masturbation, is prolonged or accompanied by a production of forms, a veritable aesthetic activity, each stage of rapture inscribing a resonant vision, a composition, something beautiful. Beauty will no longer be forbidden.

I wished that that woman would write and proclaim this unique empire so that other women, other unacknowledged sovereigns, might exclaim: I, too, overflow; my desires have invented new desires, my body knows unheard-of songs. Time and again I, too, have felt so full of luminous torrents that I could burst—burst with forms much more beautiful than those which are put up in frames and sold for a stinking fortune. And I, too, said nothing, showed nothing; I didn't open my mouth, I didn't repaint my half of the world. I was ashamed. I was afraid, and I swallowed my shame and my fear. I said to myself: You are mad! What's the meaning of these waves, these floods, these outbursts? Where is the ebullient, infinite woman who, immersed as she was in her naiveté, kept in the dark about herself, led into self-disdain by the great arm of parental-conjugal phallocentrism, hasn't been ashamed of her strength? Who, surprised and horrified by the fantastic tumult of her drives (for she was made to believe that a well-adjusted normal woman has a . . . divine composure), hasn't accused herself of being a monster? Who, feeling a funny desire stirring inside her (to sing, to write, to dare to speak, in short, to bring out something new), hasn't thought she was sick? Well, her shameful sickness is that she resists death, that she makes trouble.

And why don't you write? Write! Writing is for you, you are for you; your body is yours, take it. I know why you haven't written. (And why I didn't write before the age of twenty-seven.) Because writing is at once too high, too great for you, it's reserved for the great—that is for 'great men'; and it's 'silly'. Besides, you've written a little, but in secret. And it wasn't good, because it was in secret, and because you punished yourself for writing, because you didn't go all the way, or because you wrote, irresistibly, as when we would masturbate in secret, not to go further, but to attenuate the tension a bit, just enough to take the edge off. And then as soon as we come, we go and make ourselves feel guilty—so as to be forgiven; or to forget, to bury it until the next time.

Write, let no one hold you back, let nothing stop you: not man; not the imbecilic capitalist machinery, in which publishing houses are the crafty, obsequious relayers of imperatives handed down by an economy that works against us and off our backs; and not *yourself*. Smug-faced readers, managing editors, and big bosses don't like the true texts of women—female-sexed tests. That kind scares them.

I write woman: woman must write woman. And man, man. So only an oblique consideration will be found here of man; it's up to him to say where his masculinity and femininity are at: this will concern us once men have opened their eyes and seen themselves clearly.[1]

Now women return from afar, from always: from 'without', from the heath where witches are kept alive; from below, from beyond 'culture'; from their childhood which men have been trying desperately to make them forget, condemning it to 'eternal rest'. The little girls and their 'ill-mannered' bodies immured, well-preserved, intact unto themselves, in the mirror. Frigidified. But are they ever seething underneath! What an effort it takes—there's no end to it—for the sex cops to bar their threatening return. Such a display of forces on both sides that the struggle has for centuries been immobilized in the trembling equilibrium of a deadlock.

Here they are, returning, arriving over and again, because the unconscious is impregnable. They have wandered around in circles, confined to the narrow room in which they've been given a deadly brainwashing. You can incarcerate them, slow them down, get away with the old Apartheid routine, but for a time only. As soon as they begin to speak, at the same time as they're taught their name, they can be taught that their territory is black: because you are Africa, you are black. Your continent is dark. Dark is dangerous. You can't see anything in the dark, you're afraid. Don't move, you might fall. Most of all, don't go into the forest. And so we have internalized this horror of the dark.

Men have committed the greatest crime against women. Insidiously, violently, they have led them to hate women, to be their own enemies, to mobilize their immense strength against themselves, to be the executants of their virile needs. They have made for women an antinarcissism! A narcissism which loves itself only to be loved for what women haven't got! They have constructed the infamous logic of antilove.

We the precocious, we the repressed of culture, our lovely mouths gagged with pollen, our wind knocked out of us, we the labyrinths, the ladders, the trampled spaces, the bevies—we are black and we are beautiful.

---

[1] Men still have everything to say about their sexuality, and everything to write. For what they have said so far, for the most part, stems from the opposition activity/passivity from the power relation between a fantasized obligatory virility meant to invade, to colonize, and the consequential phantasm of woman as a 'dark continent' to penetrate and to 'pacify'. (We know what 'pacify' means in terms of scotomizing the other and misrecognizing the self.) Conquering her, they've made haste to depart from her borders, to get out of sight, out of body. The way man has of getting out of himself and into her whom he takes not for the other but for his own, deprives him, he knows, of his own bodily territory. One can understand how man, confusing himself with his penis and rushing in for the attack, might feel resentment and fear of being 'taken' by the woman, of being lost in her, absorbed or alone.

We're stormy, and that which is ours breaks loose from us without our fearing any debilitation. Our glances, our smiles, are spent; laughs exude from all our mouths; our blood flows and we extend ourselves without ever reaching an end; we never hold back our thoughts, our signs, our writing; and we're not afraid of lacking.

What happiness for us who are omitted, brushed aside at the scene of inheritances; we inspire ourselves and we expire without running out of breath, we are everywhere!

From now on, who, if we say so, can say no to us? We've come back from always.

It is time to liberate the New Woman from the Old by coming to know her —by loving her for getting by, for getting beyond the Old without delay, by going out ahead of what the New Woman will be, as an arrow quits the bow with a movement that gathers and separates the vibrations musically, in order to be more than her self.

I say that we must, for, with a few rare exceptions, there has not yet been any writing that inscribes femininity; exceptions so rare, in fact, that, after plowing through literature across languages, cultures, and ages,[2] one can only be startled at this vain scouting mission. It is well known that the number of women writers (while having increased very slightly from the nineteenth century on) has always been ridiculously small. This is a useless and deceptive fact unless from their species of female writers we do not first deduct the immense majority whose workmanship is in no way different from male writing, and which either obscures women or reproduces the classic representations of women (as sensitive—intuitive—dreamy, etc.).[3]

Let me insert here a parenthetical remark. I mean it when I speak of male writing. I maintain unequivocally that there is such a thing as *marked* writing; that, until now, far more extensively and repressively than is ever suspected or admitted, writing has been run by a libidinal and cultural—hence political, typically masculine—economy; that this is a locus where the repression of women has been perpetuated, over and over, more or less consciously, and in a manner that's frightening since it's often hidden or adorned with the mystifying charms of fiction; that this locus has grossly exaggerated all the signs of sexual opposition (and not sexual difference), where woman has never *her* turn to speak—this being all the more serious and unpardonable in that writing is precisely *the very possibility of change*, the space that can serve

---

[2] I am speaking here only of the place 'reserved' for women by the Western world.

[3] Which works, then, might be called feminine? I'll just point out some examples: one would have to give them full readings to bring out what is pervasively feminine in their significance. Which I shall do elsewhere. In France (have you noted our infinite poverty in this field?—the Anglo-Saxon countries have shown resources of distinctly greater consequence), leafing through what's come out of the twentieth century—and it's not much—the only inscriptions of femininity that I have seen were by Colette, Marguerite Duras . . . and Jean Genet.

as a springboard for subversive thought, the precursory movement of a transformation of social and cultural structures.

Nearly the entire history of writing is confounded with the history of reason, of which it is at once the effect, the support, and one of the privileged alibis. It has been one with the phallocentric tradition. It is indeed that same self-admiring, self-stimulating, self-congratulatory phallocentrism.

With some exceptions, for there have been failures—and if it weren't for them, I wouldn't be writing (I-woman, escapee)—in that enormous machine that has been operating and turning out its 'truth' for centuries. There have been poets who would go to any lengths to slip something by at odds with tradition—men capable of loving love and hence capable of loving others and of wanting them, of imagining the woman who would hold out against oppression and constitute herself as a superb, equal, hence 'impossible' subject, untenable in a real social framework. Such a woman the poet could desire only by breaking the codes that negate her. Her appearance would necessarily bring on, if not revolution—for the bastion was supposed to be immutable—at least harrowing explosions. At times it is in the fissure caused by an earthquake, through that radical mutation of things brought on by a material upheaval when every structure is for a moment thrown off balance and an ephemeral wildness sweeps order away, that the poet slips something by, for a brief span, of woman. Thus did Kleist expend himself in his yearning for the existence of sister-lovers, maternal daughters, mother-sisters, who never hung their heads in shame. Once the palace of magistrates is restored, it's time to pay: immediate bloody death to the uncontrollable elements.

But only the poets—not the novelists, allies of representationalism. Because poetry involves gaining strength through the unconscious and because the unconscious, that other limitless country, is the place where the repressed manage to survive: women, or as Hoffmann would say, fairies.

She must write her self, because this is the invention of a *new insurgent* writing which, when the moment of her liberation has come, will allow her to carry out the indispensable ruptures and transformations in her history, first at two levels that cannot be separated.

(*a*) Individually. By writing her self, woman will return to the body which has been more than confiscated from her, which has been turned into the uncanny stranger on display—the ailing or dead figure, which so often turns out to be the nasty companion, the cause and location of inhibitions. Censor the body and you censor breath and speech at the same time.

Write your self. Your body must be heard. Only then will the immense resources of the unconscious spring forth. Our naphtha will spread, throughout the world, without dollars—black or gold—nonassessed values that will change the rules of the old game.

To write. An act which will not only 'realize' the decensored relation of woman to her sexuality, to her womanly being, giving her access to her native strength; it will give her back her goods, her pleasures, her organs, her immense bodily territories which have been kept under seal; it will tear her away from the superegoized structure in which she has always occupied the place reserved for the guilty (guilty of everything, guilty at every turn: for having desires, for not having any; for being frigid, for being 'too hot'; for not being both at once; for being too motherly and not enough; for having children and for not having any; for nursing and for not nursing . . .)—tear her away by means of this research, this job of analysis and illumination, this emancipation of the marvelous text of her self that she must urgently learn to speak. A woman without a body, dumb, blind, can't possibly be a good fighter. She is reduced to being the servant of the militant male, his shadow. We must kill the false woman who is preventing the live one from breathing. Inscribe the breath of the whole woman.

(b) An act that will also be marked by woman's *seizing* the occasion to *speak*, hence her shattering entry into history, which has always been based *on her suppression*. To write and thus to forge for herself the anti-logos weapon. To become *at will* the taker and initiator, for her own right, in every symbolic system, in every political process.

It is time for women to start scoring their feats in written and oral language.

Every woman has known the torment of getting up to speak. Her heart racing, at times entirely lost for words, ground and language slipping away —that's how daring a feat, how great a transgression it is for a woman to speak—even just open her mouth—in public. A double distress, for even if she transgresses, her words fall almost always upon the deaf male ear, which hears in language only that which speaks in the masculine.

It is by writing, from and toward women, and by taking up the challenge of speech which has been governed by the phallus, that women will confirm women in a place other than that which is reserved in and by the symbolic, that is, in a place other than silence. Women should break out of the snare of silence. They shouldn't be conned into accepting a domain which is the margin or the harem.

Listen to a woman speak at a public gathering (if she hasn't painfully lost her wind). She doesn't 'speak', she throws her trembling body forward; she lets go of herself, she flies; all of her passes into her voice, and it's with her body that she vitally supports the 'logic' of her speech. Her flesh speaks true. She lays herself bare. In fact, she physically materializes what she's thinking; she signifies it with her body. In a certain way she *inscribes* what she's saying, because she doesn't deny her drives the intractable and impassioned part they have in speaking. Her speech, even when 'theoretical' or political, is never simple or linear or 'objectified', generalized: she draws her story into history.

There is not that scission, that division made by the common man between the logic of oral speech and the logic of the text, bound as he is by his antiquated relation—servile, calculating—to mastery. From which proceeds the niggardly lip service which engages only the tiniest part of the body, plus the mask.

In women's speech, as in their writing, that element which never stops resonating which, once we've been permeated by it, profoundly and imperceptibly touched by it, retains the power of moving us—that element is the song: first music from the first voice of love which is alive in every woman. Why this privileged relationship with the voice? Because no woman stockpiles as many defenses for countering the drives as does a man. You don't build walls around yourself, you don't forgo pleasure as 'wisely' as he. Even if phallic mystification has generally contaminated good relationships, a woman is never far from 'mother' (I mean outside her role functions: the 'mother' as nonname and as source of goods). There is always within her at least a little of that good mother's milk. She writes in white ink.

Woman for women.—There always remains in woman that force which produces/is produced by the other—in particular, the other woman. *In* her, matrix, cradler; herself giver as her mother and child; she is her own sister-daughter. You might object, 'What about she who is the hysterical offspring of a bad mother?' Everything will be changed once woman gives woman to the other woman. There is hidden and always ready in woman the source; the locus for the other. The mother, too, is a metaphor. It is necessary and sufficient that the best of herself be given to woman by another woman for her to be able to love herself and return in love the body that was 'born' to her. Touch me, caress me, you the living no-name, give me my self as myself. The relation to the 'mother', in terms of intense pleasure and violence, is curtailed no more than the relation to childhood (the child that she was, that she is, that she makes, remakes, undoes, there at the point where, the same, she mothers herself). Text: my body—shot through with streams of song; I don't mean the overbearing, clutchy 'mother' but, rather, what touches you, the equivoice that affects you, fills your breast with an urge to come to language and launches your force; the rhythm that laughs you; the intimate recipient who makes all metaphors possible and desirable; body (body? bodies?), no more describable than god, the soul, or the Other; that part of you that leaves a space between yourself and urges you to inscribe in language your woman's style. In women there is always more or less of the mother who makes everything all right, who nourishes, and who stands up against separation; a force that will not be cut off but will knock the wind out of the codes. We will rethink womankind beginning with every form and every period of her body. The Americans remind us, 'we are all Lesbians'; that is, don't denigrate woman, don't make of her what men have made of you.

Because the 'economy' of her drives is prodigious, she cannot fail, in seizing the occasion to speak, to transform directly and indirectly *all* systems of exchange based on masculine thrift. Her libido will produce far more radical effects of political and social change than some might like to think.

Because she arrives, vibrant, over and again, we are at the beginning of a new history, or rather of a process of becoming in which several histories intersect with one another. As subject for history, woman always occurs simultaneously in several places. Woman un-thinks[4] the unifying, regulating history that homogenizes and channels forces, herding contradictions into a single battlefield. In woman, personal history blends together with the history of all women, as well as national and world history. As a militant, she is an integral part of all liberations. She must be farsighted, not limited to a blow-by-blow interaction. She foresees that her liberation will do more than modify power relations or toss the ball over to the other camp; she will bring about a mutation in human relations, in thought, in all praxis: hers is not simply a class struggle, which she carries forward into a much vaster movement. Not that in order to be a woman-in-struggle(s) you have to leave the class struggle or repudiate it; but you have to split it open, spread it out, push it forward, fill it with the fundamental struggle so as to prevent the class struggle, or any other struggle for the liberation of a class or people, from operating as a form of repression, pretext for postponing the inevitable, the staggering alteration in power relations and in the production of individualities. This alteration is already upon us—in the United States, for example, where millions of night crawlers are in the process of undermining the family and disintegrating the whole of American sociality.

The new history is coming; it's not a dream, though it does extend beyond men's imagination, and for good reason. It's going to deprive them of their conceptual orthopedics, beginning with the destruction of their enticement machine.

It is impossible to *define* a feminine practice of writing, and this is an impossibility that will remain, for this practice can never be theorized, enclosed, coded—which doesn't mean that it doesn't exist. But it will always surpass the discourse that regulates the phallocentric system; it does and will take place in areas other than those subordinated to philosophico-theoretical domination. It will be conceived of only by subjects who are breakers of automatisms, by peripheral figures that no authority can ever subjugate.

Hence the necessity to affirm the flourishes of this writing, to give form to its movement, its near and distant byways. Bear in mind to begin with (1) that sexual opposition, which has always worked for man's profit to the point of reducing writing, too, to his laws, is only a historico-cultural limit. There is, there will be more and more rapidly pervasive now, a fiction that produces irreducible effects of femininity. (2) That it is through ignorance that most

---

[4] *Dé-pense*, a neologism formed on the verb *penser*, hence 'unthinks', but also 'spends' (from *dépenser*). [Translator]

readers, critics, and writers of both sexes hesitate to admit or deny outright the possibility or the pertinence of a distinction between feminine and masculine writing. It will usually be said, thus disposing of sexual difference: either that all writing, to the extent that it materializes, is feminine; or, inversely—but it comes to the same thing—that the act of writing is equivalent to masculine masturbation (and so the woman who writes cuts herself out a paper penis); or that writing is bisexual, hence neuter, which again does away with differentiation. To admit that writing is precisely working (in) the in-between, inspecting the process of the same and of the other without which nothing can live, undoing the work of death—to admit this is first to want the two, as well as both, the ensemble of the one and the other, not fixed in sequences of struggle and expulsion or some other form of death but infinitely dynamized by an incessant process of exchange from one subject to another. A process of different subjects knowing one another and beginning one another anew only from the living boundaries of the other: a multiple and inexhaustible course with millions of encounters and transformations of the same into the other and into the in-between, from which woman takes her forms (and man, in his turn; but that's his other history).

In saying 'bisexual, hence neuter', I am referring to the classic conception of bisexuality, which, squashed under the emblem of castration fear and along with the fantasy of a 'total' being (though composed of two halves), would do away with the difference experienced as an operation incurring loss, as the mark of dreaded sectility.

To this self-effacing, merger-type bisexuality, which would conjure away castration (the writer who puts up his sign: 'bisexual written here, come and see', when the odds are good that it's neither one nor the other), I oppose the *other bisexuality* on which every subject not enclosed in the false theater of phallocentric representationalism has founded his/her erotic universe. Bisexuality: that is, each one's location in self (*repérage en soi*) of the presence —variously manifest and insistent according to each person, male or female —of both sexes, non-exclusion either of the difference or of one sex, and, from this 'self-permission', multiplication of the effects of the inscription of desire, over all parts of my body and the other body.

Now it happens that at present, for historico-cultural reasons, it is women who are opening up to and benefiting from this vatic bisexuality which doesn't annul differences but stirs them up, pursues them, increases their number. In a certain way, 'woman is bisexual'; man—it's a secret to no one —being poised to keep glorious phallic monosexuality in view. By virtue of affirming the primacy of the phallus and of bringing it into play, phallocratic ideology has claimed more than one victim. As a woman, I've been clouded over by the great shadow of the scepter and been told: idolize it, that which you cannot brandish. But at the same time, man has been handed that grotesque and scarcely enviable destiny (just imagine) of being reduced to a single idol with clay balls. And consumed, as Freud and his followers note, by a fear of being a woman! For, if psychoanalysis was constituted from woman, to repress femininity (and not so successful a repression at that—men have made it clear), its account of masculine sexuality is now hardly refutable; as with all the 'human' sciences, it reproduces the masculine view, of which it is one of the effects.

Here we encounter the inevitable man-with-rock, standing erect in his old Freudian realm, in the way that, to take the figure back to the point where linguistics is conceptualizing it 'anew', Lacan preserves it in the sanctuary of the phallos (φ) 'sheltered' from *castration's lack*! Their 'symbolic' exists, it holds power—we, the sowers of disorder, know it only too well. But we are in no way obliged to deposit our lives in their banks of lack, to consider the constitution of the subject in terms of a drama manglingly restaged, to reinstate again and again the religion of the father. Because we don't want that. We don't fawn around the supreme hole. We have no womanly reason to pledge allegiance to the negative. The feminine (as the poets suspected) affirms: '. . . And yes,' says Molly, carrying Ulysses off beyond any book and toward the new writing; 'I said yes, I will Yes.'

The Dark Continent is neither dark nor unexplorable.—It is still unexplored only because we've been made to believe that it was too dark to be explorable. And because they want to make us believe that what interests us is the white continent, with its monuments to Lack. And we believed. They riveted us between two horrifying myths: between the Medusa and the abyss. That would be enough to set half the world laughing, except that it's still going on. For the phallologocentric sublation is with us, and it's militant, regenerating the old patterns, anchored in the dogma of castration. They haven't changed a thing: they've theorized their desire for reality! Let the priests tremble, we're going to show them our sexts!

Too bad for them if they fall apart upon discovering that women aren't men, or that the mother doesn't have one. But isn't this fear convenient for them? Wouldn't the worst be, isn't the worst, in truth, that women aren't castrated, that they have only to stop listening to the Sirens (for the Sirens were men) for history to change its meaning? You only have to look at the Medusa straight on to see her. And she's not deadly. She's beautiful and she's laughing. . . .

Flying is woman's gesture—flying in language and making it fly.[5] We have all learned the art of flying and its numerous techniques; for centuries we've been able to possess anything only by flying; we've lived in flight, stealing

---

[5] Also, 'to steal'. Both meanings of the verb *voler* are played on, as the text itself explains in the following paragraph. [Translator]

away, finding, when desired, narrow passageways, hidden crossovers. It's no accident that *voler* has a double meaning, that it plays on each of them and thus throws off the agents of sense. It's no accident: women take after birds and robbers just as robbers take after women and birds. They (*illes*) go by, fly the coop, take pleasure in jumbling the order of space, in disorienting it, in changing around the furniture, dislocating things and values, breaking them all up, emptying structures, and turning propriety upside down.

What woman hasn't flown/stolen? Who hasn't felt, dreamt, performed the gesture that jams sociality? Who hasn't crumbled, held up to ridicule, the bar of separation? Who hasn't inscribed with her body the differential, punctured the system of couples and opposition? Who, by some act of transgression, hasn't overthrown successiveness, connection, the wall of circumfusion?

A feminine text cannot fail to be more than subversive. It is volcanic; as it is written it brings about an upheaval of the old property crust, carrier of masculine investments; there's no other way. There's no room for her if she's not a he. If she's a her-she, it's in order to smash everything to shatter the framework of institutions, to blow up the law, to break up the 'truth' with laughter.

4 *Rootedness: The Ancestor as Foundation**

TONI MORRISON

. . . If anything I do, in the way of writing novels or whatever I write, isn't about the village or the community or about you, then it isn't about anything. I am not interested in indulging myself in some private exercise of my imagination . . . which is to say yes, the work must be political. . . .

There is a conflict between public and private life, and it's a conflict that I think ought to remain a conflict. Not a problem, just a conflict. Because they are two modes of life that exist to exclude and annihilate each other. It's a conflict that should be maintained now more than ever because the social machinery of this country at this time doesn't permit harmony in a life that has both aspects. I am impressed with the story of—probably Jefferson, perhaps not, who walked home alone after the presidential inauguration. There must have been a time when an artist could be genuinely representative *of* the tribe and *in* it; when an artist could have a tribal or racial sensibility and an individual expression of it. There were spaces and places in which a single person could enter and behave as an individual within the context of

* Toni Morrison, 'Rootedness: The Ancestor as Foundation', *Black Women Writers (1950–1980): A Critical Evaluation*, ed. Mari Evans, Anchor Books, New York, 1984, pp. 339–45.

the community. A small remnant of that you can see sometimes in Black churches where people shout. It is a very personal grief and a personal statement done among people you trust. Done within the context of the community, therefore safe. And while the shouter is performing some rite that is extremely subjective, the other people are performing as a community in protecting that person. So you have a public and a private expression going on at the same time. To transfer that is not possible. So I just do the obvious, which is to keep my life as private as possible; not because it is all that interesting, it's just important that it be private. And then, whatever I do that is public can be done seriously.

The autobiographical form is classic in Black American or Afro-American literature because it provided an instance in which a writer could be representative, could say, 'My single solitary and individual life is like the lives of the tribe; it differs in these specific ways, but it is a balanced life because it is both solitary and representative.' The contemporary autobiography tends to be 'how I got over—look at me—alone—let me show you how I did it'. It is inimical, I think, to some of the characteristics of Black artistic expression and influence.

The label 'novel' is useful in technical terms because I write prose that is longer than a short story. My sense of the novel is that it has always functioned for the class or the group that wrote it. The history of the novel as a form began when there was a new class, a middle class, to read it; it was an art form that they needed. The lower classes didn't need novels at that time because they had an art form already: they had songs, and dances, and ceremony, and gossip, and celebrations. The aristocracy didn't need it because they had the art that they had patronized, they had their own pictures painted, their own houses built, and they made sure their art separated them from the rest of the world. But when the industrial revolution began, there emerged a new class of people who were neither peasants nor aristocrats. In large measure they had no art form to tell them how to behave in this new situation. So they produced an art form: we call it the novel of manners, an art form designed to tell people something they didn't know. That is, how to behave in this new world, how to distinguish between the good guys and the bad guys. How to get married. What a good living was. What would happen if you strayed from the fold. So that early works such as *Pamela*, by Samuel Richardson, and the Jane Austen material provided social rules and explained behavior, identified outlaws, identified the people, habits, and customs that one should approve of. They were didactic in that sense. That, I think, is probably why the novel was not missed among the so-called peasant cultures. They didn't need it, because they were clear about what their responsibilities were and who and where was evil, and where was good.

But when the peasant class, or lower class, or what have you, confronts the middle class, the city, or the upper classes, they are thrown a little bit into disarray. For a long time, the art form that was healing for Black people was music. That music is no longer *exclusively* ours; we don't have exclusive rights to it. Other people sing it and play it; it is the mode of contemporary music everywhere. So another form has to take that place, and it seems to me that the novel is needed by African-Americans now in a way that it was not needed before—and it is following along the lines of the function of novels everywhere. We don't live in places where we can hear those stories anymore; parents don't sit around and tell their children those classical, mythological archetypal stories that we heard years ago. But new information has got to get out, and there are several ways to do it. One is in the novel. I regard it as a way to accomplish certain very strong functions—one being the one I just described.

It should be beautiful, and powerful, but it should also *work*. It should have something in it that enlightens; something in it that opens the door and points the way. Something in it that suggests what the conflicts are, what the problems are. But it need not solve those problems because it is not a case study, it is not a recipe. There are things that I try to incorporate into my fiction that are directly and deliberately related to what I regard as the major characteristics of Black art, wherever it is. One of which is the ability to be both print and oral literature: to combine those two aspects so that the stories can be read in silence, of course, but one should be able to hear them as well. It should try deliberately to make you stand up and make you feel something profoundly in the same way that a Black preacher requires his congregation to speak, to join him in the sermon, to behave in a certain way, to stand up and to weep and to cry and to accede or to change and to modify—to expand on the sermon that is being delivered. In the same way that a musician's music is enhanced when there is a response from the audience. Now in a book, which closes, after all—it's of some importance to me to try to make that connection—to try to make that happen also. And, having at my disposal only the letters of the alphabet and some punctuation, I have to provide the places and spaces so that the reader can participate. Because it is the affective and participatory relationship between the artist or the speaker and the audience that is of primary importance, as it is in these other art forms that I have described.

To make the story appear oral, meandering, effortless, spoken—to have the reader *feel* the narrator without *identifying* that narrator, or hearing him or her knock about, and to have the reader work *with* the author in the construction of the book—is what's important. What is left out is as important as what is there. To describe sexual scenes in such a way that they are not clinical, not even explicit—so that the reader brings his own sexuality to the scene and thereby participates in it in a very personal way. And owns it. To construct the dialogue so that it is heard. So that there are no adverbs attached to them: 'loudly', 'softly', 'he said menacingly'. The menace should be in the sentence. To use, even formally, a chorus. The real presence of a chorus. Meaning the community or the reader at large, commenting on the action as it goes ahead.

In the books that I have written, the chorus has changed but there has always been choral note, whether it is the 'I' narrator of *Bluest Eye*, or the town functioning as a character in *Sula*, or the neighborhood and the community that responds in the two parts of town in *Solomon*. Or, as extreme as I've gotten, all of nature thinking and feeling and watching and responding to the action going on in *Tar Baby*, so that they are in the story: the trees hurt, fish are afraid, clouds report, and the bees are alarmed. Those are the ways in which I try to incorporate, into that traditional genre the novel, unorthodox novelistic characteristics—so that it is, in my view, Black, because it uses the characteristics of Black art. I am not suggesting that some of these devices have not been used before and elsewhere—only the reason why I do. I employ them as well as I can. And those are just some; I wish there were ways in which such things could be talked about in the criticism. My general disappointment in some of the criticism that my work has received has nothing to do with approval. It has something to do with the vocabulary used in order to describe these things. I don't like to find my books condemned as bad or praised as good, when that condemnation or that praise is based on criteria from other paradigms. I would much prefer that they were dismissed or embraced based on the success of their accomplishment within the culture out of which I write.

I don't regard Black literature as simply books written *by* Black people, or simply as literature written *about* Black people, or simply as literature that uses a certain mode of language in which you just sort of drop *g*'s. There is something very special and very identifiable about it and it is my struggle to *find* that elusive but identifiable style in the books. My *joy* is when I think that I have approached it; my misery is when I think I can't get there.

[There were times when I did.] I got there in several separate places when I knew it was exactly right. Most of the time in *Song of Solomon*, because of the construction of the book and the tone in which I could blend the acceptance of the supernatural and a profound rootedness in the real world at the same time with neither taking precedence over the other. It is indicative of the cosmology, the way in which Black people looked at the world. We are very practical people, very down-to-earth, even shrewd people. But within that practicality we also accepted what I suppose could be called superstition and magic, which is another way of knowing things. But to blend those two worlds together at the same time was enhancing, not limiting. And some of those things were 'discredited knowledge' that Black people had; discredited only because Black people were discredited therefore what they *knew* was 'discredited'. And also because the press toward upward social mobility would mean to get as far away from that kind of knowledge as possible. That kind of knowledge has a very strong place in my work.

I have talked about function in that other question, and I touched a little bit on some of the other characteristics [or distinctive elements of African-American writing], one of which was oral quality, and the participation of the reader and the chorus. The only thing that I would add for this question is the presence of an ancestor; it seems to me interesting to evaluate Black literature on what the writer does with the presence of an ancestor. Which is to say a grandfather as in Ralph Ellison, or a grandmother as in Toni Cade Bambara, or a healer as in Bambara or Henry Dumas. There is always an elder there. And these ancestors are not just parents, they are sort of timeless people whose relationships to the characters are benevolent, instructive, and protective, and they provide a certain kind of wisdom.

How the Black writer responds to that presence interests me. Some of them, such as Richard Wright, had great difficulty with that ancestor. Some of them, like James Baldwin, were confounded and disturbed by the presence or absence of an ancestor. What struck me in looking at some contemporary fiction was that whether the novel took place in the city or in the country, the presence or absence of that figure determined the success or the happiness of the character. It was the absence of an ancestor that was frightening, that was threatening, and it caused huge destruction and disarray in the work itself. That the solace comes, not from the contemplation of serene nature as in a lot of mainstream white literature, nor from the regard in which the city was held as a kind of corrupt place to be. Whether the character was in Harlem or Arkansas, the point was there, this timelessness was there, this person who represented this ancestor. And it seemed to be one of those interesting aspects of the continuum in Black or African-American art, as well as some of the things I mentioned before: the deliberate effort, on the part of the artist, to get a visceral, emotional response as well as an intellectual response as he or she communicates with the audience.

The treatment of artists by the people for whom they speak is also of some interest. That is to say, when the writer is one of them, when the voice is not the separate, isolated ivory tower voice of a very different kind of person but an implied 'we' in a narration. This is disturbing to people and critics who view the artist as the supreme individual. It is disturbing because there is a notion that that's what the artist is—always in confrontation with his own society, and you can see the differences in the way in which literature is interpreted. Whether or not Sula is nourished by that village depends on your view of it. I know people who believe that she was destroyed by it. My own special view is that there was no other place where she could live. She would have been destroyed by any other place; she was permitted to 'be' only in that context, and no one stoned her or killed her or threw her out. Also it's difficult to see who the winners are if you are not looking at it from that point of view. When the hero returns to the fold—returns to the tribe—it is seen by certain white critics as a defeat, by others as a triumph, and that is a difference in what the *aims* of the art are.

In *Song of Solomon* Pilate is the ancestor. The difficulty that Hagar [youngest of the trio of women in that household] has is how far removed she is from the experience of her ancestor. Pilate had a dozen years of close, nurturing relationships with two males—her father and her brother. And that intimacy and support was in her and made her fierce and loving because she had that experience. Her daughter Reba had less of that and related to men in a very shallow way. Her daughter had even less of an association with men as a child, so that the progression is really a diminishing of their abilities because of the absence of men in a nourishing way in their lives. Pilate is the apogee of all that: of the best of that which is female and the best of that which is male, and that balance is disturbed if it is not nurtured, and if it is not counted on and if it is not reproduced. That is the disability we must be on guard against for the future—the female who reproduces the female who reproduces the female. You know there are a lot of people who talk about the position that men hold as of primary importance, but actually it is if we don't keep in touch with the ancestor that we are, in fact, lost.

The point of the books is that it is *our* job. When you kill the ancestor you kill yourself. I want to point out the dangers, to show that nice things don't always happen to the totally self-reliant if there is no conscious historical connection. To say, see—this is what will happen.

I don't have much to say about that [the necessity to develop a specific Black feminist model of critical inquiry] except that I think there is more danger in it than fruit, because any model of criticism or evaluation that excludes males from it is as hampered as any model of criticism of Black literature that excludes women from it. For critics, models have some function. They like to talk in terms of models and developments and so on, so maybe it's of some use to them, but I suggest that even for them there is some danger in it.

If anything I do, in the way of writing novels (or whatever I write) isn't about the village or the community or about you, then it is not about anything. I am not interested in indulging myself in some private, closed exercise of my imagination that fulfills only the obligation of my personal dreams—which is to say yes, the work must be political. It must have that as its thrust. That's a pejorative term in critical circles now: if a work of art has any political influence in it, somehow it's tainted. My feeling is just the opposite: if it has none, it is tainted.

The problem comes when you find harangue passing off as art. It seems to me that the best art is political and you ought to be able to make it unquestionably political and irrevocably beautiful at the same time.

VIII *Literature and History*

Most of the critics and writers whose voices have been heard so far have had something to say, implicitly or explicitly, about the relationship between literary or dramatic texts and history—understood as a specific history of events. This is inevitable, given the continuing struggle we are engaged in here: to understand past works in the present. According to R. G. Collingwood, who is quoted in Laurence Lerner's opening extract on the subject, to understand a work from another time and place is to understand the questions it asks, and the answers it gives. This helps to define our task: not only in terms of understanding what we want to ask, but in terms of what the first and later readers wanted to ask.

According to Lerner this task avoids the 'glib scepticism' of those structuralists and post-structuralists who do not allow any certain or settled knowledge of the past. Lerner identifies three contexts to any text: 'its ideology, its strategies of writing, and social reality'. To eliminate any of these completely 'is a dogmatic oversimplification'. But there remain difficulties, as the extract from Hayden White's Metahistory *suggests. Like other recent American historiographers, White argues that while historians believe their narratives to be objective, their narration itself cannot escape the implications of 'textuality': that is, of the medium of language. By analysing, or 'deconstructing', historians' texts, White claims to show how they are silently organized according to familiar narrative and hence fictive patterns, such as 'plot'.*

In this way, the foundation of traditional history, the document, can become one text among many; and the one chosen for analysis becomes an issue in itself, by focusing attention upon what the choice excludes, raising questions of race, gender, class, and institution. The awareness of the voices of 'others', however, needs to be brought back to a recognition of the forces—historical if nothing else—which have shaped that exclusion. And so we return to a sense of the overriding importance of history as an accessible reality. This position, sometimes simply unexamined, can be felt expressed in the extracts by, significantly, a group of European voices: George Steiner, who returns to one aspect of the questions posed by Jean-Paul Sartre and Theodor Adorno, namely, the problem of a language contaminated by its association with a certain history; Joseph Brodsky and Czeslaw Milosz, who argue in different ways that at certain periods only poetry can deal with reality; and Walter Benjamin, whose attempt to grasp the deeper 'theses' of history in our times led him to a richly suggestive, but fragmentary, form of utterance.

1 *History and Fiction**

LAURENCE LERNER

TEXT AND REALITY

The very title of *The Condition of the Working Classes in England in* 1844 [by Friedrich Engels] invites us to relate it to housing and sanitary conditions, population growth and factory work, crime statistics (and the difficulty of knowing them), and all the research subsequent to its publication. If the book is a contribution to economic and social history, this is how historians will treat it; and if they do so, their aim is to make it disappear. Their object of study is the past, and they will wish to retain the true facts and the valid analysis, confirmed by the work of others, and throw away the rest. When the wheat has been sorted from the chaff, the original ear of corn has been destroyed.

Such an approach clearly believes that the past is knowable. We no longer believe, now, that such knowing is unproblematic: the days of positivist history, of *wie es eigentlich geschehen [ist]*,[1] are now over, and it has become a commonplace to argue that history cannot give us direct access to objective facts, since the ideology and the verbal strategies of the historian will determine what he chooses to notice and how he describes it, to say nothing of the connections between events that he then establishes. In fact, the reaction against positivism is now so strong that we are often told that to regard a text like *The Condition* as a response to the society it purports to be describing is outmoded and naïve, for history is simply the result of the writing and (even more) the ideology of the historian. This would mean that the past is unknowable. Since what happened a moment ago belongs to the past, it is hard to credit that such an extreme view is tenable, yet it is often stated. The following is one example among scores of a view that can be heard at innumerable academic conferences:

Enough of the past is lost, and looks in any case so different from different points of vantage, for history itself to be regarded as no more (and indeed, no less) than a present fiction which must be constructed obliquely or directly according to the often only half-apprehended order of contemporary needs and struggles.[2]

The same doctrine is asserted more playfully by Malcolm Bradbury in the Author's Note to *The History Man*, which describes his novel as 'a total invention with delusory approximations to historical reality, just as is history

---

* From Laurence Lerner, *The Frontiers of Literature*, Basil Blackwell, Oxford, 1988, pp. 60–8.
[1] i.e. how it actually happened—alluding to the German positivist historical tradition. [Ed.]
[2] Francis Barker, *1642: Literature and Power in the Seventeenth Century*, University of Essex, 1981, p. 9.

itself'. If the past (including the writings of the past) simply provides raw material for the ideologically motivated writings of historians, as Francis Barker appears to be here maintaining, and thus is not in itself knowable, it must also be the case that historians' writings, which belong to the past as soon as they are written, are not knowable either, and we are faced with an infinite regress: even Barker's own statement would result from contemporary needs and struggles, so that it would not be possible to know whether it is true.

The basis of Barker's position is stated in more general terms by Terence Hawkes:

The world does not consist of independently existing objects, whose concrete features can be perceived clearly and individually, and whose nature can be classified accordingly. In fact, every perceiver's *method* of perceiving can be shown to contain an inherent bias which affects what is perceived to a significant degree. A wholly objective perception of individual entities is therefore not possible: any observer is bound to *create* something of what he observes. Accordingly, the *relationship* between observer and observed achieves a kind of primacy. It becomes the only thing that can be observed.[3]

After asserting the great structuralist insight that unmediated perception of objects is impossible, he shifts to asserting that no perception of objects is possible, claiming (for instance) that a kinship system, when seen as a language, involves 'no reference (*sic*) to a "reality" or "nature" beyond itself'.[4] After showing the untenability of naïve empiricism, Hawkes has swung to the opposite extreme of naïve scepticism. But if perception is not wholly objective, it does not follow that it must be wholly subjective: that would be to ignore the more complex possibility that it results from an interaction between the external world and our method of perceiving.

I have claimed that any text can be related to at least three contexts: its ideology, its strategies of writing, and social reality. To eliminate any of these completely is a dogmatic oversimplification; and a total rejection of positivism would be as naïve—and as fanatical—as its total acceptance.

Steven Marcus, it should be added, believes that the past is knowable. He shows no wish to brush aside the reality of nineteenth-century Manchester, and we do not need to point out to him, as we might to some, that when Engels writes 'it is almost impossible to get from the main streets a real viewing of the working class districts themselves',[5] he means *real*: his purpose is to convey knowledge of an extra-textual referent. It is most important to say that Engels himself would favour the approach that causes his book to disappear: though since his purpose is political first and scholarly second, the

[3] *Structuralism and Semiotics*, Methuen New Accents, 1977. p. 17.
[4] Ibid., p. 38.
[5] *The Condition of the Working Classes in 1844*, transl. F. K. Wischnewetzky, 1855, reprinted 1952, p. 47.

disappearance he would most favour would be that resulting not from the acceptance of his findings by other historians, but from the disappearance of Manchester's slums after the socialist revolution.

Dickens, Kingsley and Elizabeth Gaskell would all have rejected indignantly the charge that they were not interested in the condition of England, and that everything in their books was made up. They—and their readers—would have had no difficulty in distinguishing, in principle, the fictitious elements —the invented characters and incidents—from the account of slum conditions or (this is less straightforward) of Chartism and trade unionism. All of them showed concern, outside the boundaries of their fictional text, for the truth of their depiction. Kingsley wrote two prefaces to *Alton Locke*, one to the Working Men of Great Britain, and the other to the undergraduates of Cambridge, in which he admitted without hesitation the political purpose of his novel, and at the same time assumed that it dealt with social reality, remarking, for instance, that his disappointments with working-class movements since its appearance 'have strengthened my conviction that this book, in the main, speaks the truth'. Dickens never hesitated to cite his own novels when making political speeches, trampling down the difference of genre with far less scruple than I am trying to display. Elizabeth Gaskell defended *Mary Barton* by saying 'Some say the masters are very sore, but I'm sure I *believe* I wrote truth', or claiming 'that some of the men do view the subject in the way I have tried to represent I have personal evidence'.[6] These modest claims to truth refer to the controversial politics of the novel; *a fortiori* it would have seemed to her obvious that the descriptions of slum life were 'true'.

It is necessary to state the obvious. Fiction differs from history in not making a claim to truth. If Engels or Simon or a modern economic historian tells us something that can be refuted by evidence, he has broken faith, and will be censured by professionals. But to sign a contract is not the same as to carry it out; the historian, who undertakes to tell the truth, may be careless, or ignorant, or a liar, and the novelist, who does not undertake it, may be scrupulous. It is perfectly possible to maintain that the best historians of the condition of England in the 1840s were the novelists—as long as the claim is settled by historical and not by aesthetic criteria. The novelists would then be carrying out a contract they had not subscribed to.

COLLINGWOOD ON HISTORY

The best account I know of the relation between history and fiction is that of Collingwood. In developing his central concept of the historical imagination, Collingwood compares it to 'the pure or free but by no means arbitrary imagination of the novelist': 'Each of them makes it his business to construct

---

[6] *The Letters of Mrs Gaskell*, ed. J. A. V. Chapple and A. Pollard, 1966, nos. 35 and 36.

a picture which is partly a narrative of events, partly a description of situations, exhibition of motives, analysis of characters.' What then is the difference? Collingwood begins his answer with what to the structuralist will seem a question-begging naïvety: 'the historian's picture is meant to be true'—not even putting the term in the now fashionable quotation marks—but this turns out to be the beginning of a careful examination of the consequences of this claim. In doing this, I suggest, he anticipates and uses all that is valuable in the structuralist case, without driving it to the extreme of an untenable scepticism.[7]

The consequences flow from the fact that history tries to be true. First, the historian's picture 'must be localised in space and time': in contrast, Collingwood congratulates Hardy on the 'sure instinct' that led him in his novels to replace Oxford by Christminster, Wantage by Alfredson, and so on in 'what should be a purely imaginary world'. This is on the right lines, but a trifle crude. The world of fiction is not *purely* imaginary, but overlaps with the world of history; in the case of realistic fiction, the overlap is especially large, and welcomed. The fact that Elizabeth Gaskell locates *Mary Barton* in Manchester and *North and South* in 'Milton' is in the end trivial: in every important sense, they are the same town. Hardy's careful alteration of the place names of Wessex is the result of aesthetic rather than epistemological considerations.

Second, 'all history must be consistent with itself . . . ; there is only one historical world'. Here we need a distinction similar to that drawn in the previous section, where I proposed that to the writer of autobiography there is an *hors-texte*, but not to the reader. To the responsible historian, there is only one historical world; if there were not, disagreements with other historians would simply be alternative, and compatible, constructs. But to us, as we read historians of differing schools, it often grows painfully obvious that they have not succeeded in adjusting their constructs to one another. Ideological difference leads historians to select from and even to observe the past so differently that the patent nonfulfilment of this aim lends to the Barker–Hawkes point what degree of plausibility it has.

Third, 'the historian's picture stands in relation to something called evidence'. This is the crucial difference, though there are occasions on which the novelist uses evidence too. But whereas the novelist uses evidence only in particular cases, the historian must always use it. Now Collingwood makes it quite clear that evidence is not something extra-textual—or, as he puts it, 'there is nothing other than historical thought itself, by appeal to which its conclusions may be verified'. It is obvious that historical inquiry could never

[7] R. G. Collingwood, *The Idea of History*, 1946, p. 246.

proceed if the historian stopped to question the validity of every piece of evidence he had; in practice, he works from data. But what this means is that

for the purposes of a particular piece of work there are certain historical problems relevant to that work which for the present he proposes to treat as settled; though if they are settled, it is only because historical thinking has settled them in the past, and they remain settled only until he or someone else decides to reopen them.[8]

There is, in other words, no *hors-texte* for the historian, except provisionally. But Collingwood does not use this as an argument for scepticism, for denying that there is any difference between history and fiction. Instead, he draws a crucial distinction between the critic and the sceptic. The former is willing to re-enact the historian's thoughts, 'to see if they have been well done': he it is who may query the data, that is, reopen a problem which the first historian had accepted as settled. But he will do this because he has reason to suspect the settling: which clearly implies that he is willing to leave other data standing, if he has no good reason to question them. The sceptic gives himself a much easier task: without taking the trouble to examine which solutions to problems can stand and which must be reopened, he makes the general observation that since any of them could be reopened, none can ever be regarded as settled, and therefore there is no knowledge of the past. It is his refusal of this glib scepticism that leads Collingwood to say (without inverted commas) that history strives to be true, and then to go on to discuss the difficulties entailed by that attempt. Next to this careful thinking, how superficial the sceptic appears.

REALISM

All this is connected with an issue internal to literature, the question of realism. The novelists we have discussed all see themselves as realists, and there is a close parallel between the structuralist criticism of realism, and the theory just cited that history is a form of fiction. As a starting point for investigating realism, I will choose an observation of Stendhal's:

Pour être intelligible . . . j'aurais du diminuer les faits. C'est à quoi je n'aurais pas manqué, si j'avais eu le dessein un seul instant d'écrire un livre généralement agréable. Mais le ciel m'ayant refusé le talent littéraire, j'ai uniquement pensé à décrire avec toute la maussaderie de la science, mais aussi avec toute son exactitude, certains faits.[9]

(In order to be intelligible I should have modified the facts. And I would not have failed to do this if I had had the slightest intention of writing a book that would be found charming. But heaven having refused me all literary talent, my only thought was to describe, with all the sombre gloom of science, but also with all its precision, certain facts.)

[8] R. G. Collingwood, *The Idea of History*, 1946, p. 244.
[9] *De l'Amour*, 1822, ch. 24.

To make one's book generally acceptable, one needs to follow certain stereo-types which have little to do with reality itself. The faculty that enables us to do that is 'talent littéraire', and Stendhal will have none of it.

Now Barthes attacks realism on the grounds that 'le vraisemblable' [accepted-as-probable] simply corresponds to what the public believes possible, that the 'va-sans-dire' [goes-without saying] is simply the imposition (the violent imposition, he weirdly claims) of a set of conventions that society pretends are natural in order to constrain our thinking.[10]

The resemblance between this defence of realism and this attack on realism is surely very striking: in both cases, what is being pleaded for is the under-mining and rejection of stereotypes. In *Adam Bede*, for instance, George Eliot interrogates the stereotype of the pretty tender-hearted milkmaid. Hetty Sorrel, with whom both young men in the novel fall in love, has walked straight out of a ballad, a rustic idyll or a pastoral etching. 'Ah, what a prize the man gets who wins a sweet bride like Hetty! . . . the dear, young, round, soft flexible thing! Her heart must be just as soft, her temper just as free from angles.' That is the version of Hetty we can call *vraisemblable*; to show her like that requires only *talent littéraire*. George Eliot sets out to subvert this picture, to show that Adam and Arthur really know very little about Hetty, to suggest that the reader (and the self-mocking persona of the narrator) also 'find it impossible not to expect some depth of soul behind a deep grey eye with a long dark eyelash'. But the purpose of this is not to show that we cannot know one another, cannot escape from the stereotypes we use in seeing, it is to tell us that Hetty was not like that at all. One ruthless sentence disposes of her: 'Hetty did not understand how anybody could be very fond of middle-aged people' —though I have had to extract that icy statement from a long moralizing paragraph (this is early George Eliot). Molly the housemaid, we are told, 'was really a tender-hearted girl, and as Mrs Poyser said, a jewel to look after the poultry, but her stolid face showed nothing of this'.[11]

The negative programme of George Eliot is exactly that of Barthes, but her positive aim is something like the opposite. For he regards *le vraisemblable* as a device for concealing from us our inability to attain real knowledge of the extra-textual world. Literature should therefore cease to strive for mimesis, and should become semiosis, 'an adventure of the linguistically impossible',[12] freeing itself from the tyranny of the referent. Her aim, however, is to replace worn-out mimesis by a truer version, just as Stendhal wished to replace *agré-ment* by *les faits*. They set out to free literature from the tyranny of the signifier.

[10] Roland Barthes, *Critique et verité*, 1966, p. 15; *Roland Barthes par lui-même*, 1975, p. 88.
[11] *Adam Bede*, 1859, ch. 15.
[12] *Roland Barthes par lui-même*, p. 123.

To claim that realism simply replaces one set of conventions by another is to deny the central point of what George Eliot is doing. Realism is the claim that in the interaction between convention and observation that lies behind every piece of writing, a shift ought to take place, reducing the role of convention, and increasing that of observation. The structuralist who dismisses this does so because he does not really believe in observation. There is a parallel here between the rejection of realism and the denial that history gives us real knowledge of the past. Just as George Eliot is committed to the possibility of helping us to see milkmaids more shrewdly, so Engels is committed to the possibility of learning about Manchester. Knowledge of the extra-textual world is the result of an interaction between that world and our methods of perceiving it (including our language); the fact that the realist cannot get rid of language, cannot offer us naked objects untouched by our categories, is important, and explains the error of the simple-minded scholars of Laputa; but it need not lead us to abandon the possibility of observation.

The weakness of realism as a theory has always been that it does not show what is specific to art. Stendhal, offering us 'facts', and describing them with 'toute la maussaderie de la science', appears to be announcing that he is deserting literature for sociology; and indeed *De l'Amour*, written before Stendhal had become a novelist, is a kind of study in sociology and psychology, as we would laboriously say nowadays. The case of Zola is even more notorious: defining the novelist as a mixture of 'l'observateur' and 'l'experimentateur', he sums up the writing of fiction as follows:

En somme, toute l'opération consiste à prendre les faits dans la nature, puis à étudier le mécanisme des faits, en agissant sur eux par la modification des circonstances et des milieux, sans jamais s'écarter des lois de la nature.[13]

(In sum, the whole operation consists in taking one's facts from nature, then in studying the mechanism of facts, by modifying circumstances and environment to produce an effect on them, without ever departing from the laws of nature.)

It is easy to see why Zola was accused of reducing the task of the novelist to that of the mere social scientist (he virtually says as much himself). Yet this weakness is the obverse of a strength: no one could accuse Stendhal and Zola of not taking seriously the social world they are studying and representing. The view that accepts an overlap between fiction and history is likely to accept realism too, for that is a literary doctrine designed to encourage literature to step over the frontier.

The condition-of-England novels were a response to what was happening in English society, to the feeling that 'the condition and disposition of the Working Classes is a rather ominous matter at present; that something ought

---

[13] Émile Zola, *Le Roman expérimental*, 1880, I.

to be said, something ought to be done, in regard to it'.[14] Those parts of the novels that render this condition and disposition to us ought not to be dismissed as 'background' or as local colouring. They mattered to the novelist, and they matter in the novel. Their style is plain, their method realistic, their aim is truth. They are continuous at one edge with the fictitious elements of the novel, at the other with the work of historians.

2 *Introduction to Metahistory**

HAYDEN WHITE

I begin by distinguishing among the following levels of conceptualization in the historical work: (1) chronicle; (2) story; (3) mode of emplotment; (4) mode of argument; and (5) mode of ideological implication. I take 'chronicle' and 'story' to refer to 'primitive elements' in the *historical account*, but both represent processes of selection and arrangement of data from the *unprocessed historical record* in the interest of rendering that record more comprehensible to an *audience* of a particular kind. As thus conceived, the historical work represents an attempt to mediate among what I will call the *historical field*, the unprocessed *historical record, other historical accounts*, and an *audience*.

First the elements in the historical field are organized into a chronicle by the arrangement of the events to be dealt with in the temporal order of their occurrence; then the chronicle is organized into a story by the further arrangement of the events into the components of a 'spectacle' or process of happening, which is thought to possess a discernible beginning, middle, and end. This *transformation of chronicle into story* is effected by the characterization of some events in the chronicle in terms of inaugural motifs, of others in terms of terminating motifs, and of yet others in terms of transitional motifs. An event which is simply reported as having happened at a certain time and place is transformed into an inaugurating event by its characterization as such: 'The king went to Westminster on June 3, 1321. There the fateful meeting occurred between the king and the man who was ultimately to challenge him for his throne, though at the time the two men appeared to be destined to become the best of friends. . . .' A transitional motif, on the other hand, signals to the reader to hold his expectations about the significance of the events contained in it in abeyance until some terminating motif has been provided: 'While the king was journeying to Westminster, he was informed

---

[14] Thomas Carlyle, *Chartism*, 1839, ch. I.

* From Hayden White, *Metahistory: The Historical Imagination in Nineteenth Century Europe*, Johns Hopkins University Press, Baltimore, 1973, pp. 5–8, 11–13.

by his advisers that his enemies awaited him there, and that the prospects of a settlement advantageous to the crown were meager.' A terminating motif indicates the apparent end or resolution of a process or situation of tension: 'On April 6, 1333, the Battle of Balybourne was fought. The forces of the king were victorious, the rebels routed. The resulting Treaty of Howth Castle, June 7, 1333, brought peace to the realm—though it was to be an uneasy peace, consumed in the flames of religious strife seven years later.' When a given set of events has been motifically encoded, the reader has been provided with a story; the chronicle of events has been transformed into a *completed* diachronic process, about which one can then ask questions as if he were dealing with a *synchronic structure* of relationships.[1]

Historical *stories* trace the sequences of events that lead from inaugurations to (provisional) terminations of social and cultural processes in a way that *chronicles* are not required to do. Chronicles are, strictly speaking, open-ended. In principle they have no *inaugurations*; they simply 'begin' when the chronicler starts recording events. And they have no culminations or resolutions; they can go on indefinitely. Stories, however, have a discernible form (even when that form is an image of a state of chaos) which marks off the events contained in them from the other events that might appear in a comprehensive chronicle of the years covered in their unfoldings.

It is sometimes said that the aim of the historian is to explain the past by 'finding', 'identifying', or 'uncovering' the 'stories' that lie buried in chronicles; and that the difference between 'history' and 'fiction' resides in the fact that the historian 'finds' his stories, whereas the fiction writer 'invents' his. This conception of the historian's task, however, obscures the extent to which 'invention' also plays a part in the historian's operations. The same event can serve as a different kind of element of many different historical stories, depending on the role it is assigned in a specific motific characterization of the set to which it belongs. The death of the king may be a beginning, an ending, or simply a transitional event in three different stories. In the chronicle, this

---

[1] The distinctions among chronicle, story, and plot which I have tried to develop in this section may have more value for the analysis of historical works than for the study of literary fictions. Unlike literary fictions, such as the novel, historical works are made up of events that exist outside the consciousness of the writer. The events reported in a novel can be invented in a way that they cannot be (or are not supposed to be) in a history. This makes it difficult to distinguish between the chronicle of events and the story being told in a literary fiction. In a sense, the 'story' being told in a novel such as Mann's *Buddenbrooks* is indistinguishable from the 'chronicle' of events reported in the work, even though we can distinguish between the 'chronicle-story' and the 'plot' (which is that of an Ironic Tragedy). Unlike the novelist, the historian confronts a veritable chaos of events *already constituted*, out of which he must choose the elements of the story he would tell. He makes his story by including some events and excluding others, by stressing some and subordinating others. This process of exclusion, stress, and subordination is carried out in the interest of constituting *a story of a particular kind*. That is to say, he 'emplots' his story. On the distinction between story and plot, see the essays by Shklovsky, Eichenbaum, and Tomashevsky, representatives of the Russian School of Formalism, in *Russian Formalist Criticism: Four Essays*, ed. Lee T. Lemon and Marion J. Reis (Lincoln, Neb., 1965); and Northrop Frye, *Anatomy of Criticism*, pp. 52–3, 78–84.

event is simply 'there' as an element of a series; it does not 'function' as a story element. The historian arranges the events in the chronicle into a hierarchy of significance by assigning events different functions as story elements in such a way as to disclose the formal coherence of a whole set of events considered as a comprehensible process with a discernible beginning, middle, and end.

The arrangement of selected events of the chronicle into a story raises the kinds of questions the historian must anticipate and answer in the course of constructing his narrative. These questions are of the sort: 'What happened next?' 'How did that happen?' 'Why did things happen this way rather than that?' 'How did it all come out in the end?' These questions determine the narrative tactics the historian must use in the construction of his story. But such questions about the connections between events which make of them elements in a *followable* story should be distinguished from questions of another sort: 'What does it all add up to?' 'What is the point of it all?' These questions have to do with the structure of the *entire set of events* considered as a *completed* story and call for a synoptic judgment of the relationship between a given story and other stories that might be 'found', 'identified', or 'uncovered' in the chronicle. They can be answered in a number of ways. I call these ways (1) explanation by emplotment, (2) explanation by argument, and (3) explanation by ideological implication.

EXPLANATION BY EMPLOTMENT

Providing the 'meaning' of a story by identifying the *kind of story* that has been told is called explanation by emplotment. If, in the course of narrating his story, the historian provides it with the plot structure of a Tragedy, he has 'explained' it in one way; if he has structured it as a Comedy, he has 'explained' it in another way. Emplotment is the way by which a sequence of events fashioned into a story is gradually revealed to be a story of a particular kind.

Following the line indicated by Northrop Frye in his *Anatomy of Criticism*, I identify at least four different modes of emplotment: Romance, Tragedy, Comedy, and Satire. There may be others, such as the Epic, and a given historical account is likely to contain stories cast in one mode as aspects or phases of the whole set of stories emplotted in another mode. But a given historian is forced to emplot the whole set of stories making up his narrative in one comprehensive or *archetypal* story form. For example, Michelet cast all of his histories in the Romantic mode, Ranke cast his in the Comic mode, Tocqueville used the Tragic mode, and Burckhardt used Satire. The Epic plot structure would appear to be the implicit form of chronicle itself. The important point is that every history, even the most 'synchronic' or 'structural' of them, will be emplotted in some way. The Satirical mode provided the formal principles by which the supposedly 'non-narrative' historiography of Burckhardt can be identified as a 'story' of a particular sort. For, as Frye has shown, stories cast in the Ironic mode, of which Satire is the fictional form, gain their effects precisely by frustrating normal expectations about the kinds of resolutions provided by stories cast in other modes (Romance, Comedy, or Tragedy, as the case may be). . . .

EXPLANATION BY FORMAL ARGUMENT

In addition to the level of conceptualization on which the historian emplots his narrative account of 'what happened', there is another level on which he may seek to explicate 'the point of it all' or 'what it all adds up to' in the end. On this level I can discern an operation which I call explanation by formal, explicit, or discursive argument. Such an argument provides an explanation of what happens in the story by invoking principles of combination which serve as putative laws of historical explanation. On this level of conceptualization, the historian explains the events in the story (or the form of the events which he has imposed upon them through his emplotment of them in a particular mode) by construction of a nomological-deductive argument. This argument can be analyzed into a syllogism, the major premise of which consists of some putatively universal law of causal relationships, the minor premise of the boundary conditions within which the law is applied, and a conclusion in which the events that actually occurred are deduced from the premises by logical necessity. The most famous of such putative laws is probably Marx's so-called law of the relationship between the Superstructure and the Base. This law states that, whenever there is any transformation in the Base (comprised of the means of production and the modes of relationship among them), there will be a transformation in the components of the Superstructure (social and cultural institutions), but that the reverse relationship does not obtain (e.g., changes in consciousness do *not* effect changes in the Base). Other instances of such putative laws (such as 'Bad money drives out good', or even such banal observations as 'What goes up must come down') are usually at least tacitly invoked during the course of the historian's efforts to explain such a phenomenon as, say, the Great Depression or the Fall of the Roman Empire. The commonsensical or conventional nature of these latter generalizations does not affect their status as the presumed major premises of nomological-deductive arguments by which explanations of events given in the story are provided. The nature of the generalizations only points to the protoscientific character of historical explanation in general, or the inadequacy of the social sciences from which such generalizations, appearing in an appropriately modified and more rigorously stated form, might be borrowed.

The important point is that, insofar as a historian offers explanations by which the configurations of events in his narrative are explained in something like a nomological-deductive argument, such explanations must be distinguished from the explanatory effect gained by his *emplotment* of his story as *a story of a particular kind*. This is not because one might not treat emplotment as a kind of explanation by nomological-deductive means. In fact, a Tragic emplotment might be treated as an application of the laws that govern human nature and societies in certain kinds of situations; and, insofar as such situations have been established as existing at a certain time and place, those situations might be considered to have been explained by the invocation of the principles alluded to, in the same way that natural events are explained by identification of the universal causal laws that are presumed to govern their relationships.

I might want to say that, insofar as a historian provides the 'plot' by which the events in the story he tells are given some kind of formal coherence, he is doing the same kind of thing a scientist does when he identifies the elements of the nomological-deductive argument in which his explanation has to be cast. But I distinguish here between the emplotment of the events of a history considered as elements of a story and the characterization of those events as elements in a matrix of causal relationships presumed to have existed in specific provinces of time and space. In short, I am for the moment taking at face value the historian's claim to be doing *both* art and science and the distinction usually drawn between the historian's *investigative operations* on the one hand and his *narrative operation* on the other. We grant that it is one thing to represent 'what happened' and 'why it happened as it did', and quite another to provide a verbal model, in the form of a narrative, by which to explain the *process of development* leading from one situation to some other situation by appeal to general laws of causation.

But history differs from the sciences precisely because historians disagree, not only over what are the laws of social causation that they might invoke to explain a given sequence of events, but also over the question of the form that a 'scientific' explanation ought to take. There is a long history of dispute over whether natural scientific and historical explanations must have the same formal characteristics. This dispute turns on the problem of whether the kinds of laws that might be invoked in scientific explanations have their counterparts in the realm of the so-called human or spiritual sciences, such as sociology and history. The physical sciences appear to progress by virtue of the agreements, reached from time to time among members of the established communities of scientists, regarding what will count as a scientific problem, the form that a scientific explanation must take, the kinds of data that will be permitted to count as evidence in a properly scientific account of reality. Among historians no such agreement exists, or ever has existed. This may merely reflect the protoscientific nature of the historiographical enterprise, but it is important to bear in mind this congenital disagreement (or lack of agreement) over what counts as a specifically historical explanation of any given set of historical phenomena. For this means that historical explanations are bound to be based on different metahistorical presuppositions about the nature of the historical field, presuppositions that generate different conceptions of the *kind of explanations* that can be used in historiographical analysis.

Historiographical disputes on the level of 'interpretation' are in reality disputes over the 'true' nature of the historian's enterprise. History remains in the state of conceptual anarchy in which the natural sciences existed during the sixteenth century, when there were as many different conceptions of 'the scientific enterprise' as there were metaphysical positions. In the sixteenth century, the different conceptions of what 'science' ought to be ultimately reflected different conceptions of 'reality' and the different epistemologies generated by them. So, too, disputes over what 'history' ought to be reflect similarly varied conceptions of what a proper historical explanation ought to consist of and different conceptions, therefore, of the historian's task.

3 *The Hollow Miracle**

GEORGE STEINER

NOTE: Understandably, this essay caused much hurt and anger. Discussion and misquotation of it have continued in Germany to the present time. The journal, *Sprache im technischen Zeitalter*, devoted a special number to the debate, and controversy arose anew at the meeting in the United States in the spring of 1966 of the German writers known as the *Gruppe 47*. The academic profession took a particularly adverse view of the case.

If I republish 'The Hollow Miracle', it is because I believe that the matter of the relations between language and political inhumanity is a crucial one; and because I believe that it can be seen with specific and tragic urgency in respect of the uses of German in the Nazi period and in the acrobatics of oblivion which followed on the fall of Nazism. De Maistre and George Orwell have written of the politics of language, of how the word may lose its humane meanings under the pressure of political bestiality and falsehood. We have scarcely begun, as yet, to apply their insights to the actual history of language and feeling. Here almost everything remains to be done.

* From George Steiner, *Language and Silence: Essays 1958–1966*, Penguin Books, Harmondsworth, Middlesex, 1979, first publ. 1959.

I republish this essay also because I believe that its general line or argument is valid. When I wrote it, I did not know of Victor Klemperer's remarkable book: *Aus dem Notizbuch eines Philologen*, published in East Berlin in 1946 (now reissued by Joseph Melzer Verlag, Darmstadt, under the title: *Die unbewältigte Sprache*). In far more detail than I was able to give, Klemperer, a trained linguist, traces the collapse of German into Nazi jargon and the linguistic-historical background to that collapse. . . . In Hochhuth's *The Representative*, particularly in the scenes involving Eichmann and his business cronies, Nazi German is given precise, nauseating expression. The same is true in Peter Weiss's *Interrogation* and in Günter Grass's *Hundejahre*. . . .

Brecht, Kafka and Thomas Mann did not succeed in mastering their own culture, in imposing on it the humane sobriety of their talent. They found themselves first the eccentrics, then the hunted. New linguists were at hand to make of the German language a political weapon more total and effective than any history had known, and to degrade the dignity of human speech to the level of baying wolves.

For let us keep one fact clearly in mind: the German language was not innocent of the horrors of Nazism. It is not merely that a Hitler, a Goebbels, and a Himmler happened to speak German. Nazism found in the language precisely what it needed to give voice to its savagery. Hitler heard inside his native tongue the latent hysteria, the confusion, the quality of hypnotic trance. He plunged unerringly into the undergrowth of language, into those zones of darkness and outcry which are the infancy of articulate speech, and which come before words have grown mellow and provisional to the touch of the mind. He sensed in German another music than that of Goethe, Heine and Mann; a rasping cadence, half nebulous jargon, half obscenity. And instead of turning away in nauseated disbelief, the German people gave massive echo to the man's bellowing. It bellowed back out of a million throats and smashed-down boots. A Hitler would have found reservoirs of venom and moral illiteracy in any language. But by virtue of recent history, they were nowhere else so ready and so near the very surface of common speech. A language in which one can write a 'Horst Wessel Lied' is ready to give hell a native tongue. (How should the word '*spritzen*' recover a sane meaning after having signified to millions the 'spurting' of Jewish blood from knife points?)

And that is what happened under the Reich. Not silence or evasion, but an immense outpouring of precise, serviceable words. It was one of the peculiar horrors of the Nazi era that all that happened was recorded, catalogued, chronicled, set down; that words were committed to saying things no human mouth should ever have said and no paper made by man should ever have been inscribed with. It is nauseating and nearly unbearable to recall what was wrought and spoken, but one must. In the Gestapo cellars, stenographers (usually women) took down carefully the noises of fear and agony wrenched, burned or beaten out of the human voice. The tortures and experiments carried out on live beings at Belsen and Matthausen were exactly recorded. The regulations governing the number of blows to be meted out on the flogging blocks at Dachau were set down in writing. When Polish rabbis were compelled to shovel out open latrines with their hands and mouths, there were German officers there to record the fact, to photograph it, and to label the photographs. When the SS élite guards separated mothers from children at the éntrance to the death camps, they did not proceed in silence. They proclaimed the imminent horrors in loud jeers: '*Heida, heida, juchheisassa, Scheissjuden in den Schornstein!*'[1]

The unspeakable being said, over and over, for twelve years. The unthinkable being written down, indexed, filed for reference. The men who poured quicklime down the openings of the sewers in Warsaw to kill the living and stifle the stink of the dead wrote home about it. They spoke of having to 'liquidate vermin'. In letters asking for family snapshots or sending season's greetings. Silent night, holy night, *Gemütlichkeit*[2]. A language being used to run hell, getting the habits of hell into its syntax. Being used to destroy what there is in man of man and to restore to governance what there is of beast. Gradually, words lost their original meaning and acquired nightmarish definitions. *Jude, Pole, Russe*[3] came to mean two-legged lice, putrid vermin which good Aryans must squash, as a party manual said, 'like roaches on a dirty wall'. 'Final solution', *endgültige Lösung*, came to signify the death of six million human beings in gas ovens.

The language was infected not only with these great bestialities. It was called upon to enforce innumerable falsehoods, to persuade the Germans that the war was just and everywhere victorious. As defeat began closing in on the thousand-year Reich, the lies thickened to a constant snowdrift. The language was turned upside down to say 'light' where there was blackness and 'victory' where there was disaster. Gottfried Benn, one of the few decent writers to stay inside Nazi Germany, noted some of the new definitions from the dictionary of Hitler German:

In December 1943, that is to say at a time when the Russians had driven us before them for 1,500 kilometres, and had pierced our front in a dozen places, a first lieutenant, small as a hummingbird and gentle as a puppy, remarked: 'The main thing is that the swine are not breaking through.' 'Break through', 'roll back', 'clean up', 'flexible, fluid lines of combat'—what positive and negative power such words have; they can bluff or they can conceal. Stalingrad—a tragic accident. The defeat of the U-boats—a small, accidental technical discovery by the British. Montgomery chasing Rommel 4,000 kilometres from El Alamein to Naples—treason of the Badoglio clique.

---

[1] Literally, 'Hey, hey, hooray, Jewish shits up the chimney!' [Ed.]
[2] Commonplace for 'geniality', 'comfort'. [Ed.]
[3] 'Jew Pole, Russian'. [Ed.]

And as the circle of vengeance closed in on Germany, this snowdrift of lies thickened to a frantic blizzard. Over the radio, between the interruptions caused by air-raid warnings, Goebbels's voice assured the German people that 'titanic secret weapons' were about to be launched. On one of the very last days of Götterdämmerung, Hitler came out of his bunker to inspect a row of ashen-faced fifteen-year-old boys recruited for a last-ditch defence of Berlin. The order of the day spoke of 'volunteers' and élite units gathered invincibly around the Führer. The nightmare fizzled out on a shameless lie. The *Herren-volk*[4] was solemnly told that Hitler was in the front-line trenches, defending the heart of his capital against the Red beasts. Actually, the buffoon lay dead with his mistress, deep in the safety of his concrete lair.

Languages have great reserves of life. They can absorb masses of hysteria, illiteracy and cheapness (George Orwell showed how English is doing so today). But there comes a breaking point. Use a language to conceive, organize, and justify Belsen; use it to make out specifications for gas ovens; use it to dehumanize man during twelve years of calculated bestiality. Something will happen to it. Make of words what Hitler and Goebbels and the hundred thousand *Untersturmführer*[5] made: conveyors of terror and false-hood. Something will happen to the words. Something of the lies and sadism will settle in the marrow of the language. Imperceptibly at first, like the poisons of radiation sifting silently into the bone. But the cancer will begin, and the deep-set destruction. The language will no longer grow and freshen. It will no longer perform, quite as well as it used to, its two principal functions: the conveyance of humane order which we call law, and the communication of the quick of the human spirit which we call grace. In an anguished note in his diary for 1940, Klaus Mann observed that he could no longer read new German books: 'Can it be that Hitler has polluted the language of Nietzsche and Hölderlin?' It can.

But what happened to those who are the guardians of a language, the keepers of its conscience? What happened to the German writers? A number were killed in the concentration camps; others, such as Walter Benjamin, killed themselves before the Gestapo could get at them to obliterate what little there is in a man of God's image. But the major writers went into exile. The best playwrights: Brecht and Zuckmayer. The most important novelists: Thomas Mann, Werfel, Feuchtwanger, Heinrich Mann, Stefan Zweig, Hermann Broch.

This exodus is of the first importance if we are to understand what has happened to the German language and to the soul of which it is the voice. Some of these writers fled for their lives, being Jews or Marxists or otherwise

---

[4] 'Master-race'. [Ed.]
[5] S.S. rank, equivalent to second lieutenant. [Ed.]

'undesirable vermin'. But many could have stayed as honoured Aryan guests of the régime. The Nazis were only too anxious to secure the lustre of Thomas Mann's presence and the prestige that mere presence would have given to the cultural life of the Reich. But Mann would not stay. And the reason was that he knew exactly what was being done to the German language and that he felt that only in exile might that language be kept from final ruin. When he emigrated, the sycophantic academics of the University of Bonn deprived him of his honorary doctorate. In his famous open letter to the dean, Mann explained how a man using German to communicate truth or humane values could not remain in Hitler's Reich:

The mystery of language is a great one; the responsibility for a language and for its purity is of a symbolic and spiritual kind; this responsibility does not have merely an aesthetic sense. The responsibility for language is, in essence, human responsibility. . . . Should a German writer, made responsible through his habitual use of language, remain silent, quite silent, in the face of all the irreparable evil which has been committed daily, and is being committed in my country, against body, soul and spirit, against justice and truth, against men and man?

Mann was right, of course. But the cost of such integrity is immense for a writer.

The German writers suffered different degrees of deprivation and reacted in different ways. A very few were fortunate enough to find asylum in Switzerland, where they could remain inside the living stream of their own tongue. Others, like Werfel, Feuchtwanger, and Heinrich Mann, settled near each other or formed islands of native speech in their new homeland. Stefan Zweig, safely arrived in Latin America, tried to resume his craft. But despair overcame him. He was convinced that the Nazis would turn German into inhuman gibberish. He saw no future for a man dedicated to the integrity of German letters and killed himself. Others stopped writing altogether. Only the very tough or most richly gifted were able to transform their cruel condition into art.

Pursued by the Nazis from refuge to refuge, Brecht made of each of his new plays a brilliant rearguard action. *Mutter Courage* was first produced in Zurich in the dark spring of 1941. The further he was hounded, the clearer and stronger became Brecht's German. The language seemed to be that of a primer spelling out the ABC of truth. Doubtless, Brecht was helped by his politics. Being a Marxist, he felt himself a citizen of a community larger than Germany and a participant in the forward march of history. He was prepared to accept the desecration and ruin of the German heritage as a necessary tragic prelude to the foundation of a new society. In his tract 'Five Difficulties in the Telling of the Truth', Brecht envisioned a new German language, capable of matching the word to the fact and the fact to the dignity of man.

4 *The Keening Muse**

JOSEPH BRODSKY

No one absorbs the past as thoroughly as a poet, if only out of fear of inventing the already invented. (This is why, by the way, a poet is so often regarded as being 'ahead of his time,' which keeps itself busy rehashing clichés.) So no matter what a poet may plan to say, at the moment of speech he always knows that he inherits the subject. The great literature of the past humbles one not only through its quality, but through its topical precedence as well. The reason why a good poet speaks of his own grief with restraint is that, as regards grief, he is a Wandering Jew. In this sense, Akhmatova was very much a product of the Petersburg tradition in Russian poetry, the founders of which, in their own turn, had behind them European classicism as well as its Roman and Greek origins. In addition, they, too, were aristocrats.

If Akhmatova was reticent, it was at least partly because she was carrying the heritage of her predecessors into the art of this century. This obviously was but a homage to them, since it was precisely that heritage which made her this century's poet. She simply regarded herself, with her raptures and revelations, as a postscript to their message, to what they recorded about their lives. The lives were tragic, and so was the message. If the postscript looks dark, it's because the message was absorbed fully. If she never screams or showers her head with ashes, it's because they didn't.

Such were the cue and the key with which she started. Her first collections were tremendously successful with both the critics and the public. In general, the response to a poet's work should be considered last, for it is a poet's last consideration. However, Akhmatova's success was in this respect remarkable if one takes into account its timing, especially in the case of her second and third volumes: 1914 (the outbreak of World War I) and 1917 (the October Revolution in Russia). On the other hand, perhaps it was precisely this deafening background thunder of world events that rendered the private tremolo of this young poet all the more discernible and vital. In that sense again, the beginning of this poetic career contained a prophecy of the course it came to run for half a century. What increases the sense of prophecy is that for a Russian ear at the time the thunder of world events was compounded by the incessant and quite meaningless mumbling of the Symbolists. Eventually these two noises shrunk and merged into the threatening incoherent

* From Joseph Brodsky, *Less Than One: Selected Essays*, Penguin Books, Harmondsworth, Middlesex, 1987, pp. 34–43, 47–52; first publ. 1986.

drone of the new era against which Akhmatova was destined to speak for the rest of her life.

Those early collections (*Evening, Rosary and White Flock*) dealt mostly with the sentiment which is *de rigueur* for early collections: with that of love. The poems in those books had a diary-like intimacy and immediacy: they'd describe no more than one actual or psychological event and were short—sixteen to twenty lines at best. As such they could be committed to memory in a flash, as indeed they were—and still are—by generations and generations of Russians.

Still, it was neither their compactness nor their subject matter that made one's memory desire to appropriate them: those features were quite familiar to an experienced reader. The news came in the form of a sensibility which manifested itself in the author's treatment of her theme. Betrayed, tormented by either jealousy or guilt, the wounded heroine of these poems speaks more frequently in self-reproach than in anger, forgives more eloquently than accuses, prays rather than screams. She displays all the emotional subtlety and psychological complexity of nineteenth-century Russian prose and all the dignity that the poetry of the same century taught her. Apart from these, there is also a great deal of irony and detachment which are strictly her own and products of her metaphysics rather than shortcuts to resignation.

Needless to say, for her readership those qualities seem to come in both handy and timely.

More than any other art, poetry is a form of sentimental education, and the lines that Akhmatova readers learned by heart were to temper their hearts against the new era's onslaught of vulgarity. The comprehension of the metaphysics of personal drama betters one's chances of weathering the drama of history. This is why, and not because of the epigrammatic beauty of her lines only, the public clung to them so unwittingly. It was an instinctive reaction: the instinct being that of self-preservation, for the stampede of history was getting more and more audible.

Akhmatova in any case heard it quite clearly. The intensely personal lyricism of *White Flock* is tinged with the note that was destined to become her imprimatur: the note of controlled terror. The mechanism designed to keep in check emotions of a romantic nature proved to be as effective when applied to mortal fears. The latter was increasingly intertwined with the former until they resulted in emotional tautology, and *White Flock* marks the beginning of this process. With this collection, Russian poetry hit 'the real, non-calendar twentieth century' but didn't disintegrate on impact.

Akhmatova, to say the least, seemed better prepared for this encounter than most of her contemporaries. Besides, by the time of the Revolution she was twenty-eight years old: that is, neither young enough to believe in it nor too old to justify it. Furthermore, she was a woman, and it would be equally unseemly for her to extol or condemn the event. Nor did she decide to accept the change of social order as an invitation to loosen her meter and associative chains. For art doesn't imitate life if only for fear of clichés. She remained true to her diction, to its private timbre, to refracting rather than reflecting life through the prism of the individual heart. Except that the choice of detail whose role in a poem previously was to shift attention from an emotionally pregnant issue presently began to be less and less of a solace, overshadowing the issue itself.

She didn't reject the Revolution: a defiant pose wasn't for her either. Using latter-day locution, she internalized it. She simply took it for what it was: a terrible national upheaval which meant a tremendous increase of grief per individual. She understood this not only because her own share went too high but first and foremost through her very craft. The poet is a born democrat not thanks to the precariousness of his position only but because he caters to the entire nation and employs its language. So does tragedy, and hence their affinity. Akhmatova, whose verse always gravitated to the vernacular, to the idiom of folk song, could identify with the people more thoroughly than those who were pushing at the time their literary or other programs: she simply recognized grief.

Moreover, to say that she identified with the people is to introduce a rationalization which never took place because of its inevitable redundancy. She was a part of the whole, and the pseudonym just furthered her class anonymity. In addition, she always disdained the air of superiority present in the word 'poet'. 'I don't understand these big words,' she used to say, 'poet, billiard.' This wasn't humility; this was the result of the sober perspective in which she kept her existence. The very persistence of love as the theme of her poetry indicates her proximity to the average person. If she differed from her public it was in that her ethics weren't subject to historical adjustment.

Other than that, she was like everybody else. Besides, the times themselves didn't allow for great variety. If her poems weren't exactly the *vox populi*, it's because a nation never speaks with one voice. But neither was her voice that of the *crème de la crème*, if only because it was totally devoid of the populist nostalgia so peculiar to the Russian intelligentsia. The 'we' that she starts to use about this time in self-defense against the impersonality of pain inflicted by history was broadened to this pronoun's linguistic limits not by herself but by the rest of the speakers of this language. Because of the quality of the future, this 'we' was there to stay and the authority of its user to grow.

In any case, there is no psychological difference between Akhmatova's 'civic' poems of World War I and the revolutionary period, and those written a good thirty years later during World War II. Indeed, without the date underneath them, poems like 'Prayer' could be attributed to virtually any moment of Russian history in this century which justifies that particular poem's title. Apart from the sensitivity of her membrane, though, this proves that the quality of history for the last eighty years has somewhat simplified the poet's job. It did so to the degree that a poet would spurn a line containing a prophetic possibility and prefer a plain description of a fact or sensation.

Hence the nominative character of Akhmatova's lines in general and at that period in particular. She knew not only that the emotions and perceptions she dealt with were fairly common but also that time, true to its repetitive nature, would render them universal. She sensed that history, like its objects, has very limited options. What was more important, however, was that those 'civic' poems were but fragments borne by her general lyrical current, which made their 'we' practically indistinguishable from the more frequent, emotionally charged 'I'. Because of their overlapping, both pronouns were gaining in verisimilitude and Akhmatova, a poet of strict meters, was using it precisely to that end. But the more she did so, the more inexorably her voice was approaching the impersonal tonality of time itself, until they merged into something that makes one shudder trying to guess —as in her *Northern Elegies*—who is hiding behind the pronoun 'I'.

What happened to pronouns was happening to other parts of speech, which would peter out or loom large in the perspective of time supplied by prosody. Akhmatova was a very concrete poet, but the more concrete the image, the more extemporary it would become because of the accompanying meter. No poem is ever written for its story line's sake only, just as no life is lived for the sake of an obituary. What is called the music of a poem is essentially time restructured in such a way that it brings this poem's content into a linguistically inevitable, memorable focus.

Sound, in other words, is the seat of time in the poem, a background against which its content acquires a stereoscopic quality. The power of Akhmatova's lines comes from her ability to convey the music's impersonal epic sweep, which more than matched their actual content, especially from the twenties on. The effect of her instrumentation upon her themes was akin to that of somebody used to being put against the wall being suddenly put against the horizon.

The above should be kept very much in mind by the foreign reader of Akhmatova, since that horizon vanishes in translations, leaving on the page absorbing but one-dimensional content. On the other hand, the foreign reader may perhaps be consoled by the fact that this poet's native audience also has been forced to deal with her work in a very misrepresented fashion. What translation has in common with censorship is that both operate on the basis of the 'what's possible' principle, and it must be noted that linguistic barriers can be as high as those erected by the state. Akhmatova, in any case, is surrounded by both and it's only the former that shows signs of crumbling.

Anno Domini MCMXXI was her last collection: in the forty-four years that followed she had no book of her own. In the postwar period there were, technically speaking, two slim editions of her work, consisting mainly of a few reprinted early lyrics plus genuinely patriotic war poems and doggerel bits extolling the arrival of peace. These last ones were written by her in order to win the release of her son from the labor camps, in which he nonetheless spent eighteen years. These publications in no way can be regarded as her own, for the poems were selected by the editors of the state-run publishing house and their aim was to convince the public (especially those abroad) that Akhmatova was alive, well, and loyal. They totaled some fifty pieces and had nothing in common with her output during those four decades.

For a poet of Akhmatova's stature this meant being buried alive, with a couple of slabs marking the mound. Her going under was a product of several forces, mostly that of history, whose chief element is vulgarity and whose immediate agent is the state. Now, by MCMXXI, which means 1921, the new state could already be at odds with Akhmatova, whose first husband, poet Nikolai Gumilyov, was executed by its security forces, allegedly on the direct order of the state's head, Vladimir Lenin. A spin-off of a didactic, eye-for-eye mentality, the new state could expect from Akhmatova nothing but retaliation especially given her reputed tendency for an autobiographical touch.

Such was, presumably, the state's logic, furthered by the destruction in the subsequent decade and a half of her entire circle (including her closest friends, poets Vladimir Narbut and Osip Mandelstam). It culminated in the arrests of her son, Lev Gumilyov, and her third husband, art-historian Nikolai Punin, who soon died in prison. Then came World War II.

Those fifteen years preceding the war were perhaps the darkest in the whole of Russian history; undoubtedly they were so in Akhmatova's own life. It's the material which this period supplied, or more accurately the lives it subtracted, that made her eventually earn the title of the Keening Muse. This period simply replaced the frequency of poems about love with that of poems in memoriam. Death, which she would previously evoke as a solution for this or that emotional tension, became too real for any emotion to matter. From a figure of speech it became a figure that leaves you speechless.

If she proceeded to write, it's because prosody absorbs death, and because she felt guilty that she survived. The pieces that constitute her 'Wreath for the Dead' are simply attempts to let those whom she outlived absorb or at least join prosody. It's not that she tried to 'immortalize' her dead: most of them were the pride of Russian literature already and thus had immortalized themselves enough. She simply tried to manage the meaninglessness of existence, which suddenly gaped before her because of the destruction of the sources of its meaning, to domesticate the reprehensible infinity by inhabiting it with familiar shadows. Besides, addressing the dead was the only way of preventing speech from slipping into a howl.

The elements of howl, however, are quite audible in other Akhmatova poems of the period and later. They'd appear either in the form of idiosyncratic excessive rhyming or as a *non sequitur* line interjected in an otherwise coherent narrative. Nevertheless, the poems dealing directly with someone's death are free of anything of this sort, as though the author doesn't want to offend her addressees with her emotional extremes. This refusal to exploit the ultimate opportunity to impose herself upon them echoes, of course, the practice of her lyric poetry. But by continuing to address the dead as though they were alive, by not adjusting her diction to 'the occasion,' she also refuses the opportunity to exploit the dead as those ideal, absolute interlocutors that every poet seeks and finds either in the dead or among angels.

As a theme, death is a good litmus test for a poet's ethics. The 'in memoriam' genre is frequently used to exercise self-pity or for metaphysical trips that denote the subconscious superiority of survivor over victim, of majority (of the alive) over minority (of the dead). Akhmatova would have none of that. She particularizes her fallen instead of generalizing about them, since she writes for a minority with which it's easier for her to identify in any case. She simply continues to treat them as individuals whom she knew and who, she senses, wouldn't like to be used as the point of departure for no matter how spectacular a destination.

Naturally enough, poems of this sort couldn't be published, nor could they even be written down or retyped. They could only be memorized by the author and by some seven other people, since she didn't trust her own memory. From time to time, she'd meet a person privately and would ask him or her to recite quietly this or that selection as a means of inventory. This precaution was far from being excessive: people would disappear forever for smaller things than a piece of paper with a few lines on it. Besides, she feared not so much for her own life as for that of her son, who was in a camp and whose release she desperately tried to obtain for eighteen years. A little piece of paper with a few lines on it could cost a lot, and more to him than to her, who could lose only hope and, perhaps, mind.

The days of both, however, would have been numbered had the authorities found her *Requiem*, a cycle of poems describing the ordeal of a woman whose son is arrested and who waits under prison walls with a parcel for him and scurries about the thresholds of state offices to find out about his fate. Now, this time around she was autobiographical indeed, yet the power of *Requiem* lies in the fact that Akhmatova's biography was all too common. This requiem mourns the mourners: mothers losing sons, wives turning widows, sometimes both, as was the author's case. This is a tragedy where the chorus perishes before the hero.

The degree of compassion with which the various voices of *Requiem* are rendered can be explained only by the author's Orthodox faith; the degree of understanding and forgiveness which accounts for this work's piercing, almost unbearable lyricism, only by the uniqueness of her heart, her self, and this self's sense of time. No creed would help to understand, much less forgive, let alone survive this double widowhood at the hands of the regime, this fate of her son, these forty years of being silenced and ostracized. No Anna Gorenko would be able to take it.[1] Anna Akhmatova did, and it's as though she knew what was in store when she took this pen name.

At certain periods of history it is only poetry that is capable of dealing with reality by condensing it into something graspable, something that otherwise couldn't be retained by the mind. In that sense, the whole nation took up the pen name of Akhmatova—which explains her popularity and which, more importantly, enabled her to speak for the nation as well as to tell it something it didn't know. She was, essentially, a poet of human ties: cherished, strained, severed. She showed these evolutions first through the prism of the individual heart, then through the prism of history, such as it was. This is about as much as one gets in the way of optics anyway.

These two perspectives were brought into sharp focus through prosody, which is simply a repository of time within language. Hence, by the way, her ability to forgive—because forgiveness is not a virtue postulated by creed but a property of time in both its mundane and metaphysical senses. This is also why her verses are to survive whether published or not: because of the prosody, because they are charged with time in both those senses. They will survive because language is older than state and because prosody always survives history. In fact, it hardly needs history; all it needs is a poet, and Akhmatova was just that.

5 *On Hope**

CZESLAW MILOSZ

It is possible that we are witnessing a kind of race between the lifegiving and the destructive activity of civilization's bacteria, and that an unknown result awaits in the future. No computer will be able to calculate so many pros and cons—thus a poet with his intuition remains one strong, albeit uncertain, source of knowledge. Putting economy and politics aside, I will now return to my own reasons for, if not optimism, then at least opposition to hopelessness.

---

[1] As Brodsky points out earlier on in this essay, Anna Gorenko took on her pseudonym of Akhmatova for its 'distinct Oriental, Tatar to be precise, flavor'. [Ed.]

* From Czeslaw Milosz, *The Witness of Poetry*; The Charles Eliot Norton Lectures 1981–2, Harvard University Press, Cambridge, Mass., 1983, pp. 107–12, 114–16.

We can do justice to our time only by comparing it to that of our grand-fathers and great-grandfathers. Something happened, whose importance still eludes us, and it seems very ordinary, though its effects will both last and increase. The exceptional quality of the twentieth century is not determined by jets as a means of transportation or a decrease in infant mortality or the birth-control pill. It is determined by humanity's emergence as a new elemen-tal force; until now humanity had been divided into castes distinguished by dress, mentality, and mores. The transformation can be clearly observed only in certain countries, but it is gradually occurring everywhere and causing the disappearance of certain mythical notions, widespread in the past century, about the specific and presumably eternal features of the peasant, worker, and intellectual. Humanity as an elemental force, the result of technology and mass education, means that man is opening up to science and art on unprecedented scale.

My late friend, the Polish writer Witold Gombrowicz, was well aware of this. He had a gift for making insolently simple formulations. 'I am generally classified as a pessimist, even a "catastrophist",' he said in 1968 in Vence, a year before his death.[1] 'Critics have grown accustomed to thinking that a contemporary literature of a certain standard must necessarily be black. Mine is not black. On the contrary, it is more of a reaction against the sardonic-apocalyptic tone currently in fashion. I am like the baritone in the Choral Symphony: "Friends, enough of this song. Let more joyous melodies be heard."' And further:

alienation? No, let us try to admit that this alienation is not so bad, that we have it in our fingers, as pianists say—in our disciplined, technical fingers which, apart from alienation, give the workers almost as many free and marvelous holidays a year as work days. Emptiness? The absurdity of existence? Nothingness? Don't let's exaggerate. A god or ideals are not necessary to discover supreme values. We only have to go for three days without eating anything for a crumb to become our supreme god: it is our needs that are at the basis of our values, of the sense and order of our lives. Atomic bombs? Some centuries ago, we died before we were thirty—plagues, poverty, witches, Hell, Purgatory, tortures . . . Haven't your conquests gone to your head? Have you forgotten what we were yesterday?

To this one may answer that today's hell and today's tortures are not inferior to those of the Middle Ages. Nevertheless, the change Gombrowicz had in mind is real. The difficulty of appraising it correctly comes from a peculiar debasement that follows everything new. Citizens in a modern state, no longer mere dwellers in their village and district, know how to read and write but are unprepared to receive nourishment of a higher intellectual order. They are sustained artificially on a lower level by television, films, and

---

[1] *A Kind of Testament*, edited by Dominique de Roux (Philadelphia: Temple University Press, 1973).

illustrated magazines—media that are for the mind what too small slippers were for women's feet in old China. At the same time, the élite is engaged in what is called 'culture', consisting mostly of rituals attended out of snobbery and borne with boredom. Thus elemental humanity's openness to science and art is only potential, and much time will pass before it becomes a fact everywhere.

A poet, however, presupposes the existence of an ideal reader, and the poetic act both anticipates the future and speeds its coming. Earlier I spoke of the lessons of biology and of a reductionist Weltanschauung professed universally today. I expressed the hope that it will be superseded by another vision better adapted to the complexity of the world and of individuals. It seems to me that this will be connected, in one or another way, with a new dimension entered on by elemental humanity—and here I expect some surprise from my audience—the dimension of the past of our human race. This would not seem too probable, since mass culture appears quickly inclined to forget important events and even recent ones, and less and less history is taught in the schools. Let us consider, though, what is happening at the same time.

Never before have the painting and music of the past been so universally accessible through reproductions and records. Never before has the life of past civilizations been so graphically recreated, and the crowds that now visit museums and galleries are without historical precedent. Thus technology, which forces history out of the classroom, compensates, perhaps even generously, for what it is destroying. Daring to make a prediction, I expect, perhaps quite soon, in the twenty-first century, a radical turning away from the Weltanschauung marked principally by biology, and this will result from a newly acquired historical consciousness. Instead of presenting man through those traits that link him to higher forms of the evolutionary chain, other of his aspects will be stressed: the exceptionality, strangeness, and loneliness of that creature mysterious to itself, a being incessantly transcending its own limits. Humanity will increasingly be turning back to itself, increasingly contemplating its entire past, searching for a key to its own enigma, and penetrating, through empathy, the soul of bygone generations and of whole civilizations.

Premonitions of this can be found in the poetry of the twentieth century. In 1900 education was of course the privilege of a small élite and included training in Latin and Greek, remnants of the humanist ideal. Some acquaintance with the poets of antiquity read in the original was also required. That period is closed, and Latin has even disappeared from the Catholic liturgy, with not much chance for revival. But, at the same time, judging by poetry, say Robert Graves's, the past of the Mediterranean—Jewish, Greek, Roman —has begun to have an even more intense existence in our consciousness than it had for our educated predecessors, though in a different way. One could multiply examples from poets. Also, the presence of mythical figures taken from European literature or from literary legend is more vivid than at any previous time, figures such as Hamlet, Lear, Prospero, François Villon, Faust.

From this perspective, it is worthwhile to mention the adventures of one poet, at least a few of whose poems belong to the canon of twentieth-century art and who deserves the name of forerunner, even though his work as a whole is uneven. A Greek from Alexandria, Constantin Cavafy was born in 1863. After many attempts at writing in the spirit of fin-de-siècle, he dared to embrace an idea alien to the highly subjectivist literary fashion of his contemporaries. He identified himself with the entire Hellenic world, from Homeric times up through the dynasty of the Seleucids and Byzantium, incarnating himself in them, so that his journey through time and space was also a journey into his own interior realm, his history as a Hellene. Maybe the impulse came from his familiarity with English poetry, primarily with Robert Browning and his personae taken from Renaissance Italy. Perhaps he had also read the poems of Pierre Louys, *Songs of Bilitis*. Be that as it may, Cavafy's best poems are meditations on the past, which is brought closer so that characters and situations from many centuries back are perceived by the reader as kindred. Cavafy seems to belong in the second half of this century, but this is an illusion resulting from his late arrival in world poetry, through translations. In fact, nearly unknown in his lifetime (though T. S. Eliot published him in his *Criterion*) and only gradually discovered after his death in 1933, he wrote his most famous poems before World War I. 'Waiting for the Barbarians' dates from 1898; 'Ithaka' in the first version from 1894, in the second from 1910; 'King Dimitrios' from 1900; 'Dareios' and 'In Alexandria, 31 BC, came a little later, in 1917.

Since I have tried to present my Polish background and have used examples taken from Polish poetry in these lectures, it would perhaps be proper to note that the presence of the Hellenic past in Cavafy is particularly understandable for a Polish poet. The true home of the Polish poet is history, and though Polish history is much shorter than that of Greece, it is no less rich in defeats and lost illusions. In Cavafy's decision to exploit his own Hellenic history, his Polish reader recognizes the idea he had already discovered when reading poets of his own tongue: that we apprehend the human condition with pity and terror not in the abstract but always in relation to a given place and time, in one particular province, one particular country. . . .

'From where will a renewal come to us, to us who have spoiled and devastated the whole earthly globe?' asks Simone Weil. And she answers, 'Only from the past, if we love it.' At first sight this is an enigmatic formulation, and it is difficult to guess what she has in mind. Her aphorism acquires meaning in the light of her other pronouncements. Thus she says elsewhere: 'Two things cannot be reduced to any rationalism: Time and Beauty. We should start from them.' Or: 'Distance is the soul of beauty.' The past is 'woven with time the color of eternity'. In her opinion, it is difficult for a man to reach through to reality, for he is hindered by his ego and by imagination in the service of his ego. Only a distance in time allows us to see reality without coloring it with our passions. And reality seen that way is beautiful. This is why the past has such importance: 'The sense of reality is pure in it. Here is pure joy. Here is pure beauty. Proust.' When quoting Simone Weil I think of what made me personally so receptive to her theory of purification. It probably was not the work of Marcel Proust, so dear to her, but a work I read much earlier, in childhood, and my constant companion ever since—*Pan Tadeusz* by Adam Mickiewicz, a poem in which the most ordinary incidents of everyday life change into a web of fairytale, for they are described as occurring long ago, and suffering is absent because suffering only affects us, the living, not characters invoked by all-forgiving memory.

Humanity will also explore itself in the sense that it will search for reality purified, for the 'color of eternity', in other words, simply for beauty. Probably this is what Dostoevsky, skeptical as he was about the fate of civilization, meant when he affirmed that the world will be saved by beauty. This means that our growing despair because of the discrepancy between reality and the desire of our hearts would be healed, and the world which exists objectively —perhaps as it appears in the eyes of God, not as it is perceived by us, desiring and suffering—will be accepted with all its good and evil.

I have offered various answers to the question why twentieth-century poetry has such a gloomy, apocalyptic tone. It is quite likely that the causes cannot be reduced to one. The separation of the poet from the great human family; the progressing subjectivization that becomes manifest when we are imprisoned in the melancholy of our individual transience; the automatisms of literary structures, or simply of fashion—all this undoubtedly has weight. Yet if I declare myself for realism as the poet's conscious or unconscious longing, I should pay what is due to a sober assessment of our predicament. The unification of the planet is not proceeding without high cost. Through the mass media poets of all languages receive information on what is occurring across the surface of the whole earth, on the tortures inflicted by man on man, on starvation, misery, humiliation. At a time when their knowledge of reality was limited to one village or district, poets had no such burden to bear. Is it surprising that they are always morally indignant, that they feel responsible, that no promise of the further triumphs of science and technology can veil these images of chaos and human folly? And when they try to visualize the near future, they find nothing there except the probability of economic crisis and war.

This is not the place to say what will happen tomorrow, as the fortune tellers and futurologists do. The hope of the poet, a hope that I defend, that I advance, is not enclosed by any date. If disintegration is a function of development, and development a function of disintegration, the race between them may very well end in the victory of disintegration. For a long time, but not forever—and here is where hope enters. It is neither chimerical nor foolish. On the contrary, every day one can see signs indicating that now, at the present moment, something new, and on a scale never witnessed before, is being born: humanity as an elemental force conscious of transcending Nature, for it lives by memory of itself, that is, in History.

6 *Theses on the Philosophy of History**

WALTER BENJAMIN

V

The true picture of the past flits by. The past can be seized only as an image which flashes up at the instant when it can be recognized and is never seen again. 'The truth will not run away from us': in the historical outlook of historicism these words of Gottfried Keller mark the exact point where historical materialism cuts through historicism. For every image of the past that is not recognized by the present as one of its own concerns threatens to disappear irretrievably. (The good tidings which the historian of the past brings with throbbing heart may be lost in a void the very moment he opens his mouth.)

VI

To articulate the past historically does not mean to recognize it 'the way it really was' (Ranke). It means to seize hold of a memory as it flashes up at a moment of danger. Historical materialism wishes to retain that image of the past which unexpectedly appears to man singled out by history at a moment of danger. The danger affects both the content of the tradition and its receivers. The same threat hangs over both: that of becoming a tool of the ruling classes. In every era the attempt must be made anew to wrest tradition away from a conformism that is about to overpower it. The Messiah comes not only as the redeemer, he comes as the subduer of Antichrist. Only that historian will have the gift of fanning the spark of hope in the past who is firmly convinced that *even the dead* will not be safe from the enemy if he wins. And this enemy has not ceased to be victorious.

* From *Illuminations*, transl. H. Zohn 1968, Fontana/Collins, 1977, pp. 257–60; first publ. as *Schriften*, 1955.

VII

Consider the darkness and the great cold
In this vale which resounds with misery.

(Brecht, *The Threepenny Opera*)

To historians who wish to relive an era, Fustel de Coulanges recommends that they blot out everything they know about the later course of history. There is no better way of characterizing the method with which historical materialism has broken. It is a process of empathy whose origin is the indolence of the heart, *acedia*, which despairs of grasping and holding the genuine historical image as it flares up briefly. Among medieval theologians it was regarded as the root cause of sadness. Flaubert, who was familiar with it, wrote: '*Peu de gens devineront combien il a fallu être triste pour ressusciter Carthage.*'[1] The nature of this sadness stands out more clearly if one asks with whom the adherents of historicism actually empathize. The answer is inevitable: with the victor. And all rulers are the heirs of those who conquered before them. Hence, empathy with the victor invariably benefits the rulers. Historical materialists know what that means. Whoever has emerged victorious participates to this day in the triumphal procession in which the present rulers step over those who are lying prostrate. According to traditional practice, the spoils are carried along in the procession. They are called cultural treasures, and a historical materialist views them with cautious detachment. For without exception the cultural treasures he surveys have an origin which he cannot contemplate without horror. They owe their existence not only to the efforts of the great minds and talents who have created them, but also to the anonymous toil of their contemporaries. There is no document of civilization which is not at the same time a document of barbarism. And just as such a document is not free of barbarism, barbarism taints also the manner in which it was transmitted from one owner to another. A historical materialist therefore dissociates himself from it as far as possible. He regards it as his task to brush history against the grain. . . .

IX

Mein Flügel ist zum Schwung bereit,
ich kehrte gern zurück,
denn blieb ich auch lebendige Zeit,
ich hätte wenig Glück.

(Gerhard Scholem, 'Gruss vom Angelus')[2]

[1] 'Few will be able to guess how sad one had to be in order to resuscitate Carthage.'
[2] My wing is ready for flight.
I would like to turn back.
If I stayed timeless time,
I would have little luck.

A Klee painting named 'Angelus Novus' shows an angel looking as though he is about to move away from something he is fixedly contemplating. His eyes are staring, his mouth is open, his wings are spread. This is how one pictures the angel of history. His face is turned toward the past. Where we perceive a chain of events, he sees one single catastrophe which keeps piling wreckage upon wreckage and hurls it in front of his feet. The angel would like to stay, awaken the dead, and make whole what has been smashed. But a storm is blowing from Paradise; it has got caught in his wings with such violence that the angel can no longer close them. This storm irresistibly propels him into the future to which his back is turned, while the pile of debris before him grows skyward. This storm is what we call progress.

Acknowledgements

We are grateful for permission to include the following copyright material in this volume.

Chinua Achebe, 'Colonialist Criticism', from *Hopes and Impediments: Selected Essays, 1965–87* (Heinemann, 1988).

T. Adorno, 'Commitment' from *Aesthetics and Politics*, pp. 177–95. Reprinted by permission of Verso.

Bill Ashcroft et al, excerpt from *The Empire Writes Back: Theory and Practice in Post-Colonial Literatures* (1989). Reprinted by permission of Routledge.

W. H. Auden, 'Introduction' to 'The Poet's Tongue', copyright 1935 by W. H. Auden, from *The English Auden: Poems, Essays and Dramatic Writings 1927–1939*, edited by Edward Mendelson. Reprinted by permission of Faber & Faber Limited and Random House, Inc.

Etienne Balibar & Pierre Machery, 'On Literature as an Ideological Form: Some Marxist Propositions', reprinted with permission from *The Oxford Literary Review* 3:1 (1978), pp. 4–12, © 1978 *Oxford Literary Review*.

John Barrell, 'Introduction' from *Poetry, Language and Politics*, Manchester University Press, 1988, © John Barrell 1988. Reproduced by permission of the publisher.

Roland Barthes, 'The Death of the Author' from *Image–Music–Text*, Essays Selected and Translated by Stephen Heath (1977). Copyright © 1977 by Roland Barthes. Reprinted by permission of Collins Publishers and Hill & Wang, a division of Farrar, Straus & Giroux, Inc.

Simone de Beauvoir, 'Introduction' from *The Second Sex*, translated & edited by H. M. Parshley. Copyright 1952 by Alfred A. Knopf Inc. Reprinted by permission of Jonathan Cape and Alfred A. Knopf on behalf of the Estate of Simone de Beauvoir.

Walter Benjamin, excerpts from 'Theses on the Philosophy of History', in *Illuminations*, English translation © 1968 by Harcourt Brace Jovanovich, Inc. and reprinted with their permission. Reprinted by permission of Suhrkamp Verlag from their edition *Gesammelte Schriften* vol. 1.2, © Suhrkamp Verlag Frankfurt am Main 1974.

Asa Briggs, 'The English: Custom and Character' from *The English World*, ed. R. Blake (1982). Reprinted by permission of Thames and Hudson Ltd.

Joseph Brodsky, excerpt from 'The Keening Muse' from *Less Than One*, copyright © 1986 by Joseph Brodsky. Reprinted by permission of Penguin Books Ltd., and Farrar, Straus & Giroux, Inc.

Marilyn Butler, 'Repossessing the Past: the Case for an Open Literary History' from *Rethinking Historicism: Critical Readings in Romantic History*, ed. M. Levinson et al (Blackwell, 1989).

I. Calvino, from 'Right and Wrong Political Uses of Literature' from *The Uses of Literature*, © 1982, 1980 by Giulio Einaudi editore s.p.a., Torino, English translation © 1986 by Harcourt Brace Jovanovich, Inc. Copyright © Palomar, Srl. Reprinted by permission of Harcourt Brace Jovanovich, Inc., and Wylie, Aitken & Stone Inc.

Neville Cardus, excerpt from *Good Days* (Cape, 1934). Reprinted by permission of Margaret Hughes.

Seymour Chatman, reprinted from *Story and Discourse: Narrative Structure in Fiction and Film*. Copyright © 1978 by Cornell University. Used by permission of the publisher, Cornell University Press.

Chinweizu et al, 'The African Novel and Its Critics' and 'Issues and tasks in the Decolonization of African Literature', from *Toward the Decolonization of African Literature: African Fiction and Poetry and Their Critics*. Reprinted by permission of Kegan Paul International Ltd.

Hélène Cixous, 'The Laugh of the Medusa', trans. Keith and Paul Cohen, first appeared in translation in *Signs* 1:4 (Summer, 1976). © 1976 by The University of Chicago. All rights reserved.

Terry Eagleton, 'Introduction: What is Literature?' and 'The Rise of English' from *Literary Theory: An Introduction* (1983). Reprinted by permission of Basil Blackwell on behalf of the author; excerpt from *Marxism and Literary Criticism* (Methuen & Co. 1976). Reprinted by permission of Routledge.

Umberto Eco, 'The Semiotics of Theatrical Performance' was originally published in *The Drama Review*, Volume XXI, Number 1, March 1977. Copyright 1977 by New York University. All rights reserved. This abridged version is reprinted by permission of Umberto Eco and MIT Press, Cambridge, Massachusetts.

Martin Esslin, 'The Signs of Drama: Icon, Index, Symbol' and 'The Signs of Drama: The Actor' from *The Field of Drama* (Methuen, 1987). Copyright Martin Esslin. Reproduced by permission of Curtis Brown, London, and Methuen London, on behalf of Martin Esslin.

Frantz Fanon, 'On National Culture' from *The Wretched of the Earth*, trans. Constance Farrington. © 1963 by Presence Africaine. Reprinted by permission of Grafton Books, a division of William Collins Publishing Group and Grove Weidenfeld.

Elaine Fido. 'Value Judgements on Art and the Question of Macho Attitudes: the Case of Derek Walcott'. *The Journal of Commonwealth Literature*, vol. 21, No. 1, 1986, pp. 109–19 and extracts from Notes. Reprinted by permission of Hans Zell Publishers, an imprint of Bowker-Saur Ltd.

Stanley Fish, 'Interpreting the *Variorum*', *Critical Inquiry* 2: 465–86. © 1976 by The University of Chicago. All rights reserved.

E. M. Forster, 'Notes on the English Character' from *Abinger Harvest* (1936). Reprinted by permission of Edward Arnold.

Gérard Genette, 'Order' from *Narrative Discourse* (1986). Reprinted by permission of Basil Blackwell.

Sandra Gilbert and Susan Gubar, from *Shakespeare's Sisters: Feminist Essays on Women Poets* (Indiana University Press, 1979), pp. xvi–xxii. © Sandra Gilbert and Susan Gubar 1979. Reprinted by permission of the authors.

Seamus Heaney, 'Englands of the Mind' from *Preoccupations: Selected Prose 1968–1978*. Copyright © 1980 by Seamus Heaney. Reprinted by permission of Faber & Faber Limited and Farrar, Straus and Giroux, Inc.

E. D. Hirsch, Jr., 'The Babel of Interpretations' and 'Understanding, Interpretation and Criticism' from *Validity and Interpretation*, pp. 128–33, 134–9. Copyright © 1967 by Yale University. Reprinted by permission of Yale University Press.

Hans Robert Jauss, 'Literary History as a Challenge to Literary Theory' translated by
E. Benzinger, in *New Directions in Literary History*, ed. R. Cohen (1974). Reprinted
by permission of Routledge.

Cora Kaplan, 'Language and Gender' from *Sea Changes: Culture and Feminism*,
pp. 69–72, 79–86. Reprinted by permission of Verso.

Frank Kermode, 'Canon and Period' from *History and Value: Clarendon Lectures* (OUP,
1988), pp. 113–17. Reprinted by permission of the Peters Fraser & Dunlop Group
Ltd.

Lawrence Lerner, 'History and Fiction' from *The Frontiers of Literature* (1988), Chapter
1, History: The Condition of England. Reprinted by permission of Basil Blackwell on
behalf of the author.

Georg Lukács, 'The Ideology of Modernism', translated by John and Necke Mander,
from *The Meaning of Contemporary Realism* (1963). Reprinted by permission of The
Merlin Press Ltd.

John McGrath, 'Behind the Clichés of Contemporary Theatre' from *A Good Night Out:
Popular Theatre, Audience Class and Form* (1981). Reprinted by permission of
Methuen London.

Pierre Machery, 'Rule and Law', 'Implicit and Explicit', 'The Spoken and the
Unspoken' and 'The Two Questions' from *A Theory of Literary Production* (1978).
Reprinted by permission of Routledge.

Czeslaw Milosz, 'On Hope' reprinted by permission of the publishers from *The Witness
of Poetry* by Czeslaw Milosz, Cambridge, Mass.: Harvard University Press, Copyright
© 1983 by the President and Fellows of Harvard College.

Toni Morrison, 'Rootedness: The Ancestor as Foundation', reprinted from *Black
Women Writers 1950–1980: A Critical Evaluation*, ed. Mari Evans (1984). Reprinted
by permission of Pluto Press.

George Orwell, 'The Lion and the Unicorn', from *The Collected Essays*, Volume II. ©
1968 by Sonia Brownell Orwell. Reprinted by permission of A. M. Heath on behalf
of the estate of the late Sonia Brownell Orwell and Secker & Warburg. Published in
the US by Harcourt Brace Jovanovich Inc.

Edward Said, 'Introduction' and 'Style, Expertise, Vision' from *Orientalism*. © 1978 by
Edward W. Said. Reprinted by permission of Routledge and Pantheon Books, a
division of Random House, Inc. 'Yeats and Decolonization', excerpts from *Nationalism, Colonialism and Literature*, Field Day Pamphlet #15 (1988). © Edward Said
1988.

Jean-Paul Sartre, 'What is Writing?' and 'For Whom Does One Write?' and 'Situation
of the Writer in 1947', translated by B. Frechtman, both from *What Is Literature?*
(Methuen & Co. 1967). Reprinted by permission of Routledge.

Robert Scholes, 'Towards a Semiotics of Literature', *Critical Inquiry* 4 (1977), 105–20.
© 1977 The University of Chicago. All rights reserved. Used with permission. 'Who
Cares about the text?' from *Textual Power: Theory and the Teaching of English*, pp.
150–6. Reprinted by permission of Yale University Press.

Wole Soyinka, 'Drama and the African World-View' and 'Ideology and the Social
Vision' from *Myth, Literature and the African World*, pp. 37–9, 61–3 (1976). Reprinted by permission of Cambridge University Press.

George Steiner, 'The Hollow Miracle' from *Language and Silence: Essays and Notes*

1958–1966. Reprinted by permission of Faber & Faber Limited. Published in the US by Atheneum.

Sara Suleri, 'The Geography of *A Passage to India*', reprinted in *E. M. Forster's A Passage to India: Modern Critical Interpretations*, ed. Harold Bloom (Chelsea House, 1987). Reprinted by permission of the author.

Lionel Trilling, 'Freud and Literature' from *The Liberal Imagination*. Reprinted by permission of Diana Trilling.

Paul Valéry, 'Remarks on Poetry' from *Symbolism: An Anthology*, ed. T. G. West (Methuen & Co., 1980). Reprined by permission of Routledge.

Hayden White, from *Metahistory* (1973). Reprinted by permission of Johns Hopkins University Press.

Raymond Williams, 'Metropolitan Perceptions and the Emergence of Modernism' from *Politics of Modernism: Against the New Conformists*, pp. 44–7, 32–5. Reprinted by permission of Verso.

Virginia Woolf, from *A Room of One's Own* (1929), copyright 1929 by Harcourt Brace Jovanovich, Inc., and renewed 1957 by Leonard Woolf; and from *Three Guineas* (1938), copyright 1938 by Harcourt Brace Jovanovich, Inc., and renewed 1966 by Leonard Woolf. Reprinted by permission of The Hogarth Press as publisher on behalf of the Executors of the Virgina Woolf Estate, and Harcourt Brace Jovanovich, Inc.

Although every effort has been made to secure permission prior to publication this has not been possible in some instances. If notified the publisher will rectify any errors or omissions at the earliest opportunity.

Subject Index

Index of People and Books